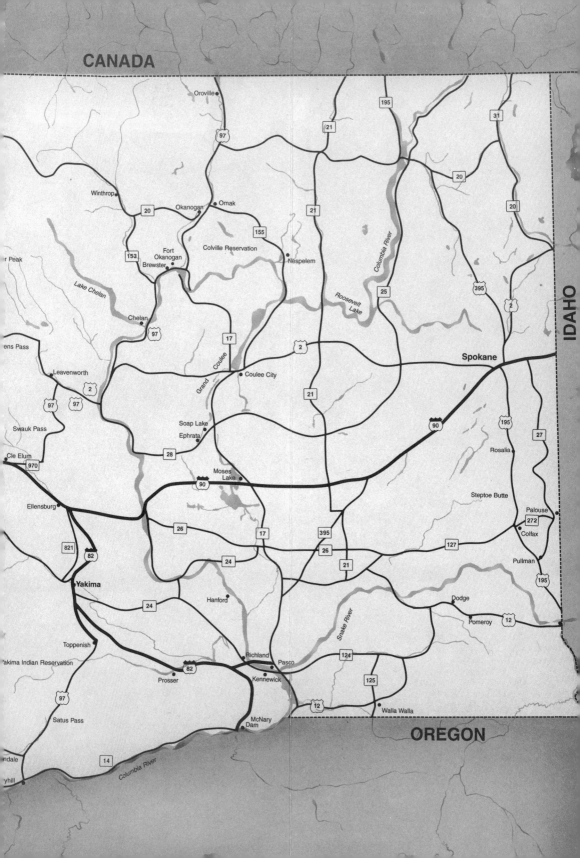

A Traveler's History
of
Washington

A Traveler's History
of
Washington

Bill Gulick

The Caxton Printers, Ltd.
Caldwell, Idaho
1996

Library of Congress Cataloging-in-Publication Data

Gulick, Bill, 1916–
    A traveler's history of Washington / Bill Gulick.
        p.   cm.
    Includes bibliographical references and index.
    ISBN 0-87004-371-4 (alk. paper)
    1. Washington (State)--History, Local. 2. Washington
    (State)--Guidebooks. 3. Historic sites--Washington (State)--
    Guidebooks.
I. Title.
F891.G85   1996
917.9704'43--dc20   96-3586
                                                                CIP

Lithographed and bound in the United States of America by
The Caxton Printers, Ltd.
Caldwell, Idaho
160617

To the Memory of my good friend,
Dave Flaccus,
who left us too soon.

Contents

Illustrations

INTRODUCTION

The Mountains Unite Us

The first thing a newcomer to Washington must understand is that the state is split in the middle, on a north–south axis, by a magnificent range of mountains called the Cascades. Some years ago, a regional writer coined a catchy phrase describing the difference between people living east or west of the mountains that proclaimed, "Divided we stand!"

This was intended to mean that whichever side of the mountains we lived on and however much we disliked our city or country cousins who resided on the other side, whenever outlanders criticized us we stood together, ready to beat the tar out of them.

Having lived both west and east of the Cascades for a number of years, I agreed with that statement until eighteen months ago, when my wife, Jeanne, and I began to travel extensively over all areas of the state in researching and writing this book. Gradually, it dawned on me that the statement was outmoded for several reasons. First, it did not take into account the fact that to a growing number of people the Cascade Mountains are not only a wall between two distinct climate zones and ways of life but an in-between area in which they prefer to live as neither rain-side nor dry-side inhabitants. These Cascade mountain dwellers feel that they have the best of both worlds.

Second, the statement did not consider that without the waters of the Columbia and the Snake, which are the second and sixth greatest rivers in the United States south of Alaska and originate east of the mountains, metropolitan areas west of the Cascades would not have the cheap hydroelectric power, the fish, grain, fruit, and other foods which not only feed western

Courtesy Washington State Library
MOUNT RAINIER NATIONAL PARK ROAD, 1923

Washington people but are exported from Puget Sound ports to hungry Pacific Rim countries.

Third, simply by being there the Cascades give Washington a diversity that few other states possess. Not only can a person go from "sea level to ski level" in an hour or two, he may also go from desert to rain forest, from freeway gridlock to wide open back–country driving, or from whitewater rafting in mile–deep Hells Canyon to riding a high-speed ferry from Seattle to Victoria, British Columbia—all in a short day's driving time.

Statistically, Washington ranks twentieth in size among the nation's states, covering 68,192 square miles, a good-sized portion of which, 1,622 square miles, is water. Population of the state is 5,257,320 (1996 estimate), most of it living west of the Cascades.

With a number of peaks topping 9,000 feet, the Cascades are a rugged range, crossed by only five highway passes: White, Chinook, Snoqualmie, Stevens, and North Cascades. Of these, both Chinook and North Cascades are closed during the winter because of heavy snowfall.

HISTORY OF SETTLEMENT

The year of 1792 was a very important one in the history of the Pacific Northwest. For three centuries, intrepid explorers of four great nations had been poking the bows of their frail sailing ships into the mouths of rivers, inlets, coves, and straits along the west coast of North America in hopes of finding the mythical Northwest Passage that would shorten the voyage from Europe to the fabled East Indies by many months.

Spain, England, Russia, and finally the brash young new nation, the United States, all had sent explorers to the Northwest Coast. Even a Greek pilot named Apostolos Valerianos. Valerianos got into the act, though, like the Italian, Cristofo Columbo, he did it under the alleged auspices of Spain and adopted a pseudonym to suit, Juan de Fuca. The word "alleged" is used with good reason, for no facts regarding his voyage have ever been verified. Even so, he got credit for discovering and mapping the most important strait in the Pacific Northwest, which ever after has borne his name.

In 1592, he claimed, he entered a broad inlet between the forty-seventh and forty-eighth degrees of north latitude. Published in an English book *Purchas, his Pilgrimes*, 1625, it was sufficient to give the Spanish name—Juan de Fuca—to the fifteen mile-wide, forty-five mile-long strait between the Olympic Peninsula and Vancouver Island.

By 1792, explorers of the four nations had pretty much given up on finding an easy passage to the Orient. Led by the monolithic Hudson's Bay Company, whose "company of gentlemen" had been chartered by the Crown, the prize sought in the wilds of North America now was fur. Russia tried to claim the west coast as far south as San Francisco Bay, then backed off and settled for the southern border of Alaska. Spain established a trading post on Nootka Sound in what would become British Columbia, but, when challenged by the British, agreed to sell out and retreat to the forty-second parallel in northern California.

Backed by a strong naval force and several vessels, British Captain George Vancouver sailed to the eastern end of the Strait of Juan de Fuca in 1792 and was busy drawing maps and naming mountains when a young American sea captain, Robert Gray, in charge of a small ship called *Columbia Redidiva,* met the renowned British explorer in Puget Sound and told him about having discovered the mouth of what appeared to be a great river near the forty-sixth parallel.

Gentleman that he was, Captain Vancouver smiled, shook his head, and told Captain Gray that the great river he thought he had discovered wasn't a river at all; it was merely an inlet whose currents and tides had fooled even such an experienced Spanish explorer as Bruno Heceta, who, a few years earlier, also thought he had discovered a river there. Inexperienced young sea captains, Vancouver suggested gently, should stick to commanding their vessels, leaving exploring and map-making to men who knew their business.

Chastened but still curious, Captain Robert Gray returned to the mouth of the river that wasn't there, found its current strong and its waters fresh far out to sea, and at last took advantage of a favorable wind and friendly tide to cross the tumultuous six mile-wide sandbar at its mouth and sail up the river twenty-five miles. There, near a spot called Tongue Point, he dropped anchor and modestly named the river "Columbia after his ship.

Hearing about this, Captain Vancouver sent an assistant, Lieutenant William Broughton, down the coast, who rediscovered the great river, sailed up it in the brig *Chatham* for one hundred miles, and dropped anchor on the north shore near a headland he named Point Vancouver. He then claimed the river and all the lands surrounding it in the name of His Royal Majesty, stating that to the best of his knowledge, "...no citizen of a civilized nation has ever entered this country before..."

In the same important year 1792, events transpiring half a world away also had a bearing on the fate of the region. After serving as Ambassador to France for ten years, Thomas Jefferson observed its Revolution first-hand and came to know its people and leaders well. As he prepared to return to the United States, where he would be elected Vice President in 1796 and President in 1800, he had good reason to believe that a bargain piece of real estate in the Pacific Northwest might be coming on the market soon.

Migrating from Germany to America at about the same time Jefferson left for Paris, John Jacob Astor, a butcher by trade, had found the fur trade far more profitable than meat-cutting and was well on his way toward becoming the wealthiest man in the United States. Both Jefferson and Astor were empire builders,

Courtesy Bureau of Reclamation, BPA Photo
GRAND COULEE DAM, COLUMBIA RIVER

though each man had a different goal. Jefferson dreamed of establishing a nation stretching from sea to sea. Astor schemed to create an empire based on fur.

Following the Louisiana Purchase in 1803, President Jefferson sent the Lewis and Clark party on their epic mission to the Pacific. Soon after its return to St. Louis in 1806, Astor organized the Pacific Fur Company, which, with President Jefferson's approval, sent by sea and by land contingents to the west coast in 1811–12.

At the same time, British companies headquartered in Montreal were sending fur traders and explorers west across the Canadian wilderness, the vanguards of which reached the lower Columbia and Fraser Rivers only weeks after the arrival of the Americans.

For a time, the War of 1812 interrupted the peaceful rivalry between the United States and Great Britain as to who should own the Pacific Northwest. Agreeing that a few thousand furs a year weren't worth fighting another war over, the two nations signed an agreement unique for that place and time. Beginning with the signing of the Treaty of Ghent in 1818, citizens of both nations would be granted free and equal access to the region called the "Oregon Country" for a period of ten years. If need be, the Joint Occupancy Treaty could be extended for another ten years. Eventually, ownership of the country would be decided by the people who liked it well enough to live in it.

Other than the fact that the western border of the Oregon Country was the Pacific Ocean, the eastern the Rocky Mountains, the southern the Spanish territory south of the forty-second parallel, and the northern the Russian lands somewhere around 54 degrees north, the area in question was not closely defined. In the opinion of many Americans, it was a howling wilderness inhabited by Indians and trappers. In the 1830s, Secretary of State Daniel Webster allegedly offered to trade all of Oregon for a codfish bank off the coast of Newfoundland, but the deal fell through because of an argument between the principals as to the size of the codfish bank.

Because of a number of reasons we will explore later in this book, expansion–minded Americans began to believe that there were things more valuable than beaver in the Oregon Country. In 1846, the United States gave notice that it wished to end the Joint Occupancy Treaty. After a few months of polite discussion, the

TEPEE MADE OF REED MATS, CA 1900
Major Moorhouse Photo, Courtesy Penrose Library, Whitman College

ENTRANCE OF THE COLUMBIA RIVER
Ship *Tonquin*, crossing the bar, March 25, 1811

END OF THE *BEAVER*
Working as a tug for the Hudson's Bay Company from 1836 to 1888, the first
steamer in the northwest was wrecked near Vancouver Harbor.

Click Relander Collection, Courtesy Yakima Valley Regional Library
INDIAN FISH NET TRAPS
The scene is near LaConner, on Puget Sound.

boundary between Canada and the United States was set at the forty-ninth parallel as far west as Georgia Strait, where it jogged south and then west again in order to give each country its share of the lovely San Juan Islands, let Canada keep all of Vancouver Island, and split the Strait of Juan de Fuca westward to the Pacific Ocean so that both nations would have access to it.

In 1853, Washington Territory was organized, its north and south borders being pretty much where they are now, though its far eastern limit still was the summit of the Rocky Mountains. Ten years later in 1863, Idaho Territory was organized and chopped off; in 1865, Montana Territory was created; and the boundaries of the State of Washington were reduced to their present locations.

A physically diverse state, Washington may conveniently be divided for purposes of history and travel into six regions. These are:

1. PUGET SOUND

With cities such as Olympia, Tacoma, Seattle, Everett, and Bellingham situated within sight and smell of the beautiful inland sea, this is the most heavily populated region in the state. It has

Ashael Curtis Photo, Courtesy Washington State Historical Society
MOUNT OLYMPUS CREST

the most industry, the most traffic, and in some ways the most problems related to size and congestion. But in the minds of many of its residents, it also has the most beauty and a well-deserved rating of being the most desirable place to live in the whole country.

2. OLYMPIC PENINSULA
Though the rugged mountains and wild stretches of ocean beaches lying west and south of Puget Sound are just across from the most heavily populated section of the state, the traveler seeking solitude does not have to go very far to find it in this area. The seventy-nine hundred foot high Olympic range is mostly National Park and Forest; Indian reservations such as those of the

Quillayute and Quinault tribes preserve a large area in a primitive, isolated condition; and one of the finest rain forests in North America, upon which as much as 140 inches of rainfall a year nourishes huge old Sitka spruce, hemlock, fir, cedar, and other varieties of trees, make the region unique and priceless.

3. SOUTHWEST WASHINGTON

Between Grays Harbor, which is two-thirds of the way down the coast, to the mouth of the Columbia, lies a more open, less rugged country. The large inlet called Willapa Bay supports a thriving oyster industry. In the Long Beach area, there is a stretch of many miles of straight, level, sandy beach noted for its variety of clams—including the incredible geoduck, whose neck is three feet long.

Eastward to the foot of the Cascade Mountains 150 miles away, there are a series of pleasant, lightly timbered valleys where the rainfall is not as heavy as it is further north, containing cities such as Longview, Centralia, Chehalis, and Vancouver, where the Hudson's Bay Company post of Fort Vancouver was established in 1823 by the British factor, Dr. John McLoughlin.

"CHINOOK TURKEY" (KING SALMON)
Near the mouth of the Columbia in the early 1900s.
Courtesy Ilwaco Heritage Museum

Courtesy Washington State Library
PARADISE LODGE
Mount Rainier National Park, in the 1930s.

4. CASCADE MOUNTAINS

From Mount Baker near the Canadian border to Mount Saint Helens overlooking the Columbia River, the spectacular Cascade Range splits the State of Washington from north to south near its center, dividing it into two distinctly different regions called "East and West of the Mountains."

West of the Cascades lies rainy, well-watered country, where trees grow thick and tall, and the weather seldom gets very hot or very cold. East of the Cascades lies dry plateau and open range country, much of which would be classified as desert, were it not for the abundance of irrigation water which makes its fertile soil produce some of the finest grains and fruits in the world.

5. COLUMBIA BASIN

Dominating the eastern half of the state is the Columbia River which, with its tributaries, ranks second in the nation for the vol-

Courtesy Yakima Nation Collection
INDIANS FISHING AT CELILO FALLS, ON THE COLUMBIA

ume of water it carries to the ocean. Because of the 161 dams on its watershed, it ranks first in the amount of electric power it generates. Born in the snowfields of the Canadian Rockies, its peak flow comes during the summer months when this land of little rain needs it most for irrigation.

On both the Columbia and its main tributary, the Snake, dredged channels and navigation locks which lift tugs and barges one hundred vertical feet at each dam make the river system navigable as far inland as Lewiston, Idaho, 470 miles from the Pacific Ocean.

6. SOUTHEAST WASHINGTON

Remote as it is from the large centers of population west of the Cascades, the Walla Walla Valley in the southeast corner of the state was where the history of Washington began. At the Cayuse Indian Mission established by Marcus and Narcissa Whitman in 1836, the first white child born west of the Rockies came into the world; this was the most important way-station on the Oregon Trail between Fort Laramie and the Willamette Valley; and it was here that the tragic massacre of fourteen white people in 1847 dra-

Bill Gulick Photo
MODERN–DAY STERN-WHEELER
Cruises from Portland upriver to Cascade Locks may be taken on this boat.

matically turned the attention of the rest of the nation west and made it certain that the Oregon Country would become part of the United States rather than Great Britain.

Embraced by the Snake River, the southeastern Washington region known as the Palouse Hills is one of the world's most prolific grain producers. In the extreme corner of the state, the sector of the Snake River flowing through a spectacular, mile-deep gorge called Hells Canyon fueled a long-running, bitter battle between private and public power advocates over who would build the last and highest dam on the river.

Much to the surprise of both parties, the dispute was settled when the US Supreme Court ruled that no dam at all should be built. Instead, this ninety-mile stretch of free-flowing river has been preserved as the Hells Canyon National Recreation Area, which has become one of the few places in the Pacific Northwest where a river can be seen and enjoyed in its natural condition.

Having now established the fact that Washington is a beautiful state with a wide variety of scenery and a colorful history, we will begin our journey on Puget Sound just south of the Canadian

Click Relander Collection, Courtesy Yakima Valley Regional Library
PEACE ARCH, BUILT BY SAM HILL, AT BLAINE

border at Blaine, where the first bit of history to be learned is that the Peace Arch, which rises majestically in a lovely, flower-filled park on the border between the two nations, contains an ancient timber which once was part of the hull of the ship *Mayflower*, which carried the first band of Pilgrims to the New World in 1620.

PART I

Puget Sound

Sitting squarely astride the border between Canada and the United States, the imposing white concrete Peace Arch bears two legends. Engraved on the Canadian side are the words, "Brothers Dwelling Together in Unity." On the American side, "Children of a Common Mother."

Just south of the Peace Arch, the lovely, flower and shrub filled Samuel Hill Memorial Park commemorates peace and good will between the two countries, the gift of a flamboyant railroad-builder and good roads enthusiast in the Pacific Northwest who spent many years following World War I promoting the cause of world peace.

While in England helping Europe recover from the ravages of war by supplying food to starving people, Sam Hill came across an old barn which was said to have been built out of timbers taken from the *Mayflower*. Securing one, he shipped it to the United States and had it placed in the south side of the Peace Arch as a symbol of unity between Great Britain, Canada, and the United States. Matching it on the north side, Canada embedded a piece of iron salvaged from the Hudson's Bay Company ship *Beaver*, the first steamer to ply Northwest waters in 1836.

On I–5, the distance between Blaine and the turnoff to Anacortes, where a tour of the San Juan Islands begins, is just forty miles. But there is little of scenic or historic interest to be seen from the freeway, which stays several miles inland from Puget Sound. As always, it is on the back roads that places of interest may be seen by the traveler who is not in a hurry.

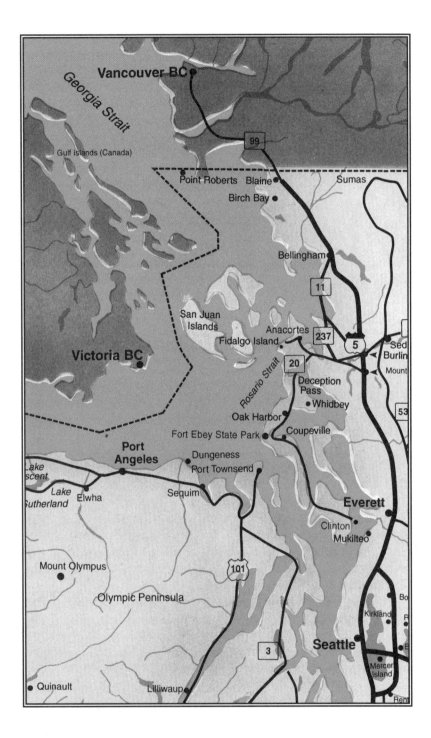

Birch Bay, which was named by British Captain George Vancouver in 1792 for the many black birch trees growing along its shore, is a wide, curving, shallow bay where the tide goes far out, known for many years as a family vacation spot and for its clams.

Visible on a clear day twenty miles to the northwest is one of the most unique spots in the State of Washington, Point Roberts. Though attached to the mainland, this small peninsula is part of Canada but extends two miles south of the forty-ninth parallel, which marks the northern border of the United States. It cannot be reached by land from Blaine without crossing the line into Canada. By road, this means a round trip of eighty-some miles and four border crossings, which can be an infernal nuisance when traffic is heavy—as it usually is. From time to time over the years, small ferries have made the trip direct, but never have generated enough revenue to support them.

During the days when smuggling Chinese or liquor into the United States was profitable, business thrived in this isolated spot, though now most of the traffic across the line increases or dwindles according to the exchange rate or the price of gasoline, food, and legal liquor. This freak of geography came about back in 1846 when the Joint Occupancy Treaty between the United States and Great Britain ended, and the two countries agreed on the forty-ninth parallel for the boundary as far west as the waters of the Pacific Ocean, where it then would turn south, southeast, and then west to follow the center of the main channel through Georgia Strait, Puget Sound, and the Strait of Juan de Fuca.

When it later developed that not one but three "main channels" existed between the countries, a dispute ensued—so serious that it almost led to war. The result was that Point Roberts became an "orphan" —and apparently is destined to remain one forever.

OLD FORT BELLINGHAM

Shortly after the Territory of Washington was established in 1853, an ambitious young army officer who had distinguished himself

---

I–5—Blaine to Bellingham
20 miles
State 11, 237, 20—Bellingham to Anacortes
30 miles

Click Relander Collection, Courtesy Yakima Valley Regional Library
BLOCKHOUSE ON WHIDBEY ISLAND, NEAR FORT CASEY

during the Mexican War a few years earlier, Isaac Ingalls Stevens, was appointed governor and given the twin tasks of exploring a railroad route west from St. Paul to the Pacific and "extinguishing Indian title" to the lands in the country he passed through and would govern.

During a whirlwind tour of the Territory, he made treaties with all the tribes, persuaded the chiefs to sign them on behalf of their people, then "settled" the Indians for what he thought was the foreseeable future on designated reservations where they could live unmolested while the white newcomers took over their lands. Much to his surprise, peace lasted only long enough for word of what the signing chiefs had given away to spread among dissident tribesmen, causing the outbreak of a series of local wars.

For the most part, little blood was shed. But all over the Pacific Northwest blockhouses were built to protect the settlers from Indian raids—that never came. Small contingents of federal troops backed by local volunteers manned them, and recent West Point graduates (eager to distinguish themselves in action) were given commands that would prepare them for the greater conflict soon to come, the Civil War.

One of these officers was Captain George Pickett, who later would win renown by leading his troops in a charge at Gettysburg. As early as 1856, he demonstrated his eagerness to charge while stationed on Puget Sound, though with considerably less success.

The two blockhouses he built and commanded at Fort Bellingham never were used or really needed as defenses against the local Indians, most of whom were peacefully inclined. But they did serve as a deterrent against the deadly raiders of the North, the Haidas of British Columbia and Alaska, who since time immemorial had rowed their swift, sea-worthy war canoes down into Puget Sound, creating terror and panic among Indians of the region as they sought wives, slaves, booty, and heads to take home as trophies. When the San Juan Island dispute heated up to the point of imminent war, Fort Bellingham also made a convenient staging area for troops and a temporary headquarters for visiting generals and newspaper reporters come to promote the cause of peace or war.

With the regional Indian troubles settled by 1858, Bellingham briefly became a different kind of staging area when a gold discovery in the lower Fraser River country brought thousands of Americans seeking land or water transport to the Canadian mainland or across the Sound to Victoria, on Vancouver Island, which British provincial capital city at one time was so full of Americans that they threatened to take over the local government.

When the Alaska gold rush of 1898 made Seattle boom, Bellingham shared in the prosperity of that era for a time. But for most of the present century it has existed as a rather quiet, peaceful city whose main industries were related to fishing, timber processing, dairying, and bulb culture. Of recent years, the city has invested millions of dollars in its port facility, and has been rewarded by being made the southern terminus of the ferry system between Puget Sound and Alaska, which moved there from Seattle. Being a hundred miles closer and in less congested waters, the Port of Bellingham now has established a monopoly on the Alaska passenger traffic.

Just south of Bellingham on State 11, what has long been called Chuckanut Drive offers a pleasant scenic route south well removed from freeway traffic. Winding along a shelf cut into the rocky face of Chuckanut Mountain high above the brilliant blue waters of Puget Sound, the frequent turnouts and picnic spots (such as Larabee State Park) provide stunning views of the San Juan Islands to the west. There are 172 of these islands on the American side of the channel defining the border between the United States and Canada, with a hundred more on the Canadian side, which, in Georgia Strait, are called the Gulf Islands.

Ferries from half a dozen points in both countries carry cars, trucks, and foot passengers across to island or mainland destinations, with sailings scheduled hourly during daylight in the peak traveling season, daily on the less traveled routes. With beautiful scenery always in sight on these sheltered waters, which seldom are rough though often foggy, riding the ferries is a delightful way to travel, with kibitzing passengers standing high on upper decks dividing their comments equally between admiration of the captain's skill as a pilot and the skill of the deckhands in stashing the last possible car or truck in the last possible square foot of space without denting a fender or breaking a taillight.

Anacortes, twenty miles west of Mount Vernon, is the main point of embarkation for a ferry tour of the San Juan Islands. Though many of the islands, points, and inlets bear names given them by Spanish explorers, the town was named, so the *WPA Guide* tells us, "...for Anna Curtis, wife of Amos Bowman, an early settler..."

Of the 172 habitable islands clustered in the northern waters of Puget Sound and the southern extension of Georgia Strait, the largest is Orcas Island, which is 58 square miles in extent; it also boasts the highest peak, Mount Constitution, which rises 2,454 feet above sea level. Second in size by only a whisker is San Juan Island, which covers fifty-seven square miles.

Historically, of course, San Juan Island ranks far above its somewhat larger neighbor, for it was on it that the pig was killed that almost started what was called the "Pig War."

THE PIG WAR

The 1846 agreement setting the border between Canada and the United States at the forty-ninth parallel was based on a fifty-year-old map drawn by Captain George Vancouver. The agreement simply stated that the water boundary should jog south, then southeast, then west "...through the main channel..." between the islands.

Trouble was, there were *three* channels, not one, and the two nations could not agree on which was the "main" one. Given the whole of Vancouver Island as its private preserve, the Hudson's Bay Company claimed that the "main channel" was the one closest to the continental United States, which would give Canada practically all of the islands. Without making any claims at all, Americans living in the newly established Territory of Washington simply moved onto and occupied land on whichever island they happened to like, no matter which channel ran between it and the mainland or Vancouver Island. As in days of Joint Occupancy, they felt that the lightly settled country was free and open to citizens of both nations.

Encouraged by the Hudson's Bay Company, a Britisher named Charles J. Griffin transported a band of 1,300 sheep and a crew of Hawaiian shepherds to the south side of San Juan Island aboard the small Hudson's Bay Company side-wheeler *Beaver* on December 13, 1853. Hearing of their presence, an American Collector of Customs for the Port Townsend district, Colonel Isaac N. Ebey, notified Governor James Douglas in Victoria that the sheep were there illegally, thus were subject to seizure for non–payment of American taxes. In response, Douglas appointed Griffin, who owned the sheep, Justice of the Peace for the San Juan District and told him to arrest Ebey, if he came around "...as a common offender..."

On May 2, 1854, Ebey did come around aboard the chartered schooner *Sarah Stone*, accompanied by a friend named Henry Webber. Summoning Griffin to their camp, Ebey told him he was in violation of US Revenue laws. Griffin temporized until Governor Douglas steamed across from Victoria on the *Otter*, bringing with him the Collector of Customs at Victoria, James Sangster. Ebey had his men raise the US flag atop the nearest hill. The British countered by hoisting the Union Jack on Griffin's farm.

After several polite protests were made by both parties, an invitation to share a friendly drink was offered and refused, and a not so polite threat was made by Sangster to arrest Webber. When six British stalwarts approached within three paces of Webber:

> "...the American produced four six-barreled revolvers," one local historian writes, "and aimed one of them directly at the constable's head. `One more foot and you are a dead man,' he said calmly. `I have no ill will toward you; on the other hand, the first one who steps toward me I will blow his brains out.'"

Recognizing the fact that a man who could produce four six-shooters with such ease was not to be trifled with, the constable did the sensible thing, retreating a pace or two and then ordering his men to advance and disarm the "prisoner." When they refused, he repeated the order to a Negro servant, who similarly declined.

Now that a temporary peace had been declared, Webber sat down on a convenient stump, the constable did likewise, and they talked for a while. Presently the constable withdrew his posse and asked for further instructions from his superiors. After a couple of hours, he returned, informed Webber that nothing more would be done until the return of Governor Douglas, and that the British sheep owner, Griffin, had sent along a leg of mutton for Webber's supper. Webber replied he was much obliged but he was sailing back to the mainland that evening in order to pick up his own supplies, following which he intended to return to San Juan Island and make a permanent camp.

By the time he came back four days later, he had decided to go to Victoria and take care of some other business. In order to be given free transportation, he asked Charles Griffin to arrest him and take him to Victoria as a prisoner of the Crown. By then Governor Douglas had changed his mind and decided he no longer wanted Webber apprehended, so Griffin declined. Still wanting to go to Victoria, the American paid his own passage there and back—and was never taken prisoner. Returning to San Juan Island, he remained there for a year, during which time he and Griffin became good friends.

When the Indian war of 1856 broke out in the Puget Sound area, Governor Douglas and the Hudson's Bay Company joined forces with the United States to protect the settlers of both nations from the natives, suspending hostilities with each other. Hearing that a large party of head-hunting Haidas from the North intended to stage a raid on the American settlements, Governor Douglas not only warned the Americans of the impending attack but also sent troops to protect the alleged trespassers on British soil. This so surprised the hostiles that they withdrew in confusion.

With the Indian problem pretty well settled in April of 1858, some sixteen Yankee "squatters" took up claims on San Juan Island. One of them was a lanky Ohioan named Lyman Cutler. After taking an Indian wife, he built a cabin, spaded up and

Click Relander Collection, Courtesy Yakima Valley Regional Library
INTERIOR OF OLD SMOKEHOUSE, NEAR TULALIP

fenced a small garden spot, planted a patch of potatoes, and settled down to a life of relative ease in the balmy San Juan Island
climate. The fact that the place he "squatted" on was squarely in
the center of Charles Griffin's best sheep pasture did not bother
him in the least.

By mid–June, the potatoes were looking good, and Lyman
Cutler was looking forward to a bountiful harvest. Like other settlers on the island, he kept a few pigs, but managed to put up a
good enough fence to keep them out of the potato patch.
Sheepman Charles Griffin, on the other hand, owned a big,
aggressive black boar, who had never encountered a fence he
could not go over, under, or through. And his favorite food was
potatoes.

After finding the big black boar in his potato patch several
times, taking a switch to it, and driving it back where it belonged,
Cutler went to Griffin and warned him in no uncertain terms of
what would happen if he didn't keep the boar out of the potato
patch. Pointing out the poor quality of Cutler's fence, Griffin
replied that the island always had been open range country, so far
as roaming boars were concerned, and that rather than it being his

duty to keep his pig out of the potato patch, it was Cutler's job to keep his potatoes out of reach of Griffin's pig.

Thus the seeds of conflict were sown.

Early one bright summer morning, Lyman Cutler was awakened by snorting sounds in his garden. Going to the door of his cabin, he saw the big black boar rooting gluttonously in his potato patch. At that very moment, Griffin's black servant—a man named Jacob—happened to be riding by. When Cutler yelled at him, demanding that he shoo the boar out of the potato patch and drive it home with him, the servant laughed and rode on. To Cutler, that was the last straw.

"Upon the impulse of the moment," he said later, "I seazed [sic] my rifle and shot the hog."

Regretting his action after he had cooled off a bit, Cutler rode over to Griffin's place, told him what he had done, and offered to replace the dead pig with one of his own. Now it was Griffin's turn to lose his temper.

"It's no more than I expected," he stormed. "You Americans are nothing but a nuisance on the island and you have no business here."

Now he intended to do what he should have done long ago, he said, which was to write Governor Douglas and request that all the Americans on the island be removed.

"Cutler replied that he wasn't there to discuss international politics," writes local historian David Richardson, "but to settle up for shooting the hog. How much did Griffin figure it was worth?"

One hundred dollars, Griffin answered. Indignantly, Cutler replied that the Britisher was more likely to be struck by lightning than to get that kind of money for his hog. Ten dollars should be plenty. If that didn't seem right, Cutler added, why didn't they ask a committee of three neighbors to arbitrate a fair price. No, Griffin raged, he had his own way of dealing with the matter. Well, Cutler replied angrily, so did he, which Griffin later claimed to mean "...he would as soon shoot me as he would a hog if I trespassed on his claim..."

From that point on, the dispute quickly escalated. By coincidence, the Hudson's Bay Company vessel *Beaver* chanced to call on the island that afternoon, with several officers aboard. One of them allegedly told Cutler that he had committed a serious offense against the Company and the Crown, and might have to be taken to Victoria for trial. Caressing his Kentucky rifle, Cutler allegedly told the official he'd like to see him try. Hearing about the incident, the American representative of government on the island, Paul K. Hubbs, wrote an ominous letter to the Collector of Customs in Port Townsend, saying, "Collision is imminent, and that of such a character as may produce the most serious result to the two governments."

The threatened difficulties could only be avoided by a settlement of the Boundary question, he warned, or by "...placing immediately a large military force to protect the American Settlers from being carried off at the will of the Hudson Bay Company and shut up in the prison of British Columbia, which is somewhat worse than Dartmoor was in 1813."

In order to post his letter, Hubbs had to go to Fort Bellingham, where his long-time friend Captain George Pickett was in command. Eager to do something more interesting than supervising the planting and weeding of a vegetable garden to supply the troops, Captain Pickett promised to pass on word of the San Juan Island crisis to his superior, General William S. Harney, who soon would be touring the northern Puget Sound posts.

Before returning to San Juan, Hubbs and a settler friend bought the largest American flag they could find and a good supply of gunpowder and fireworks with which to make the approaching Fourth of July celebration a real humdinger.

After the flag had been run up to the top of the fifty-five foot pole erected in front of Hubbs' cabin, a volley of rifle fire followed as a salute, one bullet of which pierced the star-studded field. No matter; it flew just as well with a bullet hole in it. Everyone present made a speech, each one of which as the afternoon waned and the spirits waxed grew more and more patriotic. Toward the end, one patriot proposed that the citizens present declare war and take on the whole British Empire.

"Completely carried away," says historian David Richardson, "one orator—a Welshman—suggested that they declare their independence not only of Great Britain, but of the United States as well, and start a country of their own on such a beautiful island."

GENERAL HARNEY TAKES OVER

Just as Captain Pickett had promised, General William S. Harney, aboard the new warship *Massachusetts*, steamed into Bellingham

Click Relander Collection, Courtesy Yakima Valley Regional Library
MODELS OF A LUMMI INDIAN SMOKEHOUSE AND CANOES

Bay two days after the Fourth of July celebration on San Juan Island. He was quite impressed with what he saw, writing:

> Puget's Sound is a most remarkable sheet of water, and is destined to be eminent in the annals of commerce. Its entrance is fifteen miles wide and as deep as the sea from shore to shore, yet so sheltered by high mountains on its islands and shores that its waters are as smooth as those of a river or lake.

After talking to Captain Pickett about the San Juan situation, Harney passed through Haro Strait and entered Victoria Harbor, where Governor Douglas met him with all due courtesy, giving him a salute from the guns of the Hudson's Bay Company fort and a formal dinner in the governor's home. Digesting the information he gathered during his stay on Vancouver Island, Harney wrote in his report to Lieutenant General Winfield Scott, commanding general of the US Army:

> The population of British Columbia is largely American and foreigners; comparatively few people from the British Isles emigrate to this region. The English cannot colonize successfully near our people; they are too exacting. This, with the pressing necessities of our commerce on this coast, will induce them to

yield, eventually, Vancouver's Island to our government. It is as important to the Pacific States as Cuba is to those on the Atlantic.

Next morning, General Harney and his battleship steamed out of Victoria Harbor and crossed the Sound for his first look at San Juan Island. Still thinking in military terms, he reported that the island:

> ...contains fine timber, good water and grass, and is the most commanding position we possess on the Sound...completely sheltered, offering the best location for a naval station on the Pacific Coast.

In a secret conference with Paul Hubbs, the American representative on the Island, General Harney suggested that he draw up a petition to be signed by all the settlers requesting protection against marauding Indians. The petition then could be used as justification for the landing of troops. Acting swiftly as he went south, he stopped at Fort Steilacoom, where he left the *Massachusetts* and gave orders that the warship be put at the disposal of Captain Pickett in order to expedite the redisposition of troops from Fort Bellingham to San Juan Island.

He then conferred with Isaac Ingalls Stevens, who had just resigned as governor after having been elected to the National Congress, telling the ex–West Point officer (who was as militant as Harney) what he had done.

MILITARY OCCUPATION OF SAN JUAN

On July 26, 1859, Paul Hubbs was wakened before dawn by a persistent knocking on the door of his cabin. Rising sleepily, he opened the door and was greeted by a uniformed orderly, who saluted and gave him Captain Pickett's respects. The captain was down on the beach, he said, in need of advice as to where to land the sixty men in his command, who were about to disembark from the warship *Massachusetts*, which was anchored in the bay.

Getting dressed, Hubbs went down to the beach, conferred with Captain Pickett and his aide Lieutenant Howard, then after they had agreed to the site he suggested—a gravel pit next to the Hudson's Bay Company dock—took a nip of brandy out of the flask the aide produced and joined the two officers in a toast to the success of their landing.

Not at all by coincidence, Her Britannic Majesty's corvette *Satellite* also had arrived during the night, dropping anchor in Griffin Bay. Accompanying it was the British side-wheeler *Shubrick*, with a hastily appointed magistrate, Major John Fitzroy de Courcy, aboard.

Suspecting that the magistrate had come to arrest the almost-forgotten American involved in the pig dispute, Hubbs hastened to alert Lyman Cutler. When he came out of his cabin in the dawn's early light to wash up for breakfast, the pig-killer was told it might be best if he permitted himself to be taken into protective custody.

After the situation had been explained to him, Cutler laughed, surrendered, strapped on a six-shooter, and walked down the hill with Hubbs toward the camp of the American soldiers. At about the halfway point, they met Magistrate de Courcy and three British officers coming from the opposite direction. For a few paces, neither party gave way, but finally the British stepped aside and permitted Hubbs to escort his "prisoner" to the American camp. After being entertained there for a day or two, some of his settler friends urged him to disappear into the hills for a few days—which he did.

Captain Pickett wasted no time taking measures to consolidate his gains. Entitled "Orders No. 1," he had a proclamation tacked to a tree near the beach. It read:

Military Post, San Juan Island
Washington Territory July 27, 1859
1. In compliance with the orders and instructions from the general commanding, a military post will be established on this island, on whatever site the commanding officer may select.
2. All the inhabitants of the island are requested to report at once to the commanding officer in case of any incursion of the northern Indians, so that he may take such steps as are necessary to prevent any future occurrence of same.
3. This being United States territory, no laws, other than those of the United States, nor courts, except such as are held by virtue of said laws, will be recognized or allowed on this island.

Soon after this notice was posted, the *Satellite* weighed anchor and headed for Vancouver. Next afternoon, the British frigate *Tribune*, its decks bristling with cannon, entered Griffin Bay, swung broadside, and dropped its hook. Its guns were trained on

Click Relander Collection, Courtesy Yakima Valley Regional Library
TOTEM POLES CARVED BY CHIEF SHELTON, PUGET SOUND AREA

Pickett's camp. Shortly thereafter, Agent Griffin, whose roving boar had started the trouble, wrote Captain Pickett a letter:

> Sir: I have the honor to inform you that the island of San Juan, on which your camp is pitched, is the property and in the occupation of the Hudson's Bay Company, and to request that you and the whole of your party who have landed from the American vessels will immediately cease to occupy the same. Should you be unwilling to comply with my request, I feel bound to apply to the civil authorities. Awaiting your reply, I have the honor to be, sir, your obedient servant.

CHAS. JNO. GRIFFIN

Captain Pickett's reply was equally polite and equally forceful:

> Sir: Your communication of this instant has been received. I have to state in reply that I do not acknowledge the right of the Hudson's Bay Company to dictate my course of action. I am here by virtue of an order from my government, and shall remain until recalled by the same authority.
> I am, Sir, very respectfully, your obedient servant.

GEORGE E. PICKETT

In Victoria, excitement reached a fever pitch. Vessels of all kinds came and went between the islands, bringing as many as five hundred reporters and sightseers a day to what the Victoria *Gazette* called "the seat of war." Two more British ships, the *Plumper* and *Satellite* anchored in Griffin Bay and trained their guns on the American camp.

If ever there were a military situation designed for creating a hero or a martyr, this was it. Captain Pickett made the most of it. Appealing to the settlers for help, every one of whom volunteered to defend the island with his last drop of blood, Pickett stationed his troops in the woods overlooking the bay, giving each man sixty rounds of ammunition and three days rations. All were crack rifle shots, he knew. He ordered them to pick off the British officers as they alighted from their boats, then fall back to defensive positions in the trees.

"Don't be afraid of their big guns," Pickett told the troops. "We will make a Bunker Hill of it."

Receiving the dispatch in Fort Vancouver, Washington Territory, which was headquarters for the Department of the Pacific in the Northwest, General Harney fired a long-range volley north at Governor Douglas in Victoria, British Columbia, in the *other* Vancouver (Island). In a blunt letter, he stated that he had sent troops to San Juan in order to protect the Americans living there "from the insults and indignities" of the British and the Hudson's Bay Company authorities. Commending Captain Pickett for bravery in the face of overwhelming odds, the general alerted all federal troops stationed on Puget Sound, notified the new governor of Washington Territory, Richard Gholson, that he might need to raise a force of volunteers if the situation worsened, then sent a dispatch to the War Department in Washington, DC, detailing what he had done.

Secretary of War, W.R. Drinkard, and President James Buchanan were appalled. General Harney had been sent out to Washington Territory to put down Indian troubles, they thought, not to embroil his country in a war with a friendly nation over a few paltry islands. Bluntly ordering Harney to take no action until given further instructions, Secretary Drinkard summoned Harney's commanding officer and long-time nemesis from Mexican War days, Lieutenant General Winfield Scott, and asked him to go west to Puget Sound and straighten out the situation. Scott was seventy-two years old and known to be in poor health. But when President Buchanan told him that a war with England

Click Relander Collection, Courtesy Yakima Valley Regional Library
BLOCKHOUSE AT ENGLISH CAMP, SAN JUAN ISLAND

must be prevented at all costs and that Scott was the only man who could accomplish that task, the old soldier agreed to go.

A WARRIOR MAKES PEACE

"The President has been much gratified at the alacrity with which you have responded to his wish that you would proceed to Washington Territory to assume the immediate command, if necessary, of the United States forces on the Pacific coast," Secretary of War Drinkard wrote General Scott, September 16, 1859. "It is impossible, at this distance from the scene, to give you positive instructions as to your course of action. Much, very much, must be left to your own discretion, and the President is happy to believe that discretion could not be entrusted to more competent hands..."

Sailing by fast steamer from New York harbor to Panama, crossing the Isthmus to the Pacific coast, then taking the speedy mail steamer *Northerner* to the Columbia River and Fort Vancouver, General Scott completed the voyage in just a month, the vessel dropping anchor half a mile below General Harney's headquarters a little after midnight October 20. Wakened at 2 a.m. with word that Scott had arrived, a somewhat thunderstruck Harney said he would go see him at once. Told not to disturb the old gentleman's sleep but to report at 8 o'clock in the morning with all his orders and correspondence related to the San Juan affair, Harney did so.

To his surprise, he was greeted not by the ill, tired old man he had expected to see but by a healthy, vigorous general in full command of his faculties. Whether the long sea voyage or the call to action had restored the general's health no one could say, but he certainly was full of vim and vigor.

Relieved to hear that hostilities had not yet broken out, General Scott asked that an aide read some of the San Juan letters aloud, but soon said he had heard enough. When Harney offered the opinion that the state of affairs on San Juan should be continued as it was "...until further advices from the government could be received," Scott's cordial manner changed abruptly.

His course was already decided upon, he said, which was to offer the British a joint military occupation of the island, until the dispute could be solved at the diplomatic level. Harney objected angrily.

"General Scott, I have maintained the honor of my country up to this moment and if you consent to a joint occupancy I shall consider it a disgrace to the country!"

Thumping his cane on the floor as he rose to his feet and glared down at Harney, General Winfield Scott said in an icy tone of voice, "We have both got our superiors and we've got to obey them."

The interview was over. So was Harney's career in the army as far as General Winfield Scott was concerned, for he never saw him again during the two weeks Scott's tour of the Pacific Northwest lasted.

Writing Governor Douglas in Victoria, Scott proposed that each nation should occupy a separate portion of San Juan Island, pending a settlement of the question by the two governments. Douglas cautiously replied that he was "...at a glance satisfied that no obstacle exists to a completely amicable and satisfactory adjustment..." but that he needed time to study the proposal.

General Scott reluctantly agreed to give Governor Douglas a little more time.

While maneuvering to exchange dispatches in British waters near Victoria, the warship *Massachusetts* and the mail steamer *Northerner* accidentally collided, causing the warship to lose her jib boom and the mail steamer her flagstaff and ensign, which broke off and fell into the bay. Though the damage was minor, the mail steamer looked somewhat bedraggled as it headed back to San Francisco, while the appearance of the *Massachusetts* as the ship steamed past San Juan Island without stopping on her way to Bellingham Bay to be repaired made the Americans there wonder if war had begun.

Meanwhile, Governor Douglas, who still was smarting over some of the belligerent statements made by Captain Pickett and General Harney, wrote Scott saying that he could not accept the proposal for joint military occupancy of the island "...without the sanction and express instructions of my government..."

Though this was obviously meant to be a rejection of the proposal, the cagey old general turned probable defeat into possible victory by regarding the above-quoted phrase and several other conciliatory sentences as grounds for drawing up a document titled, *Project of a Temporary Settlement, etc.*

Following the first WHEREAS with phrase after phrase of involved syntax, General Scott laid a trail of verbal flypaper in which what was meant to be a firm "No" was turned into a mushy "Yes." Thanking Governor Douglas for his cooperative attitude and good judgment, General Scott then issued an order removing all American troops and armed vessels except Captain Pickett's force of one hundred men from the island. Confronted with such a gesture of good will, Governor Douglas could only do likewise. He did send a private note to General Scott requesting that the firebrand commander of the American contingent, Captain George Pickett, be transferred to some post well removed from San Juan Island—where an imprudent act on his part could not start a war.

General Scott obliged. The "Pig War" was over.

BOUNDARY SETTLEMENT

Meanwhile, the two camps on San Juan Island—English and American—existed side by side in relative peace. Each contained one hundred marines or infantrymen, who drilled, paraded, exchanged visits, and now and then fielded teams to play cricket

Click Relander Collection, Courtesy Yakima Valley Regional Library
MARIE WILBUR, WITH HER SON JIMMY
Click Relander says they are a mixture of three races: Chinese, Indian, and White.

or baseball. Relations between Great Britain and the United States cooled during the Civil War because England was providing safe harbors for Dixie raiders on Yankee shipping, but the friction did not extend to San Juan. There, soldiers' wives gave tea parties for each other, shared recipes, and traded fruits and vegetables grown in adjacent gardens.

After the War ended, the two nations continued to disagree as to which of the three channels through the islands should be the boundary. Finally, in 1871 they agreed that a committee of German geographers and jurists chosen by Kaiser Wilhelm the First should arbitrate the dispute. One condition of the agreement was that only Haro Strait, nearest Vancouver Island, or Rosario Strait, nearest the United States, could be chosen, thus eliminating the possibility of picking the middle channel.

While the Kaiser's committee was debating its choice, a baseball team from Olympia, Washington Territory, was scheduled to play a rival team from Victoria, British Columbia. Mysteriously, a fake telegram apparently sent from Washington, DC appeared and was published in the newspapers of both cities. It read:

> Emperor William has decided to let the result of the coming baseball game between Olympia and Victoria dictate his decision to the international boundary question.

Both the baseball players and the townspeople knew it was just a joke, but it did add zest to the game. Oddly enough, the American team won—and the Kaiser's decision making Haro Strait the dividing line was announced shortly thereafter, which also was something of a victory for the Americans. Still, the Canadians had no great reason to complain, for over one hundred of the Gulf Islands were awarded to them, while the United States was granted title to 172 of the San Juans.

Today, the area is preserved as San Juan Historical Park on the sites of the old English and American camps. Authorized by Congress to commemorate the Pig War events of 1859–72, the Park comprises some 1,200 acres on the southern end of the island, including the old Hudson's Bay Company Bellevue Farm, San Juan Town, Pickett's brave redoubt overlooking Griffin Bay, and Lyman Cutler's farm-site, where the pig-shooting episode occurred.

Because both the San Juans and the Gulf Islands are so beautiful and the climate so benign, more and more tourists pass through them every year—and many of them like the atmosphere so well that they buy land, build homes, and become Islanders for the rest of their days. While a reasonable amount of tourism and development is welcome, both are becoming difficult to control without excessive long range urban planning—which is the very thing the old settlers and the newcomers want to avoid.

If a poll were taken today, the sentiment so rabidly expressed by the Welshman in his Fourth of July speech back in 1859—that the islands secede from both the United States and Great Britain and form a country of their own—probably would win in a landslide.

WHIDBEY ISLAND

For the traveler interested in history, the inland route south from Anacortes and Mount Vernon to Everett by way of I–5 is far less intriguing than State 20, which stays within sight and smell of saltwater. This route traverses the length of Whidbey Island,

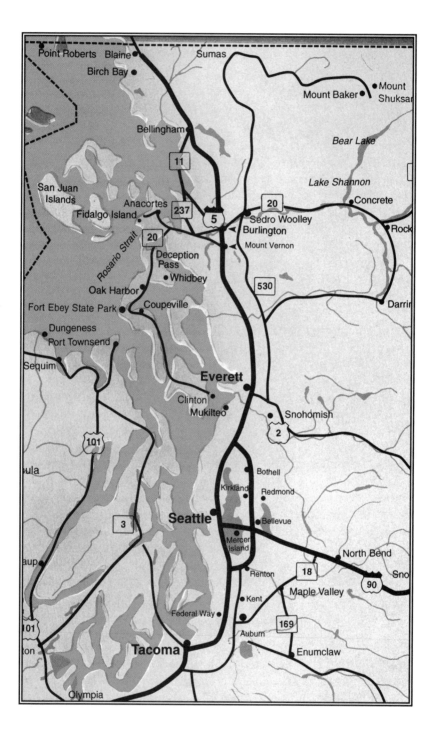

which ranks as the second largest island in the United States. Separated from the mainland at its northern end by a shallow slough and a short bridge, this highway has access to Everett at its southern end by means of a two-mile ferry ride across Possession Bay between Clinton and Mukilteo.

Fidalgo Island, which lies between the mainland and much larger Whidbey Island, was named for the Spanish explorer Salvador Fidalgo whose small ship cruised through the area in 1790–91.

Eighteen miles to the south, Deception Pass Bridge, which was completed in 1935, once was the marvel of its day and still is a sight worth seeing. The bridge has a total length of 1,350 feet, a 22–foot wide roadway bordered by railed pedestrian walks, and offers a spectacular view of two tidal races below, narrow Canoe Pass and wider Deception Pass.

Confined to the sheer-walled gorge directly beneath the bridge, approximately 2.5 billion gallons of water an hour surges and boils when the tide changes, as levels between Rosario Strait to the west and the much smaller inner channel to the east try to equalize each other. When Captain George Vancouver first viewed the bay in 1792, he judged it to be the entrance to a calm, safe harbor, but when he learned its true nature he decided that the name Deception Pass suited it much better. Tidal velocity of waters seething in and out has been measured as high as eight knots an hour through channels which vary from four to thirty-seven fathoms deep. It is no place to be caught in a small boat with an under-powered engine.

Oak Harbor, halfway down the island, was named for the many oak trees that once grew in the area. Like other communities in the Puget Sound region, its first settlers, who were Dutch, encouraged relatives and friends to come and settle there, so the town used to be full of names such as Fakkema, Koetje, and Van Wieringer. Today the outstanding event is the Holland Days

I–5—Mount Vernon to Everett
   33 miles
State 20—Mount Vernon to Clinton
   66 miles

Festival, in which Dutch costumes are worn and old–country games are played.

INDIAN WAR CANOES

Along the Strait of Juan de Fuca and into the sheltered waters of Puget Sound, then north through Georgia Strait along the coast of British Columbia and the Inside Passage to Alaska, the art of canoe-making has been known and refined by these salt water-dwelling Indians since time beyond knowing. Of all the tribes, the Makahs on the northwestern edge of the Olympic Peninsula and the Haidas in the Queen Charlotte Island area off the coast of British Columbia were the best. The Makahs were so skilled at canoe-building that they went out to sea and hunted gray whales in their craft, while the Haidas cruised hundreds of miles to the south in canoes manned by fifty or more paddlers on raids aimed at taking slaves, vengeance, or heads.

The method of manufacturing the seagoing craft was the same all along the coast. First, a man with an expert eye chose a cedar tree as nearly flawless as possible, had it felled with obsidian bladed axes called *pe-yah-cuds,* and then had it dragged to a convenient spot. Ideally, the tree would be seventy or eighty feet long.

The head canoe-maker or *tyee* (Chinook Jargon for "chief"), scored the bark, then his helpers trimmed the branches and peeled the trunk. The hull was shaped slowly and carefully. After hot rocks had been used to burn out the interior and the hull had been roughly formed, the *tyee* went over it inch by inch, chipping and smoothing until the finished craft would trim properly in the water.

Some hulls were preserved against warping and checking by charring the surfaces, but the favored practice was to apply several coats of dogfish-liver oil, hand-rubbing the surface after each application until a glossy polish was secured. Plentiful in the area, "dogfish" were one of several varieties of small, voracious sharks that were easy to catch, eaten only when no other fish were available, but useful in many other ways—such as for their liver-oil.

Though the oil application made the war canoes smell to high heaven, it did a remarkable job of preserving the canoes, some of which have proved serviceable a hundred years after they were built.

Crucial in the construction process was the spreading of the craft's interior in order to make it exactly the right width, which

Courtesy Washington State Library
STEAMBOAT *WHIDBEY* WRECKED AND BURNED IN OAK HARBOR, 1940.

was a delicate balance between load capacity and seaworthiness. After the hull was hollowed out, it was filled with water which then was heated with red-hot stones. As the still unseasoned wood softened, carefully measured thwarts were placed so that they would act as spreaders, producing a flare. Too little spread reduced stability in a heavy sea; too much might split the wood. Working without blueprints or printed directions, the only guide was the judgment of the *tyee* whose skills had been handed down to him through a long line of canoe-builders.

Sketches of the canoes seen by the first white explorers in the 1790s show them to be rather crude and clumsy-looking, despite their seaworthiness. But the Indian canoe-makers had an excellent eye for beauty as well as utility. Soon after they got their first look at the Bedford whalers, the Gloucester fishing vessels, and the Yankee Clippers, they incorporated their clean lines into their own craft, which became things of beauty as well as utility. After 1850, practically all of the canoes built by the Indians of the Northwest Coast reflect the influence of New England ship designers.

Today at Coupeville, halfway down Whidbey Island, examples of the best of the native craft may be seen in historical museums.

HAIDA VENGEANCE
As has happened too often during contacts between white new-comers and Indians native to a region, an act of injustice that occurred in lower Puget Sound soon after the Territory of Washington was formed in 1853 poisoned relations between the Haidas and the settlers for many years thereafter.

Curious to see how the white men lived, several Haida Indians from the far north made a peaceful journey down to a set-tlement called Budd's Inlet, only a couple of miles away from the newly-established capital of Olympia, where they traded some native craft work they had brought along for some white goods. When offered work by two white men named Butler and Burt, they accepted, did the labor required of them, and, when it was done, asked to be paid.

An argument ensued, with its result being they were first insulted, then ordered to leave with no wages at all. When they protested too vigorously, Butler and Burt attacked and killed them. Other settlers living in the area, some of whom had wit-nessed the killings, agreed that the two white men were cold-blooded murderers who should be made to pay for their crimes. Indeed, they were arrested, charged with murder, and brought before a magistrate for examination.

But before they could be indicted, the prosecuting attorney who was supposed to try them moved for the discharge of the accused because, "Thurston County has no jail, and it would be an expense to the county to keep them in custody."

So they were discharged and never brought to trial, an act which many white people in the community felt was a miserable travesty on law and justice. What the Haidas felt was much stronger—and eventually it inspired an imposition of Haida-style justice that the residents of Puget Sound would remember for a long time.

One of the murdered Indians was chief of a band of Haidas that lived in the Sitka area of Russian Alaska, and his people swore vengeance. In the latter part of May, 1855, Indians of that nation came from their northern homes in large numbers to avenge that death. In ten large war canoes, each of which carried fifty to sixty well-armed warriors, they cruised south to Vancouver Island, looking for victims. Though the first person they killed, Charles Bayley, was a British settler whom they mis-took for an American, they soon corrected that error by raiding a settlement on the shores of Bellingham Bay. There, they killed two Americans named David Melville and George Brown, cut off their heads, and sent them home as trophies to show that their mission had been successful.

Still not satisfied, they moved on to Whidbey Island, where they struck terror into the hearts of the settlers by attacking, looting, and burning. Though no more Americans lost their lives in this series of raids, the panic-stricken Americans appealed to the federal and territorial governments for warships and troops with which to repel the invaders. By the time help arrived, of course, the raiding Indians were long since gone.

Imaginative writers have called the Haidas the Pacific Northwest version of the Vikings. But Ivan Doig, who has written extensively about them in his book *Winter Brothers: A Season at the Edge of America*, feels that they deserve attention strictly as Haidas. He says:

> Undo the past and disperse a few hundred thousand Haidas along this coast from their home islands of northern British Columbia, the Queen Charlottes, south as far as the mouth of the Columbia River between Washington and Oregon, prime them with firepower equal to ours, and white civilization still might be waiting to set its first foot ashore here. The Haidas from all I can judge would have warred implacably as long as we could have stood it, then negotiated us to a frazzle.

Sad to say, though they were never conquered by force of arms, the white man's more deadly weapons—alcohol and smallpox, to neither of which were they immune—so debilitated their numbers that the estimated six thousand Haidas living in the Queen Charlotte Islands region in 1835 had dwindled to less than eight hundred in 1885. The worst killer was a smallpox epidemic in 1862. But until that happened, they were the terror of the Northwest Coast.

Near Coupeville on the west side of Whidbey Island, markers denoting Fort Ebey and Ebey's Landing commemorate the spot where one of the most macabre examples of Haida vengeance took place. As mentioned in an earlier chapter, Isaac N. Ebey in his capacity of tax collector had attempted in the spring of 1857 to establish American sovereignty on San Juan Island, with no success. Now a member of the Territorial Legislature and a trader on Whidbey Island, he was accustomed to dealing with far northern Indians, so when members of a party of two hundred or so Haidas came to his house August 11, 1857, he met them on what he thought were amiable terms. Certainly, he had never abused this or any other band of Indians. But white men had killed their chief a few years ago. And their vengeance was not complete.

At midnight, they again went to his house, called him out, shot him, cut off his head, and made their escape, carrying away the head, which was never recovered despite efforts of relatives to retrieve it.

A few miles north of Coupeville, which is on the east side of Whidbey Island, a road turns west to Fort Ebey State Park. In 1942, a coastal gun was installed here as part of a defensive system against a Japanese attack that never came. All that remains of the fortification today is a shallow concrete pit containing a circular iron ring on which the long-range gun, which has been removed, once tracked. Nearby are underground concrete bunkers in which ammunition was stored.

DAY OF THE ROBBER BARONS

On the mainland across from the southern end of Whidbey Island at Port Gardner Bay, the site that was to become Everett slumbered for one hundred years after its first discovery by Captain George Vancouver. Then in February, 1892, big doings were in the rain-drenched wind, for two of the nation's greatest capitalists, James Jerome Hill and John Davison Rockefeller, had taken an interest in the area and were about to make it the most important city north of San Francisco.

Following completion of the Northern Pacific Railroad from Lake Superior west across the Rockies to the lower Columbia River and then north to Tacoma in the 1880s, nearly one hundred thousand people came into Washington Territory. In 1889, Washington became a state. Now Jim Hill, the Empire Builder, was bringing the Great Northern Railroad to tidewater in Everett, where in conjunction with John D. Rockefeller and other eastern capitalists, he would build a thriving metropolis based on the unlimited timber and mineral resources of the region that would far surpass all the other cities in the Pacific Northwest. Or so it was hoped.

The fact that the Everett Land Company, which was controlled by the capitalists, owned every square foot of land in the area, surprised no one, for in that place and time that was the way the world was run.

Among other capitalists interested in the area were lumber barons such as Frederick Weyerhaeuser, who were planning to make Everett the timber capital of the world. Running out of trees with which to supply their sawmills back in Minnesota and Wisconsin, they were buying up all the virgin forest land they could gain title to—and buying it cheap. The westward-building railroads had been given huge grants of land by the federal government to encourage construction—land which the railroads then could sell to homesteaders or timber companies in order to build up passenger and freight traffic.

Judging from the size of the trees covering the country, the soil which nourished them must be extremely rich and fertile, said the experts. When the trees had been cut down and sunlight permitted to fall on the land, farm crops should do very well. And sawmills meant jobs.

With Everett booming and James Hill due to arrive in June, 1893, on the first through train from Lake Superior, a group of town boosters inscribed a solid silver plate to honor the Empire Builder during his visit to what they proudly called the "city of smokestacks." Unfortunately, the Panic of 1893, which caused lumber prices to collapse, made the Great Northern stop all construction, bankrupted the Northern Pacific, brought on the failure of three of the five local banks, and forced Hill to postpone his trip for a while. The partners in the Everett Land Company issued bonds, in the amount of $1.5 million at eight percent interest, in order to keep operating. With most of the bonds being purchased by John D. Rockefeller himself, local capitalists breathed a sigh of relief. "Rockefeller never loses money," people said, "so his stake in Everett is a guarantee of success"

It was also a guarantee that Rockefeller now owned all the assets worth having in the town, which he could and would take over when he wished to do so.

After 1893, wages fell sixty percent. By 1897, the Everett Land Company was in receivership, stripped of its assets by Rockefeller, and auctioned on the courthouse steps for $15,000 in cash and $750,000 of its own worthless bonds. Of the original capitalists who had believed in the town, only one remained—James J. Hill. But he still had plans to build a Northwest Empire.

Key to those plans was timber.

FANTASTIC BARGAIN

In St. Paul, James Hill and Frederick Weyerhaeuser had long been friends. With the availability of usable trees declining in the Mississippi Valley area and an unlimited supply of prime trees to be had in the Pacific Northwest, Weyerhaeuser, encouraged and aided by Hill, negotiated one of the largest financial transactions in the history of the country. This was the purchase of 900,000 acres of land grants (which had been given to the Northern Pacific Railroad Company) for six dollars an acre. The price paid for the timber standing on this expanse of land was estimated at ten cents a thousand board feet.

In order to utilize the trees cut off his company's holdings, Weyerhaeuser built the largest sawmill in the world in Everett. From its initial capacity of 28 million board feet in 1902, the mill expanded steadily, reaching a capacity of 70 million board feet in 1912. Following his example, other timber barons came to Everett and built mills, encouraged by cheap timber, free mill sites, and reduced rail rates to markets in the East.

"By 1910 there were ninety-five manufacturing plants in Everett," writes historian Norman Clark, "including eleven lumber mills, sixteen shingle mills, and dozens of minor industries subordinate to the sawdust economy. Over five thousand of the thirty-five thousand men, women, and children in Everett earned wages in mills and factories."

In a day when there were few safeguards in an extremely hazardous industry, the brotherhood of shingle weavers was bonded in the grim realities of blood and sawdust, Clark writes.

It was not at all uncommon for shingle mill workers to lose four to eight fingers in accidents. One State Bureau of Labor survey found that over fifty percent of them had suffered serious injuries. Though their $4.50 a day wage was twice the $2.25 earned by other sawmill workers, the extreme danger of their jobs forced them to organize into the most militant of the unions. "Shingle Weavers," they proudly called themselves, after their talent for putting bundles of shingles together so fast that they appeared to be weaving them. The fact that the employers did not recognize their union mattered not at all to them. To a man, they all belonged to the International.

THE WOBBLIES

Founded in the 1890s and soon becoming the most radical union of all, the Industrial Workers of the World took pride in being front line soldiers in the ask-no-quarter-give-no-quarter battle between Labor and Capital. Contemptuously called "Wobblies" and "I Won't Work" by the employers, they were harassed, clubbed, shot at, and forcibly driven out of every logging camp or sawmill in which they appeared. On their part, they advocated the complete overthrow of the capitalistic system and its replacement by a society owned and operated by the workingman.

If the only way to achieve their ends was by planting bombs on the gateposts or under the beds of the politicians, judges, and capitalists who opposed them, so be it. On the other hand, more than one man of wealth and power bragged that with his money he could "hire half of the working class to club the other half into line."

By the use of strike-breakers, Pinkertons, and hired goons, he often did just that.

It was into this atmosphere of growing conflict that the Reverend Billy Sunday came to Everett in 1910. Before becoming a hell-and-brimstone evangelist, Billy Sunday had been a better than average professional baseball player—a pitcher. When he launched into a sermon, he preached like he had pitched.

Leaning forward to get his sign from the catcher, which now was the entire audience, he scowled, appeared to shake off signs for a curve or a change of pace, then nodded, reared back, and threw what everybody in the park knew he intended to throw in the first place—-his high, hard one.

"If some of the guns that you young bucks carry in your hip pockets were to explode," he would thunder at the youth in the audience, "it would blow your brains out. Card playing and dancing in so-called Christian homes have ruined more young men than all the saloons the devil has ever licensed."

Since there were forty licensed saloons along downtown Everett's Hewitt Avenue alone, the devil had all he could do to keep up with renewals. Sponsored by the city's Protestant churches, which were mounting a campaign to turn Everett dry, volunteer labor built a tabernacle to seat sixty-five hundred souls. In his first sermon, titled *Home, Booze, and Native Land*, which he delivered three times the first day to over twelve thousand people, Billy Sunday struck the keynote for his five-week revival appear-

Courtesy BPA
DIABLO DAM, CITY OF SEATTLE LIGHT COMPANY

ance in Everett. Though he expressed disappointment in the city's lack of Christian response, he increased church membership by twenty-five hundred people during his stay.

Much to the chagrin of the good people of Everett, the devil was busy in Seattle, too, which was just twenty miles away. With the Klondike Gold Rush over and the city suffering a mild recession, Seattle Mayor Hiram Gill promised his business friends to restore prosperity by luring loggers and millworkers from the entire Puget Sound area to the flesh pots of Seattle by keeping the saloons and other attractions of Skid Road open twenty-four hours a day. Hearing that one red-light house that had recently opened for business was employing seven hundred women, workmen from Everett jammed every car of the interurban lines.

Though a mild moral revival following Billy Sunday's tour endured for a few months after his visit, a drop in demand for lumber brought on serious unemployment in the winter of 1913. When the only work loggers could find was shoveling snow off the tracks of the Great Northern in the mountains at miserable wages, the Wobblies marched through the streets of Everett in protest. Tossing their shovels into drifts beside the right of way, many of them came down from the hills to hear their national leader, Big Bill Haywood.

Not too many years before, Haywood was indicted and tried in Boise, Idaho, on the charge that he had conspired to plant a bomb on the gatepost of an ex–governor, Frank Steunenberg. Attorney for the prosecution was Senator William Borah. Attorney for the defense was advocates around the world, Haywood was acquitted. Now he was the hero of the more radical sector of the Labor movement.

"The IWW is without morals!" He roared to an audience of four hundred rabid supporters, "To hell with reform! We want revolution!"

With other Wobbly leaders, he declared that the plight of workers in the Pacific Northwest justified violence. The governments of every state, he predicted, would soon collapse under the strain of a nationwide general strike.

Thus, when the Shingle Weavers went out on strike, as they did May 1, 1916, the stage was set for the most violent act of the conflict between Labor and Capital ever to take place in Washington State.

THE EVERETT MASSACRE

Though the depression of 1914–15 hurt the efforts of more moderate trade unions to win pay raises and the eight-hour day, war in Europe increased demand for lumber and upped prices. As yet, no IWW heads had been cracked in Everett, as had happened in other cities, but the town was far from being a bastion for free speech.

When James Rowan, an IWW spokesman, mounted the speaker's stand and attacked conservative trade unionism by shouting that the AFL "promotes organized scabbery," he was first called a liar, then arrested by Sheriff Donald McCrae and accused of "peddling literature without a license." After a night in jail, he was given the choice of a thirty-day sentence or a free ride out of the county. He took the interurban to Seattle.

With the shingle weavers still on strike and jeering at the "scabs" imported by the mill owners to replace them, tension rose. By July 1916, patience was wearing thin on both sides. Some of the more imaginative pickets noted that while the mills were being guarded along the city streets, many of them had been built

Courtesy Washington State Library
SKAGIT CHIEF, IN FREIGHT SERVICE ON PUGET SOUND IN 1952

on pilings and were partially above water, which was in federal jurisdiction; so the pickets borrowed boats which they rowed under the windows of the mills, shouting obscenities at the non–union workers within.

Ten pickets were surrounded and beaten. In retaliation, 150 angry union men returned and approached the strike-breakers. Apparently feeling that an invisible line had been crossed, the police, who had stood impassively by while the pickets were being beaten, intervened; shots were fired, with one striker being wounded as he and his comrades were driven away from the plant.

In its Seattle headquarters, the IWW decided to counter by sending its most colorful agitator to Everett. This spell-binding firebrand, James P. Thompson, had led the Wobblies so-called "free speech fight" in Spokane in 1909, which had been a classic triumph of passive resistance. When Spokane police started arresting speakers for violating a city ordinance against street meetings, Wobblies led by Thompson appeared like a plague of locusts, willing to mount soapboxes and be carted off to jail. Called the "soldiers of discontent," they poured out of the woods and the harvest fields in such numbers that they soon filled the jails to overflowing. Over twelve hundred Wobblies were arrested and jailed. By the time the city fathers finally got around to repealing the ordinance, the jails were so packed that all other criminals had to be released and the city was forced to spend a quarter of a million dollars housing and feeding its unwanted guests.

Written as a model of liberal intent, Everett's street-meeting ordinance decreed that speakers could use the cross streets along Hewitt Avenue if they stayed fifty feet back from the thoroughfare. Before bringing in twenty members from Seattle on August 22, the Wobblies carefully measured off exactly that distance, then erected their platform. But in spite of this precaution, Sheriff McCrae came into the IWW office that morning and ordered them all to leave the county.

They refused. That evening, following a concert by the Salvation Army band, Wobbly speaker James Thompson invited the crowd to stay and hear the truth about American industry. In his speech, he declared that the Industrial Workers of the World supported the shingle weavers in their strike and urged other people in Everett to do likewise. After he had spoken for twenty minutes or so, city police moved in and seized him.

One by one the rest of the twenty Wobblies got onto the platform and began to speak; one by one they were arrested and hauled away. Even an Everett woman sympathetic to the union cause, Mrs. Letelsia Frye, who mounted the platform and tried to read the Declaration of Independence, was grabbed and taken away. When the local Trades Council representative, Jake Michel, moved out of the crowd to protest, he too was hauled off to the city jail.

Day by day, tension increased. Deciding to link the striking shingle weavers with the IWW, mill owner David Clough appeared at a meeting of the Everett Commercial Club and verbally painted a terrifying picture of what the Wobblies could do to the economy of their fair city, which they might destroy just for the hell of it. They were in many cases not even Americans, he said, but men whose mad leaders encouraged them to befoul their own bunks, defile the flag, burn wheat fields, and sand the bearings of expensive machinery. Such men should not be allowed to steal Everett's future.

The only way to save the city, he suggested, was to authorize Sheriff McRae to deputize a force of several hundred club members.

Click Relander Collection, Courtesy Yakima Valley Regional Library
FLOATING BRIDGE ACROSS LAKE WASHINGTON, EAST OF SEATTLE

In a word, Everett prepared for war, with Sheriff Donald McCrae the general in charge of the defending army. The first skirmish was not long in coming.

THE BATTLE OF EVERETT

Discovering that land access to the city by railroad, interurban, auto, or foot was denied them, a party of Wobblies decided to attack by sea. Getting off the train at Mukilteo, just south of Everett, ten members were loaned a small boat, the *Wanderer*, by a friend, while the other ten found seats in a dory, which was towed behind the *Wanderer* as it set out across Port Gardner Bay.

Sheriff McCrae was ready for the invading force. In a tugboat with sixty deputies, McCrae first fired a warning shot, then another into its muffler, disabling the smaller boat and bringing it to a stop. Taking the Wobblies aboard his tug, the sheriff confronted the skipper of the *Wanderer*, who later told his story:

> ... they had made fast my stern line and as I bent over with the line McCrae struck me with his revolver on the back of the head. I said something to him and then he ran the revolver right here in my groin and he ruptured me at the same time.
> I told him, "It's a fine way of using a citizen."
> He says, "You're a hell of a citizen bringing a bunch like that

to cause a riot in this town."

I says, "Well, they are all union men anyway."

He says, "You shut your damn head or I will knock it clean off." And I guess he would, because he had enough whiskey in him at the time to do it.

After being held for nine days in the county jail, allegedly without beds or blankets, the invading force from the *Wanderer* was sent back to Seattle.

Meanwhile on the streets of Everett, companies of club-swinging deputies continued to terrorize the Wobblies and anyone in sympathy with their cause. But a few local pro–union men spoke out in protest against what they felt was the basic cause of the violence. Ernest Marsh, long a voice of reason in an unreasonable place and time, wrote in an editorial in the *Labor Journal* that the Trades Council:

> ... holds no brief with the IWW, who foolishly or otherwise persist in speaking on Wetmore Avenue, but the real agitators are the business and professional men who have allowed themselves to be buncoed into a private standing army.

By early November, it was clear that a climactic battle was imminent. Speaking to the Everett Commercial Club November 3, the manager of the Employers' Association of Washington State told the five hundred assembled deputies how a similar group of five hundred in Detroit had taken the law into their own hands to put down "the Wobbly menace." He urged the men in his audience to do the same, to show the world that "...a city of red-blooded Americans would not be bullied and cowed by a handful of men...the only way to combat force is with force... "

In Seattle, the editors of the *Industrial Worker* were equally militant, calling for an army of two thousand men to assemble and march to Everett in support of radical unionism and free speech. By Sunday morning, the call had brought forth about four hundred men. Marching from the IWW hall to the dock, half of them boarded the steamer *Verona* while the other half waited for a second steamer, the *Calista*.

"Laughter and jest were on the lips of the men who crowded the *Verona*," one witness described the scene, "and songs of One Big Union rang out over the sparkling waters of Puget Sound. Loyal soldiers were these in the great class war, enlightened work-

VIRGINIA VI
This boat was popular on the run between Tacoma and Seattle, prior to the 1950s.

ers who were willing to give their all in the battle for bread, happiness, and liberty... "

Historian Norman Clark doubts the statement that the men were prepared "to give their all." More likely, he writes, they carried a kind of tribal memory of Spokane, in which their peaceful protest of their rights of free speech had led to a peaceful ending, which had greatly embarrassed the authorities. To resist passively, to go to jail, even to be bloodied a bit—these were things a Wobbly could count on sooner or later.

But they counted also on their strength in numbers and on their public support this day to humble a sheriff and a clan of bosses who, their speakers assured them, so richly deserved humiliation.

Scattered through the crowd were a few men who were in no mood to laugh or jest. These were the workers that had suffered the wrath of Sheriff Donald McCrae, who, if reports were to be believed, was incredibly brutal when drunk, as he often was. With pistols smuggled in a coat pocket or belted under overalls against the belly, they were grimly determined not to suffer his kicks or clubs again.

It would later be alleged that at least two or three Pinkerton spies and agent provocateurs were in the crowd, one of whom had kept urging violence, while the other had loudly offered to buy phosphorous—a favorite tool of professional arsonists. Either or both of these men, it was later said, had been in telephone contact with Sheriff McCrae before the boats left Seattle.

In Everett, rumors spread like wildfire. One prominent citizen later declared, "The IWW came here to burn Everett and to burn the mills. The citizens had to arm to repel the invasion."

The commander of the United States Naval Militia in Everett, who was also a businessman and a deputy, reported that he had heard that the Wobblies intended to raid the naval armory and seize arms and ammunition. "I therefore took the precaution to safe-guard same and had them removed to a room in the commercial club." During his brief absence from that room, he later sheepishly admitted, the arms and ammunition were again removed—this time by the deputies to the city dock.

As the *Verona* approached the dock, it became a scene of utter confusion. On the hillside above the waterfront, thousands of people stood watching in the bright afternoon sunshine. Cheers from pro–union people filled the air; jeers from the anti–Wobbly crowd were just as loud. As the engines slowed and grew quiet, people ashore could make out the words of the Wobbly hymn which was being sung enthusiastically:

We meet today in freedom's cause
And raise our banners high!
We'll join our hands in union strong,
To battle, win, or die!

As the bowline was thrown and secured and the gangplank lowered to the dock, Sheriff McCrae, brandishing two pistols, stepped forward and demanded, "Boys, who's your leader?"

"We're all leaders!" a strong Wobbly voice jeered back.

"You can't land here!"

"The hell we can't!" a Wobbly shouted.

The crowd of men aboard the boat surged forward. Suddenly somewhere to the sheriff's right a shot rang out, then another and another, with three shots being deliberately fired by a man whose position or identity could not later be determined. Both aboard the ship and on the docks, hundreds of men ran around screaming and firing their weapons indiscriminately.

Sheriff McCrae and two of his deputies fell to the dock, wounded. Aboard the ship, a man who had climbed a mast in order to wave to the crowd lost his grip, slipped, and fell to the deck, where he died instantly. In terror, the Wobblies ran to the side of the ship away from the guns on shore, causing the ship to tilt to the overweighted side; a number of the living, wounded, and dead slid overboard into the water.

The exchange of gunfire lasted no more than two minutes. Then the engines of the *Verona* gave a surge of power, the lines broke, and the ship churned away from the dock. Ashore two men were dead and at least twenty were wounded, while the casualties aboard the boat were equally high. Worried that the Wobblies might send reinforcements by land, Sheriff McCrae, who had been shot in the legs, telegraphed the governor:

> Terrible riot in Everett. At least twenty-five citizens shot. Some dead and others mortally wounded. Send militia at once without fail and plenty of them.

Governor Lister responded by sending two National Guard units to Everett and Seattle. When the *Verona* docked in Seattle, the authorities refrained from arresting its passengers for fear of more violence. But it was a quiet group of men that left the ship, for they now realized, as one observer wrote "... that class struggle was not all jokes and songs..."

On the ship, four were dead, one was dying, and twenty-seven were wounded, historian Clark writes. The number that went overboard when the ship tilted and slid into the sea was guessed to be between six and twelve. Almost all of the dead and wounded were young men under twenty-six years of age.

"The bitterness drawn across Everett during that afternoon would linger for at least a full generation," Norman Clark writes. "Among the survivors and partisans even today, there are many who see the events of November 5 as the result of a necessary, if tragic, police action that revolutionaries had forced upon the sheriff and other loyal citizens who accepted the responsibility for keeping law and order in a terrified city."

Others with equal sincerity, he then adds, reject any challenge to the phrase now fixed in regional history— "The Everett Massacre." He concludes:

> If a historian searching for truth examines critically the first-hand accounts of participants, he can stack such accounts

Courtesy Washington State Library
PUGET SOUND EXCURSION BOAT IN TACOMA HARBOR, CA 1940

into impressive heaps of mutually contradictory evidence, which often conceal more than they reveal.

Following a trial held five months later, in which the Wobblies were charged with murder, the jury found the accused men not guilty. No charges were ever brought against Sheriff McCrae and his army of citizen deputies.

FOUNDING OF SEATTLE

By nature, the two men credited with founding Seattle were complete opposites, writes Nard Jones in his affectionate, personal history of Seattle. Arthur Armstrong Denny was pragmatic, close-fisted, and a teetotaler. Dr. David Swinton Maynard was outgoing, friendly, and a hard drinker. Yet somehow they always got along well together as they worked in different ways to build a great city, disagreeing only once. This was on the plan by which the streets of the growing village were to be laid out.

Doc Maynard stubbornly insisted that the streets on his plat run foursquare on a north–south, east–west grid, while Denny, who recognized the importance of the waterfront, dogmatically platted his streets so that they followed the shoreline, no matter

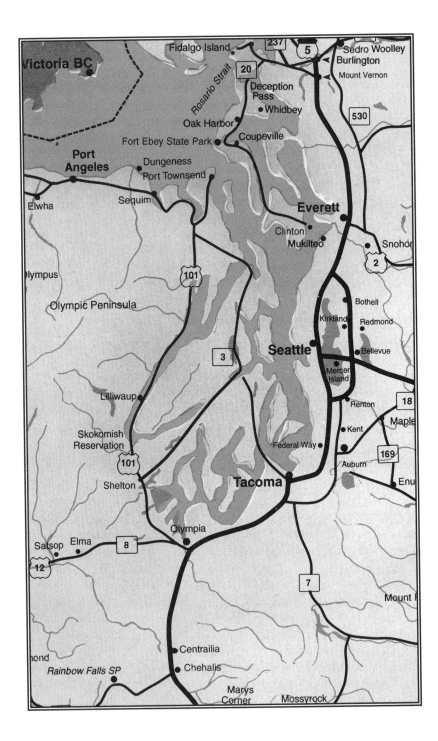

which direction it wandered. Though city engineers later did their best to meld the two patterns where they joined, the result eventually proved to be a puzzle that still remains unsolved.

The son of Irish immigrant parents, Arthur Denny came west from Illinois in 1851 during the peak of emigration to the Oregon country. Though he planned to take a Donation Claim in the Willamette Valley, he found the growing city of Portland too big for his tastes, so turned his eyes north toward Puget Sound. On February 15, 1852, he found a site he liked on Elliott Bay just below Alki Point. There, the twelve adults and twelve children in the party filed their claims and began to build their homes.

Shortly thereafter, Doctor David Maynard arrived and was shown around the area by a big, friendly, intelligent local Indian named Sealth.

At about this same time, another industrialist arrived, Henry L. Yesler, with plans to build a steam sawmill. Denny and Maynard were laying out streets and selling or giving away lots on plats that did not jibe, but since both men recognized the value of having a sawmill in the town, they quickly adjusted their plats to make room for Yesler. Because Maynard was generous when in his cups, he gave away many of his lots, so his part of town grew more quickly than Denny's did. On the other hand, Denny was shrewder and his plans usually were broader in scope.

Though the entire Puget Sound area was full of good harbors and new settlements, the fact that Elliott Bay boasted a sawmill, an energetic businessman, and a public–minded doctor, made it attractive to new settlers. Even so, few vessels visited Puget Sound during the winter of 1852–53 and basic supplies of food such as pork, butter, flour, and sugar, which had to shipped around the Horn or imported from Chile or China, were extremely scarce. For instance, Denny wrote:

> That fall I paid $90 for two barrels of pork, and $20 for a barrel of flour. I left one barrel of pork on the beach in front of my cabin, as I supposed at high tide, until it would be needed. Just about the time to roll it up and open it there came a high tide

I–5—Everett to Seattle
25 miles

and heavy wind at night, and like the house that was built on sand, it washed away and disappeared. It was the last barrel of pork in King County and the loss of it was felt by many as a very serious matter.

Two of the original settlers, John Low and Charles Terry, were New Yorkers, so when they suggested that the town be called New York, it was so christened. But the name was too pretentious for a settlement of log cabins and muddy streets, so it was altered to New York Alki, the added Indian word meaning "New York by-and-by."

When Washington Territory was organized in 1853 and its first governor, Isaac Ingalls Stevens, met and made treaties with the leaders of local Indian tribes, one of the most impressive and articulate of the native Americans was a chief named Noah Sealth. Recognizing the fact that his people must adapt to the white man's ways, whether they wanted to or not, he was so friendly and helpful that his name, slightly altered for ease of pronunciation and spelling, was given to the growing village, which became Seattle.

Chief Sealth's claim to lasting fame has come, Nard Jones writes, from a speech he supposedly made during talks at the Stevens' Treaty discussions in 1854. As a newspaperman, Jones long was skeptical as to the authenticity of the speech, which was translated and recorded some years after it was made. But as time passed, he came to believe that it expressed the feelings, if not the exact wording, of the wise old chief, concluding, "No book with the city of Seattle as its subject would be complete without it."

The much-quoted (and misquoted) speech begins:

Yonder sky that has wept tears of compassion upon our fathers for centuries untold, and which to us looks eternal, may change. Today it is fair, tomorrow it may be overcast with clouds...

And ends:

At night, when the streets of your cities will be silent and you think them deserted, they will throng with returning hosts that once filled and still love this beautiful land.
The white man will never be alone. Let him be just and deal kindly with my people, for the dead are not powerless.
Dead—did I say?
There is no death.
Only a change of worlds!

NARD JONES

Because I frequently quote him in this book, I should explain the special relationship that existed between the late Nard Jones and myself over a period of many years. In my opinion the finest writer the state of Washington has produced, he was thirteen years older than I. Though Nard was a third–generation Washingtonian, while I did not migrate to the state until 1945, we had a number of things in common.

We both were full-time professional writers, who shared the same New York publisher and agent. In our youth, we both had lived in Greenwich Village as bachelors, then later had returned to the big city with our wives to show them what life was like in New York. Because we found it different and disagreeable, we both eventually returned to what we felt was the better life in Washington state.

Nard Jones graduated from Whitman College in Walla Walla, thus retained a warm spot in his heart for the college and the town. Getting interested in the history of the interior Pacific Northwest, about which both Nard and I wrote for most of our careers, I spent some time doing research in the excellent Whitman College Library, coming to like it and Walla Walla so well that Jeanne and I moved from Tacoma to the "dry" side of the mountains. We have lived here ever since. Eventually, Jeanne went to work at the Whitman College Library as Pacific Northwest Librarian, remaining there for thirteen years.

At about this time, Nard moved back to Seattle, where, as an editor and book-reviewer for first the *P–I (Post–Intelligencer)* and then the *Seattle Times,* he reviewed fiction and nonfiction books I wrote on the Pacific Northwest, while as a reviewer for *Union–Bulletin* in Walla Walla, I reviewed books he wrote about Washington state and Seattle.

Though we did not meet face to face for ten years, we crossed each other's tracks in print and through friends in the trade many times, developing a mutual respect for each other's writings. On one occasion, I gave a verbal review of a book into which Nard had put his heart and soul, *The Great Command,* at a luncheon where he was the honored guest of the Marcus Whitman Society. A naturally shy man, he squirmed a bit when I prefaced my review by asking him if he recalled the kind of review he had given my most recently published book. But his concern was needless—he had been kind to me, as I was to him.

Published in 1947 by Dodd Mead, his *Evergreen Land* gives the best overall view of the state of Washington that I have ever read; while his *Seattle*, issued by Doubleday in 1972 is the most entertaining and informative book I have found on that city. When first published many years ago, several of his regional novels were so realistic and true to life that—though not banned completely—they were under-the-table or behind-the-desk items at local bookstores and libraries.

His historical novel on the Columbia, *Swift Flows the River*, which was a best-seller in its day, remains a classic and is still in print. His dramatized but true account of the martyred missionaries, *Marcus and Narcissa Whitman*, whose murders in 1847 by grief-stricken Indians dramatically turned the attention of the nation to the Pacific Northwest, is the best thing in its field.

It was Nard Jones' firm belief that history written in the form of dramatic narrative need never be dull. I heartily agree—and hereby give him credit for the example he has set for regional writers who have followed in his footsteps...

THE MERCER GIRLS

Like all frontier communities, Seattle was full of energetic, ambitious young single men but suffered a lack of young single women. Back East, big cities such as Boston and New York were full of lovely, virtuous young ladies, but with a wide continent lying between in a day when virtuous single women almost never traveled alone, chances that the twain should meet were small. In order to remedy that problem, Charles Prosch, editor of the *Puget Sound Herald*, ran an ad in his paper on February 24, 1860:

> Attention, Bachelors: Believing that our only chance of a realization of the benefits and early attainments of matrimonial alliances depends upon the arrival in our midst of the fair sex from the Atlantic States, and that, to bring about such an arrival a united effort and action are called for on our part, we respectfully request a full attendance of all eligible and sincerely desirous bachelors in this community to assemble on Tuesday evening next in Delin and Shorey's building to devise ways and means to secure this much needed and desirable emigration to our shores.

Though the first meeting produced little other than the suggestion that Charles Prosch send clippings of his editorials to eastern papers, in hopes they would reprint them and inspire a response, the field had been prepared for a young genius in public relations who did know how to get results. This was Asa Mercer, whose older brother, Judge Thomas Mercer, had first come to the town in 1852. Arriving a year after the first bachelor meeting was held, Asa was brash, well educated, personable, and ready to tackle any project that interested his lively mind, no matter how impossible it seemed.

After grubbing out stumps, clearing land, and helping build the first structure on the site of what was proposed to be a university of higher learning, he cheerfully accepted the positions of both president and entire faculty of the institution. A bachelor himself, he became interested in Prosch's project.

"Clothed in the dignity of the university presidency he discussed a plan with Territorial Governor Pickering and with members of the legislature," Jones writes. "He insisted that the way to get suitable white women onto the shores of Elliott Bay was to go East and bring them back in groups of a hundred, two hundred, five hundred. But no politician supported the idea actively, and anyhow the territorial treasury was empty."

With no resources himself, he went from cabin to cabin and from merchant to merchant to raise money for his passage East. Once there, he managed to persuade eleven young women, ranging in age from fifteen to twenty-five, to accompany him back to Seattle. They arrived at midnight on May 16, 1864.

Leading the greeting party were the married ladies of Seattle, while the newly washed and shaved bachelors hung around nearby, hoping to be noticed. A reception was held in the common meeting hall, which lasted until dawn. Taken into respectable homes until they found employment as school teachers or other genteel trades, the young ladies were awed with the beauty of their surroundings and the warmth of their welcome.

Though Asa Mercer was disappointed in having brought out only eleven young ladies, his neighbors were so impressed with his achievement that they elected him to the legislature with a thumping majority despite the fact he made no campaign at all.

"They did it without my spending a nickel," he said in a daze. "I never bought a cigar or a glass of whiskey for anybody."

Encouraged by his friends, he undertook a second expedition a year later. This time he raised funds in advance, requesting three hundred dollars from each bride-hungry bachelor in exchange for a promise to bring him back a mate. He had hoped to appeal to President Lincoln's known weakness for great humanitarian projects, but was stunned when about to catch a train from New York to Washington to learn that the president had been assassinated the night before.

For weeks, he hung around the nation's capital, shunted from one politician to another, being told by all how brilliant his plan was and how greatly it would contribute to the welfare of the nation, then being given sincere regrets and limp reasons why they could give him no help at this present moment.

Then he ran into General Grant. Unlike many Washington politicians and bureaucrats, Grant knew Washington Territory well, for he had served at Fort Vancouver just across the river from Portland as a lowly, impecunious lieutenant back in 1853. "I'm to appear at a cabinet meeting this morning," Grant told Mercer. "You wait here and I'll try to bring the whole matter to a head, one way or another."

He was back within an hour, writing out an order to Mercer on the United States Army for a vessel completely fitted out and manned for Puget Sound. But when Mercer literally ran with it to the office of the Quartermaster General, he struck a snag.

"This is absolutely illegal and Grant knows it," the Quartermaster said firmly. "I cannot honor this order. You'll get no vessel from the Army."

With Grant pulling such strings as he could and by use of all his own powers of persuasion, Mercer finally got the Quartermaster to agree to provide him with a vessel if he would make a payment of eighty thousand dollars to the federal government. In his desperate scramble for funds and a commitment by five hundred young ladies to go to Seattle, he came to the attention of the stagecoach and steamship magnate, Ben Holladay. They made a deal in which Holladay would furnish the money, Mercer would supply the five hundred young ladies, and Holladay would transport them to Seattle at the going rate.

When Mercer provided only two hundred young women, Holladay boosted the per capita rate, with Mercer reluctantly agreeing. Receiving the news in Seattle, frantic efforts to build housing for two hundred ladies were begun, while the five hundred bachelors who had put up three hundred dollars for a bride worried over the problem of dividing two hundred young ladies among five hundred men.

Accompanied by a reporter from the *New York Times*, who recorded the stormy journey through the Strait of Magellan and then north toward Seattle with its homesickness, seasickness, bickering, and even a bit of hair-pulling, the unique cargo reached San Francisco, which was as far as Holladay's skipper would go without further payment.

Mercer telegraphed Governor Pickering for passage money to Elliott Bay. The return message came collect and Mercer could not pay for it. Telling the Western Union man he thought it was a money order from the Governor of Washington Territory, Mercer offered to gamble. "If it is, I can pay you. If it isn't, you need not read it to me."

The telegrapher looked at the message and laughed. Governor Pickering had sent several hundred words of congratulations—collect—and no money.

But Asa Mercer did not give up. In New York he had bought several farm wagons, which he hoped to take to Seattle and sell at a profit. Instead, he sold them here. With the proceeds and a bit of bargaining, he managed to ship his "cargo of brides" piece-meal on several craft during the next few days. Following their arrival in Seattle, all the Mercer girls married in a relatively short period of time, including one lovely young lady who married Asa himself.

But the effort had taken a lot out of Asa Mercer's spirit of innovative adventure. No longer did he yearn to be a university president or a member of the Washington Territorial Legislature. Jones writes, "Soon with his bride he headed for the western foothills of the Rocky Mountains to become a rancher. Meanwhile, the Mercer Girls and their descendants carried on, modestly and quietly."

GOLD IN ALASKA

During the 1880s, Seattle grew by fits and starts as the lumber industry, fishing, and railroad-building suffered ups and downs, with only two notable events occurring. These were the anti–Chinese riots in 1886 and the disastrous fire of 1889 which wiped out a good-sized section of the waterfront business establishments. While both the riots and the fire raged with considerable intensity for brief periods of time, neither did much lasting

damage. In the case of the fire, it did clear out a lot of flimsy buildings that had needed burning for years. In addition, the rebuilding of the businesses along the waterfront, whose structures were
erected of more solid material several feet higher above tide level,
improved plumbing functions remarkably, while at the same time
creating a tourist attraction that would not be discovered and
developed until the 1960s.

When the city was first built in the 1850s, "water closets," as
they were called, simply dumped their contents into a convenient
hole, ditch, or stream. Those built along the waterfront deposited
directly into the bay. But if built too close to the high tide level,
there could be a problem.

William C. Speidel, publisher of the *Seattle Guide* and *Sons of
the Profits*, who is good-naturedly cynical about the ancestors of
Seattle's present-day businessmen, not only discovered a vast network of tunnels underlying the waterfront where new buildings
were built above the old, but also claims that going to the bath-
room in the "good old days" was something of an adventure.

"Kids were raised on the tide tables instead of Doctor Spock,"
he says, "for toilets flooded and backed up at high tide. Some
ingenious settlers solved the problem by raising the water closet
to such a height that three or four steps were required to climb
aboard."

According to one early settler, Ezra Meeker, "You can smell
Seattle a couple of miles before you can see it."

A TON OF GOLD

In 1893, a nation-wide depression had buried the Pacific
Northwest deep in the doldrums. Conditions were so desperate
that a mob of unemployed men seized a hotel in Tacoma, stole all
the food in the kitchen and storerooms, then began hauling out
the furniture with the hope of selling it for passage money to
Washington, DC, where they intended to demand help from the
federal government. Only the use of troops by the governor
brought the disorder to an end.

Seattle's unemployed were more easily controlled, Nard
Jones says, because they were confined to the Skid Road district
along the waterfront. Because the term "Skid Road" is so often
misused by writers who either don't know or don't care about its
origin, I will here digress long enough to join the late Stewart

Holbrook, Jim Stevens, Nard Jones, and other regional writers who knew the timber industry and used its vocabulary correctly in their long-standing campaign to kill the more modern term "Skid Row."

In the days when sections of felled trees were pulled out of the woods by teams of oxen or horses, a trail was cut through the big timber just wide enough to let a team and a log be hauled out. To make sure that the big log did not hang up, a narrow road of small logs was laid down, placed at right angles and coated with axle grease in order to make the big logs skid more easily.

This was called a "skid road."

Before long, the term was applied on an ever-widening scale to mean a man, a district, or anything else that was deteriorating so rapidly that a greased road leading in that direction must have been laid down to assist it.

But the term "skid row" is meaningless and a sure sign that its user is an effete city-dweller who has no respect for a logger, who, as any native to Seattle knows, stirs his coffee with his thumb, shaves with a double-bitted ax, and cuts his hair with a chain saw. In any event, Seattle was a badly depressed area during the summer of 1897. Then a piece of news reached it that made everybody sit up and take notice. Returning from Alaska, the steamer *Portland* sent a wireless shortly after she cleared Cape Flattery inbound through the Strait of Juan De Fuca. As word of her cargo spread, crowds of wild-eyed men swarmed down to the Seattle docks to meet the ship. Soon newspapers all over the Puget Sound were screaming the sensational headlines:

GOLD! GOLD! GOLD! GOLD!
Sixty-Eight Rich Men on the Steamer Portland
STACKS OF YELLOW METAL!
Some have $5,000, Many Have More
A Few Bring Out $100,000 Each
A TON OF GOLD ARRIVES!

Actually, the $700,000 in gold placed in the ship's safe would have weighed slightly less than a ton at the price of gold those days, but since many of the returning passengers were carrying their treasure on their persons or in their cabins, the total probably was close. But nobody quibbled.

The first strikes had been made on the Yukon River in Canadian Territory. But soon Alaska, just across the border, would prove equally rich in gold as far north as Nome. A stampede the likes of which had never been known before ensued—with Seattle the jumping-off place where every prospector headed north would buy the ton of food, supplies, and equipment required before he disembarked at Skagway and started the terrible climb up and over Chilkoot Pass, across Bennett Lake, and then down the rapids of the Yukon River to Dawson City and the fabled riches of the Klondike.

From that day on, the prosperity of Seattle was tied closely to that of Alaska, for it was through Seattle that most of the wealth of the forty-ninth state passed in one form or another.

One of the legends of the time was that tenderfeet—"cheechakos"—fared better than experienced miners who had been prospecting for years. As the first reporter to cover the Yukon strike put it:

> Fortune seemed to favor the inexperienced men who went into the district only late last year. The stories they tell seemed beyond belief. Instances are noted where single individuals have taken out in two and a half months gold to the value of $150,000 or more.

During the Gold Rush, Seattle prospered and grew. There was a tremendous upsurge of commerce and of highly profitable sin, Nard Jones writes:

> Seattle was getting a reputation that rivaled that of the Barbary Coast in San Francisco. Bankers, if unaccompanied by wives, tipped their derbies to the likes of Diamond-Tooth Lil, a leading madam who had decided that a large diamond embedded in a front tooth would add something to her smile. It certainly did, and well might the bankers lift their hats to Lil. The accounts of the houses were not to be overlooked, and neither were the girls.

Whenever Lil received a shipment of new girls, she dressed them up in fashion so ladylike that the real ladies were infuriated. Because the newspapers would not accept her advertising, Lil paraded her flock up and down Second Avenue in the finest open carriages available for rental.

"A petition to the mayor, signed by more than a hundred women who considered themselves respectable, pleaded that this blatant public appearance of prostitutes be confined to the vicinity of Yesler's mill and similar areas," Jones writes, after apparently having researched the story with commendable zeal. "But somehow the petition was mislaid among the mayor's official papers."

GROWTH OF SEATTLE

The discovery of gold in Alaska made Seattle boom. "Even before the *Portland* docked she was booked full for her passage back north," historian Murray Morgan writes. "Half of Seattle seemed to expect to make its fortune by going to Alaska, the other half by outfitting the prospectors."

Seeking ways and means to profit from trade with the far north, the Chamber of Commerce appointed an out-of-work newspaperman, Erastus Brainerd, chairman of a Gold Rush committee. He proved to be exactly the right person for the job.

Among the many ingenious ways he thought up by which to get free publicity was the "letters home" ploy. Whenever he heard of a newcomer to town he gave him a form letter full of information and had him send it to the editor of his hometown paper. His aim was, "Anything to link the two words: Seattle and Alaska. Alaska and Seattle."

He had a staff of stenographers write personal letters to every governor and to the mayor of every city of five thousand or more. The letters gave information about the goods anyone would need in Alaska and mentioned that anyone wanting further information should write to Seattle. He had folders printed containing pictures of Alaska, the Klondike, and Seattle, which he sent to every library in the country. When the *Post–Intelligencer* printed a special Klondike edition, Brainerd's committee paid for nearly a hundred thousand copies and sent them to every postmaster in the United States, to every library, and to five thousand public officials.

"Seattle and Alaska. Alaska and Seattle."

As the publicity went out, the prospectors came in—by the thousands. The streets were crowded with men, hotels overflowed, and men rented out their barns, displaying signs, "Flop in the hay, six bits."

The innocents would buy anything. The only thing tenderfeet—called "Cheechakos" by veteran Alaskans—knew for sure about Alaska was that it would be cold, so they were suckers for devices guaranteed to keep them warm. One of the products offered was a burner that would operate on coal, oil, gas, or most any other fuel.

"I bought one for $18," a prospector ruefully reported, "and we set it up in our tent. It roared like a small Vesuvius in full eruption. Flames shot from every crack and opening in that stove. I worked the pump with frantic haste—it was no use, the whole thing was going to blow up. I started for the door of the tent, but a lad who had seen the burners work before said, `There's no danger.' He coolly took out his pocket knife, cut the lead connecting pipe, took the burner on a stick, and threw it outdoors. There were a good many suckers in Seattle in those days."

Another good seller was a "still" the size of a fifty-pound lard can with which to distill water. Apparently it did not occur to the tenderfeet that after disembarking at Skagway they would be climbing over snow-covered mountains, poling rafts or rowing boats across large fresh-water lakes, and then descending the rapids of rivers containing immense quantities of the coldest, purest water on earth.

Because of the demand for ships, one of Brainerd's friends, Robert Moran, who at the time of the great fire had been mayor of Seattle, expanded his small boat-building business into a much larger enterprise. After successfully building a harbor tug and a torpedo boat for the government, he constructed fourteen river steamboats for the Yukon River trade. Upon their completion, he personally piloted the stern-wheelers, which had a draft of three and one-half feet, from Seattle through the North Pacific and the Bering Sea to St. Michael at the mouth of the Yukon River—an astounding feat of navigation.

As always happens in a boom town, the operators of the saloons, brothels, and dance halls along Skid Road prospered, for the thousands of single men pouring into the city had time to kill and money to spend.

In a decade, the population of Seattle tripled, exploding from 80,671 in 1900 to 237,194 in 1910. During that brief period of time Seattle changed from being merely a growing city to becoming the metropolis of the Pacific Northwest.

At the turn of the century one major problem remained, so far as the movement of traffic was concerned. This was the steepness of the hills over which the city streets had been built. The most awkward of these was Denny Hill, which blocked the city's expansion toward Lake Union; Dearborn Hill, which stood between the business district and expansion toward Lake Washington; and Jackson Hill. Because the grades were twenty per cent on some hills, they were impossible for horse-drawn vehicles.

City Engineer Reginald H. Thomson solved the problem with typical frontier ingenuity by applying the sluicing methods being used in Alaska. He literally washed the tops off the hills.

By 1910 the city was level enough to take advantage of the automobile, which greatly increased land transportation. But before that could happen, Seattle decided to show the country how grown-up it was by putting on a World's Fair.

ALASKA–YUKON–PACIFIC EXPOSITION

In 1905 when the Lewis and Clark Exposition was staged in Portland, a former Seattle resident, Godfrey Chealander, was in charge of the small Alaska exhibit there. He was Grand Secretary of an organization called the Arctic Brotherhood, whose chief purpose was to create ties between Puget Sound cities and the far north. Despite its small space and budget, the Alaska exhibit attracted a great deal of attention at the Portland Fair.

For many years Portland and Seattle had been bitter rivals, with each city extolling its virtues as a business and trade community to all the world it could reach. Certainly Portland had stolen a march on Seattle when it put on the Lewis and Clark Exposition, celebrating the party's reaching the Pacific one hundred years earlier, just a year after St. Louis had staged its 1904 fair commemorating the one-hundredth anniversary of the beginning of the epic journey.

When the Portland Fair closed, Chealander came back to Seattle and called on the city editor of the *Seattle Times,* James A. Wood. He urged Wood to support the building of some sort of permanent exhibit that would keep alive the ties between Seattle and Alaska.

"I've been thinking about something that would tie in with your idea," Wood said. "If Portland can have a successful exposition, why can't we? Let me test it out with the public through the paper."

Over a period of several weeks, the paper carried interviews with prominent citizens; they all were favorable. With so many former Alaskans in town, hundreds of letters came in to the *Times.* Wood printed all that his space would allow. It was decided to form a committee with the purpose of financing a full-fledged exposition to be staged in 1907, the tenth anniversary of the discovery of gold in the Klondike.

Edmund S. Meany, a popular professor of history at the University of Washington, proposed the university campus as a site for the fair. Because this was in a large, forested area on the shores of Lake Washington and Lake Union, which could be reached only by trolley car, the idea was considered "far out" both literally and figuratively. The campus consisted of only three buildings, and these were so well-hidden in the trees that a freshman getting off the trolley for the first time had difficulty finding them.

"Many believed that the site was too far away for out-of-town visitors and that attendance would be affected seriously by the distance," Nard Jones writes. "Meany did not agree. He insisted that the forest park itself was an attraction, and people were accustomed to the trolley cars. Besides, he said, the trip would be a sightseeing tour for non–Seattleites."

Meany had the foresight to believe that the exposition could do a lot for the campus. A large part of the wilderness would need to be landscaped, and surely some of the buildings would be permanent and of practical use to the University in years to come. After the state showed its good faith by putting up enough money to construct four buildings, Congress promised $600,000 if the city of Seattle would raise a million dollars, which the city quickly did. King County then came forward, agreeing to build a $300,000 forestry exhibit with an additional $78,000 for displays.

The name of the fair began to grow. Beginning simply as the Alaska Exposition, it accepted the suggestion that, since the first big strikes that created the gold rush had been in the Yukon Territory, which was in Canada, that name should be included, too. Then Professor Meany reminded his fellow citizens that the whole Pacific Rim was involved in Seattle's commerce and culture, and that Washington's own coastline on the far side of the Olympic Peninsula was part of the Pacific Rim.

"As long as we're doing it," Seattleites responded, "let's do it big."

So the fair became the Alaska–Yukon–Pacific Exposition.

The famous AYT Exposition, Nard Jones says, probably was more loved by Seattleites than any other project in the history of the city. In a gentle jibe at other cities whose expositions had not been completed on opening day, the Seattle Fair was widely advertised to be "the fair that will be ready on time." But through no fault of the sponsors it did suffer a two-year delay.

Early in 1906 the governor of the Jamestown Exposition in Virginia pointed out that they had 1907 in mind as it was the tercentenary of the landing at Jamestown. Would it be possible for Seattle to postpone the Alaska–Yukon–Pacific Exposition?

Though Seattle could have competed with the Jamestown celebration or followed it up in 1908, the sponsors wisely chose to do neither, sending a telegram to Jamestown wishing them well and informing them that the Seattle Fair would be postponed until 1909. This turned to to be a fortunate decision, for in 1907 one of those "panics" that now and then swept over the country occurred and the recession that ensued no doubt would have affected attendance from other regions.

Given plenty of time, the architects who designed the overall plan for the fair did a superb job. One of them, James Frederick Dawson, took full advantage of the spaciousness of the grounds and of the natural forest.

A central feature (underlighted at night) was a long pool which descended gently by means of a series of short waterfalls. This was fascinating to visitors, who watched it for hours at a time and returned again and again to succumb to its magic. Dawson's whole plan resulted in what many visiting reporters called the most beautiful exposition ever held anywhere in the world.

Most of the big-city newspaper writers sent to cover the fair were so astonished at the accomplishments of an infant frontier community that there were few adverse reports—and of course Seattleites saw no reason why there should be any. As Professor Meany had foreseen, the exposition left in its wake one of the most unusual university campuses in the country.

For a time the question of whether or not the fair should have a popular entertainment section caused a lively discussion. Earlier, St. Louis had its "Pike" and Chicago its "Midway," whose belly dancer, Little Egypt, was a sensation to be remembered for a long time. Seattle was not willing to go that far, but it did install a section called the "Pay Streak," which included games of chance. When visitors complained that the pay-offs were few and far between, the proprietors pointed out that not every cheechako had struck it rich in the Gold Rush, either. June 1, 1909, dawned clear, with only a slight overcast. At ten o'clock, bells began to ring and whistles screamed. In Washington, DC President William Howard Taft pressed a key made of an Alaska gold nugget, activating a telegraph signal which set the Alaska–Yukon–Pacific

Exposition in motion. Though he was not there for opening day, he would be along later to see it all, and to beat capitalist A.S. Kerry in a game of golf.

It was reported later that the President's white knickers were the most capacious ever seen on the Seattle links.

1962 WORLD'S FAIR

On a cold, rainy winter day in January, 1955, four men got to talking over drinks in the bar of the Washington Athletic Club. They agreed that business in Seattle was in the doldrums and needed a shot in the arm. Only one of them had seen the AYP Exposition in 1909, but he remembered it vividly, even though he had been only a child at the time. When the idea of putting on another fair was proposed half in jest, they decided to take a closer look at it. Thus, what came to be called "the exposition in a jewel box" was born.

With the importance of tourism beginning to be recognized, businessmen in Seattle were hoping to develop a civic center that would attract out-of-town people. The city owned property committed to a center, but progress on the project had been slow. Without a site, without money, and without an organization, the fair was only an idea far out in the blue. To help it along, an advertising executive, Gerald Hoeck, suggested giving it a name.

"How about calling it the Twenty-First Century Exposition?"

"Not a bad idea," one of his associates, Marlowe Hartung said. "But suppose we turn it around and maybe it will sound better. Make it Century 21 Exposition."

The idea flew, as they used to say in advertising circles. Thus, Century 21 was born.

Certainly the name was timely, for on October 4, 1957, Russia put *Sputnik I* in orbit, a feat that electrified the world. "Our exposition," Hoeck said, "should take a giant leap into the next century."

By this time, fifty years after the AYP Exposition, there was little undeveloped land available in downtown Seattle. At a minimum, the fair grounds would need sixty-five acres in the metropolitan district on which to build the fair. Though the city of Seattle did own some downtown property on which it long had talked of building a civic center, the land-holdings were not nearly that large and the project so far had been moving very slowly. In order to obtain the additional space needed, the city would have to purchase tracts of land owned by both the Masonic Order and the Catholic Church. When approached by Ed Carlson, chairman of the Century 21 committee, both entities refused to sell at any price.

"Well, nobody can say we haven't made any progress at all," Carlson said wryly. "We've got the Catholics and the Masons together at last."

Eventually a compromise was reached under the terms of which the city acquired the sixty-five acres needed to create "a fair in a jewel box" and planning of the buildings and grounds got under way.

Unlike the AYP Exposition, the public attitude toward this fair ranged from mildly interested to indifferent. But strangely enough, when the City Council put a $7.5 million civic center bond issue on the ballot, the voters passed it with a thumping three to one majority. Nard Jones writes, "Their attitude seemed to be, `If they can put on even a little fair for $7.5 million, let them go ahead and try.'"

Like Alaskan prospectors given a grubstake during the Gold Rush, the Century 21 committee accepted the dare. Telling Governor Arthur Langlie, who until then had been lukewarm toward the proposed fair, about the backing the voters had given them, they challenged him to put some state money into the pot.

"How much do you think we ought to come in for?"

"We think Washington State and the city of Seattle ought to be fifty–fifty partners," Ed Carlson said.

After a bit of political broken-field running through the halls of the legislature, a $7.5 million bond issue was passed. The fair was launched and under way.

Because the fair grounds were compact and within walking distance of scores of hotels and motels, getting there was neither a problem nor a challenge. But soon a proposition made to the fair's sponsors by a foreign company put some excitement into the matter of transportation.

All over the country a number of companies were promoting their version of the monorail. Out of the blue came a proposition from Alweg of Sweden. This firm was ready to build a monorail installation of two high-speed trains, to be financed by taking twenty-five cents off the top of each admission ticket. When the fair was over and the cost amortized, the monorail would revert to the city.

Traveling slightly over a mile, the smooth, quiet, delightful ride took only ninety-five seconds; most people who came to the fair took it not just once but several times. It still does a brisk business today, particularly in the summer time. Symbolically, it curves around the fountain statue of Chief Seattle, whose spirit must regard it with pleasure, for the white man's trinkets and technology always did fascinate him.

SPACE NEEDLE

When Ed Carlson visited Stuttgart, Germany, a few years earlier, he was intrigued by the revolving television tower there. Immediately there leaped to his mind a tower restaurant and observation platform for the fair. It should revolve once every hour, giving diners a leisurely 360–degree view of what Carlson thought was the most beautiful sight in the world. The name came to him at the same time. It would be called the Space Needle.

Flying home, he conferred with architects and engineers, who told him the concept was feasible. They came up with a flame-topped tower more than six hundred feet high. The Needle supports a restaurant shaped like a flying saucer, which seats two hundred and sixty diners. The observation platform is just above. Both are supported by three gracefully curved steel legs and are reached by two high-speed elevators ascending the outside of the central support. The anchor which holds the structure is bolted together in concrete thirty feet below the ground.

Soon becoming a symbol of Seattle, the Space Needle on a clear day may be seen from as far away as Cape Flattery at the entrance to the Strait of Juan de Fuca to the west and from the foothills of the Cascade Range to the east.

Speaking of clear days, Nard Jones chuckles a bit as he refutes a slander of long-standing against Seattle's climate, where it is supposed to "rain all the time." He suggests that a good way to win a few dollars from a visiting New Yorker in a bar is to casually turn the conversation around to the weather. Inevitably, he says, the Easterner will make a derogatory comment about the rain. To which, the Seattleite responds, "Yes, we do get considerable rain here. But New York City probably gets more rain than we do."

After the wager has been made, the native obligingly looks up the phone number of the Weather Bureau and supplies a coin for the call. Hearing a juke box blaring in the background, the weatherman sighs and answers the question he is asked from bars several times a week.

"The average annual rainfall in Seattle is 34.10 inches. The rainfall in New York City is 42.37 inches."

Opening at noon April 21, 1962, when President John F. Kennedy pressed the same gold nugget key that had set the Alaska–Yukon–Pacific Exposition in motion back in 1909, this signal, in keeping with the theme of the fair, traveled a longer route than the earlier one, though it arrived just as quickly.

President Kennedy's touch activated a computer in Andover, Maine, which focused a radio-telescope on the star Cassiopeia A. The star was 60,000,000,000,000,000 miles away. The telescope picked up the vibration from that star which had started across space ten thousand years before and relayed it to Seattle, where bells rang and whistles shrieked along the waterfront. The fair had begun.

ENTERTAINMENT AT THE FAIR

At first, it was thought that fun and games should be omitted, with the only entertainment to be a theater and an opera. "Then the cry went up that no city—absolutely no city—could hold a fair that ignored the kiddies and those who liked a bit of the risque. So there came into being Show Street and the Gayway."

Gracie Hanson's Paradise International, which was a plush 700-seat restaurant, was at the end of Show Street. Though its young ladies were topless, it was a class act—for both the costumes and the young ladies were beautiful.

"How many local laws this venture broke nobody knew or cared to find out," Nard Jones writes. "Somehow the law never got around to Show Street in its official capacity."

Yet curiously enough, when the fair was over the fine arts had drawn more people than all the girlie shows combined. "The rise of science and the arts over fun and sex caused Seattleites to take a new look at themselves. Fine arts became `the thing' and the fair, the Seattle Repertory, the Seattle Opera, and the Seattle Symphony Orchestra climbed in popularity and in settings the likes of which the town had never seen."

Though President Kennedy scheduled a visit to the fair, it had to be canceled because of the Cuban Missile Crisis. In his place he sent Vice President Lyndon Johnson, who, much to the embarrassment of fair officials, was so overshadowed by his companion, John Glen, who had recently become the first United States astronaut to go into space and circle the globe, that few people even noticed Johnson's presence.

By any measure, the small, compact Seattle World's Fair, which ran for six months, was a smashing success, Nard Jones writes. "The city, as planned, was left with the legacy now known as the Seattle Center. Intact and flourishing are such things as the Opera House, the Coliseum, a huge fountain, a refurbished Arena, pools, playhouses, and lovely tree-lined boulevards."

The Science Center alone draws 250,000 paying customers a year, while the entire complex draws 7.5 million people, ranging from strollers and gawkers to paying customers for the various events staged there.

"Truly, the center is a jewel in the city."

BIG KITE FACTORY

Even before Seattle began sluicing away the tops of its hills to make way for the age of the automobile, a young man whose eyes were raised to a higher level passed up his final year at Yale and came west to seek his fortune. His name was William E. Boeing. The town had never known any man quite like him. Twenty-two years old, tall, handsome, quiet, and studious, he arrived in 1903 and began looking around for business opportunities.

He acquired timber holdings. He outfitted expeditions to Alaska. He bought a shipyard in order to finish a yacht whose building was not coming along to his liking. Then one day he discovered a new marvel called flight.

With a friend named Conrad Westerveldt, who was in ship-building, Bill Boeing went out to watch a touring pilot named Torah Maroney show off a Curtis–type hydroplane by giving passengers a brief ride above the waters and hills near Lake Washington.

"The skinny wings were covered with muslin," Nard Jones writes, "and the whole machine was supported by rods anchored to the sled–type float. The little engine hung between the two wings. Only one passenger could be managed, and Boeing volunteered to be the first."

Climbing onto the lower wing, the passenger had to brace his feet on a metal footrest and hang on with both hands. Maroney's speed is not recorded, but he took Boeing to an altitude of one thousand feet. Later, Bill Boeing admitted to being a little nervous, but the brief ride convinced him that man was meant to fly.

"The question is," he added practically, "is there a future in aviation?"

Conrad Westerveldt was not at all certain about that, but he was ready to find out. One thing he did know.

"We could build a plane a hell of a lot better than that one."

"All right," Boeing said. "Let's do it!"

COMPANY TOWN

In the 1880s when Henry Yesler's sawmill was practically the only industry in the area, Seattle was called "a company town." Because the Boeing Company is by far the biggest employer—in a metropolitan region stretching from Everett on the north to Tacoma on the south—Seattle sometimes is called the same thing today. Certainly the common saying "Every time Boeing sneezes, Seattle comes down with a cold" long has been true. Nard Jones writes:

> In the early seventies when Boeing 747 sales came in below expectations and the SST program was scuttled by Congress, Boeing employment dropped to about 30,000 from a peak of 100,000. The effect of Boeing's cutbacks was traumatic. We didn't like being called "a major disaster area." It hurt our pride.

Even so, enough Seattle people retained their sense of humor so that a sign could be painted and posted on a billboard visible from the freeway at the edge of town. Showing a glowing bare light bulb with a pull-chain switch, the legend read, "Will the last person to leave Seattle please turn out the light?"

So far, that has not been necessary.

TACOMA NARROWS BRIDGE

Though much of Puget Sound is criss-crossed with a system of colorful, scenic ferries which carry a great deal of auto and passenger traffic, there long has been agitation for bridges between heavily populated areas on the mainland and the Olympic Peninsula because of their much greater carrying capacity. The most spectacular of these was and is the Tacoma Narrows Bridge, which connects the mainland city of Tacoma with towns on the Olympic Peninsula. The verbs "was" and "is" must be used because the first bridge—not so affectionately known as "Galloping Gertie"—lasted only four months before doing its final twisting dance and collapsing into the deep waters of Puget Sound.

Costing $5.5 million in 1940 dollars, the extremely embarrassing engineering mistake was replaced in 1950 by a wider, stronger, and much more expensive bridge that is still standing. As the

Courtesy Washington State Library
LOOKING LIKE AN OVERGROWN PUMPKIN
This vacuum chamber at the Boeing Space Center can simulate altitudes 400 miles above the earth.

designers learned after the first bridge fell into the water, its structural failure was caused by two relatively simple and long-known factors working together—wind resistance and resonance.

Because strong winds frequently blew through the Tacoma Narrows, which lies between steep ranges of hills, the engineers knew that the vertical faces of the bridge which supported the roadway would often be blasted horizontally by strong winds. They also knew that the mile–long structure, which was supported by massive stranded steel cables strung over two tall towers and anchored at both ends, would be subject to up and down motions like that of a narrow wooden foot bridge strung under ropes in primitive countries where most of the traffic consists of men on foot and an occasional pack animal.

When crossing such a bridge, it long has been standard practice for a column of men such as an infantry company, which customarily marches in step so that each man's left foot, then his right foot, strikes the ground at the same time, to be given the order, "Break cadence!" This is done so that the rhythm of the column's march will not set up a vibration that will start the bridge to bouncing so wildly up and down that it tears loose from its moorings and falls into the depths.

In physics, the definition of resonance is, "the reinforced vibration of a body exposed to the vibration, at about the same frequency, of another body."

As the bridge was originally designed in 1938, these two factors were taken into consideration, but for reasons of economy the first design was changed. According to a later report supervised by Charles E. Andrew, Principal Consulting Engineer, published June 30, 1952:

> Preliminary plans for the structure consisted, in brief, of a suspension bridge with a central span of 2800 feet and side spans of 1100 feet each with an open stiffening truss twenty-five feet in depth. The bridge provided a two-lane roadway and two sidewalks; deep piers of the cellular caisson type were used.

The key words here are "open stiffening truss," which meant that the device used to baffle the up and down bouncing effect would not present a solid surface against which strong winds could work but would be an open web of steel cables through which the winds could blow with little resistance. But when a board of independent consultants was hired to review the plans, it recommended a drastic change:

> ...in both the superstructure and substructure, substituting an entirely different type of foundation and using a shallow plate girder, eight feet in depth, for the stiffening of the superstructure instead of the deep, open truss contemplated by the State on the grant application.

Before final approval was given to the amended plans, the foundation of the main piers was changed back to the original design but the eight-foot solid stiffening plate girder was approved. Built at a cost of $5,594,730, the bridge was opened to traffic on July 1, 1940. Even before completion, indications of serious problems became visible. Principal Consulting Engineer Charles E. Andrew wrote in his 1952 report:

Click Relander Collection, Courtesy Yakima Valley Regional Library
TACOMA'S OLDEST HOUSE, NOW IN POINT DEFIANCE PARK

During the construction period and prior to steel fabrication, evidence of aerodynamic instability was reported on the Bronx–Whitestone Bridge (in New York City), which was of similar form and construction. The last appointed Board of Consultants and the Director of Highways at once questioned the advisability of proceeding with the bridge superstructure, as then designed, because of its even more slender and lighter construction than that of the Bronx–Whitestone Bridge. They were assured, however, by the original designer and consultant, who was considered to be the highest authority on suspension bridges, that a simple means had been devised to correct the instability of the Whitestone Bridge which could be applied, if necessary, to the Tacoma Narrows Bridge.

Upon such advice, construction proceeded according to plan; however, as soon as floor forms were started, noticeable oscillation occurred. This oscillation steadily increased while the bridge floor was placed, varying in intensity in accordance with wind conditions. Finally on November 7, 1940, the superstructure failed and a large part of the bridge floor and the stiffening girders fell into the Sound, leaving the cables and towers with the side span floor system still standing.

For a time following the collapse of the bridge, wild rumors circulated that the broker who had been given the half-million dollar premium with which he was supposed to insure the bridge had not insured it, pocketing the money on the rather sound theory that such a well-designed structure could not possibly fail. This proved to be the case, but before he could be prosecuted for his crime he committed suicide. Because he was an agent for the company, to whom the State of Washington had paid the premium in good faith, the underwriters accepted liability and made an offer to pay $4,000,000 plus salvage. The State accepted, and the money was promptly paid.

During the four months in which automobiles, buses, and trucks had crossed the bridge between Tacoma and the small Olympic Peninsula town of Gig Harbor, no engineer was needed to tell the vehicle drivers that the bridge was in trouble. Not only was its up and down motion so tangible that a driver whose car was climbing the slight incline at one end could see a car approaching from the other end rise and fall as if floating on a wave, the horizontal twisting motion was evident, too. When strong winds blew and the road surface of the bridge started moving in two different directions at the same time, the crossing became so dangerous that the bridge had to be closed to traffic until the winds subsided.

Thus the name "Galloping Gertie," which the Tacoma Narrows Bridge earned several months before its collapse. With a forty-two mile-an-hour wind blowing on November 7, 1940, the bridge, which had been closed to traffic several hours earlier, went into its final twisting dance, which was well recorded by still and movie cameras, then fell into the deep waters below. Having been amply warned of its imminent failure, no lives were lost.

NEW NARROWS BRIDGE

Because the towers and cables left standing and hanging had no value except for salvage, and at the same time constituted a menace to navigation, the decision was made to remove them.

Bill Gulick Photos
COLLAPSE OF THE
FIRST NARROWS BRIDGE,
NOVEMBER 7, 1940

This could have been accomplished by simply cutting the strands at the anchorages and allowing them to fall into the Sound, the water being of such great depth that no menace to navigation would have remained. However, because of the great need of metal and scrap in the war effort existing at the time, it was decided to salvage the steel and wire...The removal of the cables was an extremely hazardous and difficult operation requiring ingenuity on the part of the engineers and contractor. It was the first time a suspension bridge cable of any magnitude had been removed without the use of catwalks. The dismantling was accomplished without the loss of life or major injury.

Cost of the removal was $646,661, with the salvaged wire and metal valued at $295,726, resulting in a net cost to the State of $350,935. If salvage work had been delayed until World War II ended and plans for a new bridge were drawn up, the increased cost of labor and the decreased value of scrap metal would have made the effort much more expensive.

In designing a new bridge, one of the first problems to be confronted was the question of aerodynamic stability, which had not been properly addressed before. Because of the great advances made by the Boeing Company and other aircraft builders during the war, the "cut and try" method by which an airplane was built, test flown, then had its shortcomings corrected by changes in its design, no longer need be used. The process now was greatly simplified by building scale models and testing them in wind tunnels.

"It seemed logical to follow the latter process in the design of the bridge," Engineer Andrew writes. "A wind tunnel sufficiently large to test a 1 to 50 scale model was built at the University of Washington. As bridge designs were developed they were tested in the tunnel. Many changes in design were necessary before the desired degree of stability was obtained by test."

Because the new bridge would carry four rather than two lanes of traffic, a number of changes in its design were required. As many of the former main piers and cable anchorages, which were valued at $3 million, were preserved and used as possible. The old tower legs, which had been fifty feet apart, were removed and new pedestals installed with sixty-foot centers. The old piers, one of which was 175 feet and the other 225 feet below water level, proved to be capable of carrying the increased weight, which, because it was distributed over a wider area, proved to be only six per cent greater than that of the old bridge.

Every effort was made to restore public confidence in major bridge construction in particular and the engineering profession in general by building a structure that would not fail.

One of the main contributing factors causing collapse of the former bridge was its extreme flexibility. In the final design for the new bridge, the stiffening trusses are on 60 foot centers with a depth of 33 feet center to center of chords. Trusses of the new bridge had an average moment of inertia of 6,890,000 ins. as compared to 120,400 ins. for the original bridge....All parts of the suspended structure were designed with the view of reducing areas exposed to the wind as much as possible...

Construction of the new bridge, which cost $11.2 million, got under way on April 8, 1948. Before its completion and opening to traffic on October 14, 1950, it was subject to some unusual stresses and strains, not the least of which was a major earthquake. Living in Tacoma as we did at the time, I can vouch for the fact that the following account in the report by Engineer Charles Andrew is an accurate one.

On April 13, 1949, during the erection of Tower 5, an unusual incident occurred. Both tower legs were erected to full height with the exception of the top cross struts. Just before noon of that day the most severe earthquake of modern times in the Northwest occurred, reaching an acceleration of 8% of gravity (now expressed as 8.0 on the Richter scale).

The contractor had lifted the cable saddle to the top of the south leg and had blocked it on timber cribbing about four feet above the tower top some 510 feet above the water level. The free standing tower was of course subject to a considerable amplitude in vibration, which dislodged the saddle weighing about twenty-one tons and pitched it into the Sound in approximately 140 feet of water. In its descent the saddle crashed through a large work barge anchored to the south end of the pier, sinking it and losing a considerable amount of the contractor's equipment. Fortunately no fatalities occurred and only two men were slightly injured.

At the time of the earthquake, I was personally acquainted with one of riggers who happened to be working on that tower just fifty feet below the cable saddle when it fell. As he described it to me a couple of days later, when the tower began to shake all he could do was hang onto his safety belt with both hands and pray. Looking up, he saw the twenty-one ton saddle falling toward him and knew there was nothing he could do to get out of its way.

"It missed me by six inches," he said shakily, as he finished another of several drinks. "When the earthquake finally ended, I climbed down from that tower and I haven't gone back up it since. Maybe I never will."

Whether he did or not, I never knew. During the rebuilding of the New Tacoma Narrows Bridge, four men were killed in accidents, which for such a dangerous job was not a bad record. And inevitably after the new bridge was opened to traffic, the collectors of tolls were asked by drivers pausing at their booths, "Think it'll stay up till we get across?"

"If it doesn't," the toll collector answered solemnly, "we'll give you your money back."

To date, nobody has gotten a refund.

Recently, there has been some talk of raising what is left of the fallen bridge for its salvage value as scrap metal. Preservationists have voiced strong opposition to such a project. Their underwater explorers say that the nooks and crannies of the bridge's skeletal remains have become homes and havens for all sorts of marine life, thus should not be disturbed. They are so serious about this that they have made a formal request that the area be declared an Underwater National Historic Site. If their application is granted, it will be the first of its kind in the nation.

EZRA MEEKER, PIONEER

Typical of the first pioneers to migrate to the Puget Sound area was Ezra Meeker, though during his long, active, colorful life, nothing about him could be called "average." By his own admission at the age of seventy, he was too busy living until then to begin writing about his adventures. But unlike most people who do not start to record their experiences until their twilight years, he had the gift of total recall and the ability not only to relive the experiences of his younger days in his mind but also the capacity and the vocabulary to set them down on paper in vivid, colorful style.

Living to the age of ninety-eight, he stayed physically active and mentally sharp all his life. He was one of the few men ever to travel in a single lifetime over the Oregon Trail by oxen, railroad, highway, and airplane. Born in 1830 and dying in 1928, it may truthfully be said that he not only wrote history—he made it.

"The story of the trip across the plains in 1852 is both interesting and pathetic," he began his *Reminiscences* in 1905, "but I have planned to write of life after the journey rather than much about the journey itself."

This he does so well that following him during the final and most dangerous section of the journey west—rafting through the terrors of the Columbia River Gorge between The Dalles and Fort Vancouver—is like being there to share the adventure with him and his fellow emigrants.

Starting out with his young wife and their seven week old son from the small settlement of Eddyville, Iowa, (southeast of Des Moines), Ezra was just twenty-two years old at the time. Also traveling in the party was his brother Oliver, age twenty-four, who was still a bachelor and so compatible that Ezra could claim fifty years later "we never had a disagreement in our lives."

While the oxen, milk cows, and horses belonging to the sixty people in the wagon train were herded along the steep, rocky slopes adjacent to the Columbia River, the cold, weary men, women, and children risked their lives on the hastily built scow-like rafts put together just down river from The Dalles. For the next fifty miles the Columbia River literally turned on edge as the tremendous volume of its waters was confined to the sheer-walled gorge it had cut through the ten-thousand-foot-high Cascade Mountains. With autumn at hand, rain fell for days on end, clothes and footwear never dried out, and danger was ever-present. But as so many other people had done and would do, Ezra, his wife, and child made it through the Gorge to the stump-and-mud-puddled town of Portland, just across the river from what they hoped would be the Promised Land. With his wife too weak to walk, he sought shelter for her and the baby.

> About nine o'clock at night, with a bright moon shining, on October 1st, 1852, I carried my wife in my arms up the steep bank of the Willamette River, and three blocks away in the town of Portland, to a colored man's lodging house.

Depositing his wife and baby "in the nice, clean bed in a cozy room," Ezra consulted with his brother Oliver on their financial assets. Discovering that they had $3.75 between them, Ezra took two dollars, Oliver kept the rest, and shortly after daylight next morning they both started looking for work. In busy, bustling Portland, whose sawmills were running at full capacity to supply the Gold Rush towns of California, there was plenty of work to be done; Ezra soon found the newly arrived bark *Mary Melville* about to load a cargo of recently milled lumber. As a land-lubber from the dry plains of Iowa, Ezra had never even seen a ship before, let alone been aboard one, but he wasted no time walking up the gangplank and asking the captain, "Do you want any men?"

Apparently one of those masters used to treating deckhands as veritable slaves, the captain gave him a contemptuous look, then grunted between phrases of profanity, "Yes. Go below and get your breakfast."

When Ezra said that he must go and tell his wife where he was before he either ate or worked, the captain glared at him dubiously, as if doubting that he would return. But Ezra did come back, and without asking about hours or rate of pay, worked from dawn until dark for three days. Enduring blistered hands and a steady stream of profanity from the captain and the first mate, he kept at it steadily until, on the third evening, the black owner of the lodging house politely requested another payment on the rent. Fully expecting to be fired for his brashness, Ezra timidly asked the captain if he could have a few dollars as an advance against his wages.

> When I told him what I wanted the money for, the old man's eyes moistened, but without a word, he gave me more money than I had asked for, and that night the steward handed me a bottle of wine "for the missus," which I knew instinctively came from the old captain.

Invited by the captain to bring his wife and baby to Sunday dinner aboard the ship, Ezra did so, learning a lesson that served him well the rest of his life in this far western country: that one must not judge people by outward appearances and that young men who were willing to work could soon make friends who would help them in many ways.

HUNT FOR A LAND CLAIM

Though his brother Oliver had found work in the nearby booming river settlement of Saint Helens, Oregon, and urged him to quit his ship-loading job and come there, Ezra stayed with the *Mary Melville* "until the last stick of lumber was stowed, the last pig put in the pen...", for which he was paid forty dollars in cash, before he checked out the prospects in Saint Helens. For a time, he

Click Relander Collection, Courtesy Yakima Valley Regional Library
CELILO FALLS
The area was a great Indian fishery on the Columbia before The Dalles Dam
was built in 1955.

and his brother ran a boarding house for sixty lodgers who were
building ship-loading facilities that supposedly would excel those
of Portland, but when the project was suddenly abandoned and
the workmen laid off, Ezra and his wife recalled the dream that
had made them leave Iowa.

"But claims we must have. That was what we had come to
Oregon for; we were going to be farmers."

Crossing the broad Columbia River in January, 1853, to what
soon would become Washington Territory, they found a piece of
land near what would develop into town of Kalama (an Indian
word meaning "Pretty Maiden"). There, he built a small log cabin,
the first home he and his wife had ever owned. Because there was
little forage for the cattle they had brought with them and the cost
of feeding them would be high, they sold all their cattle except a
milk cow due to have a calf soon and the two big steers, Buck and
Dandy, which Ezra had bought before leaving Iowa and trained
so well to pull their wagon and obey his commands that they had
become pets; both were so tame that often on chilly nights on the

trail Ezra would bed down with one of them and use its amiable bulk for warmth.

With the Pacific Ocean only sixty miles away and the Columbia River a mile-and-three-quarters wide at this spot, the tide rose and fell twice a day. In late spring each year the river flooded the lowlands, making it impossible to plant a garden on the low-lying plains until the high water subsided. But these same floods brought large quantities of uprooted trees and large logs into eddies near the Meeker cabin. These, Ezra, his wife, and his brother rounded up as if they were strayed range cattle, putting together a raft in seven weeks time which, when floated across the river to a sawmill, sold for a substantial sum.

"We marketed eight hundred dollars worth of logs," he writes, "that enabled us to obtain flour, even if we did pay fifty dollars a barrel, and two dollars a bushel for potatoes, and sometimes more."

Thrifty soul that she was, Mrs. Meeker saved and dried every piece of potato peeling that contained an eye. Though these little triangular segments were no larger than the end of her finger, she insisted that they would grow and thus save buying seed potatoes, whose price was out of sight because so many potatoes were being shipped south to the San Francisco market. Knowing that the lowlands would flood in June and that planting a garden would be pointless until the land dried out, she experimented by placing a few of the dried eyes in a box of moist soil indoors. When they sprouted, she was sure that her idea would work. But before she could test it, Ezra got restless and talked of moving on.

"In April, the word began to pass around that we were to have a new Territory to embrace the country north of the Columbia River, with its capital on Puget Sound."

Here at Kalama, Ezra complained, they were not on the Sea Board they had come west to settle near, but on the bank of a river sixty miles inland. True, the Columbia was a great river, but its mouth was impeded by a wide, hazardous bar which was difficult to cross. He wanted his claim to be on salt water, which would make the nations of the entire Pacific Rim his neighbors. Until the Washington Territorial Legislature was elected, met, and made laws for the land north of the Columbia River, those of Oregon Territory would be in effect—including the Donation Claims Act under which a married man could gain title to a square mile of land. Both he and his brother wanted to be among the first to file claims in the new Territory—and they wanted them to be on the inland sea called Puget Sound.

"So, one bright morning in May, my brother Oliver and myself made each of us a pack of forty pounds and took to the trail, bound for Puget Sound."

Whatever concern he may have felt for leaving his wife, child, and new home in the lonely forest on the north side of the Columbia River for an indefinite period of time, Ezra expressed in the simple statement: "Had not the little wife and I made a solemn compact before we were married that we were going to be farmers?"

That they had. Nothing else mattered.

Reaching the southern waters of Puget Sound at the raw, new settlement of Olympia, which contained only one hundred souls but had been designated capital of the newly organized Territory, Ezra and Oliver gazed out over the tide flats with more than a little fear. Watching the native Indians paddle casually here and there in their ungainly-looking dugout canoes, aware of the fact that neither of them had ever ventured onto a body of water larger than an Iowa creek without a river-wise person to guide them (as had happened crossing the Platte, Snake, and Columbia coming out the Oregon Trail), and knowing that there were sixteen hundred miles of shoreline to be explored in Puget Sound in their search for the farm of their dreams, they were sorely tempted to abandon their adventure and retrace their steps.

"I said I would not go out in one of those things, the Indian canoe," Ezra declared, "that we would upset it before we were out half an hour. Brother Oliver pointed to the fact the Indians navigated the whole Sound in these canoes, and were safe, but I was inexorable and would not trust my carcass in a craft that would tip so easily as a Siwash canoe."

When he came to know the Indians better, he adds, he stopped using the term "Siwash," (which originally came from the French word *Sauvage*, meaning "savage" or "aborigine" but later degenerated into a term of contempt many whites used when referring to coastal or river Indians). "And afterwards when I saw the performances of these apparently frail craft, my admiration was greater in degree than my contempt had been."

Click Relander Collection, Courtesy Yakima Valley Regional Library
BEACON ROCK NEAR VANCOUVER
The formation is a landmark on the lower Columbia.

Meantime, not trusting Indian canoes, Ezra and Oliver undertook to build a boat of their own—despite the fact that neither of
them had the slightest notion of how to design it.

TWO INNOCENTS AT SEA

Like the native American canoe-maker of Puget Sound who used
no blueprints other than those in his mind, the Meeker plans for
their craft were simple. Of course the native tyee came from a long
line of canoe-builders, whose art had been passed down from
generation to generation, while the Meeker brothers maritime
industry was just beginning. They give no dimensions or specifi-
cations for the craft they built, saying only:

> We determined to have a skiff broad enough to not upset easily,
> and long enough to carry us and our light cargo of food and
> bedding...We did not really know whether we would go twenty
> miles or a hundred; whether we would find small waters or
> large; straight channels or intricate by-ways; in a word we knew
> but very little of what lay before us. If we had known a little
> more, we would not have encountered the risks we did...Poor
> innocent souls, we thought we could follow the shore line and

thus avoid danger, and perhaps float with the tide, and thus minimize the labor, and yet keep our bearings.

As any modern weekend sailor who has ventured to navigate the tricky, dangerous waters of Puget Sound—even with the best of charts, tide and current tables, and electronic gear designed to make the task easier—knows, this is a formula for sure disaster. As Ezra later sheepishly admitted, their flat-bottomed skiff did not even have a keel, for the simple reason that neither he nor his brother knew what a keel was for; a sail, of course, was out of the question. About the only thing that could be said in favor of the boat they built and launched was that it floated.

After wandering around the placid lower end of the Sound, making some forward progress as their boat drifted north on the ebbing tide, then losing almost all they had gained when the tide turned and carried them back south despite their best efforts with the oars, evening of the first day found them just twelve miles from the spot where they had launched the boat. Because the pebbly beach, the grassy spit, and the background of giant fir trees made this look like a pleasant place for a camp, they pulled into it for the night. Apparently, the natives liked the spot, too, for soon several Indian canoes were beached nearby and a party of dusky strangers paid a visit to their camp. A matronly looking Indian woman approached them and began talking in what they guessed to be Chinook Jargon.

"*Mika tik-eh clams?*"

"What is she saying, Oliver?" Ezra asked his older brother.

"Blessed if I know, but she evidently wants to sell us some clams."

Because they were hungry and eager to try what they had heard was the prime delicacy of Puget Sound, they agreed to trade her a few trinkets for the basket of clams she was carrying. Since the clams were still in the shell, they had no idea how to go about cooking them. As the woman started to leave, they stopped her and asked by grunts and gestures, "How do you cook them?"

For a moment she and the natives accompanying her stared blankly at the two young white men, obviously wondering: Can anyone be so ignorant as not to know how to cook clams?

"The idea that there lived a person that did not know how to cook clams brought some merriment in the camp," Ezra writes. "Without saying by your leave or anything else the motherly looking native began tearing down our camp fire."

After Oliver cautioned Ezra to leave her alone, the two brothers watched as the woman took over their outdoor kitchen. Covering the hot sand, where the fire had been built for breadmaking purposes, with a light layer of pebbles, the woman deposited first the clams then a scattering of fine twigs and a thin layer of earth over them. While her husband watched and nodded approvingly, she eyed her work and grunted, *"Kloshe!"*

"Hyas-kloshe!" muttered her husband, nodding his approval.

"What did they say?" Ezra asked.

"I know what they said, but I don't know what they meant," Oliver answered, "unless it was she had done a good job, which I think she has."

A few minutes later the Indian woman uncovered the steaming mass of clams, placed them on a flat slab of driftwood, and served them to the two hungry men, saying, *"Yah-kah kloshe alta, delate kloshe; muck-a-muck alta."*

They still did not understand her words, but they did understand that she meant for them to eat and enjoy. Which they did, partaking in their first of many clambakes with gusto. Hospitably, they shared the bread Oliver had baked and the potatoes he had boiled with their new Indian friends. In time to come, they would discover that every turn of the tide uncovered a new supply of delicious clams in this country and that, if treated like human beings, the friendly, generous natives of these inland waters were harmless.

While crossing the plains in the wagon train, Ezra writes, the emigrants always had watched the Indians warily, guns at their sides if not in their hands, taking it for granted that the Indians were enemies, without ever studying their character. But here the natives went out of their way to be neighborly and helpful, he admits, and he and Oliver reciprocated in kind.

> We took a lesson in Chinook, and by signs and words combined held conversation until a late hour, when, upon getting ready for taking leave, a slice of venison was handed us, sufficient for several meals. Upon offering to pay for it we were met with a shake of the head, and with the words: *"Wake, wake, kultus potlatch,"* which we understood to mean they made us a present of it.

AROUND THE SOUND

For the next two months, the Meeker brothers toured Puget Sound in their clumsy skiff, which, to paraphrase a recent modern warning, was "unsafe in any waters." In extremely dangerous places like the Tacoma Narrows and Deception Pass, where strong tidal bores against which even skilled Indian canoe-handlers dared not risk their craft, the Meeker brothers cruised boldly through. They survived mainly because they had sense enough to watch what the Indians traveling ahead of or toward them did. If an Indian canoe nearing a narrow channel pulled in to the shore and waited for the tide to change, so did they. *Chuck* meant water or sea, they soon learned. If it were *klosche*, it was good or safe; if it were *cultus*, it was bad or unsafe. If it were *skookum*, it was strong, so if the two words *skookum kloshe* were combined, it was very good or very safe, while if the water passage was *skookum cultus*, it was bound to be very bad.

In late spring, 1853, the Hudson's Bay Company was closing out its operations in the United States and withdrawing to Canada, as it had agreed to do following the 1846 setting of the border between the two countries at the forty-ninth parallel. However, in anticipation of the change in sovereignty it had established an entity called the Puget Sound Agricultural Company managed by a shrewd gentleman by the name of Dr. William Tolmie, which in theory at least was entitled to own land, raise crops, and do business as if it were an American company. As such, it laid claim to thousands of acres of good farm and grassland near the mouth of the Nisqually River and the lower end of Puget Sound, warning the brash American settlers who were coming north from the Columbia River to respect its rights or else...

Since the recent organization of Washington Territory, some of the bolder newcomers had begun to test the "or else" part of the warning. Ezra Meeker noted that one enterprising settler who lived near pasture lands claimed by the Puget Sound Agricultural Company, managed his thirteen-cow herd so well that it produced a crop of thirty-three calves in a single summer. Whether the handy lasso rope habitually carried on the settler's saddle had anything to do with the fine calf crop, Ezra did not venture to say.

Working their way north by easy stages, the Meeker brothers examined one of the world's finest harbors in Commencement Bay, where the city of Tacoma would soon be built; viewed a muddy, grubby settlement called "New York *Alki*," which would become Seattle by-and-by; stopped for a visit on Whidbey Island with Colonel Isaac N. Ebey, who soon would lose his head to vengeful Haidas; then blithely crossed extensive open waters to Port Townsend on the south shore of the Strait of Juan de Fuca.

At that time, every tidewater settlement had its town boosters who claimed that it must become the most important port on Puget Sound for one reason or another: Port Townsend because it was closest to the open sea and therefore to the Orient; Seattle because it had the most big trees adjacent to the water, therefore must become the lumber-shipping port of the Northwest Coast; Tacoma because it was the furthest-possible inland port in Puget Sound, therefore the closest to the land markets of the United States.

But the Meekers were not interested in ports, though they did want to file their farm claim close to salt water. So, after completing their circuit of the Sound, they at last saw a location they liked better than any other. For a pair of Iowa land-lubbers, it was a strange choice: McNeil Island.

Located in the southern end of Puget Sound three miles offshore from Steilacoom, the small island, which later would become famous as the site of a federal prison from which few inmates even attempted to escape because of the treacherous currents between the island and the mainland, it at that time was uninhabited. Returning alone to Kalama while Oliver started to build a cabin, Ezra picked up his wife, baby, and all their possessions, which included the milk cow, a new calf, and the cherished pair of oxen, Buck and Dandy. In his absence, Mrs. Meeker had planted the potato eyes, which now were thriving in a crop that eventually would sell for $400.

Apparently Ezra had not lived long enough on the Kalama claim to gain title to it, nor did he "prove up" on the McNeil Island claim, either, for after his father and the rest of the Meeker family left Iowa and came out to Washington Territory in 1854, he accepted his father's verdict that the island claim was no place for plains-raised farmers. Moving across the Sound to the beautiful, fertile prairie adjacent to the sluggish Puyallup River, Ezra Meeker claimed a square mile of land there shortly before the right to file under the Donation Claims Act of Oregon Territory expired; and there he stayed for the rest of his long life.

Though he had no political ambitions and never ran for public office, this did not mean he did not take part in civic affairs. In

Curtis Photo, Courtesy Washington State Historical Society
SPIRIT LAKE AND MOUNT SAINT HELENS
The mountain was a perfect cone before the 1980 explosion.

fact, it may accurately be said that where public matters were concerned, he was outspoken—by no one. But before hearing from him again, we must review the career of the first Governor of Washington Territory, Isaac Ingalls Stevens, whose every act during the few brief years he served as Governor caused a storm of controversy.

ISAAC INGALLS STEVENS

When established as Washington Territory March 2, 1853, the area split off from Oregon was a big piece of real estate and a long ways from the *other* Washington where laws and government appointments were made. With its southern boundary the Columbia River, its northern the 49th parallel, and its eastern the summit of the Rocky Mountains, it covered the present states of Washington, Idaho, Montana, and a portion of Wyoming. Then, as now, Presidential appointments often were made for political rather than intellectual reasons: as recognition of distinguished military service; as repayment of campaign support; as a convenient means to send a rising political star to some distant hinterland where the light he shed would be wasted on the wilderness rather than glowing in the national capital where it might eclipse the luster of the current administration.

Certainly the new Governor of Washington Territory, Isaac Ingalls Stevens, was destined to become such a star, if his career to date were any indication. Born in Andovor, Massachusetts in 1819, graduating from West Point at the head of his class in the Corps of Engineers in 1839, a veteran of the Mexican War in which he had served with great distinction, the designer of fortifications and military works all along the Atlantic Coast, he was a personal friend of newly elected President Franklin Pierce, and a man destined to go far in whatever field he chose. When he offered to resign from the Army and accept the governorship of Washington Territory, he was quickly given the appointment.

A small-statured, black-haired man, with alert dark eyes and a neatly trimmed mustache-goatee, Governor Stevens at the age of thirty-four was aggressive, energetic, and politically ambitious. To this description of his character, his detractors (Ezra Meeker soon became one) added that he was also conceited and obstinate—which his actions eventually proved him to be.

An ordinary man appointed the chief executive of such a large Territory would have had more than enough to do accomplishing that one job. But not Isaac Stevens. On his way out from St. Paul to the new capital being established at the southern end of Puget Sound, he might as well survey a northern route for a transcontinental railroad, he told President Pierce. While doing this he also could make contact with the Indians encountered along the way, with the aim in mind to come back later, treat with them, and "extinguish title to their lands."

Within two years he had accomplished all his objectives.

MAN IN A HURRY

In his whirlwind tour west of the Cascades he had little trouble getting the small though numerous tribes living there to agree to accept reservations in or near where they had lived for generations. They were already "settled" Indians to a degree. Their homes were the forests, the streams, and the saltwater beaches on the rainy side of the mountains, where they need not roam far to find sustenance or neighbors with whom to trade. Furthermore, they were intimidated by the large numbers of white people who had moved into their country, built cabins, cleared fields, and established farms. Most important of all, they had been tamed and their population drastically thinned by the greatest civilizing force of all—smallpox and other white man's diseases against which they had no natural immunity.

The tribes east of the Cascades, the horse Indians, were quite another matter (which I will discuss later). But the effect of most of the treaties Governor Stevens made with Indian tribes both west and east of the Cascades was that once they understood what they had given away by touching the end of the writing stick beside the letters "X–His Mark" at the bottom of the treaty paper, they became so discontented and rebellious that they committed acts of violence that threatened full-scale Indian–white wars.

Conditioned by conflicts generations ago in the East, the white settlers of Puget Sound invariably panicked when an act of violence occurred. Now that a Territory had been established and a number of military posts built, the settlers demanded protection from one branch of government or the other, failing which they would defend themselves in the traditional way by forming their own Citizens Militia.

As a West Point trained officer and a veteran of the Mexican War, Governor Stevens knew how the military mind worked and should have been able to accurately assess how serious the scattered Indian outbreaks really were. Certainly he should have been aware of the fact that no great conspiracy for a general uprising existed among the Indians, who seldom went to war on a large scale. But because he was so proud of the speed and efficiency with which he had persuaded (forced would be a better word) the Indians to sign treaties giving up their lands, he regarded each isolated act of violence as a piece of treason against the United States as a nation and against himself as Governor of Washington Territory.

For treason, he claimed, only one penalty would suffice: death to the individual; extermination for the offending tribe.

GOVERNOR ISAAC INGALLS STEVENS

When the first outbreak occurred in the Seattle area, which soon would be followed by the killing of a few trespassing whites and Agent A. J. Bolon east of the Cascades in the Yakima country, Governor Stevens and his party were on the upper Missouri River near Fort Benton, where they had just concluded a treaty with the Blackfeet "extinguishing" their rights to a large expanse of land. By express rider, Secretary Charles Mason, Acting Governor in Stevens' absence, sent a message saying the whole Territory was aflame with an Indian war. Though he had appealed to General

Bill Gulick Photo
MOUNT RAINIER
The photo site is near Tipsoo Lake on the Chinook Pass Highway.

John E. Wool, commandant of federal troops in San Francisco for
the Pacific Northwest District, for help and a contingent of feder-
al troops to go to the upper Missouri River country and escort
Governor Stevens and his party home, he feared General Wool
might not respond favorably. Therefore, he suggested, perhaps it
would be best if Governor Stevens and his party went down the
Missouri by boat to New Orleans, Washington City, or even New
York, whence they could eventually return to Olympia via ship to
Panama, cross the Isthmus by land, then board another ship for
Puget Sound.

    While this might have been the sensible thing to do, Governor
Stevens refused even to consider it. To his way of thinking, it
would be a cowardly act of retreat when the situation demanded
a man of courage must charge. Rallying a hundred Nez Perce
Indians (a tribe friendly to the whites since the days of Lewis and
Clark) to his support, he headed back toward Olympia by the

direct overland route, determined to fight his way through the thousands of Yakima warriors supposedly blocking the way or die nobly in the attempt. Because the alleged "hostiles" did not really care what he did and certainly did not want to go to war against the Nez Perces, he and his party made their way home without encountering any opposition. But when the feisty little Governor learned what General Wool's reaction to the appeal for help had been, he literally exploded, for Wool had said, "I have neither the resources of a Territory nor the United states Treasury at my command."

Since Governor Stevens had gotten himself into his present predicament, General Wool implied, he must get himself out of it on his own initiative. Otherwise, he could come home by way of New Orleans and Panama, then try to explain that travel voucher to whoever was paying his expenses.

THE WOUNDED GENERAL

If the response seems to indicate that General Wool did not like Governor Stevens, this was certainly true. Animosity between the two men dated back to a dinner party in San Francisco in December, 1854, almost two years after Major Stevens had resigned from the Army and become Governor of Washington Territory. No doubt drinks were imbibed that evening, during which a discussion of experiences of the Mexican War in which both men had served played a prominent part.

When the talk turned to the battle of Buena Vista, Stevens said later, General Wool "loudly claimed for himself all the credit for that battle, disparaging in an offensive manner General Taylor and the part he took in it."

Stevens had been only a lowly lieutenant at the time and had served in a different area of the Mexican War. But now he was out of the military, Governor of Washington Territory, and felt it his right to speak as an equal. According to his own account, his sense of justice was so outraged by the boastful and unfair tirade, that he spoke up and said:

> General Wool, we all know the brilliant part you bore in the battle, but we all know and history will record that General Taylor fought and won the Battle of Buena Vista.

Satisfying though the statement may have been to Stevens' sense of justice and outrage, it was not a diplomatic thing to say under the circumstances, for a wounded general—like a wounded elephant—never forgets his attacker. When word reached Wool that an Indian war had broken out in Governor Stevens' bailiwick, he made a quick trip north to Fort Vancouver to analyze the situation. During his visit, he censured everybody, not omitting Captains Rains and Haller (officers of federal troops whose units had lost skirmishes with the dissident Indians), but was particularly hard on territorial officers and volunteers.

When he learned that Secretary Mason was raising a company of volunteers to go to the aid of Governor Stevens, he ordered it disbanded and made the statement quoted above. Furthermore, he declared that the war had been deliberately provoked by white businessmen eager to sell goods to the military. Claiming that the Indians were victims rather than aggressors, he closed the entire region east of the Cascades to settlement by the whites, ordering those who were there to move to the west side of the mountains. He then used whatever political power he had in Washington, DC to persuade the Senate not to ratify the treaties Governor Stevens had made. Finally, he made an amazing statement:

> The Cascade Range forms, if not an impassable barrier, an excellent line of defense, a most valuable wall of separation between two races always at war when in contact. To permit settlers to pass The Dalles and occupy the natural reserve is to give up this advantage, throw down this wall, and advance the frontier hundreds of miles to the east, and add to the protective labors of the Army.

In a word, chaos reigned supreme...

As Indian wars went in that place and time, the conflict that raged over Washington Territory between 1855 and 1858 did not amount to much. The native Americans—as always—were the losers. Raising a Territorial Militia despite General Wool's orders to the contrary, Governor Stevens put the new Territory a million dollars in debt by issuing scrip that proved to be next to worthless when the merchants, farmers, and businessmen who had sold the military supplies at inflated prices tried to collect for their merchandise. After federal troops suffered stinging defeats east of the Cascades in the Yakima country, General Wool was replaced in 1857 by General Newman S. Clarke, who moved his headquarters from San Francisco to Fort Vancouver, and instigated a campaign against the Indians that soon whipped them into submission and brought peace to the Territory.

By then, Governor Stevens had decided to expand his political horizons by running as Territorial Representative to the National Congress. When elected, he resigned as Governor, but before he left Washington Territory he instigated a brutal act against a Puget Sound Indian alleged to have been a leader in the rebellion and got embroiled in a legal squabble with the Territorial court system so marvelously complex that historians cannot satisfactorily explain it even today.

GOVERNOR STEVENS PARDONS HIMSELF

To simplify the matter as much as possible: Judge Edward Lander, Chief Justice of Washington Territory, had ruled that the establishment of Martial Law by Governor Stevens was unconstitutional and therefore invalid. Instead of accepting the ruling, Stevens ignored it, abolished the court, and put Judge Lander under military arrest. Before being restrained, Judge Lander issued a warrant against Governor Stevens charging him with contempt of court. When a US Marshal attempted to serve the warrant in the Governor's office, the marshal was ejected by force in a scuffle in which Stevens himself took part.

Later, when the marshal returned to try again, Governor Stevens did submit to arrest, then demanded ample time in which to procure counsel and enter pleadings, which was granted.

"The judge was inexorable but not vindictive," Ezra Meeker writes. "He assessed the nominal fine of fifty dollars to establish the principle that the civil law was supreme. Stevens refused to pay the fine and came into court with one of the most remarkable documents to be found in American jurisprudence..."

The document stated:

> Respite: To all persons to whom these presents shall come, greeting: Know ye: That I, Isaac I. Stevens, Governor of the said Territory, by virtue of the authority vested in me as Governor as aforesaid, in order that the President of the United States may be fully advised in the premises known thereon, do hereby respite the said Isaac I. Stevens, defendant, from execution of said judgment, and all proceedings for enforcement and collection of said fine and costs until the decision of the President of the United States can be made known thereon ...

Which was something like the mayor of a city today forgiving himself for a parking ticket, then appealing to the President to back him up.

Judge Lander refused to be governed by the so-called respite, Ezra Meeker says, "...ordering the Governor into the custody of the marshal and to close confinement, whereupon the fine was paid by the Governor's friends..."

TRIAL OF LESCHI

Though Meeker regarded the conflict between the Executive and Judicial branches of the Territorial government as one of those things that often happened in newly settled country, he could never excuse or forgive the brutal treatment Governor Stevens gave the native Americans whose claims he had "extinguished" with a series of hastily-made treaties. Because few Indian bands recognized a "chief" who was authorized to speak for the tribe as a whole, it was the custom of the white authorities to insist that each group of Indians with which treaties were negotiated point out a leader who could speak and make commitments for the entire tribe. If the Indians did not designate such a person, the white treaty-makers did it for them. Understandably, the Indian appointed to the position of "Chief" by the whites was the one who would agree to whatever proposition the white man made.

Chief Leschi belonged to the Nisqually tribe, whose traditional lands near the mouth of the lower Puget Sound river of the same name were adjacent to the former Hudson's Bay Company post, Fort Nisqually, which a few years ago had turned most of its holdings over to the Puget Sound Agricultural Company. Owning a large herd of cattle and being relatively well-to-do for an Indian, Leschi long had been on friendly terms with his American and British neighbors, was a man of peace, and was respected by all who knew him, whether red or white. So when Governor Stevens called a treaty council with the numerous bands of lower Puget Sound Indians and asked them who they regarded as their head man, it was natural that they should say, "Leschi."

At that place and time, Oregon Territory by its Donation Claims Act was giving 320 acres of land to each adult single man that filed on it, 640 acres if he were married. Other western territories were granting 160 acres of land to every white person that wanted it. In some cases (Oregon, for example) the same privilege also applied to a person who was half-Indian and half-white.

But so far as Governor Stevens was concerned in his role of Superintendent of Indian Affairs, the purpose of such treaties as he made at Medicine Creek was to "extinguish title to the Indian

Bill Gulick Photo
NORTHEAST SIDE OF MOUNT RAINIER
Ezra Meeker and other pioneers built the Naches Pass Road in this area in the 1850s.

lands." If he had been fair about it and given each native American man, woman, and child clear title to say 160 acres of productive land—which was being done for all other American citizens—there would have been more than enough land for all the people that wanted it, for this was a big, lightly settled country. Instead, he insisted that the Nisqually Indians sign away rights to *all* their traditional lands, in exchange for a rocky, timbered, inland reservation removed from their traditional saltwater fishing and clamming grounds which would give them only four acres per person.

Of course he sweetened the deal by giving each "chief" a few hundred dollars in annuities (to be paid in trade goods such as calico shirts rather than cash), the promise of being permitted to hunt and fish "in their usual and accustomed places" (providing no white men were using those places), and schools in which the Indians would be taught how to live like white men—whether they wanted to learn that dubious skill or not.

Though Leschi touched the end of the writing stick beside "X–His Mark" as a token of friendship toward the whites, once the terms of the Medicine Creek Treaty were fully explained to him, he tore it up, threw it away, and continued living where and how he had lived in the early days of white settlement on Puget Sound. When some of his people went to war, he reluctantly joined them, though later there was no firm evidence that he ever took part in any of the individual murders of white men or abuse of white women of which he eventually was accused. But since he had signed the Medicine Creek Treaty and had taken part in the war, Governor Stevens insisted that he was guilty of treason and must pay the supreme price.

As a member of the all-white jury that tried Leschi, Ezra Meeker took a keen interest in the way the trial was conducted and must be regarded as a reliable historian, for he knew both the Indians and Governor Stevens very well. For example, he writes, when James Wickersham (a pioneer attorney who later became a respected judge) was acting as an interpreter for the Indians while the Medicine Creek Treaty was being negotiated, he was asked, "Can you get the Indians to sign this treaty?"

"Yes," he answered wearily, for he knew how the process worked. "I can get the Indians to sign their death warrant."

During the Leschi trial, his innocence or guilt hinged on two factors: (1) Did a state of war exist? If so, he could no more be accused of the murder of a white man than a white man could be accused of the murder of an Indian, for in wartime the killing of an enemy is not a capital offense. (2) Did he actually kill the white militia man who had died in battle, or was he even present when the death occurred?

Because Governor Stevens had declared martial law and raised troops to defend the Territory, it seemed obvious that a state of war did indeed exist. But because Leschi had torn up his copy of the Medicine Creek Treaty, Governor Stevens claimed that he was not a party to the agreement, was acting as an individual

Bill Gulick Photo

MOUNT RAINIER
The scene is from Sunrise Viewpoint, northeast of the mountain.

rather than as a leader of his tribe, thus could not claim that the killing had taken place during a state of declared war. To this bit of specious reasoning, the court ruled that a state of war had certainly existed because Governor Stevens had declared it, though the judge was hazy as to whether or not Leschi was entitled to the benefits of that fact.

As to Leschi's presence or participation in the killing of the militia man, the one witness who testified against him was proved to be nowhere near the event when it happened and gave such perjured testimony that almost no one believed him. But as usually happened following a white–Indian war on the frontier, the attitude of the citizen jurors was that since several white people had been killed, the Indian leaders must pay.

"The judge had charged that if the deed was done as an act of war the prisoner could not be held answerable to the civil law," Meeker writes. "The secret ballot of the petit jury developed eight for conviction and four against. The balloting went on— eight–four, eight–four, eight–four—with pallor on the cheeks of more than one juror, for it was well known that the feeling on the outside was for vengeance."

After telling the judge that they were hopelessly deadlocked and could not reach a verdict, the jurors were sternly instructed by the court that they *must* reach a verdict, so they went back into session and tried again. After long hours of haggling, two jurors weakened and switched to a "guilty" verdict. But Ezra Meeker and a priest named Father William M. Kinkaid refused to join the majority. So the jury was discharged and Leschi was saved for the time being.

By the time a new trial was begun March 18, 1857, the Territory had been redistricted and the site of the trial switched to Olympia, where settler sentiment backing Governor Stevens was strong. He had left the Pacific Northwest by then and now lived in Washington, D.C., but his letters, statements, and depositions accusing Leschi of premeditated murder continued unabated. Though Meeker swore that the principal witness against the Indian chief perjured himself as blatantly as he had done in the first trial and that no facts were brought out to deny that a state of war had existed at the time of the alleged crime, Leschi was convicted and sentenced to be hanged.

On February 19, 1858, the sentence was carried out. Ten years earlier when five Cayuse leaders convicted of instigating the killings of Marcus and Narcissa Whitman and twelve other people at the Whitman Mission in 1847 they had said before being hanged in Oregon City in 1850: "Did not Christ die to save his people? So die we to save our people."

And so died Leschi to save his...

THE FALLEN STAR

Whether his brief career as the first Governor of Washington Territory would have served as a springboard to higher office—just as he hoped becoming its representative to the National Congress would do—never was known, for his political career was interrupted by the onset of the Civil War. Because of his prior military service, he became an officer in the Union Army and was given the rank of Brigadier–General.

Leading his regiment at the Battle of Chantilly, September 1, 1862, he was killed, so the question of how high he might have risen and how brightly his star might have shown in the national political sky can never be answered.

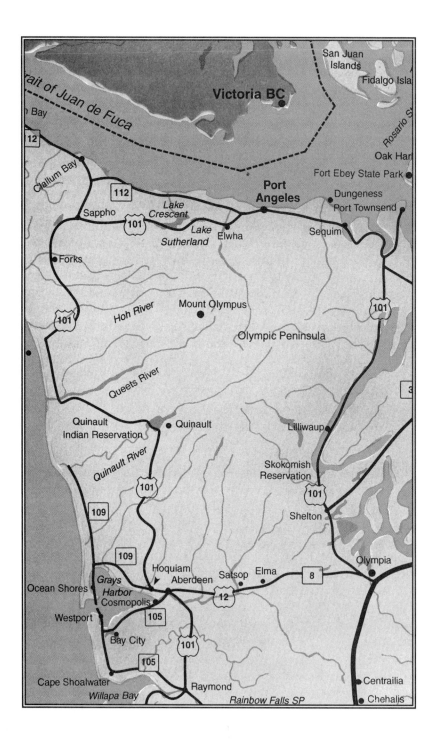

PART TWO
Olympic Peninsula

A complete circuit of the Olympic Peninsula by way of the route suggested here measures exactly five hundred highway miles. Despite the fact that the roads are good, though often crooked, this is not a distance to be traveled in a single day. Too many scenic wonders such as tranquil inland seas, immense trees, rugged mountains, and vast stretches of storm-tossed ocean beaches lie next to the road to let travelers hurry. Three days to a week is barely enough time to make the circle.

From Olympia, US Highway 101 is four-lane to Shelton, where it touches the southwestern finger of Puget Sound. Here, State 3 heads northeast toward Bremerton and eventually crosses Hood Canal on a "floating" bridge toward the historically intriguing town of Port Townsend, while 101 itself stays on the western shore of the long, narrow channel in the direction of the main city on the south side of the Strait of Juan de Fuca, Port Angeles.

Because metropolitan centers such as Tacoma, Seattle, Bellevue, and Everett lie just to the east across the Sound, the smaller settlements lining the western shores often are called "bedroom communities," from which their residents make the daily commute from homes to jobs by means of ferries, bridges, or a combination thereof—whose chronic inadequacies are subjects

---

US 101—Olympia to Port Angeles
   110 miles
State 3, 104—Shelton to Port Townsend
   81 miles

of heated discussions during coffee klatches and cocktail parties by people who use them to travel to and from the traffic-choked cities.

Despite its location in a dead-end bay on what appears to be a tiny finger of Puget Sound, Bremerton is home port for some of the largest ships in the United States Navy, while nearby Bangor shelters some of the country's largest and deadliest nuclear submarines. As was proved in the Gulf War, the air and naval power represented by planes built by Boeing in Seattle and by warships launched from the Bremerton Naval base is awesome. Yet in the wilderness of the forests, streams, and mountains lying only a few miles to the west may be found the most peaceful, tranquil countryside in Washington State, for Olympic National Park is such a relatively virgin wilderness that access roads penetrate it for only a few miles, and not a single one crosses it.

Names such as Admiralty Inlet, Puget's Sound, Port Townshend, and Hood's Channel, which were originally recorded by Captain George Vancouver during his first voyage of exploration in 1792, eventually had letters dropped or were accidentally misspelled until they took the form they retain today.

HOOD CANAL FLOATING BRIDGE

Spanning what normally is a two-mile wide strait of placid water at the northern end of Hood Canal, the so-called "floating" highway bridge here—like others of its kind—now and then breaks up, sinks, or otherwise becomes an impediment rather than an aid to traffic. Like in the first Tacoma Narrows Bridge collapse, wind invariably triggers the problem, for when the floating concrete sections—which are anchored by steel cables to the ocean floor and are designed to give a little to tides and currents—get to bouncing up and down and twisting sideways out of synchronization with choppy waves, the force generated is so tremendous that at some point in the long, flexible structure, something has to break.

This does not happen often. But when it does, as was the case in the failure of the first Tacoma Narrows Bridge, it is a disaster of major proportions. In 1979, for example, one-hundred-mile-an-hour gales roaring through the channel started the Hood Canal floating bridge to bouncing and twisting, so that a section eventually flooded and sank, pulling the western half of the bridge down with it.

More recently on November 25, 1990, the "floating" bridge spanning Lake Washington between Bellevue and Seattle, which carries a tremendous amount of traffic, also sank, causing a monstrous jam of backed-up cars and buses. After a lengthy hearing, the investigating panel of engineers announced solemnly:

> Our most basic finding is that everybody looked on that bridge as a highway on water instead of what it really was, which is a boat...It is quite clear that the construction of floating bridges involves marine-construction practices that are not the same as road-construction practices...

This bit of wisdom also could have been applied to the sinking of the Hood Canal Bridge in 1979, for here it was learned that the point of balance between the amount of water and air required to keep the pontoons stable or afloat is a relatively delicate one.

During the three years west shore commuters were forced to make roundabout detours by way of other bridges or ferries while the Hood Canal bridge was being rebuilt, the coffee klatch and cocktail discussions became quite heated—just as they later did among commuters between Seattle and Bellevue. But no one in any of these communities ever suggested a permanent solution to the problem—moving to the other side of the water. If such a thought were voiced, the immediate response would be, "Who would want to live over there?"

PORT TOWNSEND'S DREAM OF GLORY

Settled as early as 1851, two years before the creation of Washington Territory, Port Townsend and the region adjacent to it was and is one of the most interesting areas in the state. Even so, not all of its early events have been properly noted by local people. For instance, the *WPA Guide* says:

> Among the early settlers in the area was one Albert Briggs. In 1852 he decided to leave Portland; sending his family by boat, he started overland with a herd of 30 head of cattle. At Tumwater, near Olympia, he loaded his cattle on a scow and, floating with the tide by day and beaching it at night, he reached the shallow harbor opposite Port Townsend. The trip took 15 days. To commemorate his voyage, Briggs named the harbor where he landed Scow Bay.

Inelegant, perhaps. But worthy of being remembered. The *Guide* also gives its readers this intriguing historical tidbit regarding the Puget Sound Navy Yard at Bremerton:

The main gate to the yard is at the foot of 1st St., a few feet right from Pacific Avenue. An ordinance passed in 1902 made it a misdemeanor to sell or roast peanuts, loaf, tell stories, whittle, or scatter litter near this entrance.

Let the tourist be warned.

Among the first foreign visitors to the outer reaches of the Olympic Peninsula were three Japanese sailors whose story of shipwreck is a classic of worldwide wandering caused by willy-nilly winds. Sailing in a junk carrying a cargo of rice and porcelain ware between the coastal ports of Yokohama and Tokyo, they were caught by a typhoon which swept their vessel out to sea. With its rudder damaged and no way to steer, the junk drifted eastward on the Japanese Current for an entire year before it finally made landfall near Cape Flattery on the mainland of North America.

With plenty of rice and water aboard, the crew survived for a while, then disease broke out and most of the sailors died. By the time the junk smashed up on the rocks near Makah territory, only three men were left alive. After plundering the wreckage of the ship, the Indians made prisoners of the Japanese sailors, holding two of them in one village and the other in a settlement further down the coast. Though they were treated well enough, the Japanese sailors wanted to go home, so they devised a clever scheme designed at effecting their rescue.

On a piece of paper they had salvaged, they drew a picture of a wrecked ship, Indians swarming around it, and three stick figures indicating human survivors. Given to a friendly Indian who was asked to pass it along to the first white men he might encounter in the Puget Sound area, the sketch finally reached the Hudson's Bay Company post at Fort Nisqually. Realizing that a ship had been wrecked in the Cape Flattery area, Captain William McNeil, on his next trading trip, investigated.

Discovering two of the Japanese sailors in the first Makah village he visited, he ransomed them and told the local chief he would do the same for the third captive, if he were turned over. Soon this was done, with the three sailors being taken first to Fort Vancouver, then to London, and finally home to Yokohama— where presumably they told wives, children, and relatives stories that began, "A funny thing happened to me on the way to Tokyo a few years ago..."

THUNDERBIRD
This Quillayute version of the totem is at LaPush.

Unlikely though it might seem today, there was a period back in 1880s when Port Townsend hoped to become the most important metropolis in the Pacific Northwest. In his book *Steep Trails*, which was published in 1888, John Muir wrote:

> This being the port of entry, all vessels stop here, and they make a lively show about the wharves and in the bay. The winds stir the flags of every civilized nation, while the Indians, in their long-beaked canoes, glide about from ship to ship, satisfying their curiosity or trading with the crews. . .

At that time, sail still dominated the high seas so far as international freight traffic was concerned, though steam-powered ships were beginning to take over the passenger trade because of their higher speeds and greater dependability. Maneuvering in the restricted waters of Puget Sound could be tricky for sailing ships, so Port Townsend, as the first safe American harbor within the Strait of Juan de Fuca, became the off-loading point for ships whose cargos were destined for mainland cities. Thus, it seemed logical that when the transcontinental railroad reached tidewater, its terminus would be at Port Townsend.

With some of the tallest and largest trees in the country growing right down to tidewater, Port Townsend pioneers made good money cutting and shipping wood products to booming

California, which was crying for lumber. During the Gold Rush beginning in 1849 and with San Francisco suffering a rash of fires, which forced the expanding city to rebuild time and again, the price of lumber rose from $200 to $500 per thousand, while timbers cut for pilings and mine timbers at eight cents a foot sold for a dollar a foot in the California.

Cutting timbers so long that special stern ports had to be cut in the vessels to facilitate loading, a mill owner named Thomas Cranny achieved the high point of his career when he shipped a two-hundred foot long flagpole for the Paris Exposition of 1867, where it flew the Stars and Stripes aloft far above the banners of any other nation. The Port Townsend newspaper *North–West* boasted in print:

> If our Columbia River friends receive any orders for longer lumber than their shrubbery will produce, we can fall some of our tall trees in a southerly direction, and they may use the taper-ends that snap off for that purpose.

During the 1880s and '90s, Port Townsend called itself the "Key City," with boat lines radiating out from it to Victoria and Vancouver, British Columbia, to the Gulf and San Juan Islands, and to cities on Puget Sound. Like other tidewater communities, Port Townsend had its enthusiastic promoters who could prove beyond dispute that it was the most logical site for a western railroad terminus and that it was bound to become as important a city on the west coast as New York was on the east.

In 1887, town boosters incorporated the Port Townsend and Southern Railway Company and began to acquire right-of-way along Hood Canal, drawing up plans to build a railroad south to the Columbia River which would connect with a transcontinental line there. Stimulated by boom talk, property values soared, population increased to 7,000, six banks did a rushing business, and a number of office buildings and private homes were erected in a hurry. Construction was started on the rail line, a few miles of track were laid, and by September 1, 1890 trains were actually running from Port Townsend to Lake Hooker.

But when funds were exhausted and the company went into receivership in November, real estate values collapsed, the dream ended, and the town's population fell to 2,000. The *WPA Guide* says:

Attempts in the nineties to establish industries also met with indifferent success. A huge drydock was constructed but was towed elsewhere when it was nearly completed; a nail works opened in 1892 and failed soon thereafter; and several other enterprises opened only to close after a short time. The panic of 1893 filled Port Townsend Bay with ships of all kinds and tonnage; there they lay idly at anchor, until the improvement of business conditions in 1897 called them again into the channels of trade.

Though major industrial development, such as the Crown Zellerbach Corporation, did come later in 1927, the idyllic site and fine climate for the tourist and recreation trade gradually made it apparent that Port Townsend's future should and would develop in those areas.

RAIN SHADOW EFFECT

It is a curious fact that on the Olympic Peninsula the rainiest and the driest spots west of the Cascades are located only a few miles from each other. On the southwest slope of Mount Olympus, whose crest rises to an altitude of 7,965 feet, up to two hundred inches of rain a year falls. At Sequim, just above sea level and thirty-five miles northeast of the peak, the average rainfall is a meager sixteen inches.

The reason for this dramatic discrepancy is that the prevailing winds sweeping in over the warm Pacific Ocean drive clouds containing a great deal of moisture before them. When these clouds strike the mountains of the Olympic Range, they cool and deposit most of their moisture on the western slope, with little left to fall on places such as Sequim, Port Angeles, Port Townsend, and Victoria, British Columbia. In this "rain-shadow" area, the natives describe the frequent clouds that pass over without dropping anything more than a fine mist as "empties" heading back for a refill.

Pronounced as a one-syllable word *squim*, the strip of open, low-lying land called "Sequim Prairie" raised excellent potatoes, the first settlers found, though they had to be irrigated because of the lack of rainfall during the growing season. Among other distinctions, Sequim is noted for having established the first irrigation district in Washington Territory.

CHERBOURG TOWNSITE COMPANY

Just as a pair of early developers tried to name the site of Seattle "New York by-and-by," a visionary Customs Collector stationed at Port Townsend in the 1860s tried to establish a city a few miles to the west, which he hoped some day would rival the great port and naval base of Cherbourg, France. His name was Victor Smith. Arriving at the established Customs House in Port Townsend in 1861, he disliked the area and its residents on sight, just as they soon came to despise him. Soon he concocted an ambitious scheme by which he would demonstrate the powers of his office and put the people of Port Townsend in their place.

Taking an inspection tour sponsored by a group of men that were promoting a townsite in the Port Angeles area, which was thirty-five miles to the west, he became so impressed with the region that he decided to change the location of the Customs House from Port Townsend to the new settlement. In her colorful book *Untamed Olympics,* historian Ruby E. Hult, writes:

> As soon as his eye fell on the harbor formed by the natural breakwater of the spit, his decision was made. Here was the place for his future port of entry: across from Victoria, the biggest shipping port in the North Pacific area, and along the Strait where all vessels entering Puget Sound must pass close by.

That his decision was based on the hope of personal gain, as well as by "a patriotic wish to see an important government base established in the harbor..." is made clear by the fact that his first move was to buy out the claims of the defunct Cherbourg Townsite Company; his second was to write the Secretary of the Treasury, Salmon P. Chase, urging that the post be relocated.

Before the people of Port Townsend realized what he was up to, he made a trip to Washington DC, and, working through Secretary Chase and other friends, persuaded President Lincoln to sign an act June 19, 1861, setting aside five square miles of land along the Port Angeles harbor spit as a military and naval reserve. This included not only the land Smith had purchased from the Cherbourg Townsite Company but also title to some 3,600 acres owned by men with whom he had business relationships, permitting him to gain control over five square miles of prime waterfront land, to which no outsiders could lay claims that would not be contested by the government Land Office.

Over the strong objections of Port Townsend, Victor Smith moved the Customs House to Port Angeles in the autumn of 1862, building it on land he owned and leased to the federal government. Next spring, he had five hundred acres of the reserve land

Click Relander Collection, Courtesy Yakima Valley Regional Library
CATCH OF SMELT
Here a fine mesh net has been thrown around a school of smelt, near the mouth of the Quillayute River. The catch will fill two dugout canoes.

released, surveyed, and laid out as a city. Divided into 803 units comprising urban lots, suburban lots, and acreage tracts which were "sold at public outcry, the sale taking place at the door of the Customs House," only twenty-two persons bought lots, for a total of $5,000, which did not repay the government for the cost of its survey.

Though "Cherbourg on the Strait" had not gotten off to a very good start, twenty-five frame houses were built along a narrow rutted road that wandered off into the timber. Located on what was called "Main Street," these included the first hotel, Conklin House, and John Everett's "wild" meat market, where its proprietor sold pheasant, grouse, deer, and bear meat. On the bay, the only vessel usually moored to the pier was the small revenue cutter *Shubrick*.

Despite its location in a region of light annual rainfall, it was a deluge of water during a sudden flash flood on Valley Creek that washed the Customs House away, drowning two people, that marked the beginning of the end of Victor Smith's dream. Though a new Customs House was built in a different location, Smith himself was drowned two years later in a different kind of water tragedy when the steamship *Brother Jonathan*, on which he was a passenger bound from San Francisco to Portland, struck a reef off the coast of northern California and sank with a great loss of life, including his own.

UTOPIA IN PORT ANGELES

Oddly enough, some twenty years later another man named Smith brought another kind of notoriety to the Port Angeles area when he got tired of agitating against the so-called Chinese menace and turned his organizational talents toward forming a Utopian society. Moving to Seattle in the 1880s, George Venable Smith for a time published a newspaper called the *Model Commonwealth*, whose motto was, "Let the Many Combine in Cooperation as the Few Have Done in Corporations."

Hating Chinese laborers because they allegedly worked for lower wages than white men did, he sought to establish a refuge from such disastrous competition by establishing a colony in which unemployment would be unknown, rents and taxes would not be collected, medical care would be free, and where old age could be lived out in security. That Chinese laborers sometimes received higher wages than immigrant Irish, Italian, Swedish, or other foreign workmen (which was the case) because they were more dependable, worked harder, accomplished more, cost less to feed and house, stole fewer tools, and went on fewer day-after-payday sprees, were facts George Venable Smith did not mention, of course. But he was such a spellbinder as a speaker that he convinced a lot of people his Puget Sound Cooperative Colony would work. Soon two thousand members had subscribed $50,000, and were waiting only to be told where his promised Utopia would be built.

The site finally chosen by George Venable Smith was the five-square mile reserve established in the Port Angeles harbor by his namesake, Victor Smith, nineteen years earlier. Everything his colony needed was there: a mild climate, fertile soil, an excellent harbor, an abundance of fish, streams for developing water power, an unlimited supply of timber, and land available at a reasonable price. Of the original 803 units laid out by the first Smith, 700 were still for sale; so the second Smith bought five ten–acre tracts and announced that the colony was ready to do business. Hult writes:

During 1887 and 1888, the colonists gathered, a thousand or more of them...they came with different will-o'-the-wisps of desire and self-seeking, men and women from all walks of life, with greatly varying backgrounds, with different shades and hues of political opinion and religious belief...

For a time the colony prospered, Hult says, establishing industries to provide employment for all: a tin shop, two black-smith shops, a dress and shirt factory, a barber shop, a bathhouse, a brickyard, a shoe shop. A sawmill was imported from Seattle. A subscription of $4,200 was raised to build a 65–foot schooner *The Angeles* in which to carry produce marketed in Port Townsend and Seattle. A meeting place called the "Potlatch House" was built (so named because all material used in it was obtained by gift). It was dedicated to one of the basic principles of the community— Free Speech—with people of any persuasion, whether free-thinkers, atheists, Catholics, Methodists, Presbyterians, or any mixture thereof permitted to get up and express themselves.

Like many other communal societies formed in the United States at that time, this one began to fall apart because of its fail-ure to solve financial and human problems. Though it had been decreed that "all money relations between individuals shall be abrogated," it soon was found that some type of payment for the labor of the society's members was necessary. When a special script was printed and issued, it could be used readily enough in the company stores, but when the managers of these enterprises tried to purchase replenishment of their stocks outside the com-munity, the script was not honored. So real money was needed, after all.

Though most of the families were of good reputation and were hard workers, the colony attracted more than its share of "radicals," who at that time came in the form of anarchists and advocates of free love. When George Venable Smith ran for and was elected the first judge of Clallam City in 1888, he found it nec-essary to withdraw from active leadership of the society. When a man named Thomas Maloney succeeded him, dissension, bicker-ing, and charges of mismanagement began to tear the colony apart. In 1895, it went into receivership, failing, a local joke said, "Because it lacked dollars and sense."

SQUATTERS' AID SOCIETY

Meanwhile, much of the federal reserve established by President Lincoln at the urging of Customs Collector Victor Smith still lay unused and unoccupied. During the speculative boom of 1889, arriving newcomers who had come to Port Angeles looking for home sites eyed the 3,100 acres on the reserve with restive, bitter eyes. To their way of thinking, government ownership of this prime property "held the town by the throat, a menace to all progress."

Something must be done.

Not surprisingly, it was an Irishman named John C. Murphy who literally mounted a stump on a street corner and told the citizens what they ought to do.

Beginning with the first tide of immigration from Europe into the United States from the 1830s until and past the turn of the century, newspapers all over the country filled chinks in their columns with jokes poking fun at whatever race of immigrants happened to be flooding into the country during that particular decade: Dutch, Swedes, Chinese, Italians, Irish—all kinds of newcomers were butts of jokes for a time. Many of these jokes would be called racist today, but the stories had more than a grain of truth in them. One of the Irish jokes went like this, "What's the first thing an Irishman does when he lands in America?"

"He has a drink."

"Right. And the second thing?"

"He has another drink."

"Correct. And the third thing?"

"He declares himself agin' the Government."

Essentially, this was just what John C. Murphy did in his stump speeches. What was a townsite for? he demanded. For whom had it been set aside and why? What was its purpose, if not to *develop* a town? His plan was simple and direct, Hult says:

> Take the reserve by entering and squatting, then force the Government to give title. "Possession is nine-tenths of the law," says the old adage, and Murphy maintained that once the settlers were in possession of the land, the Government would be forced to give official sanction.

Patriotically, the day selected for action day was July 4th, 1890. In concert, several hundred men, women, and children moved onto the reserve, began to cut down trees, clear out brush, and drive stakes locating the boundaries of their land. Collectively, they had become claim-jumpers.

What was the United States Government going to do about this openly lawless act? Well, it *could* accept John Murphy's dare to arrest him and haul him off to jail. But it did not. In fact, it did absolutely nothing, letting a pious editorial in the Port Angeles *Times* mildly stating "a belief in the rigid and absolute maintenance of the laws of the United States..." speak for government policy. Later news stories in the same paper revealed its sympathy with the claim jumpers. One headline read:

Uncle Sam Has Not Interfered And There Are Hopes He Will Sanction the Action of his Children.

Early in August, a Squatters' Aid Society was organized, with a formal constitution and by-laws. Judge George Venable Smith was elected president, John C. Murphy vice president. A detailed record of all the claims filed on the reserve was kept by the organization—five hundred of them by the end of the year.

Statehood having come to Washington in November, 1889, the newly elected representative, John L. Wilson, was deluged by letters, telegrams, and petitions urging him to introduce a bill into Congress legalizing the claims. Delegations of "Squatters" journeyed to the National capital carrying appeals such as the "Baby McKee petition," which was signed by one hundred and fifty school children living on the reserve, telling what hardships they and their parents were enduring through the long months of delay.

To say that the Government fought the land-grab is not an accurate statement, for the only weapon it used was the weak bureaucratic one—delay. Though the Squatters offered to buy their claims for the nominal price of $10 each, the Government insisted that the claims be appraised so that their real value could be established. Following this, the Government further decreed, each Squatter must place an ad in six consecutive issues of the local paper, stating that he was filing on a specified claim.

The appraisal and the forced advertising boosted the income of the local surveyor and the newspaper publisher, but when the valuation of the "jumped" lots was set at $100, howls of outrage were heard. In the end, the Government comprised at $40, and by January, 1894, ninety percent of the Squatters had paid the required purchase price, and were given title to their land.

The work of John C. Murphy was finished. In his honor, a celebration was held, in which he was named the "Original Squatter of the Port Angeles Townsite Reserve," whose high point was a tableau showing Murphy with an axe over his shoulder and a sign above him with the motto, *"Boys, Follow Me."*

INDIAN SYMBOLS AND COSTUMES

Though the practice of carving totem poles was more common among tribes such as the Haidas and Tlinglits along the coast of British Columbia and Alaska, the Chinooks, Makahs, and Puget Sound Indians did use cedar and other woods to carve masks and symbols of their beliefs in powerful, unseen gods that they felt ruled the spirit world. The strongest and most universal of these invisible beings was the Thunder Bird, which is vividly described in the writings of James G. Swan, who served as agent to the Makahs for many years, and Myron Eells, who was both a missionary and an agent to the Skokomish and related tribes in the upper Puget Sound area during the 1870–90 period.

Keeping detailed journals and making extensive collections of native American art, handiwork, tools, and weapons at a time when institutions such as the Smithsonian welcomed such material but lacked the funds and staff to send their own qualified researchers into the field, men like Swan and Eells, who lived with the Indians and understood both their language and their customs, made a tremendous contribution to cultural knowledge that could have been gained in no other way.

The dramatic thunderbird figure, Eells says, is to be found in the mythology of tribes living in the Diomede Islands in the far north's Bering Sea; among that of the natives inhabiting the jungles of Guatemala to the south; and in that of the Indians residing to the east on the shores of Hudson's Bay in Canada. He quotes an anthropologist in the 1890s, W.H. Holmes, who writes:

> The storm bird dwells in the upper air beyond human sight, and carries on its back a lake of fresh water. When it winks its eye there is lightning, when it flaps its wings there is thunder, and when it shakes its plumage there is rain.

In the art of the Haidas, who were the best of the totem and mask carvers, the thunderbird took its most terrifying form. In his book *Haida Indians*, Swan writes:

> The bird is standing on a whale, with a fish nearby. Seven masks are used (illustrated by Swan) in the thunder-bird performance, five of which represent the human face, and the other two the heads of birds. In some of these the eyes and lower jaw are mov-

able, so that by means of string the eyes are made to move and the jaws to clatter in a hideous manner.

Another early–day anthropologist, whom Eells identifies only as "Dr. Riggs," adds considerable color to Indian lore by writing:

This thunder god is a being of terrific proportions, in shape somewhat like a bird. As it flies, hid by thick clouds, the lightnings flash forth and the thunder is its voice. There are four varieties, and they are male and female. One is black, with a long beak, and has four joints in each wing. Another is yellow, without any beak at all, and with wings like the first, but it has only six quills in each wing. The third is of a scarlet color, and has eight joints in each of its great wings. The fourth is blue and globular, with neither eyes nor ears. In place of the eyebrows [there] are semi-circular lines of lightning, from beneath which project downward two chains of lightning, zigzagging and diverging as they descend. Two plumes of soft down serve it for wings.

The home of this family of gods is at the western extremity of the earth, on the summit of a beautiful mound, which is on a high mountain. The dwelling opens toward the four cardinal

MAKAH INDIAN MASK
The mask changes shape when the strings are pulled.
Click Relander Collection, Courtesy Yakima Valley Regional Library

points, and at each doorway is stationed a watcher—a butterfly at the east, a bear at the west, a reindeer at the north, and a beaver at the south. Each of these sentries is enveloped, except the head, in scarlet down, very soft and beautiful. These are gods of war, ever on the warpath. They are ruthless, cruel and destructive, and a deadly enmity exists between them and the gods of the waters.

Thus we see that this singular belief, varied somewhat in different localities, yet based on the same underlying idea, is widespread, and is found among tribes of very diverse languages.

All of which certainly proves that the native Americans of the Pacific Northwest Coast had a long tradition of a visual art rich in symbolism and mysticism.

TWINS WERE EVIL

Among the Indians of Puget Sound and the Strait of Juan de Fuca, the birth of twins was a rare occurrence and regarded as very bad luck. In his eighteen years there, Eells says, he knew of only one pair among the Twana Indians, and one pair among the Clallams. Because the Twana Indians were educated and lived on the reservation where they had observed how the Indian Agent, whose wife had borne twins, regarded them, their own were treated well, though some of the older women did claim that they were bound to bring bad luck. Eells wrote:

> But the pair among the Clallams did not fare so well. Their parents were among old-fashioned Indians at Neah Bay, catching seals, when the twins were born. Immediately the Neah Bay Indians became hostile to them, fearing that the twins would scare the fish away. Accordingly, the parents returned to their home at Port Discovery, eighty miles away, by steamer, though the Indians were reluctant to have them go in that fashion, fearing that even aboard the ship they would frighten all the fish away, saying that they should walk the entire distance over the mountains and through the forests or on the beach, although there was neither beach nor road much of the way.
>
> When they reached home, some of the old Indians of their own tribe were very much afraid. They threatened to kill one of the twins, so that the father did not dare to leave home. Hence he could not go off and work and earn food; neither would they allow him to fish near his home, although the fish at that time were very abundant there, for fear that all the fish would leave. Hence the man was greatly troubled to get food enough for his

family to keep them from starving. They told him to live on clams. They would not go near his house if it could be avoided, and, if they had to pass it, would make quite a detour around.

Because the taboo against twins was associated with the food supply, it seems likely that this was an ancient, instinctive means of limiting population which was shared by many primitive peoples.

POTLATCH CUSTOM

In Chinook Jargon, "potlatch" means "to give away." How old the custom was, Eells could not say, but he did know that it was confined to the Pacific Northwest region bounded by the Columbia River on the south, the Cascade Mountains to the east, and Alaska, to the north. In 1877, he says, the greatest potlatch of them all had been made by a rich chief in Alaska who invited four thousand Indians to his "giveaway" party. Eells says:

> The custom may have originated when the chiefs, in order to gain and keep the good will of the people, gathered them together and made presents to them. Gradually other tribes were invited, on account of relationship or friendship, and the compliment was returned. Other persons, not chiefs, but who wished to become such, or at least to become prominent persons, followed the example, until now it has grown to its present size, so that often nearly all the surrounding tribes are invited, and almost every person of any prominence, both of the men and women, feels bound to have a share in giving a potlatch at least once in a lifetime. They have grown so large, however, that seldom does even the richest person feel able to give one, hence they combine together, sometimes twenty or thirty being concerned in the same one.

During his years as an agent, Eells was invited to attend four of these potlatch festivals, he says, "...in order to watch over the Indians, prevent drunkenness, and see that they did nothing improper, according to their ideas of impropriety."

He appears to have attended only as an observer, though he says white officials at that time were trying to discourage the custom among the natives. But some of the Indians felt that since they themselves had received gifts of goods and money at potlatches to which they were invited, it would be like stealing if they did not give potlatches in return. One of the festivals he attended was on the Skokomish Reservation in the fall of 1876. He writes:

It was the largest and longest of any, about twelve hundred persons being present, and it lasted three weeks....The distribution of gifts is about the last thing done, the previous time being spent in religious ceremonies and social intercourse, including feasting, while side shows are the procuring of wives, and gambling, the latter being very prominent.

Preparations for this potlatch had been going on for years, he says. Old women went in rags while they filled trunks with bolts of new calico cloth to be given away, depositing boxes of dry goods with him for more than a year in advance of the event, which was scheduled to take place in October. Work on building the main longhouse in which the potlatch would be held began a year earlier, was deferred for a month or two for one reason or another, then was resumed, and finally was completed at about the time the invitations were sent out. Because the longhouse could not accommodate all the people expected to attend, mat houses, tents, and other temporary shelters were erected nearby.

About the 14th of October, they sent runners to the various surrounding tribes to invite them to come. Each one who takes part in the potlatch first decides whom he wishes to invite. He then prepares tickets of invitation. These are about the size of a lead pencil, and from three to six inches long, which he entrusts to a runner. When all engaged in the potlatch have done so, the messengers start. Occasionally only one or two messengers carry the invitations from all the givers, but usually there are from three to eight, sometimes one messenger carrying the tickets of only one giver.

When the messenger reached the home of the person invited, he stood a short distance outside the dwelling place, said a few words aloud, then tossed the stick into the grass—to be picked up or ignored by the invitee as that person might choose. In some cases, families sure of an invitation and eager to accept it were already on their way to the scene of the potlatch before the messenger arrived with their invitation. Eells writes:

At the Skokomish potlatch of 1876, the first installment of guests, about a hundred Chehalis Indians, arrived on the 29th of October. They came in wagons and on horseback to within about four miles of the house—as near as they could because of water. Here they were met by the leader of the potlatch, and after considerable speech-making they camped for the night. The next day the Twanas sent six large canoes to take them to the house. At noon they rowed past the agency, one mile from camp, abreast, singing a solo and a chorus, accompanied by

Click Relander Collection, Courtesy Yakima Valley Regional Library
MAKAH INDIAN MASKS, TOTEMS, AND COSTUMES

drumming on two drums and pounding on canoes. After passing the agency they broke line and so went on for a mile or more
until they came in sight of the potlatch house, when they again
formed abreast and rowed to the house in alignment with their
music. At landing there was more ceremony, for the visitors had
brought many presents. Each present was held by the donor
while he made a speech, after which he gave it to a Twana, who
replied to the speech, when the gift was handed to the one for
whom it was intended.

These presents consisted of calico, blankets, two beeves,
dried meat, and money (sixty dollars having been counted as
coming from one canoe), and seemed to have been given to the
prominent Twanas. The Chehalis then landed and went to one
part of the house assigned them, where they took lodgings. The
whole performance occupied three hours and was longer than
that of any other tribe.

Two days later a band of Clallams arrived, though the usual
welcoming ceremony was interrupted by the news that while en
route a Clallam child had been killed by the caving in of a bank.
Because the child's family had relatives among the Twanas, a stop
was made at the burying grounds on the nearby beach, where the

corpse was placed in a box on a log and a brief mourning ceremony was held. Following the potlatch, the child's body would be taken home by the Clallams, where it would be given a proper burial service.

Other tribes kept coming every day or two for two weeks, and the reception was much like that already described. Generally, they were met two or three miles before reaching their destination by some of the Twanas, who learned their wishes about landing and directed preparations to be made accordingly; and commonly they brought some presents of cloth, food, and money, and danced and sang, but a few landed without any ceremony. When they had all arrived, it was estimated that there were from a thousand to twelve hundred present, comprising, besides those already mentioned, Squaksons, Nisqually, and Port Madison Indians, a few from the Snohomish, Lummi, and Puyallup reservations.

Those who lived farthest off had come a distance of about 150 or 175 miles, but these had relations by marriage among the givers of the potlatch.

ENTERTAINMENT AND FEASTING

Preceding the passing out of gifts, the evenings were occupied with dancing of some kind, either serious or comic.

These dances were accompanied with drumming, singing, and clapping of hands. In dancing they jumped up and down, sometimes joining hands in a circle, and sometimes each one dancing singly, jumping the whole length of the house. At times the men alone danced, and again the women joined them, generally having a part of the circle to themselves. Once almost all joined in the dance, having green branches in their hands.

At another potlatch he attended in the Dungeness area, Eells observed an outdoor, daytime dance on the beach performed by the medicine men, which apparently offended his religious sensibilities.

As I returned from my dinner, I saw a masked Indian, the same I suppose that was masked the night before, and three others similar to the two half-naked men of the previous night, dancing backward and forward for a distance of about 100 yards on the beach in front of the houses. The masked dancers went through some performances not fit to be described. Their dance consisted chiefly of running around with ropes encircling them, held by others, as on the previous night.

This dance continued until about 2 p.m., when they danced off into the woods, followed by forty or fifty of their friends, with the singing, etc. They all formed a large circle as they moved off, and did not return until five o'clock, when they reached the beach a quarter of a mile from where they left it.

Some three of them, apparently tired out, were each jerked up by six men wrapped in blankets and carried into the potlatch house. One walked in supported by attendants. I have inquired frequently the meaning of this ceremony, and could get only the answer, "It is their tamahnous." I infer it was an initiatory custom with the black tamahnous. Some of them, I heard, were starved a part of the time.

One young Clallam half-breed, it was said, was told that he would be obliged to go through some such initiatory ordeal at this potlatch, and he declared he would rather run away and hide until it was over, but the Port Discovery Indians took him some time before the festival, guarded him closely, and compelled him to submit. I suppose this was true, as he was not seen anywhere until the ceremony was over. While these scenes were being enacted the women met and sang in their usual way, and when I asked why they did so I was told they were tamahnousing in order to get strong minds towards the men.

Tahmahnawis in the Chinook tongue (the variant above is Clallam) means "a guardian or familiar spirit in its personal application," Edward Harper Thomas says in his dictionary. Every Indian had one.

"*Tahmahnawis* also means magic, ghost, spirit, or anything supernatural, and is used as the equivalent of luck, fortune and kindred words. It was applied to anything the Indians could not readily understand."

More tolerant than most missionaries, Myron Eells does not appear to have been as dogmatic in insisting that the Indians give up their spiritual beliefs, as some other ministers did; still, he was not comfortable when observing the practice close up.

Feeding their twelve hundred guests from their own resources or by using some of the presents brought to them, such as cattle, was expected of the Twanas. Eells writes:

Sometimes they gave the food to the visitors, who cooked it for themselves, but once or twice a day commonly they cooked and distributed the food. When this was done, they seated their guests in the house in two rows on mats. When the meal consisted of boiled rice, wheat, or fish, it was placed before them in large kettles, from which they helped themselves with their native ladles; but when it consisted of berries and crackers, bread, apples, potatoes, and dry food, it was placed in troughs, made of 6–inch boards, 8 or 10 feet long and three-sided. Sometimes, when the meal was over, two persons would stand, one at each end of a row of eaters, holding tightly before their faces a piece of calico cloth on which all would wipe their mouths. Then they arose and departed.

THE POTLATCH PROPER

The potlatch or distribution of gifts took place in the daytime, Eells says, two days after all the guests had arrived. The women gave first, then the men. Usually the gifts of the women were new calico cloth, with a few dresses and a little money.

> Each giver gathered those to whom she wished to make presents in two rows facing each other, in the middle of the house; next she placed her trunks at one end of the rows, took out the pieces, laid them in a pile or two, counting them over; then, taking one or two things at a time, she carried one to each woman. Each piece contained, commonly, between 5 and 9 yards. Occasionally two or three women combined together and gave at the same time, if they were not very wealthy, but the richer ones gave each by herself. About thirty women thus distributed their gifts...Three of the more prominent women gave about one hundred pieces each. If all averaged half as much, they gave away nearly 10,000 yards.

This occupied about two days and a half. A day and a half was then consumed by the men, who gave money chiefly, but occasionally blankets and a few guns. The recipients were arranged much the same as with the women, but were all men, and the distribution was conducted in much the same style.

> There were ten male donors, each of whom gave, generally, from $1 to $2 to each of his friends, so that most of the latter received from $2 to $10 each; some got more, and one who was expected to make a large potlatch in a year or two received $40. They gave on an average a little over $300 each, and the whole sums given away amounted to about $3,300. A few of the donors borrowed some of this money from their friends with considerable ceremony, promising to repay. One Indian who received a nice beaded cloak and some other articles put them on a fire, where they were consumed, in memory, it was stated, of a deceased child.

Click Relander Collection, Courtesy Yakima Valley Regional Library
LUMMI MASKS AND COSTUMES

Because it was considered bad etiquette to remain in the host community after the gifts had been distributed, the guests loaded their canoes and departed soon after the potlatch was over, the usual duration of the giveaway festival being three weeks.

BLACK TAMAHNOUS OF TENAS CHARLEY

Forcing medicine men to stop performing their magic healing rites over the sick was one of the most difficult tasks the Indian Agent had to do, Eells says.

> About 1871 or 1872 I had orders to do this from the Superintendent of Indian Affairs for Washington Territory, but it was simply impossible. The Indians would hide away, or leave the reservation, or doctor at night to cure the sick in their way, and not an Indian would dare to testify to the fact.

As an example, he cites the case of *Tenas* Charley. In Jargon Tenas means "small," which the so–named Indian may have been in stature. But among his people his power was great. When Mrs.

Mary Adams, wife of one of the chiefs, became sick and grew steadily worse despite being treated by the reservation physician and two Indian doctors, she sought help in the native way. Eells writes:

> One of these doctors had for years ruled the reservation whenever he wished to do so—Tenas Charley. He had never been a chief, but he had ruled the chiefs. If he told them to do anything, they were afraid to do differently for fear that he would kill them or their children by his tamahnous...This man was the leading Indian doctor hired at this time, and he was paid a horse for his services.
>
> The sick woman recovered, as the Indian doctors expected she would, after they had tamahnoused over her, and as the government physician expected she should do, after taking his medicine. The Indians did not try much to hide the fact that they had broken the law.

Secretly told about it, Eells felt that not much could be done, so did nothing. But when an agent in a higher position in the official hierarchy visited the reservation, he decided that the time had come to make an issue of it.

> He told them that for fourteen years he had talked to them about the foolishness of this practice and tried to reason with them, but that he would do this no longer. He would simply enforce the order. He fined the principal medicine man the horse he had received, and said the horse should be used for the police.
>
> This angered Tenas Charley, also Billy Adams, Mary's husband. Soon after, the latter resigned as chief, thus saying virtually to the Agent, "I will no longer help you."

After being confronted and given the order, Tenas Charley shook his fist in the Agent's face and declared angrily, *Cultus kopa nika kopa mika* ("I do not care anything for you.") He also added that he would never stop his tamahnous.

> It now became clear that it was to be decided who was to rule, the Agent or Tenas Charley, for although the latter had ruled many a time, he had always done it in such a way as not to have an open conflict with the Agent.
>
> After supper the Agent went to the school teacher, B.F. Laughlin, and told him as chief of police to arrest that man, and bring him in. He waited until the next morning, and then took the farmer, G.W. Coates, a heavy six-footer, and two Indian policemen, and went to Tenas Charley's house, a mile from the Agency...

As they went in, Tenas Charley was lying in bed partly covered up, and Mr. Coates afterwards said he did not know him very well and did not see exactly where he was, and so did not at once pounce on Tenas Charley with his handcuffs. Tenas Charley drew a knife, jumped from his bed across the room to his guns, and said he would shoot any one who should try to take him. The whole police force, afraid that others might help him, retreated, leaving Tenas Charley victor, in possession of the field, and reported to the Agent.

Eells says that the Agent was "nonplussed," for never in his fourteen years on the job had an Indian resisted authority in this manner. But the Agent was a stubborn man, writing out a proclamation in which he said that the law would be enforced "...even if he had to bring soldiers from Fort Townsend, seventy miles distant, to do it; that Tenas Charley was in open rebellion against the United States; and that if any other Indians should help him, they would be as liable to punishment as he was."

In reply, Tenas Charley declared:

...that he would fight before he would deliver himself up, and if the soldiers should come, he and his friends would burn all the houses, and kill all the whites they could in the region, then flee to the mountains and hide; and although they might be killed at last, they would have their revenge by doing plenty of damage at first.

Before issuing an irrevocable call for federal troops, the agent appealed to the patient, Mary Adams, to her father, who was a sub–chief, and to several of the local Indian leaders in hopes they could talk Tenas Charley into surrendering and permitting the law to take its majestic course. Reluctantly, he did so. Eells writes,

After dinner he came down and delivered himself up. He was put in jail for ten days, and fined forty dollars. It did him good, for he learned not to oppose the government, and became in many ways a better Indian.

Whether the lesson learned by Tenas Charley taught him to give up practicing medicine without a license, Eells does not say. But it probably did teach him not to get caught again.

CHINOOK JARGON

In the years following the establishment of Washington Territory in 1853, one of the first things newcomers to the area west of the Cascade Mountains needed to learn was Chinook Jargon. Though this was considered to be a simplified language employed by whites and Indians as a means of communicating for purposes of trade, it had been used by the Indians themselves long before the coming of the white man. Most users had a vocabulary of only eight hundred or so words, with which they expressed only the most basic of thoughts. But Chinook Jargon could be a rich, poetic language. For example, Myron Eells, who was both a missionary and an Indian agent for eighteen years, wrote in 1893 that he had, "... talked in it, sung in it, prayed and preached in it, translated considerable into it, and thought in it..."

In 1875, writes Edward Harper Thomas in his book *Chinook: A History and Dictionary*, over one hundred thousand people in the Pacific Northwest used Chinook Jargon in their everyday lives. At least fifty Chinook dictionaries have been published, he says, and many of its words have survived and become part of our present–day language. Yet today, only a handful of older people, anthropologists, and specialists in native American cultures have any knowledge of what once was a common tongue.

Among primitive people, trade is the great leveler, causing tribes living in different regions and speaking different languages to find some way to communicate when one band possesses something another band wants. In the case of the Chinook Indians, who lived in the lower Columbia River area, and the Nootkans, who inhabited the Vancouver Island region a few hundred miles to the north, the items they wanted to trade were slaves and seashells.

As one of the most powerful tribes in the area, the Chinook Indians did a thriving business in capturing children and young women and using them as trading material. The Nootkans, who controlled the source of scarce seashells such as dentalium, which passed as money among Northwestern tribes just as wampum had done earlier on the East Coast, coveted slaves who would perform the labor of their villages, fisheries, and camps.

Because each tribe respected the power of the other to make war, they developed the practice of trading rather than fighting. When the white man first made contact with the Indians around 1790, Comcomly, Chief of the Chinooks, and Maquinna, *Tyee* of the Nootkans, were the most powerful native American rulers in the Pacific Coast Northwest.

"Aboriginal history begins with their names," writes Thomas. "All that lies back of them is mystery."

The fact that there is no written reference to Chinook Jargon prior to 1800 means only that no white man bothered to write down what long had been a useful trade language until an British sailor named John Rodgers Jewitt spent two and one-half years as a captive on Nootka Sound, then was rescued and recorded his experiences.

CAPTIVITY OF JOHN JEWITT

The son of a Lincolnshire blacksmith and a good metal worker himself, nineteen-year-old John Jewitt joined the crew of the American ship *Boston* as an armorer at the British port of Hull, where she was taking on a cargo of goods destined to be traded to Northwest Indians for furs: "English cloths, Dutch blankets, looking glasses, beads, knives, razors, sugar, molasses, rum, and a great quantity of ammunition and firearms."

After an uneventful trip around Cape Horn, the *Boston* arrived off Vancouver Island on March 12, 1803, and started trading with the Indians. During the bartering sessions, John Jewitt was kept busy at his anvil fashioning custom–made hooks, chisels, and knives for the natives, fascinating them with his dexterity. During the dickering, unfortunately, the great Nootka chief, Maquinna, felt himself insulted. Storming ashore, he swore revenge—and the next day he took it.

Pretending to stage an entertainment aboard the ship for the officers and crew, the Nooktas suddenly threw back their outer garments, drew their weapons, and massacred every living soul on the ship—except for John Jewitt and a sail-maker named John Thompson, whom the chief felt were too useful to kill. During the looting of the *Boston*, the ship was set afire and totally destroyed. But because of their talents, the lives of John Jewitt and John Thompson were spared and they became slaves.

Making the best of the situation, John Jewitt soon won both the confidence and affection of Chief Maquinna. Though he turned down the inducements of other tribes to leave Nootka Sound and come live with them, he did make enough friends outside the village to assure that word of his plight would be spread to any British or American ship that might call on this coast. At last after two and one-half years the word reached him that the American brig *Lydia*, skippered by Captain Samuel Hill of Boston, had arrived in the area and was about to engage in trading with the Indians. Though sail-maker John Thompson was still alive, the delicate negotiations for the rescue of both men were completely in the hands of John Jewitt because of his special relationship with Maquinna, the all-powerful Nootka chief. The following are excerpts from Jewitt's book, *A Narrative of the Adventures and Sufferings of John. R. Jewitt,* (Middleton: Seth Richards, 1815):

> It was now past midsummer, and the hopes we had indulged in of our release became daily more faint, for though we had heard of no less than seven vessels on the coast, yet none appeared inclined to venture to Nootka...in the letters I wrote, imploring those who should receive them to come to the relief of two unfortunate Christians who were suffering among the heathen, I stated the cause of the *Boston's* capture and that there was not the least danger in coming to Nootka...still I felt very little encouragement that the letters would come to hand.
>
> Then on the morning of the 19th of July (1805), a day that will ever be held by me in grateful remembrance of the mercies of God, while I was employed with Thompson in forging dag-

MAKAH SMOKEHOUSE MODEL WITH THUNDERBIRD SYMBOL
Click Relander Collection, Courtesy Yakima Valley Regional Library

gers for the king (Chief Maquinna), my ears were saluted with the joyful sound of three cannon, and the cries of the inhabitants exclaiming, "Weena, weena—Mamethlee," that is, strangers—white men...

We continued our work as if nothing had happened, when in a few minutes Maquinna came in, and seeing us at work, appeared much surprised and asked if I did not know that a vessel had come. I answered in a careless manner that it was nothing to me.

"How, John," said he, "you no glad go board?"

I replied that I cared very little about it, as I had become reconciled to their manner of living and had no wish to go away. He then told me that he had called a council of his people respecting us and that we must leave off work and be present at it.

During the council, John Jewitt wrote, several opinions were expressed: putting the captives to death; sending them fifteen or twenty miles back into the country until the vessel departed; or releasing them and hoping the white men would forgive the Nootkas for having massacred the captain and crew of the *Boston* two and a half years ago. Chief Maquinna himself had a different idea—namely, to go aboard the ship, make peace with its captain so that trade could be resumed, while still keeping the extremely useful white captives. Jewitt wrote:

With regard to his going aboard the vessel, which he displayed a strong inclination to do, there was but one opinion—all remonstrating against it, telling him that the captain would kill him or keep him prisoner in consequence of his having destroyed our ship.

When Maquinna had heard their opinions, he told them that he was not afraid of being hurt from going aboard the vessel; he would, however, be guided by John, whom he had always found true...he said with much apparent satisfaction that if I would write a letter to the captain, saying that he had treated Thompson and myself kindly since we had been with him, and to use him well, he would go...

Knowing that his life depended upon how the letter was written and interpreted by the captain of the *Lydia*, John Jewitt phrased it very carefully.

Sir: The bearer of this letter is the Indian king by the name of Maquinna. He was the instigator of the capture of the ship *Boston*, of Boston in North America, John Salter captain, and of the murder of twenty-five men of her crew, the only two survivors being now on shore. Wherefore I hope you will take care to confine him according to his merits, putting in your dead-lights and keeping so good a watch over him that he cannot escape from you. By so doing we shall be able to obtain our release in the course of a few hours.

> John R. Jewitt, Armorer of the *Boston* for himself and
> John Thompson, Sail-maker of said ship.

From his long residence with the Indians, Jewitt said, he was sure that they would rather give up any number of white captives if the life of their chief depended upon their release. Still, Chief Maquinna was suspicious.

On my giving the letter to Maquinna, he asked me to explain it to him. This I did line by line, as he pointed them out with his finger, but in a sense very different from the real, giving him to understand that I had written to the captain that as he had been kind to me since I had been taken by him, that it was my wish that the captain should treat him accordingly and give him what molasses, biscuit and rum he wanted.

...Never did I undergo such a scrutiny or ever experience greater apprehension than I felt at that moment...The least mark of embarrassment on mine or suspicion of treachery on his part would probably have rendered my life the sacrifice...

Observing nothing to excite his suspicion, Chief Maquinna told John Jewitt that he believed "...what I said was true, and that he would go on board, and gave orders to get ready his canoe..."

But the wily chief made one more test. "Scarcely had the canoe put off when he ordered his men to stop, and calling to me asked me if I did not want to go on board with him. Suspecting this as a question merely intended to ensnare me, I replied that I did not wish to do it, not having any desire to leave them."

Thus reassured, Maquinna went aboard the brig *Lydia*, presented its master, Captain Samuel Hill, several beautiful furs, and then gave him the letter written by John Jewitt. After reading it, the captain invited the chief to his cabin, where he gave him some biscuits and a glass of rum, then quietly directed the first mate to go forward and return with half a dozen armed men.

"When they appeared, the captain told Maquinna that he was his prisoner and should continue so until the two men, whom he knew to be on shore, were released, at the same time ordering him to be put in irons and the windows secured, which was instantly done."

Click Relander Collection, Courtesy Yakima Valley Regional Library
CHARLEY SWAN IN THE THUNDERBIRD COSTUME, NEAH BAY

Though surprised and obviously terrified, Maquinna made
no effort to resist, requesting that one of the Indians who had
come aboard with him be summoned. When this was done, he
gave the man an order to release the two white captives and bring
them on board the ship immediately. Jewitt writes:

In a few minutes, to my inexpressible delight, I once more found
myself alongside a Christian ship, a happiness which I had
almost despaired of again enjoying.

The captain then asked me into the cabin, where I found
Maquinna in irons with a guard over him. He looked very
melancholy, but on seeing me his countenance brightened up
and he expressed his pleasure with the welcome of "Wocash

John," when, taking him by the hand, I asked the captain's permission to take off his irons...Such was the transport he felt when Captain Hill told him he was at liberty to go that he threw off his mantle, which consisted of four of the very best skins, and gave it to him as a mark of his gratitude...The captain then desired me to inform him that he should return to that part of the coast in November and that he wished him to keep what skins he should get, which he would buy of him. This Maquinna promised, saying to me at the same time, "John, when you come make *pow* (which means *to fire a gun*) to let me know and I will come down"...Then grasping both my hands, with much emotion, while the tears trickled down his cheeks, he bade me farewell and stepped into the canoe, which immediately paddled him ashore...

Sailing north with the *Lydia* for the next four months to trade and gather furs as far up the coast as Alaska, the ship, which was in need of new masts and spars after enduring some stormy weather, returned south to the mouth of the Columbia. After crossing over the bar and dropping anchor ten miles upriver in Baker Bay, Captain Hill and the crew were casually given a piece of news by the local Indians: a pair of American explorers named Lewis and Clark had recently appeared in the area, after their party had crossed the continent by land.

Since President Thomas Jefferson had authorized the explorers to return by sea, if they should happen to make contact with an American ship on the Pacific coast, the course of history might have been changed dramatically if the two groups had made contact with each other. But they did not. Finding the stretch of beach north of the mouth of the Columbia too windy, rainy, and open for their liking, the Lewis and Clark party had crossed the river, gone south a dozen or so miles, and established their winter camp at Fort Clatsop. Being a few miles inland from the sea and surrounded by big trees, this location was less exposed to the strong coastal winds, though the rain, fog, fleas, flu, and boredom between late December and March were just as dreary as they would have been on the coast north of the Columbia River

Though each party heard rumors of the other's presence, no contact was made. Which probably was just as well, for the purpose of the Lewis and Clark party was the acquisition of knowledge of the continent by a land exploration, while that of the *Lydia* was the acquisition of furs which then would be taken to China and sold to wealthy mandarins at a profit of at least one thousand percent. Since a two-year voyage around the world would be required to complete the transaction, with Lewis and Clark having no authority to compel a change of plans, it is doubtful if the two leaders would have agreed to such a long sea voyage. At any rate, it did not happen.

But thanks to John Jewitt, both trade with the Northwest Indians and the language in which it could be conducted resulted from his two and one-half years of captivity among the Indians. True to his promise, Captain Hill sailed the *Lydia* back to Nootka Sound in late November. Whether John Jewitt, who was still aboard, made the cannon go *Pow* as Chief Maquinna had asked him to do, he does not say. But from the Nootka village as soon as the brig dropped anchor:

> Inquiry was immediately made if John was there, as the king had some skins to sell them if he was. I then went forward and invited them on board, with which they readily complied, telling me that Maquinna had a number of skins with him, but that he would not come on board unless I would go ashore for him.
>
> This I agreed to, provided they (several Nootka Indians) would remain in the brig meantime. To this they consented...I then went on shore in the canoe, notwithstanding the remonstrances of Thompson and the captain, who, though he wanted the skins, advised me by no means to put myself in Maquinna's power. But I assured him that I had no fear as long as those men were on board.
>
> As I landed, Maquinna came up and welcomed me with much joy. On his inquiring for the men, I told him that they were to remain till my return. "Ah, John," said he, "I see you are afraid to trust me. But if they had come with you, I should not have hurt you, though I should have taken good care not to let you go aboard another vessel."

A PRACTICAL TONGUE

Because no scholars were involved in the creation of Chinook Jargon and it was not written down until it had existed for many generations, it became a practical, unpretentious language. As Thomas writes, "It absorbed what was useful and discarded the useless."

Since it was an oral language based on sounds pronounceable by a wide variety of linguistic groups, the spelling of the words by Jewitt, by missionaries, agents, and other literate white people who at last set them down varied widely. Whether the word meaning "trade" should be spelled makuk, makook, or mahkook mattered not at all to the Indians or to the white men who dealt with them. As a possible indication that their ancestral roots were in Asia, the Indians, like other Orientals, had trouble articulating the letter *r,* so it usually came out *l,* with "rudder " becoming *ludda* and "rum" becoming *lum.*

French words such as *la mer* for "the sea" became *lamai, lummieh,* or *lumnei.* Both an island and an Indian tribe in northern Puget Sound near Bellingham were and still are named *Lummi.* The English word "man" remains *man* in Jargon, but "old man" becomes *oleman.*

Like many Indian tribes, those in the Pacific Coast region seldom had generic names for trees, objects, or relatives. If a man referred to a relative, he used one word for "my mother," another for "your mother," and still another for "his mother." Words meaning "trees" in general did not exist; it was a "pine tree," an "alder tree," a "birch tree," and so on, with a different word for each. *Lepan* was "the bread," *lesak* was "the sack," *leseezo* was "the scissors."

If you look up the word "grog" in the English–Chinook Dictionary, you will find an awkward but intriguing combination of letters forming the Chinook Jargon word *lumpechuck,* Thomas says. Together, the two words mean rum and water, or *grog in* the parlance of the British navy. *Lum* comes from "rum," *pe* from "and," *chuck* from "water," (in the Nootkan tongue, *chauk.*)

An intriguing thing about Jargon was the way many of its words imitated the sound of the object it defined. Thus, a cow became a *moos-moos,* a wagon a *chick-chick,* a clock a *ding-ding,* a crow a *kaw-kaw,* a duck a *quack-quak,* a laugh a *tee-hee,* a heart a *tum-tum,* and a talk or speech or sermon a *wah-wah.* Early white settlers, children, and editors found the vocabulary so colorful and descriptive that they often used it in their everyday lives. Much to the despair of traditionally educated school teachers, children could and did speak it as well as their own tongue—to the extent that it replaced "proper" English much as slang and street talk do today.

Missionary–agents such as Myron Eells often gave their sermons to Indian audiences on the Skykomish and other reservations in Chinook Jargon, illustrating them with large, vivid, though somewhat crude pictures which the native Americans could relate to as they did in their own culture with clan symbols carved on totem poles. Here is an example of a sermon delivered by Eells in 1888:

ENGLISH

Two Sundays ago I spoke to you concerning that picture. There you saw two women coming to the sepulchre where Jesus lay, on Sunday, just at sunrise. Jesus had risen. He was gone. So I told you in that sermon.

CHINOOK JARGON

Moxt Sunday ahnkuttie nika memook kumtux mesika kopa okoke papeh. Yahwa mesika nanitch moxt klootchmen. Klaso chaco copa mimiloose-illahee, kah Jesus mitlite, kopa Sunday, kopa delate tenas sun. Spose klaska kap okoke mimiloose-illahee, klaska halo nanitch Jesus. Jesus get-up; yaka klatawa. Kahkwa nika wawa kopa mesika talkie Sunday.

In addition to his sermons, Myron Eells put the Ten Commandments, the Lord's Prayer, and a number of hymns—which the Indians loved to sing—into Chinook Jargon. Truly inspired was his translation of a song he composed for a Temperance meeting, titled *WHISKEY,* which he notes should be sung to the tune of a ballad called *Bounding Billows.* It goes:

1. *Ahnkuttoie nika tikegh whiskey*
   Pe alta nika mash.
        Alta nika mash.
   Formerly I loved whiskey,
     But now I throw it away.
        Now I throw it away.
2. *Whiskey hias cultus,*
   Pe alta nika mash.
        Alta nika mash.
   Whiskey is good for nothing,
     And now I throw it away.
        Now I throw it away.

And so on for several more verses. Without the music of *Bounding Billows* it no doubt loses something.

As an illustration of the depth of emotion that could be expressed in the form of poetry in Chinook Jargon, Edward Thomas quotes a poem written over a hundred years ago by Hezikiah Butterworth, attributed to a nameless old Indian woman. The Chinook Jargon word *tamala* means "tomorrow," she

Click Relander Collection, Courtesy Yakima Valley Regional Library
CHARLEY SWAN, MAKAH INDIAN, IN "CANNIBAL" COSTUME
His Granddaughter, Pauline Daniels, holds two large war whistles.

says, and to the Indian mind "tomorrow" meant eternal life. While only the single word *tamala* is Jargon in the poem, its thought as the canoe of the young Indian chief who has recently died floats down the river toward the sunset is sad and poignant:

> Aha! it is ever tomorrow, tomorrow—
> *Tamala, tamala,* sing as we row;
> Lift thine eyes to the mount;
> To the wave give thy sorrow;
> 　The river is bright, and the rivulets flow;
> 　　*Tamala, tamala,*
> 　　Ever and ever;

The morrows will come and the morrows will go
Tamala! Tamala!
Even in English and without music, this is poetry that sings in every word...

As you circle the Olympic Peninsula on US 101, access roads lead into the National Park and Forest from the east, north, west, and south. These go to resorts, campgrounds, viewpoints, and trailheads, where you can see and enjoy the scenic wonders by most any means desired. Park headquarters are located a mile south of Port Angeles, where maps and information regarding road conditions, hiking trails, fire and camping restrictions, and needed permits may be obtained.

Five miles west of Port Angeles, US 101 turns southwest, then south again through beautiful mountain and lake country past Elwha, Lake Sutherland and Lake Crescent, to Forks. Nestled at the base of steep mountain slopes, Lake Crescent contains the clearest, purest water in the region, reaching a depth of six hundred feet, which is well below sea level.

Between the western end of the lake and Forks—which in time past has been proud of its title "Logging Capital of the Olympic Peninsula"—the highway leaves the National Park and traverses National Forest and privately owned property. Standing stark and ugly here are the stumps of logged-over land, the cutting of whose giant trees since the turn of the century provided a livelihood for three generations of loggers and sawmill workers. As little as twenty years ago, these workers did not dream that the day would come when their jobs would be at risk because the region was running out of old-growth trees. But as environmentalists point out more and more vehemently as time goes on, only five percent of the ancient forest that once covered this land remains standing and must be preserved.

To them, the issue is trees. To the forest industry workers, the issue is jobs. Where, when, and how this vital controversy will be settled is a subject that will become an important facet of the history of the region eventually. But the day of resolution is not yet in sight.

EDGE OF THE CONTINENT

Before the states of Alaska and Hawaii were added to the Union, a diagonal line drawn from the southern tip of Key West to Neah

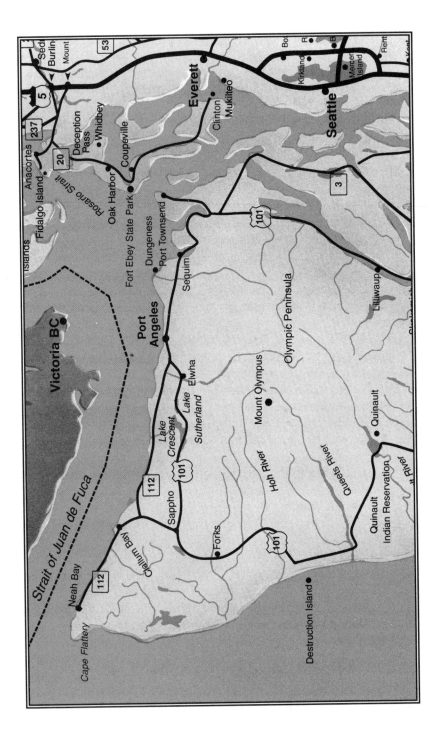

Bay on the northwest extremity of Washington would have crossed the most culturally and physically diverse land on earth. Not being familiar with the present residents of the Key West area, I cannot say who owns it now. But title to Cape Flattery and Neah Bay on the extreme northwestern tip of the continental United States is still in the hands of what are presumed to be its original residents, the Makah Indians.

Five miles west of Port Angeles, where US 101 swings left toward Forks, State 112 follows the curving shoreline of the Strait of Juan de Fuca directly west for sixty-six miles to Neah Bay, the Makah Indian Reservation, and the lighthouse standing on Cape Flattery at the extreme edge of the country. Though the light and its foghorn give visual and audible warning of a rugged coast, no shipping hazards such as those at the entrance to the Columbia River at the southern border of the state exist in the strait itself, for here it is fifteen miles wide, hundreds of feet deep, and so free of hazards that even the largest of vessels can navigate it without danger.

Like many other Indian tribes in Washington State, the Makahs have chosen to preserve their history by means of an excellent museum and visitor center at the eastern edge of the town of Neah Bay, which is headquarters for a reservation covering the northwest tip of the state. Inquiries should be made here regarding access to the beaches and anthropological dig sites in the area, some of which have been recently discovered and still are being evaluated.

Among the intriguing exhibits in the museum are a canoe manned by simulated native Americans in search of seals or whales and a dimly lit longhouse with simulated families going about their daily chores, made realistic by a sound track of chants and the cries of animals and birds.

By this time, the traveler making a circuit of the Olympic Peninsula will have accepted the fact that Washington State has preserved many unique place names of Indian origin: Lilliwaup, Skokomish, Duckabush, Dosewallips, and Pysht—to mention a

US 101, State 112—Port Angeles to Neah Bay and Forks
124 miles

few—and has given up trying to pronounce them. Since there are no overall rules for pronunciation, the only helpful advice we can offer is: listen to a native, then imitate him if you can.

Six miles east of Clallam Bay, a blue-line highway turns south off State 112 and cuts across ten miles to US 101, which it intercepts at the small settlement of Sappho. Backtracking to Lake Crescent for twenty-eight miles is well worth the time, for this is one of the most beautiful lakes in the country. It and Soleduck Hot Springs, which is in the Olympic National Park by way of a secondary road, long have been popular vacation spots for local people and tourists from all over the country.

EXPLORING THE OLYMPIC MOUNTAINS

Washington became the forty-second state to join the Union on November 11, 1889. With a population of 349,390 people and a growth rate of 365 percent during the past ten years, the new state literally was "busting its buttons" with pride in its progress and was searching for some dramatic way to celebrate its new status. At that time, the search for Dr. Livingston in Africa by a New York newspaper reporter name Stanley was making headlines all over the world. So when Governor Elisha P. Ferry told a local reporter that the State of Washington had in its northwestern corner an unexplored section of wilderness twenty-five hundred miles square, enclosed by the Olympic Mountains, "...which never, to the knowledge of old residents of the territory, has been trodden by the foot of man, white or Indian..." regional newspapers in general and the *Seattle Press* [predecessor to the *Seattle Times*] in particular jumped on the story. A *Press* reporter wrote:

> Washington has her great unknown land like the interior of Africa....Here is a fine opportunity for some of the hardy citizens of the Sound to acquire fame by unveiling the mystery which wraps the land encircled by the snow capped Olympic range.

Following publication of the article, the *Press* was flooded with letters from readers who claimed to have been "all over" the area, and who would, if properly subsidized, be glad to lead a new exploring expedition. But when asked to substantiate their claims, most of them admitted that they had seen only the outer edges of the wilderness area and that their avowed knowledge of the interior was based on rumors, legends, and hearsay.

Even local Indian tribes such as the Skokomish, Makahs, and Quinaults, whose reservations were located on salt water and the lower reaches of the mountains, knew very little about what lay in the interior. According to their legends, the high country was the abode of the mystic, terrible Thunderbird, the flapping of whose wings caused storms, whose eyes darted lightning bolts, and whose back carried a lake of water which fell as torrential rain whenever he shook his feathers. Some of them said that behind the towering outer peaks lay a broad, enchanted valley full of beautiful streams and lakes, hordes of fish and game, and all sorts of precious metals and gems. But it was said to be inhabited by a tribe of Indians so fierce and jealous of their territory that no outsider who dared to trespass had ever survived. Thus, all the coastal Indians refused to venture into that dangerous country, either on their own or as guides for white men.

Of all the responses from readers, one received on November 6, 1889, from North Yakima, Washington, which was written and signed by a man named J.H. Christie, most intrigued the interest of the *Press*. Christie wrote:

> From your article upon the Olympics I judge that we are both interested in the unveiling of the mystery ...My interest, aroused by the fact that the mountains have not as yet been penetrated by white men and an ambition to accomplish what others may have failed in, backed by an inherent love of adventure, caused me to form the resolution to penetrate the depths of the unknown range. It is now my intention to act upon this resolution by entering the mountains this next month.
>
> It is no ambitious, untried youth who now writes you, but a man tried in all the vicissitudes of mountain, forest, and plain life, schooled in the great plain of the northwest territories during the Sioux and Nez Perce wars, having met with most of the reverses that fell to the lot of frontiersmen during the years between 1871 and 1878.

Though he was ready, willing, and able to lead an exploring party across the unknown Olympics in the dead of winter, Christie expressed regret that he could not finance such an exploration himself. But surely that difficulty could be overcome, he said, if a few public-spirited citizens of means would contribute to the project. He concluded his letter, "Why not let the *Press* give its countenance and support to an expedition for clearing up of a mystery lying at the very door of Seattle?"

Ashael Curtis Photo, Courtesy Washington State Historical Society
IN THE HIGH OLYMPICS

Somehow sensing that the writer of the letter was exactly what he claimed to be, the publisher of the *Press*, William E. Bailey, and one of its sharp young reporters, Edmund S. Meany, talked it over, then invited Christie to come to Seattle and tell them more about himself. This he was happy to do.

THE *PRESS* OLYMPIC EXPEDITION

James Halbold Christie, who arrived in Seattle accompanied by three rugged companions, proved to be a unique kind of man. Just returned to the United States after three years in the Arctic, where he had explored northern Canada's Peace and MacKenzie rivers, he had paused to visit friends in Yakima, Washington. There, he had met a young cowboy named Christopher O'Connell Hayes, who had called his attention to the newspaper story about the unexplored Olympics. Though Christie and his two friends, John H. Crumback and John W. Sims, had been discussing the possibility of going to Africa, they decided they would explore the Olympics instead, if proper backing could be obtained.

Publisher Bailey was so impressed by Christie and his companions that he agreed to sponsor the expedition, suggesting only that an ex–Marine, Captain Charles A. Barnes, who was a skilled photographer and map-maker, and Harris Boyle Runnalls, a Puyallup doctor, be added to the party. To this, Christie agreed.

Click Relander Collection, Courtesy Yakima Valley Regional Library
CHARLEY SWAN, MAKAH INDIAN, IN WOLF MASK AND COSTUME

Because the *Press* was footing the bill, it had an "exclusive" on the story, which later was printed serially in the newspaper during the summer of 1890. It was not published in any other form until the various journals and diaries were edited by Robert L. Wood, (who knew the Olympics well and attempted to reconcile the sometimes conflicting accounts), and issued in book form by the University of Washington Press in 1967.

As originally constituted, the *Press* Exploring Expedition consisted of six men, four dogs, and fifteen hundred pounds of provisions. Later two mules were acquired to assist in packing supplies. Nothing is known about the dogs except that their names were Daisy, Tweed, Bud, and Dike, but considerably more has been recorded about the men.

Unloading their provisions and gear at Port Angeles on December 8, 1889, the party went by wagon to the lower Elwha

River, where it took the trail south to Meagher's Ranch, which was as far as a trail of any kind penetrated the wilderness. After considerable haggling, they managed to buy two mules named Jennie and Dollie, loaded them with 250–pound packs, then each of the six men shouldered a sixty-pound pack, and the exploration party got under way. Though winter was just beginning and snowfall in the mountains ahead of them was expected to be heavy, so many other parties were planning to attack the Olympics from all directions with the coming of spring, the *Press* Expedition was bound and determined to be first.

Information regarding the nature of the country ahead was unreliable. Told by one Port Angeles native, who was supposed to know the region well, that a mile up the Elwha from Meagher's Ranch the river widened and was navigable for at least thirty miles, the men struggled for days to drag enough heavy, green lumber with them to build a boat. When completed, the unwieldy craft was thirty feet long, five feet wide, and two feet deep. Christened *Gertie*, the boat finally was dragged through the snowdrifts down to the river and launched on the last day of the year. But instead of floating like a cork, it swam like a fish.

"I am sorry to find that she takes in a little too much water," Christie wrote in his diary, "which will compel a recaulking. Thus ends our labor for 1889."

By then, Dr. Runnalls had received a message saying that his wife was ill, so he was forced to leave the party and return to Puyallup. Though he hoped to rejoin the group in a week or two, he was never able to do so; thus, the expedition was reduced to five men and was without a doctor. Judging from the incredible hardships the men endured for the next five months, with dysentery caused by near starvation their only physical complaint, the services of a medical man were not sorely missed.

While they chopped wood, upended the boat, built a fire, and tended it day and night in order to drive the sap out of the green lumber, snow fell incessantly and it became so cold that ice froze over the outer side of the boat. By January 11, when they finally got the drying and caulking finished, the snow was three and a half feet deep and the weather bitter cold. Launched again, the *Gertie* "...floated like a duck and dry as a whistle..." so was loaded and headed upriver. Within half a mile, rapids were encountered, where the boat had to be unpacked, its cargo portaged, and the

Ashael Curtis Photo, Courtesy Washington State Historical Society
HIGH OLYMPIC CRAGS

heavy vessel itself hauled upstream by towline. After taking a header into the icy water and going completely under, Christie wrote with remarkable restraint, "Devilish cold and the party rather in a frozen-out condition. The Elwha is quite a different stream, I find, from the Elwha of common report."

By January 24, after fighting the river for two weeks and progressing only four miles, the party agreed that they had reached the "head of navigation," such it was, abandoned the boat, and sought other means to move their cargo into the mountains. These included improvised toboggans, snowshoes, hand-pulled travois, wheelbarrows on runners, and a double-ended "go-cart" designed and built by Sims and Crumback, which, though it looked like it should work, proved so contrary that "...its load was reduced to 100 pounds, and by dint of great pulling and hard pushing made a quarter of a mile. When last seen Sims was jumping with both feet up and down on the wreck and Crumback was calling for an axe wherewith effectually to end its short but troubled career."

Of another vehicle, Captain Barnes observed, "Hayes' buggy remained by the cache. Its glory was that it did not fail—it never started. Hayes, like a prudent man, profited by our experience and packed his load on his back."

With the snow getting deeper and the trail climbing sharply, the entire party turned to carrying fifty-pound packs, making as many trips up and back as were necessary, while the two mules, Jennie and Dollie, whose small hoofs were not suited to snow and ice and who suffered cruel cuts and bleeding gashes as their legs sank deep into the treacherous going, carried less and less each day.

After two months on the trail, the expedition was still in the narrow, sheer-walled canyon of the Elwha River. Here, snow lay seven feet deep, with more falling every day. At Christie's direction, a three-level blaze was chopped in the bark of standing trees at intervals along the trail they were making: one at the surface of the snow to show where its level had been at the time the party passed through, a second at waist-height, and a third at eye-level. Some of these blazes are still to be seen, mountaineers say today, though later hikers have confused their authenticity by cutting similar blazes at more recent times.

The size of the trees growing in the area impressed members of the party. Hayes measured several giant cedars that were thirty feet around, estimating them to be two thousand years old.

Despite rumors of gold in the interior, the party's occasional panning of streams along the way showed no signs of color. Game was scarce much of the time, though just as their supply of meat was running low they did encounter a herd of elk in a sheltered valley, one of which they killed, dressed, and smoked for meat. On February 26, 1890, they noted that they shot and killed "...a large gray wolf..." which they were not tempted to eat because of its leanness, toughness, and resemblance to their dogs.

Because of the deep snow and rugged country, three months had elapsed by early March and they were only one-fifth of the way across the mountains in a journey they had estimated would take six months. After traversing a gloomy, sheer-walled canyon they called "Goblins Gates" and climbing toward a divide on the eastern shoulder of Mount Olympus dubbed "Devils Backbone," they were convinced that the oft-repeated story that a broad,

Ashael Curtis Photo, Courtesy Washington State Historical Society
HERD OF ROOSEVELT ELK IN THE OLYMPICS

open, pleasant valley lay in the heart of the Olympic range was a myth. Instead, the reality was that the interior country between the Strait of Juan de Fuca on the north to Quinault Lake on the south, and from the Pacific Ocean on the west to Hood Canal on the east, was filled with a jumble of fifty or more peaks three to eight thousand feet high, which in winter were covered with snow. Naming these peaks Mounts Bailey, Hunt, McClure, Angus, Anderson, Pulitzer, Seattle, and in honor of other newspaper publishers and cities that had backed the expedition, it appeared that they would run out of sponsors before they exhausted their supply of mountains.

Tragedy struck on March 9 as the exhausted mule Jennie was picking her way along an icy trail, which was little more than a narrow ledge over a chasm four hundred feet deep.

As they were traversing the mountainside, Christie was ahead, cutting away fallen trees and other obstructions, followed by Crumback leading Jennie. At a cry from Crumback, Christie turned in time to see Jennie plunging into the gulf below. The earth beneath the mule's feet had suddenly given way, and though the animal made a desperate effort to save herself she was dragged down by the two-hundred-pound load on her back. They heard a rattle of gravel, succeeded by a sickening thud as the mule struck a cleft between the cliff and a large tree about one hundred feet below.

Tying life-lines to trees along the trail, Christie and Sims lowered themselves down to where Jennie's body had lodged. Finding her so badly injured that she could not move, they quickly put her out of her pain in an act of mercy. One hundred-fifty pounds of her load, was flour, which they salvaged, but the other fifty pounds was explosive flash powder. Called "colored fire," it had been brought along because months earlier they had agreed to ignite it as a display atop Mount Olympus on a certain date in hopes that it could be seen by observers on the east side of Puget Sound many miles away.

"But signaling from a mountaintop held little interest for them at the moment..." So, after cutting the mule's packsaddle loose and letting her body fall to the bottom of the canyon far below, they kicked the package of "hell fire," as it was familiarly known in camp, and sent it after the mule, to find a fitting resting place by her side.

Left to carry on alone, the other mule, Dollie, began showing signs that she was ready to desert the party, if only she could figure out which way to go to find good pasture. Reaching a small valley near the headwaters of the Elwha where there was plenty of fish and game, the party camped for two weeks, curing 1,500 pounds of elk meat and salmon, which they hoped would last for the rest of the journey, giving Dollie a chance to regain her flesh and strength on salal, Oregon grape, and whatever other browse she could find.

Hearing an occasional distant noise like low thunder, they took it to be the periodic eruption of boiling underground springs, so called the area "Geyser Basin." They never saw a geyser (nor did any explorers that followed them in later years), so naturalists familiar with the area have since deduced that what they heard was the drumming sound that grouse make in early spring as part of their mating ritual.

John Crumback liked the valley so well that he decided to stake out a Homestead Claim here.

"On the opening day of spring, March 21, 1890, each man took his axe and proceeded to the spot Crumback had chosen for the cabin, close by the river, in the midst of a heavy growth of timber. Four trees, each a foot in diameter, were selected and soon lay on the ground...The foundation of Crumback's cabin—which measured twenty-five by thirty feet—was in place..."

Though this spot was such a paradise for fish and game that members of the party called it "a game preserve," the man who laid the foundation logs for the first cabin within the boundaries of what would become Olympic National Park never returned to complete or live in it. But during the rest of his long, adventuresome life, he must have dreamed about this idyllic spot many times.

Moving on from their pleasant camp in misnamed Geyser Valley, Christie "...was confronted with a conundrum hard to solve. Dollie was suffering from skinned legs, and to take her over more snow-covered terrain would mean sawing her legs off from the knees. A mule without legs, he asserted, was not worth much."

Though they gave Dollie a handful of ferns they had gathered, as well as a pound of their dwindling supply of beans, while she munched on but could not digest the spruce boughs from their beds, she grew weaker day by day. After surviving a bad fall, she became so crippled that she could carry little weight. On April 21:

> This was the last day Dollie traveled. About a half mile beyond the starting place, she suddenly gave out and laid down. She had done her duty faithfully and well to that point, but there she played out.
>
> They unloaded the mule, cached the pack she had been carrying, and left her on the path. "With fair luck," they assured themselves, "she would be fat and fresh at the end of the month."

On that same day, the party lost another animal—the dog "Dike." A large, black, overly eager retriever, the dog got so excited when the party jumped a large band of elk that it "...rashly attempted to head off one of the bulls, which, striking Dike with his forefeet, nearly cut the dog in two. He was horribly mangled, and gave a most instructive object lesson upon the savage nature of the elk when brought to bay."

ACROSS THE DIVIDE

At last climbing up and out of the Elwha watershed and crossing a high ridge of land to the drainage area of the Quinault, they saw peak after rugged peak six to seven thousand feet high, where immense drifts of snow up to twenty-five feet deep lay under cor-

Ashael Curtis Photo, Courtesy Washington State Historical Society
PEAKS OF THE OLYMPICS

nices that now with the coming of warmer weather collapsed and sent huge avalanches thundering down almost vertical slopes.

Limited in the amount they could carry in back packs over the difficult terrain, they ran low on food again. On April 28, they were exasperated to discover:

> Last night the dogs got away with the bacon, leaving us only two or three pounds. In the remaining piece was very little fat, the only grease in camp. We have been very saving of bacon, and the loss amounts almost to a disaster ...As for the dogs they have had scarcely anything to eat since we left the dead elk at the Gallery, for we cannot pack for dogs. They are hardly to be blamed for last night's theft. We would probably steal ourselves if we were hungry

These remarkably tolerant words were written by Captain Charles Barnes, but the sentiment he expressed apparently was shared by the other members of the party, not one of whom ever suggested that they do as many other hungry explorers had done before them—eat their dogs. Soon, their forbearance was rewarded. Early one morning as they stood gazing in awe at the ridge of mountains forming the main divide, "One of the dogs began to give tongue in a clump of trees about 300 yards down the canyon. The other two dogs were away like a shot."

"A bear!" one of the men cried, and at that moment a black bear, harassed by the three dogs, emerged from the clump of trees. The men seized their guns and gave chase. Although Captain Barnes grabbed his camera instead of his rifle, the subjects would not hold still long enough for him to get them in focus.

> The bear was fighting the dogs, sometimes sitting back on his haunches and snapping at them and trying to reach them with his paws. Then one of the dogs would nip him behind and he would be off again. No sooner would he be off a few steps than one of the dogs would nip his heels, and that would bring him up all-standing once more, and the fighting and snapping would recommence. Meanwhile, the bear and dogs were nearing a little clump of trees, and to this we all hurried.

Afraid that the other men would kill the bear before he got his pictures, Captain Barnes managed to get three "exposures" while men held their fire in fear of hitting the dogs instead of the bear. Deciding to break free of the melee by making a charge, the bear quite sensibly went after the man carrying the camera instead of a gun. Quite sensibly, Captain Barnes sought shelter behind a tree, while at the same time yelling for someone to shoot the bear with a weapon more deadly than a camera.

This James Christie did, downing the bear with a well placed shot through the kidneys. To starving men, no food tastes better or is needed more than fat—and this proved to be a very fat bear.

> It was not more than 15 minutes before we had that bear skinned and dressed and his liver and slabs of fat frying over the fire...we sat around the fire and kept the frying pans going and drank the grease as fast as we could fry it out.

It is an indication of their starving condition that the bear meat lasted the five men and three dogs (we must assume they were given a liberal share) only three days. On a two-day climb to the top of a mountain peak and back, Captain Barnes admits he started out with a fifteen-pound piece and ate it all before he got back.

During the next few days, the dogs flushed and helped the men kill three more bears; so now, on the southwest shoulder of Mount Olympus, with the weather turning warm, the snowdrifts behind,

Ashael Curtis Photo, Courtesy Washington State Historical Society
RIDERS IN THE HIGH OLYMPICS

and following the Quinault River, which at this season of the year, Christie noted tersely, "...seemed to be one continuous long waterfall..." the first crossing of the Olympics was about to be accomplished.

Reaching the Quinault Indian Reservation Agency May 20, 1890, the men took a sloop to Grays Harbor, next day. The first thing Christie did was to wire the *Press* for money to pay the party's passage to Seattle; the second, to pose for a photo with the other four men and the three dogs; the third, fourth, and fifth, to get a haircut, a hotel-cooked meal, and a hot bath.

After reaching Seattle, James Christie complied with the request of the *Press* that he stay in a hotel room and complete his diary, so that the newspaper would have a complete account of the epic journey. Though he did not claim to to be much of a writing man, he apparently did this chore to the satisfaction of *Press* publisher William Bailey. When Christie rendered a bill for expenses while at the hotel, in the amount of sixty dollars, to the *Press*, "They generously sent me a check for $75, allowing me $15 for consideration of six months of damned hard labour for their benefit. So ho." By which he probably meant, *Sic transit gloria*—or words to that effect.

Though he would live out his days in relative obscurity in the wilds of British Columbia, James H. Christie remained hale, hearty, and a mountain man to the end, dying June 15, 1942, at the age of eighty-seven.

CAPE FLATTERY

According to marine historian James A. Gibbs in his definitive book *Shipwrecks of the Pacific Coast*, the name Cape Flattery is inappropriate for the most northwesterly corner of the United States. Because of the many ships that have been lost along this rugged, storm-racked coast, "Tombstone Cape" would have been a much more suitable name, he says.

"Over 150 deep-sea ships are known to have come to grief near Cape Flattery. No telling how many others went to the bottom unrecorded in the pages of history."

He estimates that at least sixty junks from China and Japan, crippled by storms in their home waters, eventually drifted across the Pacific Ocean and went on the rocks along the lonely northwest Washington coast. Not all of these were lost in the days of sail, for as late as 1927 a steam-powered Japanese vessel suffered such a tragic fate that it became known as the "death ship."

JAPANESE DEATH SHIP

On October 31, 1927, the freighter *Margaret Dollar* was steaming south off Cape Flattery when her master, Captain H.T. Payne, sighted a derelict fishing vessel on the horizon. Approaching it, the captain ordered a boat lowered and dispatched a boarding party. Gibbs writes:

> As they approached the mysterious craft they found her hull encrusted with four inches of barnacles. Her rigging hung limp and the masts were badly strained, with but one shred of sail remaining. A cold chill came over the intruders as they clambered over the gunwales. The smell of death was about. Their lips became silent as about them they saw decomposed bodies. Inside the cabin were the remains of the captain. Near him was a thin cedar board upon which was scrolled a list of the crew, the vessel's owner, and the name, *Ryo Yei Maru*.

When translated, the ship's log told a tragic tale. While being lashed by a sixty-mile gale seven hundred miles off the coast of

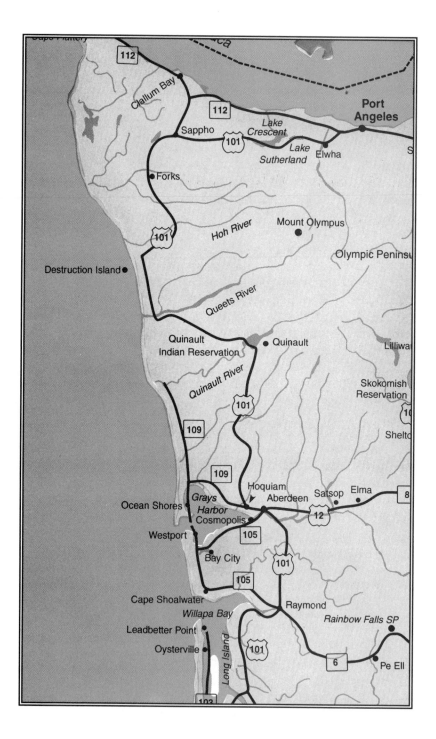

Japan, the ship's engine failed. When a freighter, the *West Isom*, came alongside and offered assistance, the captain of the crippled vessel refused to abandon ship or accept a tow, feeling that the engine could be repaired. So the freighter sailed on, leaving the *Ryo Yei Maru* to her fate. This was on December 23, 1926.

Unable to repair the engine, the crew and the ship drifted helplessly over storm-tossed seas. Improvised sails were rigged and set, but high winds soon ripped them to shreds. Wind and current carried the craft further and further away from the homeland. After six weeks of drifting, another ship was sighted in the distance but failed to recognize or respond to the distress signals. One by one, members of the crew fell ill and died, with the captain's scribe recording each name in the log. On March 9, 1927, the engineer died. Food was nearly gone, the scribe wrote, and some of the men were too weak to leave their bunks.

Between March 12 and April 1, five fishermen and the first mate perished. On April 5, Captain Tokizo Miki caught a large sea bird, which was immediately devoured. On April 14, a shark was gaffed and hauled aboard after a long, exhausting struggle, for by then the men were so weak from malnutrition and beriberi that they could hardly move. On April 19, the tenth member of the crew succumbed and on May 6 the captain became seriously ill. Four days later only he and the seaman keeping the log remained alive; both were too weak to tend the helm. Gibbs writes:

> Finally, on May 11, the last words appeared in the log. "Wind is Northwest. Weather cloudy. Wind fresh. Sea rough. Drifting with remaining sails hoisted.

Manned by a crew of dead men, the *Ryo Yei Maru* drifted on. The vessel had departed Mikasi, Japan, on December 5, 1926, and was not picked up by the *Margaret Dollar* until October 31, 1927. For eleven harrowing months, the ghost ship had drifted five thousand miles on the Japanese Current. Towed into Seattle, the vessel attracted thousands of curious sightseers, and offers were made to purchase it as a sideshow attraction. But the Japanese owners had too much respect for the dead to permit that, so, after

US 101—Forks to Aberdeen
104 miles

Ashael Curtis Photo, Courtesy Washington State Historical Society
TWO DEER WITH A RELUCTANT MOTHER NURSE

proper Buddhist ceremony, the human remains were cremated, then the vessel was saturated with oil and burned.

WRECK OF THE *ST. NICHOLAS*

Preserved in the State Library at Juneau, Alaska, an epic account of an early-day shipwreck on the Washington coast contains enough tragedy, romance, and drama to fill a long historical novel, though every word of it is true.

Under the command of Captain Nikolai Bulagnin, the *St. Nicholas* departed New Archangel (Sitka), Alaska, on September 8, 1808. Bound on a trading venture down the Northwest coast of America, the ship carried a crew of eighteen men. Also on board was the captain's beautiful wife, Anna Petrovna, who, it may be assumed, regarded the voyage as a pleasant adventure during which she would be given an opportunity to select prime pelts from the most beautiful fur-bearing animal in the Pacific Ocean, the sea otter, for which her adoring husband would be trading and later would commission a furrier to fashion her a high-style coat.

But fate decreed otherwise. In Latitude 47 degrees, 56 minutes North, just off the sheer pile of rock called Destruction Island, tragedy struck. In a dead calm that left the sails hanging limp, the ship was driven by strong currents closer and closer to the shore, then, when gale winds did arise, they came from the southwest, thrusting the ship onto the jagged reef before sail could be set and the unwieldy craft worked clear of the deadly coast.

As the stranded ship was being pounded to pieces on the beach near the mouth of the Quillayute River, Captain Bulagnin managed to get his wife, Anna Petrovna, and all members of the crew safely ashore. Before the ship broke up, the crew managed to salvage enough arms, ammunition, tents, sails, provisions, and other usable materials to assure their survival for a time. Before leaving Sitka, plans had been made to rendezvous with another Russian trading vessel, the *Kodiak*, at Grays Harbor, some distance to the south. Though the overland journey in the cold, rainy winter weather no doubt would be a rugged one, Captain Bulagnin was confident it could be made. But on this coast, not only the weather proved unfriendly.

Attacked by a band of spear-wielding Indians, the Russians drove them off with musket fire, killing two of them. But between their camp near the mouth of the Quillayute River and Grays Harbor on the southwest Washington coast lay a hundred miles of rugged country slashed by swift-flowing rivers, covered by thick growths of trees, and filled with hostile natives who coveted the weapons and tools of the white strangers. Only the guns of the Russians kept the Indians from overwhelming them.

At the Hoh River, natives had to be hired to ferry the Russians across in canoes. In the middle of the river, the savages leaped overboard and swam ashore, leaving the Russians to fend for themselves without the aid of paddles. The natives then gathered on the river banks and began throwing spears at the whites, sinking the canoes.

With Anna and her escorts taken prisoners, the remainder of the party fought the Indians, killing two of them, while losing one crew member who was struck in the groin by a sharp-edged thrown spear. Lacking shelter, possessing little food, and having trouble keeping their ammunition dry, the Russians found themselves in desperate straits. Captain Bulagnin was so despondent and heartsick over the capture of his wife that he relinquished command to Colonel Timothy Tarakanof, an experienced soldier who was more accustomed to leading men in a ground battle ashore.

Ashael Curtis Photo, Courtesy Washington State Historical Society
HEADWATERS OF THE ELWHA IN THE OLYMPICS

Ordering a raid on a nearby Indian village, the new commander found it deserted, so the Russians appropriated a quantity of
dried salmon, which the hungry men soon devoured. Presently
they were approached by a representative from the Indians seeking a ransom for the return of Anna Petrovna.

Captain Bulagnin, who conducted the bargaining, offered
everything the Russians possessed except their muskets in
exchange for his wife. The Indians demanded the muskets, too.
These the Russians refused to give up, despite the captain's desperate plea that they do so. He then begged the Indians to let him
talk with his wife. This they finally consented to do.

After a brief meeting with his wife, Captain Bulganin was
horrified as he watched the Indians drag her away into the depths
of the forest. Deciding to spend the winter in the vicinity, Colonel
Timothy Tarakanof supervised the building of a log fort whose
walls and sentry boxes would protect the crew from the Indians
and the elements until the coming of spring, thus keeping alive

Captain Bulagnin's hopes for rescuing his wife. As the long, rainy weeks passed, the Russians occupied their time by building a boat in which they hoped to make their eventual escape. They also devised a clever plan by which to effect Anna's rescue.

Sending a raiding party into a nearby Indian village, they seized two young Indian maidens, took them back to their log fort, and declared they intended to hold the young women hostage until the tribesmen produced Anna.

That got results. Deciding that the increasingly weak, frail, haggard-looking Russian woman wasn't worth two healthy young native girls, the Indians brought Anna to the fort and said they were ready to trade. But when Captain Bulagnin's wife saw the boat which the shipwrecked Russians had built and heard them tell about their plans to make the gruelling trek to Grays Harbor, she refused to go with them.

Bulagnin was so stunned that he threatened to shoot her. Still she refused and to go along, so the Indians took her away.

Having observed that none of the Russian captives had been mistreated by the Indians, Colonel Tarakanof decided that the wise thing to do was to surrender to the Indians, hoping that eventually a trading ship of friendly whites would come along and rescue them. He and four other men gave themselves up. But Captain Bulagnin was so distraught he insisted on the rest of the crew joining him in launching the boat they had built and paddling it across the river bar and out to sea in the direction of Destruction Island. A strong wind was blowing and the sea was rough. When the boat capsized, the Russians fell into the sea, from which the Indians plucked them and took them prisoners.

Now all the Russians were captives, with Captain Bulagnin separated from his wife Anna Petrovna, who had become the personal property of a chief. After wasting away month after month, she died in August, 1809, the chief apparently so displeased with her frailness during her captivity that he had her body dragged off into the forest where it was left to decay without burial.

When the news reached Captain Bulagnin, he lost his will to live and what remained of his sanity, growing weaker and more listless month by month until he too died in February of the following year.

Realist that he appears to have been, Colonel Timothy Tarakanof fared better than all the other Russian captives.

Ashael Curtis Photo, Courtesy Washington State Historical Society
OLYMPIC WILDERNESS

Becoming the property of a chief whose village was in the Cape Flattery area, he impressed his master by making tools out of pieces of metal salvaged from shipwrecks, just as John Jewitt had done a few years earlier for Chief Maquinna during his two-and-a-half years of captivity at Nootka Sound.

He also greatly impressed the Indians by building and flying kites, informing them that he was using the kites to send messages to his great white father. This gained him so much prestige that he was permitted to build his own hut and was granted many other freedoms. Eventually, a trading ship did call on a native village in the area, heard that a shipwrecked crew from a Russian vessel was hoping to be ransomed, and began inquiring around. Making good use of his freedom to go where he wished, Colonel Tarakanof found his way to the American brig *Lydia*, which, with its master, Captain Brown, was trading for furs with Indians along the Strait of Juan de Fuca, and told him about the other captives. Oddly enough, this was the same ship that had rescued John Jewitt in 1805, though it now sailed under a different master. Because the

Indians preferred weapons, tools, and goods to prisoners, a bargain was soon struck, the natives accepting for each prisoner a large quantity of cloth, a locksmith's saw, two steel knives, a mirror, five packages of gunpowder and five bags of shot.

Of the original twenty Russians aboard the ill-fated *St. Nicholas*, thirteen survivors were eventually ransomed and returned to New Archangel in the summer of 1811. Seven had perished in battle or captivity—including Captain Nikolai Bulagnin and his beautiful wife Anna Petrovna.

WORST WRECK OF ALL

Of the many shipwrecks in the Cape Flattery area, by far the worst was the sinking of the big side-wheeler, *Pacific*, in 1875. Departing Victoria, British Columbia, at mid–morning on November 4, the ship carried 277 passengers and crew members. Steaming out through the Strait of Juan de Fuca, she passed the Cape Flattery light at four o'clock in the afternoon. A strong wind was blowing from the southwest, a heavy swell was running, and cresting seas slowed her progress. Night came on cold and black.

After an evening's entertainment, most of the passengers had retired at 10 p.m. when the shock of a collision sent them sprawling from their bunks. Later, it was determined that the vessel had been struck by the sailing ship *Orpheus*, an 1,100–ton freighter headed north from San Francisco to Nanaimo, British Columbia to take on a cargo of coal. Aboard the *Orpheus*, the impact of the collision had been so light that the damage it did to the sailing vessel soon was repaired and the ship continued on its way.

But due to a number of factors never satisfactorily explained then or later, the injury done to the *Pacific* proved to be fatal. There were not enough lifeboats aboard; those that were available could not be lowered and launched by the inexperienced and undisciplined crew; unaware of the damage done, the *Orpheus* sailed on its way without lingering to see if the passenger vessel needed help.

Seas were running high; visibility was poor; the night was dark; the crew and passengers panicked; in a word, anything that could go wrong, did go wrong. As a result, of the 277 souls aboard the *Pacific*, only two survived. Though the bodies of some of the victims drifted ashore along the beaches of the Strait for weeks afterward, many—like the ship itself—sank in deep water and were never seen again.

Ashael Curtis Photo, Courtesy Washington State Historical Society
PARADISE VALLEY IN THE OLYMPICS

HOH RAIN FOREST

The rain forest on the western side of the Olympic Peninsula is unique. Cradled in the valleys of three rivers, the Hoh, Queets, and Quinault, it is best entered fifteen miles south of Forks from US 101, where a blue-line highway leads east to the Hoh Rain Forest Nature Trails Center inside Olympic National Park

In this green, wet, moss-and-fern-filled world of immense trees reaching upward three hundred or more feet, sunshine seldom touches the forest floor. All sounds are muted into a whispering silence comparable to that experienced in an old, massive, reverence-inspiring cathedral.

Among the gigantic trees are a Sitka spruce over thirteen feet in diameter, as well as the largest known western hemlock, Douglas fir, red alder, and red cedar trees. In the rain forest, trees *average* two hundred feet in height, with many of them rising over three hundred feet. In contrast to tropical rain forests, which are hot, humid, and contain fifty or more kinds of deciduous trees, the Olympic Rain Forest is cool and mild, with four varieties of evergreen trees predominant: Sitka spruce, western hemlock, western red cedar, and Douglas fir.

With a recorded high of 180 inches of rainfall a year, each square mile of surface receives fifteen vertical feet of water annually. During the winter months, it is not uncommon for six inches of rain to fall during a twenty-four hour period, with up to sixty inches falling in a month's time. As noted earlier, the moisture-laden southwest wind sweeping in off the Pacific, combined with mountain heights up to 7,900 feet in the Olympic range, cause dramatic variations in the annual rainfall, ranging from an estimated 200 inches on the face of Mount Olympus itself to a desert-like sixteen inches in the rain-shadowed Sequim Valley.

Because of the mild climate and heavy rainfall prevailing in the rain forest, the eminent naturalist Roger Tory Peterson has suggested that the area, "Probably constitutes the greatest weight of living matter, per acre in the world."

One curious feature to be seen in the rain forest is the "nurse-log." Though at first glance it seems wasteful that a huge thousand-year-old tree should die, fall, and lie rotting unused on the dank forest floor for another thousand years or so before it totally disintegrates, nothing in nature ever goes to waste, naturalists point out. Even in death, the giant creates new life.

If a tree seedling falls on the ground in the dark, wet forest, it receives little light and nourishment with which to grow. But on a nurselog, its chances are much better. There is less competition from other plants, more moisture during the dry summer months, and a substantially warmer temperature because of the moldering log under it.

A common sight in the rain forest is a tree over one hundred feet tall and three feet in diameter growing upward out of the decayed heart of a nurselog—a tree that lived for a thousand years, died and fell five hundred years ago, and in five hundred years more will be only a raised ridge on the dark forest floor, while the now-maturing giant towering two hundred feet above it can look forward to half a century of further growth until it, too, dies, falls, and carries on the eternal cycle of life, death, and renewed life in the rain forest.

THEODORE ROOSEVELT ELK

In addition to its big trees, the Olympic Peninsula also serves as a unique game preserve. It is a curious fact of history that some of the most renowned killers of wild game during the past century became the most prominent conservationists of their time.

William F. "Buffalo Bill" Cody, Stewart Edward White, Theodore Roosevelt, and even Ernest Hemingway—all of whom during their active careers as big-game hunters killed and brought home trophy heads of just about every large animal on earth—eventually decided that the best sport of all was assuring that the kinds of animals they loved to hunt would not become extinct in their native habitat.

Unique to the Olympic Peninsula is a species of elk that is slightly darker and heavier than other animals of the breed which range further east. Around the turn of the century, a fad arose among men who called themselves *real* men which decreed that they had to wear a large elk's tooth on their watch fob, preferably suspended from a heavy gold chain across their vest. The going price for such a tooth was fifteen dollars. Since it was not practical to rope and hogtie an elk, then extract its two upper canine teeth (the ones coveted) with or without the benefit of novocaine, mature bull elk by the thousands were killed throughout the mountains of the West, with only the two valuable upper canine teeth being preserved. To men such as President Theodore Roosevelt, who had become a conservationist by then, it was obvious that drastic measures must be taken. As one of the last acts of his presidency in 1909, Theodore Roosevelt proclaimed Mount Olympus National Monument a federal reserve; this area became a refuge for what were called the Roosevelt elk.

Today, an estimated seven hundred of these animals live in the Hoh valley, nine hundred in the Queets, and one thousand in the Quinault. If Theodore Roosevelt had not acted, it is highly possible that these magnificent animals would have been hunted to the point of extinction just for their teeth.

IRON MAN OF THE HOH

Before the white man came, Indians native to the region lived with the environment as they found it without attempting to change it. Bounteously supplied with food by the sea, the rivers, and occasional natural clearings in the forest where game could be found and killed, the natives now and then cut down a tree which they used to build a canoe, a shelter, or to fashion bark clothes. The thought of creating islands of sunshine by clearing the forest and planting crops such as corn, oats, pumpkins, and squash never entered their minds. But when white settlers finally began to filter into this far northwestern corner of the country, a few of them tried to fulfill the American dream by creating a "homestead" on 160 acres of this heavily-timbered land, first cutting down enough trees to build a cabin, then continuing their clearing until they let in enough sunshine to permit crops to grow.

Typical of these first homesteaders was John Huelsdonk, a man of such extraordinary strength and endurance that he became known as the "Iron Man of the Hoh." Coming ashore at Neah Bay in 1892 with his new wife Dora, he informed her that the spot where he intended to settle could be reached only by a canoe and horseback trip of several days through rugged wilderness country. Before beginning the trip, he told her, he must inspect and repack the belongings she had carried by ship up to this point. As one of their daughters would later relate:

> Pops opened her bridal trunk, pulled out her white ruffled petticoats, and wrapped the black iron pots and skillets with them. He said it wouldn't do for those pots to bang together in the panniers and scare the horses! Not with sixty miles of wilderness before they reached the ranch.

Both John and Dora Huelsdonk were immigrants from Germany. Between their arrival at what would be their lifetime home in a remote valley of the Hoh in 1892 and their deaths six months apart in 1947, Dora would bear four daughters, going "outside" (to cities such as Aberdeen) only twice. Because John supplemented their meager income by working as a government packer, guide, and hunter, he traveled more widely than his wife did, for it was also his chore to buy and pack in whatever supplies they needed at their remote homestead. A stocky, barrel-chested, powerful man, his strength was legendary. The most often told story about him is repeated by Ruby E. Hult in her book *Untamed Olympics:*

> John had to pack everything miles up a rough mountain trail, sometimes fording streams, sometimes crossing on narrow logs. One day a neighbor met John on the trail and found him packing a cook stove up to his cabin. "Isn't that a pretty heavy load?" asked the neighbor.
>
> "No," said John, "not bad at all, but it's going to be a little hard to cross over some of those foot logs the way that hundred pound sack of flour in the oven keeps shifting around."

Because he was so strong that he could pack twice the load of an ordinary man, he customarily carried and was paid double when on

Government packing jobs. His skill as a hunter and trapper was legendary; he was said to have killed over a hundred cougars.

> Many are the tales of his hunting prowess, [Hult writes] One day, they say, he saw a bear crawling out of a hollow tree, and when he shot it the carcass fell back into the hollow. John crawled into the hollow to get it and stepped on a second live bear—and had to choke it with his bare hands.

OLYMPIC NATIONAL PARK

Because of its remoteness, the need to save a portion of the Olympic Peninsula as a park was a long time in making itself evident. In 1897, President Grover Cleveland turned 2,168,320 acres into a forest reserve. Since little was known about the region other than the fact it was heavily timbered, this action set it aside so that a survey and appraisal of its resources could be made. Completed and published in 1902, the report revealed a stupendous forest empire: sixty-one billion board feet. Just outside the reserve, thick growths of trees containing another twenty billion raised this total to over eighty billion board feet.

WINTER IN THE HIGH OLYMPICS

Ashael Curtis Photo, Courtesy Washington State Historical Society

Because so much resource-rich land was being removed from the tax rolls, Clallam County was not happy about the establishment of the forest reserve, nor were private timber companies, which were eager to harvest the prime trees. Proclamations by President McKinley in 1900 and 1901 reduced the reserve from 900,000 to 750,000 acres, which cheered the local tax assessors, then in 1907, President Roosevelt added 127,000 acres, which made them unhappy.

Then, as now, the battle between public preservation and private use raged with no sudden victory for either side. What were thought to be the final boundaries of the park were set in 1938 by President Franklin Roosevelt, but they later were amended in 1940, '43, '47, and finally in 1953, when President Harry Truman signed a proclamation adding the Ocean Strip and the Queets Corridor to the park, which brought it up to its maximum authorized size of 892,000 acres.

OLYMPIC MOUNTAIN PEAKS

Ashael Curtis Photo, Courtesy Washington State Historical Society

Established as an extension to the park in order to assure access down the wilderness river westward to the sea, then north along the equally wild coast to Cape Flattery and the Makah Indian Reservation, the Queets Corridor and the Ocean Strip at one time risked being withdrawn from the ownership and administration of the Olympic National Park; but objections to such a withdrawal were so strong and unanimous from wilderness lovers that the idea was quickly abandoned and probably will not be revived.

GRAYS HARBOR COUNTRY

Although its discoverer, Robert Gray, modestly named the Columbia River in honor of his ship instead of himself, a feature he found further north up the Washington coast in that eventful year of 1792 remains as a geographical memorial to his name. Grays Harbor, a bay covering two hundred square miles, is one of only a handful of great bays along the west coast between Mexico and Canada. Because of the rich resources of the country surrounding it, the region long has been a unique world of its own.

Twelve miles wide and seventeen miles long, Grays Harbor is rimmed by tideflats and marshlands teeming with birds. Cities such as Aberdeen, Hoquiam, and Cosmopolis, which once boasted some of the largest sawmills in the world, still process and load lumber aboard ships sailing the seven seas. Smaller places such as Westport, Bay City, and Ocasta are renowned as clam, oyster, and salmon producing centers, while Ocean Shores is known as a resort and retirement community with accommodations to suit every pocketbook and taste.

Appropriately for a sawmill town, the name Hoquiam comes from an Indian word meaning "hungry for wood," while its somewhat larger neighbor, whose Scottish immigrant founder, George W. Hume, established a fish cannery there, named it after the city of his birth, Aberdeen, Scotland.

From the beginning of settlement in the early 1870s, lumbering was the key to the growth and development of the Grays Harbor region, says the WPA Guide: * by which huge sections of trees were snaked through the woods by steel cables and hand-set chokers.

The greatest stand of Douglas fir ever found in the Pacific Northwest was located here. Famous timber tracts, such as the

Ashael Curtis Photo, Courtesy Washington State Historical Society
RIDING IN THE HIGH OLYMPICS, *CA* 1920

"21–9" (meaning Township 21 N., Range 9 W.), lay adjacent to
the harbor; this one prodigious tract, 6 miles square, was logged
for over 30 years. The towering trees of the region grew so com-
pactly that they were invariably felled in one direction only, and
at times the fallen trees were so crowded together that it was difficult to saw them into log lengths.

By 1900, the great forests of New England, as well as those in
Wisconsin and Minnesota, were largely depleted; the timber-hun-
gry industry was forced to move west. Large numbers of loggers
and mill hands from the east and midwest migrated to the Grays
Harbor sector, as did Scandinavians and Finns from Europe. They
were a hardy breed, as sturdy, strong, and well-muscled as the
huge oxen whose brute strength now was being replaced by
steam-powered "donkey" engines. This brought on the era of
"high-lead" logging by which huge sections of trees were snaked
through the woods by steel cables and hand-set chokers.

> With vast profits to be made [says the *Guide*], work was speed-
> ed ahead with little heed to accident prevention, timber break-
> age, or destruction of young growth. Men who worked in the
> woods needed rare courage and toughness. Straining back
> against his safety belt, the "high rigger" walked casually up the
> side of a tall tree with an axe in his hand, stopped somewhere

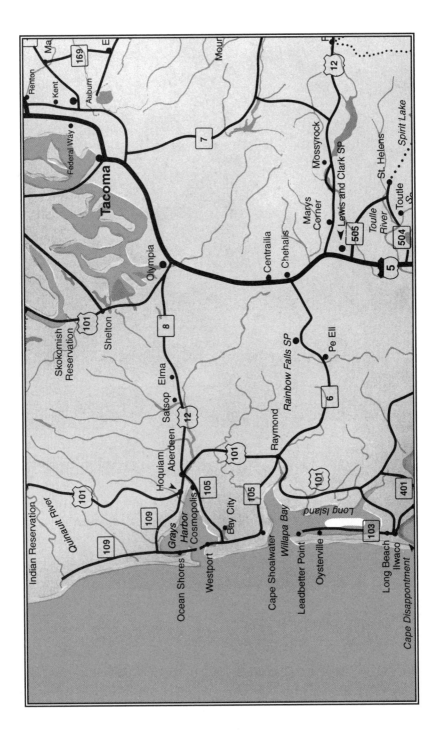

between 100 and 200 feet above the ground, braced himself at a sickening angle against the swaying trunk, and, with a flow of cheerful profanity, severed with deft strokes of his razor-edged axe the green plume that rose above him; the shock of the falling crest sent the trunk and the logger on it gyrating dizzily through the air.

Men saw their companions mutilated or killed from time to time by snapping steel cables, falling timber, rolling logs, or whirling saws; and this unremitting danger was reflected in their speech and tales and in their Saturday night blow-offs in Hoquiam and Aberdeen.

DAVID DOUGLAS, BOTANIST

Soon after he arrived in the lower Columbia River area and first saw the magnificent tree that would bear his name, the twenty-five-year-old Scottish botanist, David Douglas, toured Grays Harbor. But he was hurting so bad from a recent injury that he could think of little else but his pain. While bundling botanical specimens to be shipped to England, he had fallen upon a rusty nail, which caused a large abscess on one knee. After being laid up for three weeks at the Hudson's Bay Company post of Fort Vancouver, he heard that the ship carrying his specimens, the *William and Ann*, had been delayed inside the Columbia River bar because of bad weather, so he insisted on coming downriver to Fort George in order to make a final check on the shipment—despite the inflamed condition of his knee.

Arriving there, he found that the ship had sailed an hour earlier, so, never a man to waste a chance to explore new country, he persuaded Chief Comcomly, the renowned Chinook leader, to take him across the Columbia so that he could go up the coast. As usually happened in November, the weather was wet, cold, and windy; even the big war canoe manned by twelve of the tribe's best paddlers nearly swamped as breaking waves boarded it time and again during the crossing.

State 105, US 12—Westport to Centralia
73 miles

From Cape Disappointment, the party portaged four miles to Willapa Bay, then moved up the coast to Grays Harbor, while the pain in the injured knee grew worse and worse.

"I hardly can give an idea of my afflicted state," Douglas wrote. After a miserable day followed by a worse night, the party improvised a shelter of pine branches and bark mats. "The following day found me so broken down with fatigue and starvation," Douglas continued, "and my knee so much worse, that I could not stir out."

Despite his suffering, the young botanist—who was a crack shot because he had sharpened his eye by shooting down acorns and pine cones he wanted as specimens—bestirred himself long enough to crawl out of the shelter and provide food for the party.

"Providentially I killed five ducks with one shot, which as might be expected, were soon cooked...I made a basin of tea, on which, with a little duck, I made a good supper. Very little sufficed me."

When the chief of a band of Chehalis Indians kindly transported the party to the shelter of his village, Douglas said that he "was in no mood to find fault with the dirt, filth and stench..." in which his hosts lived; indeed, he went out of his way to praise their hospitality. But by then he was suffering so much that he did not examine the botanical wonders of the area as thoroughly as he would have liked to do, returning to Fort Vancouver on November 15, 1825 with a swollen, throbbing knee and little to show for his trip.

Because of his tragic death in the Sandwich Islands (Hawaii) a few years later, he never knew that the magnificent Douglas fir, which then covered sixty thousand square miles of mountainous country in the West as the finest stand of prime timber on earth, would be named for him.

CHARLES WILKES EXPEDITION

At a time when both British and American explorers had equal access to the country under the Joint Occupancy Treaty, it was not surprising that an American expedition under USN Commander Charles Wilkes should be the next white men to be astonished by the big trees growing around the shores of Grays Harbor. Nourished by an annual rainfall of one hundred inches, the trees seen and measured by these non–expert observers truly boggled their minds. One of them reported to Wilkes:

One [tree], that was not selected as the largest, for there were many of equal if not greater length and diameter, was measured, and that part that lay in one piece was found to be 200 feet long; another piece of the same tree was 25 feet long, and at the small end of the latter it was still 10 inches in diameter. Allowing 12 feet for the portion destroyed by fire, Mr. Eld thought 25 feet ought to be added for its top, which makes the whole length of the tree, when growing, 260 feet. Others were believed to exceed this, both in height and diameter.

While in the Grays Harbor area, the Wilkes party enlisted the services of an unusual kind of guide, an Indian woman whom they identified only as the "Squaw Chief." After promising to supply the American explorers with horses and men on a certain day:

> She brought five horses and a number of Indians who minded her "with great obedience." ...and they were soon in a condition to move. This despatch was principally owing to the directions and management of this squaw chief, who seemed to exercise more authority than any that had been met with; indeed, her whole character and conduct placed her much above those around her...Although her husband was present, he seemed under such good discipline as to warrant the belief that the wife was the ruling power, or, to express it in more homely language, "wore the breeches."

As has been noted earlier, the Chinook Indians, the most powerful tribe on the lower Columbia, did a thriving business capturing and trading slaves for shells to the Nootkas further north on Vancouver Island. According to regional historian Edwin Van Syckle, the Indian word Owahwakan meant "the river of slaves," thus might be the root of the name Oregon.

EARLY DAY FISH RUNS

Fish formed a major portion of the Indian diet, with bottom-dwelling species available in the shallow waters of Grays Harbor the year round, while five different varieties of salmon matured in the deep waters of the Pacific Ocean then returned seasonally to spawn in the five rivers emptying into the broad, inland sea.

Beginning in December and continuing their run well into April, the blueback or sockeye salmon were rich-meated and tasty, outnumbering all other species combined. King or tyee salmon came in August; the silver or coho and the dog salmon appeared from September through the middle of December.

Ashael Curtis Photo, Courtesy Washington State Historical Society
HEADWATERS OF THE QUINAULT RIVER

Steelhead ran from November to May, while a few humpbacks showed up between August and September.

Monstrous bottom-feeding sturgeon weighing two hundred to three hundred pounds and measuring twelve to fifteen feet long could be caught any time, providing the fisherman knew how to hook and drag them in—a skill which the local Indians had mastered long ago, though white newcomers would learn it more slowly.

"Indian fishermen carried special sturgeon clubs," writes Edwin Van Syckle in his intriguing book *The River Pioneers*. "And it was a fisherman and a canoeman of some skill who could haul a 200–pound sturgeon into a canoe without shipping water. Some sturgeon, even longer, were towed into the village."

Indeed, skill in handling an Indian canoe or a white man's boat of any kind was essential in this region, for the wheels that had brought the new settlers across two thousand miles of plains were of little use in this land of extensive beaches, shallow bays, flooded lowlands, and many rivers. Travel was governed by the ebb and flow of the tides. Knowing that crossing a bay and arriving at a landing on its far side while the tide was out meant walking a quarter of a mile in ankle deep mud before reaching solid ground, the traveler soon learned to time his journey so that the tide would aid rather than hinder him.

Gathering food such as oysters, clams, and crabs also was regulated by the tides. Because the local Indians had never tried to raise vegetables, fruits, or grains, food crops flourished in the rich, virgin soil, which from time immemorial had been replenished by spring floods. Bugs, worms, and other garden pests were unknown. Forty-pound rutabagas, sixty-pound cabbages, and turnips of incredible size were grown so prolifically that they were chopped up and used for cattle feed. Cranberries, which grew wild and were used by the Indians both for food and coloring purposes, showed white settlers from New England that the red berry would do well here, so they soon imported and planted cranberry bogs with cuttings brought out from Massachusetts and Rhode Island, laying the foundation for what would develop into one of biggest industries of its kind on the West Coast.

Surprisingly, considering the amount of standing water in the area, few mosquitos bothered the settlers, nor were flies a nuisance. Fleas were another matter, however, for in every Indian camp and white settlement they flourished abundantly.

Market-hunting of wild fowl by men who made no pretense of doing it for sport was an important source of income. Supplying ducks and geese for the butchers was the profession of men such as Ora Knapp, "Hickey" Belts, and John Grigsby, Van Syckle writes:

> The three men market-hunted geese and ducks as late as the winter of 1904, mostly for Jake Karshner's store in Aberdeen. The hunters received thirty-five cents each for a goose, fifty cents a dozen for teal, and seventy-five cents a dozen for most other ducks—sprig, widgeon, mallard, and canvasback.
>
> ...Grigsby on one hunt shot sixteen geese with both barrels of his ten-gauge. Belts was credited with twenty-seven sprig with a two-barrel pot-shot...

EXTERMINATION OF SEA OTTER

Although the slaughter of buffalo on the high plains of the West is well known to most students of history, the commercial killing to the point of extinction of the most beautiful fur-bearing animal along the Pacific Coast was just as tragic, though not as familiar.

Found from the Bering Sea in the frigid north to the warm waters of Baja, California off the coast of Mexico, the playful, harmless sea otter possessed a pelt prized above all others by rich Chinese mandarins, affluent Russian noblemen, and the ladies of Europe and England. From 1750 on, fortunes were made by venturesome white men sailing along the Northwest Coast, where they traded trinkets, beads, and weapons to the Indians for sea otter furs, which then would be taken to the Orient or to Europe and resold for a profit ranging from one thousand to ten thousand percent.

In the Grays Harbor area, the greatest concentration of sea otter in what would become the state of Washington dwelt just offshore in a twenty-mile-long kelp bed stretching from the harbor entrance northward to the vicinity of present–day Moclips. Large as this population was, it was completely obliterated during the years between 1860 and 1903. A haven for the sea life on which the sea otters fed, the kelp beds brought the fur-bearing animals close enough inshore that coastal Indians such as the Quinaults could shoot them with bows and arrows or spear them from the rocks. Out of a herd of several hundred otters feeding, romping, and basking off a point of land such as Point Grenville, whose rocks sheltered the animals from the surf, the Indians might bag one or two otters. But when the rifle of the white man was introduced—along with his greed and much more effective way of killing—the sea otter was doomed.

> The favorite gun was the Sharps 50 caliber [writes Van Syckle], although later there were other makes of 45–70s and 45–90s, with tremendous carrying possibilities....Each hunter as he loaded, marked the bottom of the bullet with a special insignia or brand; a cross, three slits, a circle, and so on. These marks were known up and down the beach, and whenever an otter washed up ashore bearing such a bullet, ownership was immediately established. Of course, when the bullet passed through an animal or when some finder on the beach removed the bullet surreptitiously, there was no identification, and questions and quarrels arose over ownership.

Because of the great value of sea otter pelts, "rustling" by both Indians and whites was a common occurrence along the Washington coast, bringing with it the same kind of violent retribution later common in horse and cattle country. In the early 1800s, a prime sea otter fur brought $400 in the Canton market, Van Syckle writes. He continues, "So lucrative was the trade, that in the eighty years from 1743 to 1823 some 200,839 skins found their way to market, and so devastating was the killing that only 127 skins were marketed in 1900. The last legal skin sold on the London market went for $2,000."

Like the professional buffalo hunter, the white killer worked from a solid stand set up on a high point of rocks overlooking the sea or from a platform twenty to sixty feet high from which he could spot the otter basking, feeding, or playing with its young. Looking something like a wooden derrick, the platform had three legs and was set as far out in the surf as seemed safe; now and then it collapsed because of an unusually high tide or heavy sea. It never survived the winds and waves of winter, so had to be rebuilt next spring.

Each shooter had a partner, who spotted the animal he killed or wounded, wading through the surf to claim it before an Indian or white rustler did. The shooters were expert marksmen, often making kills at a range of four hundred to six hundred yards. "A 700–yard shot was not exceptional," Van Syckle writes, "and some kills were made as far as 1,000 yards, or more than half a mile."

As any Walt Disney fan knows, the sea otter was and is a lovable creature, though commercial abalone fishermen might disagree with that statement because of the sea otter's taste for that delicious variety of shellfish. Often seen floating on its back with a youngster cradled on its breast, the sea otter does something rare in the animal world: it uses a tool in the form of a rock to crack open the shell of a clam or an abalone. On sunny days, it sometimes sleeps on its back while floating on top of the waves, which made it an easy target for the hunter. Though it reached a length of six feet and weighed up to eighty pounds, it was not an easy target to hit. But like the professional buffalo hunter, the sea otter killer was an expert marksmen.

When commercial hunting began, otters were plentiful, Van Syckle writes. A hunter named Roundtree reported that during the winter of 1863–64, he saw between one hundred to a thousand animals a day along the beach. But as time passed and the number of hunters increased, the number of sea otter seen and killed dwindled. Van Syckle writes:

> According to Ben Grigsby, "Shorty" Astell killed the last two sea otter known to have been slain near what is now Ocean City. Astell received $1,400 for one skin, $600 for the other.

Though the sea otter long has been a protected species, all efforts to reestablish it along the Pacific coast between British Columbia and Mexico have been dismal failures. It still flourishes in Alaska. But even there, like other sea life, it does not survive major oil-spills.

SPLASH DAMS

The weightiest problem faced by a man who cut down a big tree in the early days was how to get it to the sawmill where it could be sawed into usable dimension lumber. Ideally in pioneer days, the logger selected a tree growing on the downhill side of a slope inclining toward the sea, felled it in that direction, then floated it to the mill. If it needed a nudge, various kinds of jacks or levers were used to start it moving. If it were felled deep in the woods and must be dragged to the sawmill by brute force, oxen, steam-powered donkey engine drag-lines, logging trains, trucks, and eventually giant helicopters were used to transport the logs to the mill.

If a river happened to be handy to the area being cut, its current was an easy way to move logs, for wood floated, water ran downhill, and the law of gravity did all the work and rendered no bill for the energy it expended. Trouble was, short rivers tumbling down steep slopes through narrow canyons—as the five rivers emptying into Grays Harbor all did—had notoriously uneven flows. And as every logger knows, nothing on earth is harder to move than a big log jammed crosswise in the shallows of a river whose ten–foot crest has dwindled to a six–inch trickle.

Thus, the splash dam.

Like many colorful features of bygone days, when getting the job done was all that counted, with no consideration being given to the effects on the natural environment, designing and building splash dams that worked was considered to be a great talent, with the person who possessed it hailed as a true genius.

The basic principle of a splash dam was simple. Decide how big a head of water was needed to flush a deck of logs downstream to where you wanted the logs to go; build one or more dams behind which to store the water until the precise moment it was needed; install a gate that could be opened instantly; then, presto!—trip the "flush" lever and create an instant river whose raging torrent would carry the logs to the distant tidewater sawmill.

Because of the climate, the available timber, and the shape of the terrain, no region in the country was better-suited to the use of splash dams than the Grays Harbor area. In a land whose annual rainfall ranged well over one hundred inches, with five rivers—the Humptulips, the Wishkah, the Hoquiam, the Wynooche, and the Chehalis—falling steeply down through heavily timbered country toward sawmills located on salt water, only the ingenuity of men capable of designing and building such dams was needed to make the principle work. In his authoritative history *They Tried to Cut It All*, Van Syckle writes:

> Among these were Jack Byard, Nels Ess and Bob Turner. Byard was perhaps the better builder. He constructed some 30 dams in the Grays Harbor country without having a single one "blow out," that is, to have the dam wash out at the bottom or sides because of faulty construction.

To the logger eager to transport the timber he had cut to the sawmill, which then would pay him for it, a surging river was considered to be a common carrier, used as the quickest and easiest way to transport his goods from here to there. To the rancher or farmer living downstream, who saw a barn, henhouse, hayfield, or carefully tended vegetable garden suddenly washed away as a ten-foot-deep flood of water came pouring through his homestead without warning, the artificially created rivers were something else again.

"Lawsuits sprouted all along the river," Van Syckle writes, "but in many cases did not replace the rancher's washed away orchard."

The trick to building a successful splash dam was that its gate, which released the sudden flow of water, must be so constructed that the flushing action could be triggered instantaneously with a minimum of physical effort. Van Syckle cites a typical case in which the flush worked perfectly:

> It was upon one of these occasions that Joe Malinowski won fame and the adoration of the loggers. It was a dry summer, the river was full of logs, an injunction bound the river tighter than a hay-fed cow, and not a single logger could get money at the bank until he delivered his logs. Joe Malinowski surveyed the situation. He hadn't been paid either, but he did have quite a head of water in his dam. So, fiddling around on the dam one day, he "accidentally" tripped a main gate. What ensued was a

Ashael Curtis Photo, Courtesy Washington State HIstorical Society
ATOP A CRAG IN THE HIGH OLYMPICS

hat-tossing celebration, and some of the strongest language ever heard on the Wishkah.

We assume that the hat-tossing was by the loggers, the strong language by the ranchers.

To some of the big timber companies, paying damages to downstream ranchers and farmers for losses caused by the flushing of splash dams became a normal expense of doing business. In one case where a rancher routinely sued and won a damage award each year, he neglected to sue following one water release because of illness, oversight, or perhaps even because no damage had been done his property—but the timber company routinely sent him a check anyway, which he routinely accepted.

END OF AN ERA
Over the Olympic Peninsula as a whole and the Grays Harbor area in particular, the number of trees cut down and the amount of lumber produced by the sawmills between 1900 and the late 1920s, when both cutting and milling slowed down, was incredible. Exactly when the turn-of-the-century attitude that the supply of trees would last forever changed and the question how-much-more-is-left? began to be considered, is impossible to say. It is a matter of record that for six straight years, between 1924 and 1929, the average annual lumber cut in the Grays Harbor area was 1.3 billion board feet.

In this present–day controversy over the export of raw logs to the Orient, it is interesting to note that the practice is not new. In the late 1920s, Van Syckle points out:

> This was the era of the "Jap square," because it was cut exclusively for Japan. In many cases it was an entire log with but four slabs knocked off to square it. In other cases it was the heart of a log after the clear stock had been removed. It was a compact way of shipping lumber, well recognized by the Japanese, who took it across the Pacific in their own coal-burning ships and sawed it in their own mills with only half the waste in sawdust created by Grays Harbor mills. Besides, the Japanese had ready use for the sawdust. It was a lucrative trade, but it rapidly pushed back the timberline, and far outstripped nature's ability to keep pace with new growth.

Though the concept of sustained yield, tree farms, and scientific studies aimed at making better use of forest products and growing trees faster finally did begin in the 1930s, change was slow in coming to the industry, for the idea that the natural resources of this vast country had finite limits and must be conserved did not suit the "cut-and-move-on" philosophy that had existed in the United States from the time the Pilgrims landed until three hundred years later.

But at last it became clear that limits did exist. Beyond tidewater on the Washington coast, there could be no moving on. The time had come to conserve what was left—not by preserving it all, perhaps—but by using it wisely.

THE LIGHT THAT FAILED
Just off US 12 near the small towns of Satsop and Elma on the way to Centralia, what appear to be a pair of massive concrete stumps

Ashael Curtis Photo, Courtesy Washington State Historical Society
NEAR MOUNT OLYMPUS

stand as a reminder of a dramatic historic event that many people in the state of Washington and the nation as a whole would like to forget. These two round pillars are cold gray monuments of nuclear power plants that were started but never finished, creating a financial debacle recorded as the greatest default on a public bond issue in the history of the country.

Since the two uncompleted nuclear plants in the Satsop area were part of a larger project in which five plants were to be built under the supervision of a public agency called the Washington Public Power Supply System—named WPPSS for short (later, derisively, "Whoops!")—we will cover it in more detail in a later section of the book.

Suffice it to say here that back in the 1950s when the Pacific Northwest was experiencing an era of rapid industrial growth and enjoyed the cheapest electric rates in the United States, it was

Courtesy Washington State Library
SCHAFER BRIDGE, NEAR MONTESANO
View Windows can be closed by sliding doors.

thought that nuclear power could be generated at so little cost that it need not even be metered. With the use of electricity rising at an annual rate of ten percent, generating facilities in the Northwest would have to double within ten years. Because the area was running out of sites for hydro–electric dams, the region soon must turn to thermal power. The best source of this was nuclear. If building one plant was good, why not make it even better by building five? This was the logic of the planners.

Of the five plants started, two were in the Satsop area in western Washington; three were in the Richland area in eastern Washington. Of the five begun, only one was finished and is generating power today. To date, the skeletons of the four unfinished plants stand stark and lonely—monuments to a $24 billion miscalculation, say detractors, while a small, but perhaps growing number of believers say that the time yet may come when the validity of the concept should be considered again.

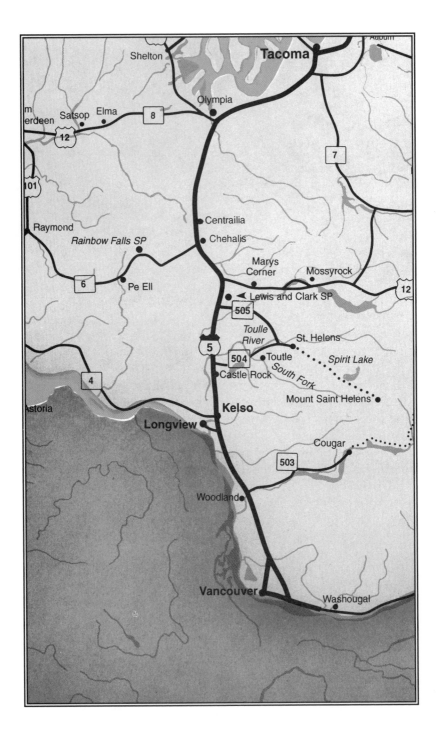

PART THREE

Southwest Washington

GEORGE WASHINGTON BUSH

One of the least-known aspects of Pacific Northwest history is the role played by people of color—then called Negroes if referred to politely—in its early development. Long before the Emancipation Proclamation was declared by President Lincoln during the Civil War, an occasional slave was freed by his master as a matter of conscience or as a dying act to express the gratitude of the white owner for the long years of service and loyalty given by the slave and his family.

Though the record is hazy, this seems to have been what happened in the case of George Washington Bush, who became one of the first Americans to settle in the area just south of Olympia, Washington Territory. In an article published in *Negro Digest* in 1963, the highly respected historian Ruby E. Hult writes:

> Details about Bush's early years are sketchy and contradictory but best information indicates that he was born in Pennsylvania in 1770. His parents were servants to a shipping magnate name Stevenson, with whose household they moved to Tennessee. When the Bushes remained faithful retainers to the end, caring for their master and his wife during their declining years, they were left the Stevenson fortune.

I–5—Centralia to Vancouver
82 miles

Granted their freedom, the parents named their son, who was half-white and an only child, after the father of the country, raised him in the Quaker faith, and gave him a good education. Enlisting in the army during the War of 1812, he fought under General Andrew Jackson during the Battle of New Orleans and acquitted himself well.

Comparing the presumed birth date 1770 with the statement made later in the same article that he remained a bachelor until he was past forty and married in 1831, I suspect that he actually was born at least twenty years later, probably in the 1790s during President Washington's second term. At any rate, he served as an American soldier during the War of 1812, then afterward took the course of adventure that many other young men pursued at that time by going to work as a trapper for first an American and then a British fur company.

Whatever other prejudices the leaders of these companies may have had, race was not one of them; they would employ anyone who could bring in the furs. Whether American or British, men like John Jacob Astor of the Pacific Fur Company and Sir George Simpson of the Hudson's Bay Company were glad to hire any able-bodied person who would risk his life for very little money to harvest the furs craved by well-to-do people in America, Europe, and Asia. Working as a "free trapper" for several years during the 1820s, George Bush became well acquainted with the mountains, streams, and meadows of the Northwest, traveling over most of the country from northern California to British Columbia, learning to know the region as only a Canadian *voyageur* or an American mountain man could know it.

STRIFE ON THE BORDER

At some time during the early 1830s, he decided to settle down in Boone County, Missouri, investing some of the money he had inherited in a farm, where he became a stock-raiser and a nurseryman. A bachelor until past forty, in 1831 he married a twenty-year-old German–American girl named Isabella James. To this union, five sons were born in rapid succession.

Though George Bush prospered in Missouri and got along well with most of his white neighbors, the conflict between pro– and anti–slavery forces, which eventually would tear the nation apart, was growing. At the same time, American missionaries were heading toward the Oregon Country to minister to the Indians: Jason Lee to the Willamette Valley in 1834; Marcus Whitman to the Walla Walla Valley in 1836.

Made uneasy by war clouds, the eyes of citizens of a restless nation were turning toward the Oregon Country. When what came to be called the Great Migration brought one hundred and twenty wagons, one thousand people, and five thousand oxen and horses to Westport in the late spring of 1843, George Bush and a few of his friends took notice and made plans.

> Bush felt that his sons would have a better opportunity in free Oregon than in the slave state of Missouri [Ruby E. Hult writes]...He took with him seeds, nursery trees, implements and herds of stock; the story is also told how he carried one hundred pounds of silver nailed under a false bottom in his wagon. But unlike many wealthy men, he was kind and generous, and he furnished teams and money out of his own pocket for some of his neighbors who started west with him.

Included in the party was a particularly close friend named Michael T. Simmons. Described as "a tall, resolute Kentuckian," Simmons was as impulsive as George Bush was cautious; as quick-tempered as Bush was placid; as aggressive in fighting for his friend's rights as the Quaker–raised Bush was willing to turn the other cheek when abused.

When the train of eighty wagons headed west in the spring of 1844, Michael Simmons was elected colonel and made second in command, charged with selecting the route each day and keeping the vehicles moving, while the elected "general" galloped hither and yon across the plains chasing buffalo. Because George Bush had traveled over the country a number of times as a mountain man, Simmons often sought the colored man's wise advice. During the long trip west, which was particularly difficult that year because of heavy rains and swollen rivers, the wagons were delayed and thrown behind schedule, which caused a number of people to run short of provisions. In the emergency, George Bush helped at least twenty destitute families out of his own stores and pockets.

Meanwhile, in the Willamette Valley where the people were setting up their own government, an attempt was made to avoid controversy by forbidding both slavery and the residence of free Negroes on Oregon soil. The Organic Law adopted by the

Click Relander Collection, Courtesy Yakima Valley Regional Library
SWEEPING THE RAPIDS WITH A DIP NET AT CELILO FALLS
The scene dates before The Dalles Dam was built in 1955.

Provisional Government in 1843 included an anti–slavery ordinance. But in 1844, a substantial number of Missourians, who were pro–slavery, pushed through a harsh amendment which not only banned slavery but proclaimed that any freed Negro who remained in Oregon more than two years would be subject to a lashing of "...not less than 20 nor more than 39 stripes..."

Learning of the new law when the wagon train reached The Dalles, George Bush decided that this was not the kind of future he was seeking for himself and his sons. Though some families in the wagon train did head south and seek claims in the Willamette Valley, Michael Simmons, who was outraged when he heard of the law, and a few other men who were indebted to George Bush for his generosity, declared that if he were not accepted in Oregon, they would not settle there either. Camping some twenty miles east of Fort Vancouver near the present site of Washougal, Washington, in an area still under the jurisdiction of the Hudson's Bay Company, the party remained there for nearly a year, the men cutting cedar shakes which Simmons and Bush traded for provisions at Fort Vancouver.

Courtesy Fort Vancouver National Historic Site, National Park Service
DR. JOHN MCLOUGHLIN, ABOUT 1851

Though the Joint Occupancy Treaty was still in effect between Great Britain and the United States, the growing tide of American emigration during the past few years had made it obvious to Dr. John McLoughlin at Fort Vancouver that when the day of reckoning did come the United States and its newly elected expansionist president, William Knox Polk, were going to demand a piece of country extending as far north as Alaska. Though England would claim that the boundary should be set at northern California, it would be happy to compromise on the Columbia River as the line between the two nations. To achieve this end, Dr. McLoughlin long had been kind and helpful to Americans wishing to settle in the Willamette Valley. To those who were curious about what kind of country lay north of the Columbia, he responded that most of it was too wet, swampy, and covered with trees to be worth anything as farming country.

To Michael Simmons, who hailed from the hills of Kentucky and was naturally suspicious of any advice given him by a Britisher, there was something fishy about the way Dr. McLoughlin denigrated (though Simmons certainly would not have used that word) the country north of the river. As the testy historian, Hubert Howe Bancroft, wrote a few years later:

> To the average American emigrant of that day the simple fact that a Britisher should wish him not to settle in any certain part of the undivided territory was of itself sufficient incentive for him to select that spot, provided it was not much worse than any other.

Therefore, wet, swampy and covered with trees though the country lying north of the Columbia River might be, Michael Simmons decided to wander up that way and eyeball it. Going as far north as Puget Sound during the late spring of 1845, he liked what he saw, returned to the Fort Vancouver area, and reported to his friends. If Dr. McLoughlin and the Hudson's Bay Company would give them the same kind of support the Company and the Doctor were giving Americans wishing to settle south of the Columbia, they would head north.

Whether Dr. McLoughlin was sympathetic toward George Bush because he was being discriminated against by the unjust law banning Negroes from Oregon, historians cannot say. Certainly McLoughlin himself, who had married and still lived with an Indian woman, had suffered from prejudice, for Sir George Simpson had sneered at him for marrying a native woman. Of course it was possible that Sir George—who was born out of wedlock himself—was sniping at the big-hearted doctor in a childish way. Whatever the case, Dr. John McLoughlin did support the Simmons–Bush party in their move north into what until then had been pristine Hudson's Bay Company territory. He even gave them a letter to Dr. William F. Tolmie, superintendent of the

Puget Sound Agricultural Company at Fort Nisqually, asking Tolmie to cooperate by providing them with supplies.

SETTLEMENT AT BUSH PRAIRIE

That the country north of the Columbia was wet, swampy, and full of trees was amply proved by the fact that Bush, Simmons, and their friends spent fifteen days cutting a road through the thick timber for their wagons. But they persisted, reaching the southern end of Puget Sound in early spring, 1846. There, Simmons claimed a piece of land at what became Tumwater Falls; Bush settled on what became Bush Prairie; and the other members of the party laid claim to adjacent pieces of land covering some six square miles. Shortly thereafter, word reached them that the British–American boundary had been set not at the Columbia River but at the 49th parallel, well to the north.

Ironically, this meant that the laws of the Oregon Provisional Government, which for the time being were recognized as the law of the region, now covered the area in which they had settled. Though it was assumed that Americans who had claimed land eventually would have their titles confirmed when Oregon Territory came into the United States, this left George Bush, a Negro, still a non–person.

In 1853, when the region north of the Columbia River was split off from Oregon Territory and organized as Washington Territory, it was stipulated that any claims made under Oregon's Provisional Government in 1843 or the Donation Claims Act of 1850 would be recognized by Washington Territory through 1854, following which laws made by the legislators of the new Territory would apply. Which still would do nothing for George Bush. But what he lacked in legal status, he made up for in friends.

"Mike Simmons, who was appointed a justice of peace under the Provisional Government, traveled to Oregon City," Ruby E. Hult writes, "where he pleaded Bush's case so earnestly that he succeeded in having a special act passed removing Bush's race disability."

Though he now could live legally in the Territory, the black pioneer still endured many other forms of discrimination. Ezra Meeker, who was a strong supporter, wrote, "He was a true American and yet without a country; he owed allegiance to the flag and yet the flag would not own him; he was firmly held to obey the law and yet the law would not protect him; he could not hold landed property; and his oath would not be taken in a court of law."

By 1854, George Bush and his family had been living on their 640–acre farm just south of Olympia for eight years and had helped many people with gifts of seeds, nursery stock, and food during times of famine. Shortly after the Washington Territorial Legislature met in 1854, friends of Simmons and Bush passed a memorial asking the US Congress to grant Bush title to his section of land. In the memorial his friends stated:

> ...his habits of life during said time have been exemplary and industrious; and that by an accommodating and laborious culti-vation of said claim by an accommodating and charitable dis-posal of his produce to immigrants, he had contributed much toward the settlement of this Territory, the suffering and needy never having applied to him in vain for succor and assistance; and that at the present time the said George Bush has a large portion of said claim under a high state of cultivation and has on it a good frame house and convenient outhouses, in all amount-ing to several hundred dollars; and in view of the premises aforesaid your memorialists are of the opinion that the case is of such meritorious nature that Congress ought to pass a special law donating to him his said claim.

Congress complied with the request, granting George Washington Bush title to his homestead on January 30, 1855. After settling in the area, a sixth son had been born to his wife. Following his death in 1863 and that of his wife in 1867, the sons and their children carried on in the tradition of their parents for over one hundred years—down to the present day. As historian George H. Himes wrote, they were and are "...among the most industrious and enterprising citizens of Thurston County."

BIRTH OF A LEGEND

In the 1870s, legends of Paul Bunyan and his blue ox Babe began to migrate from Minnesota to the big timber country of western Washington. Though told and retold by writers such as Stewart Holbrook and James Stevens, neither man foresaw that an even larger legend would be born in the rain-streaked sky between Centralia and Vancouver the night of November 24, 1971.

Unlike the tall tales of the preceding century, which built slowly as they passed from person to person, logger to logger, and camp to camp, this one was an "instant" legend, full-grown only hours after it entered the world. Created in an age of electronic communication, its birth required only that a man jump off the lowered steps of the rear exit of a commercial airliner flying 10,000 feet above the ground, then plummet through the dark night sky toward an unknown fate below.

His name was Dan Cooper. He was carrying $200,000 in twenty-dollar bills. He was wearing a borrowed military parachute that he apparently knew how to use. Beyond these facts, nothing was known about the man then. Nothing is known about him now. But the legend he created still endures.

Even though the next day was Thanksgiving, business was slow at the Portland International Airport that Wednesday afternoon in 1971 when an ordinary-looking man stepped up to the Northwest Airlines counter and said, "A one-way ticket to Seattle, please."

"Name?" asked the agent as he filled out the ticket.

"Dan Cooper."

The fare was twenty dollars, which the man paid with a twenty-dollar bill. His only luggage was a dark-colored briefcase, which he kept in his lap while waiting and carried aboard the plane. In those days, there were no X–ray machines or carry-on luggage examinations except on overseas flights or those domestic trips that came within range of Cuba.

"Flight 305 is running half an hour late," the agent said. "It'll be leaving at 3 p.m. from Gate 52."

The plane was a Boeing 727–100, with a seating capacity of 89. That day, only 36 passengers boarded the flight, walking a few hundred feet through the rain to climb the rear staircase that had been lowered from the back of the plane. Most of the passengers took seats toward the front, while the man who called himself Dan Cooper, who was last to board, took seat 18E, the middle seat in the last row on the right hand side. On the other side of the aisle, a University of Oregon student, Bill Mitchell, who was going home for the holidays, occupied the window seat.

Drinks were served while the plane was still at the gate; Cooper ordered two bourbon and water highballs from Stewardess Florence Schaffner, paying for them with a twenty-dollar bill and receiving eighteen dollars change. As the plane taxied for takeoff, Florence sat down in the jump-seat near the rear door to begin some of her paperwork. Cooper rose and offered her a white envelope, saying, "Excuse me, Miss—this is for you."

At first annoyed, Florence finally took the note out of the envelope and read it. "I have a bomb in my briefcase," it said. "I will use it if necessary. I want you to sit beside me. You are being hijacked." Soon convinced that he was not kidding, she took the seat beside him as the plane began its takeoff run. The time was 2:58 p.m. While the plane was still climbing, Cooper reached under his seat, got the briefcase, and opened it in his lap. Inside, Florence saw, were several red cylinders that looked like road flares, with a wire leading to a battery. Picking up the free end of the wire, Cooper said, "Now watch this closely. All I've got to do is touch the end of this wire to this terminal. Do you understand?"

She nodded mutely.

"Just do as I say and nobody will get hurt. You write down what I say and take it to the captain."

Using the back of the envelope that had contained the note, Florence wrote down his demands: "Two hundred thousand dollars worth of used bills in a knapsack. Two back parachutes. Two chest parachutes. After refuel passengers go free. No police. Takeoff from Seattle by 5 p.m."

Going forward to the cockpit, Florence told the three officers what was happening and gave Captain William A. Scott the note. Asked to describe the man, she said he appeared to be in his mid–forties, with brown eyes, short black hair, and an olive complexion. Despite the dimness of the day, he was wearing dark glasses.

Telling Florence and Stewardess Tina Mucklow, who by now was in the rear of the plane and aware of what was going on, to keep the hijacker calm, the captain called the chief pilot's office at the Seattle airport to inform him of the situation. He was told that getting the money and the four parachutes would be a problem on such short notice, but the office would see what could be done.

After calling the FBI, which at that time had a secret fund of marked money from which hijackers could be supplied, the $200,000 in twenty-dollar bills was promised for quick delivery to the airport. Arranging for the four parachutes proved more difficult, their only source appearing to be McChord Air Force Base south of Tacoma, where the red tape of going through military channels might cause serious delay. When this information was given to the hijacker, he became so upset that he gave one of the few clues to his background that he would reveal during the whole episode. "What do you mean `delay'?" he snarled at Tina. "Hell, McChord is only twenty minutes from the airport." Whoever he was, he knew the territory.

Trying to find a closer and less complicated source for the parachutes, the Seattle airport officer remembered a local man named Earl Cossey, who was a parachute rigger, and called him. Yes, Cossey said, he could supply the needed back chutes, which were available at Boeing Field, and knew where they could get a couple of chest chutes, but it would take a couple of hours to pick up and deliver them.

Told that all the requested items were on their way to the airport, Cooper insisted that the plane go into a holding pattern until they were delivered. Ordering all other traffic out of the 6,000 foot level, the air-controller instructed Captain Scott to fly a circle route over Puget Sound, staying clear of populated land areas. With the money and chutes finally at hand, Cooper permitted the plane to land.

Touching down at 5:43 p.m., the 727 taxied to a remote part of the airport, where, as promised, the hijacker released the thirty-five other passengers while the plane was being refueled. Checking the list, a Northwest Airlines clerk found that all the passengers had disembarked except one—"D. Cooper."

After the passengers had left, Alice Hancock, Senior Stewardess on the flight, told the hijacker that all three of the young ladies had made plans for Thanksgiving tomorrow. Could they leave the plane now?

"I don't see any problem," Cooper said. "Go ahead."

As Alice and Florence started to get off, they called to Tina, who was at the rear of the plane talking to the cockpit on the interphone. But Cooper changed his mind, saying, "No, I think Tina had better stay. I might need some help with the staircase."

Although reluctant to leave Tina behind, Alice and Florence responded to Cooper's gesture of dismissal and turned to go. He reached into his pocket, pulled out a handful of bills, and offered them to Florence, saying, "Here, I forgot to tip you when you brought my drinks."

Florence shook her head. But he was insistent. As the two young ladies started to move past him, he took out two packets of the just-delivered twenty-dollar bills, each of which contained two thousand dollars, and tried to give them to the stewardesses.

"Here, take these. I don't want them."

Again, they declined. Later, investigators realized a golden opportunity was missed: to obtain two sets of fingerprints from the hijacker. But the stewardesses, taught to refuse tips, declined.

FLIGHT TO NOWHERE

By now, it was after seven p.m., darkness had descended, and rain was falling steadily. Notified that the refueling was complete, Cooper said, "Let's get the show on the road."

After closing the rear door, Tina watched him tie the bag containing the $200,000 worth of twenty-dollar bills around his waist with a six-foot nylon cord he had stripped from one of the chest chutes. As he put on the military backpack parachute, which he had decided to use, she noted that he did it quickly and easily, as if it were a procedure he was long accustomed to.

When asked for a flight plan, Cooper ordered the pilot to fly to Reno, Nevada at an altitude of 10,000 feet, keeping the wheels down and setting the wing flaps at 15 degrees. At first, he told the pilot to leave the rear staircase extended during takeoff, but when Captain Scott said that was too dangerous, he let the steps be raised and kept in that position until the plane was airborne. When it reached the 10,000–foot level, he wanted the speed slowed to 175 miles an hour. Apparently, he planned to lower the staircase then and jump.

Flying at the relatively low 10,000–foot level, it would not be necessary to pressurize the plane, but co–pilot William Rataczak warned Tina that she might be sucked out of the stairwell when the rear door was opened. When Tina told this to Cooper, he said, "Negative on that; you'll be in no danger."

The plane took off at 7:36 p.m. At McChord Air Force Base, which had been alerted, a pair of F–106 Interceptors already had taken off, risen to the 35,000 foot level, and were ready to track the much slower 727 wherever it might be bound. As the hijacked plane climbed, Cooper opened the back door, looked down into the closed stairwell, and read the instructions for opening the staircase. Gazing apprehensively at the briefcase, Tina asked Cooper what he was going to do with the bomb.

"Don't worry. I'll either take it with me or disarm it. Now go to the cockpit and stay there. On your way, close the curtain and turn out the lights."

Tina obeyed. As she came to the curtain that separated the two sections, she turned and looked back. Cooper was standing by the open door. He raised his hand and gave her a farewell salute. She closed the curtain and snapped off the cabin lights...

D. B. COOPER, WHERE ARE YOU?

Though Tina was new to the airline business and was the junior stewardess on the flight, she had done her job well, and the cockpit crew complimented her. Looking tired and drained, she sat down in the observer's seat and told them what Cooper had said about disarming the bomb or taking it with him.

Five minutes later, at 7:45 p.m., the interphone buzzed from the rear of the plane. "Slow down a little," Cooper complained. "I can't get the staircase down."

Co–pilot Rataczak lowered the flaps from fifteen to thirty degrees, which brought the speed down from 197 mph to 167 mph. At 8:04 p.m., twenty-eight minutes after takeoff, the crew felt a slight movement. A panel light came on indicating that the stairwell was open. Wanting to know if their passenger was still aboard, the captain asked Tina to call him on the interphone. She pressed the buzzer several times, got no answer at first, then Cooper's voice could be heard yelling over the noise of the engines: "Hello."

"Are you still having trouble with the staircase?" Tina asked.

"No, everything is fine now."

Several minutes passed. Suddenly, at 8:13 p.m., the four crew members in the cockpit felt a burst of pressure in their ears. Rataczak shouted, "There he goes!"

Peering out the cockpit windows, the crew could see nothing but blackness outside. Tina's repeated pressing of the buzzer brought no response. Alerted by radio that the hijacker had jumped, the pilots in the two chase planes high above gazed down intently. But they saw nothing either.

Calling Flight Operations in Minneapolis to ask if they could send a crew member back to the cabin to make sure the hijacker had jumped, the captain was told to take no chances, continuing the flight on to Reno as planned. The flaps were reset at 15 degrees and the speed went back up to 195 mph.

When the plane landed at Reno at 11:02 p.m., the dragging staircase, which was still lowered, created a line of sparks along the runway, but otherwise the landing was made without mishap.

Shutting down the engines, Captain Scott flicked on the intercom loudspeaker. "In the cabin—are you there?"

No one answered...

Despite the massive media coverage given the hijacking and the concentrated searches made of the area in which it was thought the man named Cooper had jumped, clues to his real identify and indications of his fate were non–existent. Though the route of the plane was known and the time of his jump could be closely established, several factors complicated the problem of pinpointing the exact spot on which he had landed.

To begin with, the western foothills of the Cascades along the lower slopes of Mount Saint Helens were heavily forested, rough, slashed by several swift-flowing rivers, and dotted with several deep, long, man-made lakes which had been constructed as reservoirs for the purpose of power generation and flood control. If he were an experienced chutist—as he appeared to be—he might not have opened the parachute at once, free-falling as much as eight thousand feet before pulling the rip-cord.

He might have been thrown off balance by the 167–mile-an-hour airstream and knocked unconscious by the steps as he tried to jump, which would mean he had not opened the parachute and had died instantly upon striking the ground. If he had remained conscious and pulled the rip cord, he might have gotten hung up in the branches of a two-hundred foot tall tree; he might have accidentally hanged himself when the lines of his chute tangled; he might have landed in the middle of an icy, three-hundred foot deep lake, sinking like a rock before he could get out of the chute.

During the days and weeks that followed, a massive search of the area between Woodland and Vancouver took place. Law officers, hunters, and people from all walks of life swarmed over the region, searching for both the money and the man who by now was being called "D. B. Cooper." In the most detailed search, a contingent of four hundred soldiers from Fort Lewis spent a week of rugged duty trudging through the wet woods and the steep terrain as they followed grids laid out on large-scale maps of the area where the hijacker must have landed.

Not a shred of evidence was found. Based on the description given an artist by the clerk who had sold him the ticket, by the three stewardesses, and by the student who had sat across the aisle from him for a brief while, a sketch was made of the man who called himself "Dan

Cooper;" though it was widely circulated, not a single person came forward to say the likeness reminded them of someone they knew.

Only three facts were clear: (1) The hijacker's familiarity with parachutes indicated that he had been in the military, probably as a paratrooper; (2) He knew the flying characteristics of the 727–100, which meant he had either worked for Boeing or for an airline; (3) He knew the area, as witness his remark about McChord being only twenty minutes away from the Seattle Airport.

Because he had retrieved the note given the stewardess, had wiped his drink glass and the little bottles of bourbon clean, and had left no fingerprints on anything, there was no way in which his true identity could be established. A heavy smoker, he had gone through a number of cork-tipped Sir Walter Raleigh cigarettes, but all he had left of them were butts in the armrest ashtrays, which retained no prints.

Since the FBI had microfilmed the serial numbers of the twenty-dollar bills it had supplied, the list of these was soon published and circulated. None ever showed up.

After seven years had passed, a clue to the continuing mystery of D. B. Cooper finally did appear when a hunter found a twelve-inch plastic sign while crawling through the bushes near Silver Lake, ten miles north of Woodland. Giving large-lettered instructions on how to operate the ladder descending from the rear of a 727–100, it had been missing, investigators noted, when the hijacked plane landed at Reno.

Now it was found. But the remains of Cooper's chute, the money, or anything related to the man himself still had not appeared.

Then on Sunday, February 10, 1980, an eight-year-old boy named Brian Ingram went on a picnic with his family on a sandy beach on the north shore of the Columbia River, five miles west of Vancouver. After gathering an armload of driftwood for a fire, the boy put it down, then dropped to his knees and started smoothing out a spot in the sand on which he could pile the wood.

He felt a hump that was not sand. Something lumpy and damp. Something that felt like limp paper. Digging it up, he discovered three packets of soggy twenty-dollar bills, two of them held together with rubber bands that broke as soon as he handled them, while the third, which was not bound by a rubber band, was thinner.

Excitedly, young Brian showed the packets to his father, who, having recently moved his family to the Northwest from Oklahoma, was not familiar with the Cooper saga. But when he showed the bills to a local man who did know the story, he was told that the money probably was part of Cooper loot. He wasted no time arranging an appointment with FBI Agent Ralph Himmelsbach, a thirty-year veteran in the Portland office, who had long been hoping for just such a find.

The bills were soon identified as part of the $200,000 ransom knapsack which the hijacker had tied to his waist before he jumped out of the plane. In all, 290 of the original 10,000 twenty-dollar bills were in the packets, which meant that 9,710 of them still were missing. Though the recovered bills were held as evidence, young Brian Ingram was given a $500 reward by Northwest Airlines for finding them, which was sweetened by the *Oregon Journal* by an additional $250.

Since a private collector of rare money had offered the boy and his family $1,000 for just one of the bills, this was considerably less than fair market value, if they had been able to offer all 290 of the twenty-dollar bills. It was also considerably less than the $10,000 reward retired FBI Agent Richard T. Towsa offered for just one additional bill, when and if found, in his book about the hijacking: *D.B. Cooper Dead or Alive?* which was published in 1984.

As an aid to identifying the bills, interested parties should note, he lists them by numbers in the final chapter of his book. To date, nobody has claimed the reward.

Though any number of theories have been proposed regarding where the hijacker landed and how the 290 bills happened to turn up where they did, the best guess seems to be that the knapsack containing the bills—wherever it first fell out of the sky—washed down the Columbia River until a dredge being operated by the Corps of Engineers sucked it up, tore it open, then deposited a few packets of bills as part of the beach where the money was found.

When, where, and how D. B. Cooper got separated from the money he had gone to such lengths to acquire, is anybody's guess. But in the small town of Ariel, Washington, which is on the shores of Merwin Lake ten miles east of Woodland on State 503, his spirit is still alive and well.

Once a year on Thanksgiving eve, the local tavern puts on a celebration in his honor. As toasts are made, drinks go down, and the band plays the crowd's favorite ballad, *D. B. Cooper, Where Are You?* There is no question as to who is the hero of the people.

Some fine night, they feel sure, he will come barging through the swinging doors, dragging a knapsack full of twenty-dollar bills. They will hoist him on their shoulders and carry him to the bar. He will reach into the bag, fling bills all over the room, and shout, "Drink up, everybody! They're on me!"

BEGINNINGS OF CENTRALIA

Like the man who established the settlement of Bush Prairie a few miles to the north, the first American to claim land in the Centralia area also was a Negro and a freed slave. Coming west from Missouri in 1850 with his owner, J.G. Cochran, who filed a claim under the Oregon Territory Donation Land Act for a square mile in what would become the center of Centralia, the Negro—who also was named George Washington—was freed by Cochran, who then adopted him as his son. The *WPA Guide* says:

> In 1852 Cochran sold him [George Washington] his claim for $6,000. The new owner built a home and filed a plat for the town of Centerville, offering lots for $10 each, with one lot free to buyers who built houses.
>
> In 1891, the population—over 1,000—found its mail confused with that of another Centerville in the State, and the name of the town was changed to Centralia.

Like so many other communities being established in Washington Territory in the 1855–56 period, the threat of a general Indian uprising inspired the building of a blockhouse into which the settlers could withdraw and defend themselves. Made of solid, dovetailed fir timbers, this one was called the Fort Borst Blockhouse. If the Indian scare did nothing else, it certainly contributed a lot of solid buildings as enduring points of interest in city parks all over the state. This one, like many others, has been relocated from its original site.

Named after the public-spirited freed slave who gave the land to the city, George Washington Park now covers a square block of downtown Centralia.

Also in the park is the sculptured figure of a sentinel erected by the American Legion in honor of four Legionnaires who were killed in an Armistice Day riot November 11, 1919. As noted earlier, a radical labor organization called the Industrial Workers of the World—contemptuously dubbed the "I.W.W.s," "I Won't

Works," or the "Wobblies" by anti–labor interests—had declared war against all employers and representatives of capital, vowing to take the work force and the means of production into labor's hands by whatever means necessary, including violence.

Though the need for reform in the logging and sawmill industry was admitted by most reasonable men, brazen attempts to sabotage capitalists in general and the war effort in particular did not sit well with members of the American Legion, whose parade that day celebrated the victorious outcome of the World War. Exactly what happened to trigger the bloodshed never would be known. But these facts seemed clear:

Fearing they were about to be attacked, a number of IWW members armed themselves and holed up in their headquarters in downtown Centralia, vowing to protect themselves against what they regarded as mob violence. A number of American Legion members, who later claimed they were unarmed, stopped their parade in front of IWW headquarters and started shouting insults at the Wobblies. An attack ensued, shots were fired, and four Legionnaires fell dead.

Eleven Wobblies were arrested and jailed. That night, a number of vigilantes stormed the jail, seized a Wobbly named Wesley Everest, who reportedly had shot one of the dead Legionnaires, took him out and hanged him to a nearby railway bridge. None of the vigilantes ever were brought to trial. But the eleven Wobblies were tried, convicted, and sentenced to the state penitentiary.

Ironically, many of the reforms in working conditions, hours, and pay demanded by the Wobblies from the beginning of the movement in 1905 to its end in the 1920s already had been achieved—not by the violent means they long had advocated, but by government regulations and a more enlightened attitude on the part of employers, who were finally beginning to realize that they must change with the times.

But the Wobbly leaders did not change. For instance, Big Bill Haywood, IWW founder and longtime president, served time in a federal prison after being convicted of a wartime sedition charge. Still unrepentant following his release, he continued to fight for the cause. Embracing Communism, he finally fled to Russia and died there, requesting in his will that his ashes be buried in the Kremlin wall, spurning capitalism and the country of his birth even after his death in an alien land.

FORT VANCOUVER

Following Captain Robert Gray's discovery of the Columbia River in May, 1792, Lieutenant William Broughton, a British naval officer, confirmed the existence of the long-sought River of the West in October that same year by entering and sailing up it a hundred miles, then claiming it and all the adjacent country in the name of His Britannic Majesty on the grounds that "...no citizens of a civilized nation or state had ever entered the river before..."

One hundred miles inland, with the river still a mile wide, so deep that it offered no impediments to ocean-going ships, and so close to sea level that it rose and fell with the tides, a headland rising above the north bank was named Point Vancouver in honor of the commander of the expedition. When the War of 1812 ended, Great Britain and the United States negotiated an agreement giving both nations equal access to the Pacific Northwest under the Joint Occupancy Treaty. The British bought Fort Astoria near the mouth of the Columbia on its south shore, renamed it Fort George, then, deciding that an establishment further inland would better suit their interests, built a new post on the north side of the river, giving it the name Fort Vancouver.

In charge of the fort from its beginning in 1824 was a remarkable man, Dr. John McLoughlin. Though a British subject and loyal to the Crown, he influenced the course of Pacific Northwest history in favor of the United States for many years to come. Towering well over six feet, dressed usually in black, with a thick mass of snow-white hair, the Scottish–born Hudson's Bay Company factor was an impressive figure of a man. Called the "White-Headed-Eagle" by the Indians, who both feared and respected him, he often was caustically referred to as the "British King in Residence West of the Rockies" by the Americans who tried to do business with him.

Though an extremely moral man, he was ruthless when it came to acquiring furs from the Indians and excluding rival Americans from the trade. But so far as promoting British interests in the Pacific Northwest was concerned, he had a fatal weakness: he could not turn down a person in need, no matter what his nationality.

Favorably located on an open, fertile prairie with a large expanse of native grassland to the north, Fort Vancouver soon became self-sufficient, raising its own food and fabricating most of the tools it needed within the walls of the fort. With ships from

Click Relander Collection, Courtesy Yakima Valley Regional Library
FORT BORST, REBUILT IN BORST PARK IN CENTRALIA

England bringing amenities of the civilized world such as fine wines, newspapers, books, and occasional scientists to the post, Fort Vancouver lived up to its name "the most civilized fur-trading post west of London."

By 1826, McLoughlin had imported sawmill equipment, installed a forge, and planted the first fruit trees along the Columbia River. Legend has it that after gentlemen dining at the fort had eaten apples brought over from England, they deposited the seeds on their plates, whence frugal Indian women—many of whom were married to Hudson's Bay Company employees— saved and planted them in the fort orchard, thus starting the apple industry for which the State of Washington would become famous.

In those days, round-the-world sailing ships routinely made the Sandwich Islands (Hawaii) a port of call, filling vacancies in their crews with islanders, who were called "Kanakas." Capable as these people were in water-oriented occupations, they hated cold weather; so most of them who were brought to America as sailors or laborers soon returned to the balmier clime of their homeland. But enough of the three hundred Hawaiian men and women who visited Fort Vancouver during the next twenty years stayed on to form a district called "Kanaka Town," where some of their descendants still live in the modern city of Vancouver.

While Sir George Simpson, Director of Operations for the Hudson's Bay Company in North America, did not put the restrictive policy in writing, he made it clear to Dr. John McLoughlin that Americans should be discouraged from commerce or settlement by any means short of violence. Since he made a flying visit to the post only once a year, this was easy enough for him to say. But McLoughlin, who lived here the year round, knew from bitter experience that "discouraging" an American from doing business or settling wherever he wished was like telling a river to turn around and flow uphill.

Time and again enterprising Americans such as Hall Kelley, Nathaniel Wyeth, and Captain Benjamin Eulalie de Bonneville showed up at Fort Vancouver with one cockamamie scheme or another, which Dr. McLoughlin had to foil in some manner.

Hall Kelley was a colonizer, planning to throw the British rascals out, then give free land to all the impoverished people of New England, whose journey west would be subsidized by the federal government.

Nathaniel Wyeth was a businessman, shipping a cargo of ice and empty barrels around the Horn in hopes of filling the hold of his ship with salted Columbia River salmon caught near the fort, hauling them back East, and making a fortune in the fish markets of Boston.

Captain Bonneville was an adventurer bent on conquest, for the two-year leave he had been given by the United States Army and the seemingly endless funds supplied him by some unknown, generous backer (whose name was rumored to be Astor), meant that he probably was a spy for the American government, who, in his secret report to President Andrew Jackson, no doubt would recommend that the United States kick the British out and take over all the Oregon country south of Russian Alaska.

One by one, McLoughlin managed to defeat these invaders without resorting to violence. But in 1834 a different kind of intruder appeared on his doorstep in the form of the Methodist minister, Jason Lee. Being a man of the cloth, this newcomer required special handling.

Responding to a widely publicized plea from the Nez Perce and Flathead Indians of the interior country that they be sent holy men who would teach them the secrets written in the White Man's Book of Heaven, the Reverend Jason Lee and his party of missionaries had met their first far Western Indians at fur rendezvous on Green River, been alarmed by their wild appearance, and had taken the advice of a Hudson's Bay Company representative, who just "happened" to be there, that they might find the natives further west a bit more civilized and receptive to conversion.

At Fort Vancouver, Dr. McLoughlin confirmed that advice. In the Willamette Valley south of the Columbia River the Calapooya Indians were very tractable, he told the American missionaries; furthermore, the soil was fertile, the climate mild, and the Hudson's Bay Company would be happy to help them get started. What he did not tell them, of course, was that he was encouraging all American emigrants to settle south of the river, for despite Sir George Simpson's hope to exclude Americans from the Oregon country McLoughlin suspected that when the time came to draw a line between the United States and Great Britain in the Pacific Northwest, his country would be lucky to retain the territory north of the Columbia River.

MORE AMERICAN VISITORS

And still the Americans came. Visiting Fort Vancouver in 1836, Dr. Marcus and Narcissa Whitman and the Reverend Henry and Eliza Spalding, sponsored by the American Board for Foreign Missions of the Congregational and Presbyterian Churches, came out from Boston. They informed Dr. McLoughlin politely but firmly that as soon as they could build houses for their wives in the interior country, they intended to establish missions among the Cayuse and Nez Perce Indians in the very region Jason Lee had thought too uncivilized to be settled. Though he tried to dissuade and divert the two couples to the Willamette Valley, they refused to alter their plans. Gentleman that he was, McLoughlin let the two women stay as his guests at Fort Vancouver while their husbands, with help from the Indians, built livable winter quarters. When the cabins were ready, he supplied them food staples and material needs from Company stocks, even though he knew that Sir George Simpson would criticize him severely when he found out about it.

In 1843, an American Government exploring party under Lieutenant John C. Fremont came out the Oregon Trail, part of the

Great Migration that would bring one thousand men, women, and children to the Oregon country. All of these travelers stopped at Fort Vancouver, where Dr. McLoughlin treated them kindly and supplied them with their needs, despite his orders to the contrary.

In 1846, the boundary between Great Britain and the United States was set at the forty-ninth parallel, well to the north of the Columbia River. The Hudson's Bay Company began winding up its business affairs in what became Washington Territory in 1853. By then, Dr. John McLoughlin had decided to cast his lot with the Americans, quitting the British Company, and taking a land claim at Oregon City, in the lower Willamette Valley.

Well aware of the value of Fort Vancouver, the United States took it over as a military post in 1848. A number of officers such as Lieutenants Phil Sheridan and Ulysses S. Grant served here during the 1850s, gaining experience in regional Indian wars that would prepare them for leadership roles in the Civil War soon to come. Ironically, Benjamin Bonneville, whose efforts to gain a foothold in the area back in the late 1830s had been foiled by Dr. John McLoughlin, served a tour as commandant of the fort where he once had been considered a dangerous enemy.

Meanwhile, the settlement adjacent to the post, which first called itself Vancouver City and then simply Vancouver, flourished and grew. Incorporated in 1857, it had become such an important place that the Territorial Legislature passed a bill in 1860 authorizing the removal of the capital from Olympia to Vancouver; no date was set, so the next session of the legislature rescinded the act and the capital remained where it was.

From its beginning as a Hudson's Bay Company post in 1824 down to the present day, Vancouver was and is the most important deep-water port on the lower Columbia in the state of Washington. Following the Civil War, the military post called Vancouver Barracks housed troops used in the Indian wars of the 1870s, the Spanish–American War in 1898, World War I in 1917–19, and World War II in 1941–45.

During the First World War, Vancouver became headquarters of the "Spruce Division," in which 30,000 men logged and milled timber for the war effort on an unprecedented scale. In the Second World War, shipbuilding and the production of aluminum using electricity produced at the recently-completed Bonneville Dam thirty-five miles upriver made major contributions to the war effort.

Bill Gulick Photo
CHIEF FACTOR'S HOUSE, FORT VANCOUVER, TODAY

CHIEF FACTOR'S HOUSE, FORT VANCOUVER, MAY 1860
Courtesy Fort Vancouver National Historic Site, National Park Service

FORT VANCOUVER TODAY

First organized in 1946, the Fort Vancouver Restoration and Historical Society, in conjunction with the National Park Service, has preserved most of the buildings on the military post and has reconstructed the original Hudson's Bay Company post so that it appears to be just as it was when Dr. John McLoughlin ruled it with an iron hand and a soft heart. Administered by the National Park Service, the excellent Visitor Center contains many displays of interest to travelers intrigued by the history of the Pacific Northwest, for it was here that the Joint Occupancy Treaty demonstrated that two great nations could settle a major dispute over territory without going to war.

LEWIS AND CLARK
ON THE WASHINGTON COAST

Paddling their unwieldy dugout canoes from Point Vancouver to the Pacific Ocean, the Lewis and Clark party reached the Washington coast at the worst possible time of year. Clark wrote in his journal for November 12, 1805:

> A Tremendious wind from the S.W. about 3 oClock this morning with Lightineng and hard claps of Thunder, and Hail which Continued untill 6 oClock A.M. when it became light for a Short time, then the heavens became sudenly darkened by a black cloud from the S.W. and rained with great violence untill 12 oClock, the waves tremendious brakeing with great fury against the rocks and trees on which we were encamped.

This was the beginning of the long rainy season near the mouth of the Columbia, which Clark estimated to be five miles wide at that point, near a village of Chinook Indians. After watching the natives cross the river "...through the highest waves I ever Saw a Small vestles ride," Clark wrote, "Those Indians are certainly the best Canoe navigaters I ever saw."

Unlike today's vacationers who flock to the area whenever the sun shines (and often when it does not), Clark disliked the seacoast intensely, writing, "salt water I view as an evil in as much as it is not helthy." He even disliked its sound:

> ...the sea which is imedeately in front roars like a repeeted roling thunder and have rored in that way ever since our arrival in its borders which is now 24 days since we arrived in sight of the

Great Western Ocian, I can't say Pasific as since I have seen it, it has been the reverse.

After Captain Meriwether Lewis crossed the Columbia and found a heavily wooded site several miles inland from the Oregon coast, where the ocean could neither be seen nor heard, Captain William Clark gladly agreed that their winter camp should be built there. Celebrating Christmas at Fort Clatsop, the party stayed until March 23, 1806, with Clark's glimpses of the unpacific Pacific limited to a visit to the saltmakers camp near present-day Seaside, Oregon, and a look at a 105–foot-long whale that had died and washed up on the beach nearby.

LAND ROUTE WEST TODAY

By highway, you can travel to the mouth of the Columbia across pleasant, rolling country by leaving Interstate 5 at Kelso and taking State 4 west to Cathlamet, Long Beach, and Ilwaco. Nine miles east of Ilwaco, the Columbia is spanned by a 4.5–mile-long toll bridge to Astoria, Oregon, which stays just above water level for most of its length, then rises to a dizzying height over the ship channel near the Oregon shore so that it can clear the masts of even the tallest ocean ships sailing upriver to Portland or Vancouver.

When first discovered by white explorers and fur traders in the 1750s, this was the domain of the Chinook Indians, the most dominant tribe of the Salishan group, remarkable in many ways. First, they were so skilled at traveling on water that they often crossed the Columbia River bar and cruised north along the Pacific coast to the Strait of Juan de Fuca and Vancouver Island, where they traded captured slaves for seashells. Second, they originated a language called "Chinook Jargon" by which all the tribes living west of the Cascades could communicate with one another—a language so simple that Russian, French, Spanish, British, and American traders easily picked it up, then added words of their own. Third, they indulged in the practice of head-flattening, a mark of nobility to them, but a practice so horrifying to American missionaries that it ranked with cannibalism and nakedness as a prime reason to convert and educate yet another "benighted" heathen race.

The process was simple enough. Soon after a Chinook infant was born, a flat board was strapped to its forehead, the bindings kept tight for however long it took to give the right amount of slant to the forehead, whose soft bone covering took whatever degree of pointedness the parents thought fashionable. The head-flattening supposedly did not impair the child's mental capacity or give it a headache, but because the practice was so universally denounced by the missionaries little research regarding it was done and no firsthand accounts by its participants have survived.

Because of the abundance of seafood in the rivers, bays, and ocean; plus game such as elk and deer and wild plants and berries on land, the Chinooks were a well-fed people, with a surplus to trade. They were also well-housed, writes historian Lucile McDonald, whose book *Coast Country: a History of Southwest Washington* is by far the best source available on the region.

"The Chinooks lived in long, sturdy communal houses of cedar planks," she writes, then quotes a description by one of the first whites who saw them:

> Well formed, looking old and durable. The dwellings had a single door and no windows or chimney. An opening was left along the ridgepole to permit smoke to escape. A depressed area for a fireplace was provided for each family, and this was rimmed by an earth platform where all domestic activities were carried on. Food in the process of being cured hung from the rafters, to be dried in the smoke of the family fires. A low shelf along either wall of the building was spread with mats and furs for sleeping.

No accurate estimate of the Chinook population before their contact with the white man has been made, but it must have been in the thousands. Unfortunately, like many Indian tribes, exposure to the white man's diseases such as smallpox—against which they had no natural immunity—swept through them in epidemics that killed them off in ghastly numbers. Intermarrying with whites and other Indians, their identity as a people was almost lost for a time, Lucile McDonald says, though of recent years some of the younger people are taking pride in their heritage and are beginning to preserve it. As she aptly comments, "A people for whom a wind, a jargon, and a giant salmon were named should not be forgotten by history."

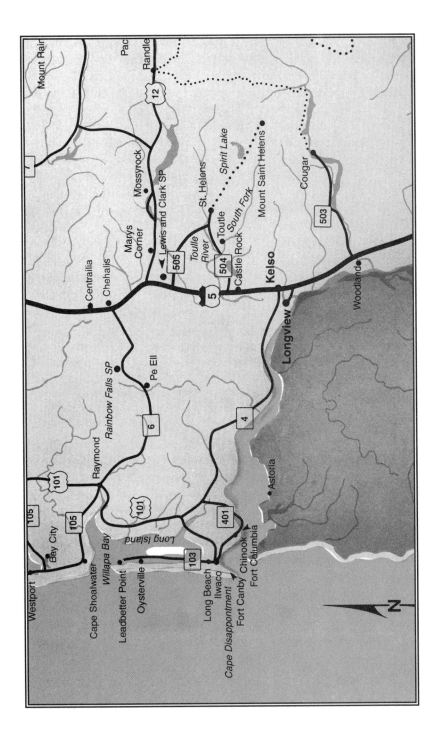

EARLY DAY FUR TRADE

As a number of historians have noted, the importance of fur on world trade cannot be overestimated. Just as beaver fueled the exploration of North America by land, sea otter inspired expeditions to the North Pacific coast, to China, Asia, and on around the world to Europe and England. The key element stimulating the fur trade was its high rate of profit. As early as 1794, for example, *Jenny* acquired two thousand sea otter pelts on the lower Columbia for an average of fifty cents apiece in trade goods, took them to China, resold them to wealthy mandarins there for goods worth twelve dollars a fur, then completed his round-the-world voyage to Bristol, England with a gross profit of $23,000—a 2400% return on his investment.

In a day when sailors were paid next to nothing, when meager rations of food were given the crew, when ships were relatively inexpensive, and the cost of a year-long voyage very small, the monetary returns to the backers of such ventures were phenomenal. Though the books of England's Crown–chartered Hudson's Bay Company and Astor's American Fur Company never were opened to public inspection, it was common knowledge in the fur trade between 1650 and 1840 that the wealthy stockholders who owned shares in those companies expected and usually got a twenty percent annual return on their investment.

Thanks to the talented pen of Washington Irving, whose book *Astoria* immortalized the establishment of the first American fur-trading post on the lower Columbia in 1811, the terrors of crossing the tumultuous bar at the mouth of the river in a small sailing ship became well known. During the next two hundred years, at least two thousand vessels and fifteen hundred lives have been lost in or near that treacherous passage despite progress from sail to steam, channel improvements, lighthouses and lightships, radar, and the latest improvements in navigational guidance equipment.

State 4, US 101—Kelso to Long Beach
72 miles

Courtesy Ilwaco Heritage Museum
SALMON CANNERY IN ILWACO AREA IN EARLY 1900s

CAPE DISAPPOINTMENT AREA

The best spot from which to see the mouth of the Columbia is the height of land on which the Cape Disappointment Lighthouse stands. Two miles southwest of Ilwaco, the headland given that inaccurate name rises two hundred and twenty feet above sea level. The narrow paved walk leading up from the parking lot of the Coast Guard Life Saving School at the foot of the hill is steep and not recommended for running by anyone over the age of eighteen; but the view of the six-mile wide mouth of the great river is so spectacular that the climb is well worth the effort, however long it takes.

First authorized in 1853, the building of the lighthouse had to be postponed for three years because the ship carrying materials for its construction—the *Oriole*—was wrecked just below the site as she attempted to cross the bar in September that same year. Thanks to the skill of professional pilot George Flavel, who had

SS IOWA, WRECKED ON PEACOCK SPIT, JANUARY 12, 1936

just established a bar-guide service in Astoria, no lives were lost, but the materials for the building of the lighthouse were not replaced until 1856, when the light first came on. Now automated, the Cape Disappointment Light has guided ships into the river for a century and a half, shooting its beam of 700,000 candlepower on the white flash and 160,000 candlepower on the red flash twenty-one miles out to sea.

As a further aid to navigation beginning in 1892, lightships were stationed off the entrances to both the Strait of Juan de Fuca and the Columbia River. Equipped with foghorns and lights, they held their positions through fair weather and foul, manned by seamen who led the loneliest, most monotonous life imaginable for six weeks at a stretch—a monotony broken only by a few hours of sheer terror when storms rolled in, seas ran high, and survival lay in the laps of the gods.

Until outmoded by the universal use of radar in the 1960s, four lightships—known by their numbers *50, 88, 93,* and *604*—held station continuously five miles out to sea southwest of the mouth of the Columbia. Out of touch with land, and stuck in a single spot without the stability of being underway, service aboard these vessels was the worst kind of sea duty imaginable.

The fourth and last of these vessels, *Columbia River Lightship No. 604*, which was in service from 1950 to the mid '60s, now is anchored next door to the Columbia River Maritime Museum in Astoria. Both it and the Maritime Museum, which is the finest ocean and river museum in the Northwest, are open for tours by the public.

NORTH HEAD LIGHTHOUSE

An increasing number of wrecks near the turn of the century resulted in the building of one of the most picturesque and powerful lighthouses on the Pacific coast in 1898. Located on the extreme end of Cape Disappointment and only two miles away from that beacon, the North Head Lighthouse stands on a conical tower 194 feet high and sends out a white-beam flash of 3.5 million candlepower. More visible to ships approaching from the north than the Cape Disappointment beacon, it became automated in 1961.

Surrounding both the North Head and Cape Disappointment lighthouse sites is the 1700–acre Fort Canby State Park. A great deal of history related to the western expansion of the United States took place in the lower Columbia River region; much of it has been preserved in the Ilwaco area and may be seen by the traveler today in museums and interpretive centers.

For example, during the Civil War when "Dixie Raiders" such as the heavily armed *Shenandoah* roamed the seas looking for Union shipping to sink or plunder, the risk that the Columbia River might be entered by a Confederate man-of-war was considered so high that fortifications were built and cannons mounted on both sides of the river in hopes of giving such an attacker the warmest possible reception.

On the Oregon side of the river, Fort Stevens was constructed, while on Cape Disappointment guns were installed at what came to be called Fort Canby. A few miles east on the Washington side of the river, Fort Columbia was built. In April, 1864, a battery of heavy guns was placed around the Cape Disappointment Lighthouse, Lucile McDonald writes, the most famous of which: "Old Betsy, standing too close to the tower, was fired four times, then moved in order to spare the lighthouse windows, some of which shattered every time the cannon boomed."

Bill Gulick Photo

CAPE DISAPPOINTMENT LIGHTHOUSE

Truth to tell, the smoothbore cannons installed at each fort had a maximum range of only two miles and were not very accurate. But against a wooden-hulled sailing ship trying to navigate the bar and the tricky channels of the lower river, even such a random bombardment might have acted as a deterrent.

Later, during the Spanish–American War of 1898, during World War I, 1917–19, and World War II, 1941–45, the type and range of the guns and their emplacements were improved so that the artillery pieces could fire a six-inch projectile at least six miles. In both world wars, the lower river was laced with underwater mines that could be fired electrically from either shore. Fortunately for the tranquility of the Pacific Northwest, neither the mines nor the long-range guns were ever fired in anger.

But the defenses were tested on one occasion. This was on June 21, 1942, when a Japanese submarine surfaced at extreme

Bill Gulick Photo
CAPE DISAPPOINTMENT US COAST GUARD TRAINING SCHOOL
The facility is Near Ilwaco.

range under cover of darkness off the mouth of the Columbia, lofted a few projectiles from its five-inch deck gun in the general direction of Fort Stevens, then submerged and ran.

Because the guns that could have reached the attacker had been cut up and sold for scrap—to the Japanese—before the war began, the fire was not returned. Many years later the commander of the Japanese submarine paid a visit to Oregon and was relieved to hear that his shells had made only a few harmless holes in the ground. Graciously, he apologized for the attack.

Still visible just below the North Head Lighthouse are the circular iron rims on which the guns tracked, the concrete ammunition storage cavities, and diagrammed placards explaining how the guns rose to be aimed and fired, then, with the gases supporting them exhausted, sank down into presumably safe hiding places for a brief time before they rose and fired again. A placard at Fort Columbia proudly relates the fact that a local gunnery crew had won a prize for speed and accuracy of firing just a day or two before the Japanese submarine launched its attack on Fort Stevens. What the prize-winning gunnery crew was doing that night, the placard does not say.

Courtesy Ilwaco Heritage Museum
NORTH HEAD NEAR MOUTH OF THE COLUMBIA

When the Coast Guard announced in 1963 that the Cape Disappointment light was no longer necessary and would be discontinued, the Columbia River Pilots' Association raised such a strong protest that the idea was quickly shelved. Even in this electronic age, the active seamen still want the light to shine—and it still does.

LEWIS & CLARK INTERPRETIVE CENTER

Located on Cape Disappointment as part of Fort Canby State Park is the Lewis and Clark Interpretive Center. Here, displays tell in visual and audio form the Indian and white history of the area, as well as the story of the expedition's journey west. This is one of three such Interpretive Centers located in the State of Washington, a second one being at Sacajawea State Park, near Pasco, Washington, the third at Chief Timothy State Park, eight miles west of Clarkston.

LIFE SAVING SCHOOL

At the base of the hill on which the Cape Disappointment Lighthouse sets, the United States Coast Guard Life Saving School is

Bill Gulick Photo

NORTH HEAD LIGHTHOUSE

the only place in the world that specializes in sea and surf rescues. Launching their rescue craft under incredibly bad weather conditions, only these specially trained men in their specially built boats dare challenge the elements on their missions of mercy. In the tradition of centuries of sea-faring men who have attempted rescues of their comrades at sea, US Coast Guard crews long have lived by the unwritten code: *You have to go out—but you don't have to come back.*

First established by the United States government in 1877, the Fort Canby and North Cove lifesaving stations were operated by the Revenue Marine, predecessor of the Coast Guard. Lucile McDonald writes:

> At first the captain of each station had to depend entirely upon volunteers to man the self-bailing lifeboat. The Fort Canby crew must have had a real test of stamina on May 3–4, 1880, when scores of gillnet fishermen narrowly missed death near the bar in a sudden severe blow.
>
> Getting together a crew of volunteers on a stormy night to risk their lives in the breakers sometimes was next to an impossibility, and several experiences in that period prompted the government to consider more adequate staffing of the stations at all seasons.

When a full-time eight-man crew under the direction of a captain began to operate in the 1880s, their quarters were spartan and their equipment minimal.

Lookouts were maintained along the coast at vantage points such as Cape Disappointment, where the old fogbell shack at the lighthouse was loaned as a shelter for the watcher when the weather was bad. A spyglass and small signal cannon were his equipment. If he saw a vessel with its ensign upside down, or a flag in the rigging, or heavy smoke—all signs of distress—he reported to the station. The captain then rang an alarm bell and his crew ran to the boathouse and were speedily on their way to the rescue. Until about 1912, the craft was either a Jersey skiff or a McClellan surfboat but, after that, thirty-six foot lifeboats were in use.

For vacationers and summer visitors to the Long Beach area, life-saving drills were feature attractions, fun for both the participants and onlookers. But on stormy nights when lives were at stake, they were in dead earnest.

Though people living along this dangerous stretch of coast were well aware of the toll in lives and property taken by the sea, they also relished the fact that the usual consequence of a wreck was booty. Because whatever prize salvaged from a grounded, abandoned ship was the property of whoever hauled it ashore, a shipwreck was like Christmas, no matter what time of year it happened.

Fine silver, exquisite table linens, fifty-pound sacks of flour, cases of fine silk dresses and well-aged liquor, farm wagons, gum boots, enough paints, nails, and tools to stock a hardware store, pianos, white Stetson hats—these were only a few of the items delivered to the coastal residents as gifts from the sea. Appropriately, the salvagers were called "sea gulls" because, like birds of that name, they gathered wherever tasty goodies were dumped into the sea.

In one instance when the huge steamer *Great Republic* went aground just inside the bar, the weather was so mild and the sea so calm that it appeared no human lives would be lost, though a few horses which had fallen over the side and tried to swim ashore did drown. Discovering that one of the Chinese cooks aboard the luxury ship still lingered behind, a rescue crew in a lifeboat rowed close under the lee rail of the listing ship, urged

Courtesy Ilwaco Heritage Museum
SALMON FISHERMEN *CA* 1900

him to don a life preserver and jump into the water, from which they were sure they could pull him without difficulty.

Whether a fear of water or a lack of understanding of what the rescuers wanted him to do made the cook hesitate so long, never was known. But at last he did don the life-preserver and jump. Unfortunately, he never came up. This puzzled his would–be rescuers, for the life-preserver certainly should have brought him back to the surface in only a matter of seconds.

Weeks later when his body washed ashore following a storm, the mystery was solved. His pockets were stuffed with the ship's silverware, which had acted like leaden weights to hold him down...

EXTREMES OF WEATHER

Even before July 17, 1841, when US Naval Commander Charles Wilkes had tried to cross the Columbia River bar in the sloop of war Peacock and ran it aground on a shoal just west of Cape Disappointment, the mouth of the Columbia River had been notorious for its bad weather. In attempting to enter the river in late March, 1811, Jonathan Thorn, captain of the *Astor* chartered ship the Tonquin, lost eight seamen in three separate efforts to cross the bar. Not until a fortunate change in the wind, the tide, and his luck favored the ship's passage did the *Tonquin* manage to enter the river.

In any kind of adverse wind, tide, current, and weather, the officers and crews of sailing ships often lashed their bodies to the masts while making the crossing of the bar in order to keep from being washed overboard; waves breaking over the ship sometimes reached halfway up to the tallest spars. Experienced seaman that he was, Commander Wilkes made the flat prediction that conditions at the mouth of the Columbia were so adverse that the river could not be entered for two-thirds of the year. Waits ranging from eight days to six weeks while ships rode out adverse winds, tides, and currents outside the river's mouth were not at all uncommon.

If crossing the bar and entering the river had been a high-risk venture during the age of sail, it became only slightly less dangerous with the advent of steam. Part of the problem lay in the fact that at low tide the river meandered at random through channels cut in the constantly shifting sand. A pilot coming through deep water one day was never sure what he might find the next. Brought in to solve the problem in 1875, the Army Engineers in charge of eliminating hazards in rivers and harbors turned it over to Colonel James Eads, who had faced the same puzzle at the mouth of the Mississippi.

In principle, the solution was simple enough, he concluded. The river must be compressed within two dikes or jetties of stone. One should be built out from the north shore, Cape Disappointment, the other from the south, Clatsop Spit. The narrow passage between the two jetties would increase the river's rate of flow, constantly scouring the channel and maintaining a safe depth for ocean-going ships.

With the expenditure of a large amount of funds over a period of years, this was done. The south jetty now reaches out seven miles from its beginning at Fort Stevens, while the north jetty extends four-and-one-half miles from a shoal called Peacock Spit in honor of the first US naval vessel to be wrecked there.

As always happens when the profile of a river mouth or a seacoast is changed artificially, there have been a few unexpected results. One that surprised a lot of Astoria people who had always regarded Sand Island as part of Oregon because it split the lower channel nearest to their side of the river, was the discovery that it

Courtesy Ilwaco Heritage Museum

FORT COLUMBIA *CA* 1900, ABOVE; *CA* 1920, BELOW

Courtesy Ilwaco Heritage Museum

Courtesy Ilwaco Heritage Museum

FORT COLUMBIA *CA* 1920

Courtesy Ilwaco Heritage Museum

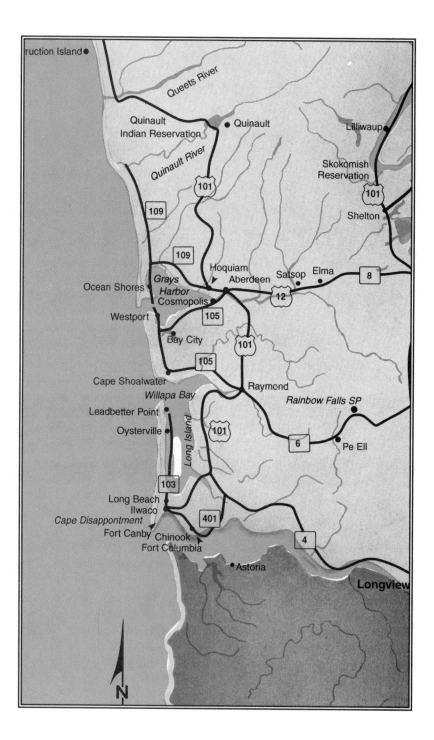

ruction Island●

Queets River

Quinault
Indian Reservation

● Quinault

Lilliwaup●

Quinault River

Skokomish
Reservation

[101]

[101]

[109]

Shelton

[109]

Hoquiam
▶ Aberdeen
Satsop Elma

[8]

Ocean Shores ● Grays
Harbor
Cosmopolis ●

[12]

Westport

[105]

● Bay City

[101]

[105]

Cape Shoalwater

Willapa Bay

Raymond

Rainbow Falls SP

Leadbetter Point ●

Oysterville ●

Long Island

[101]

[6]

● Pe Ell

[103]

Long Beach
Ilwaco
Cape Disappontment
Fort Canby Chinook
Fort Columbia

[401]

[4]

● Astoria

Longview

N

had migrated north over a period of years toward the Washington side of the river, where it now was being used by commercial fishermen and other Washington residents as *their* property. After years of suits and countersuits in state and regional courts, the United States Supreme Court finally awarded Sand Island to its original owner, the State of Oregon.

But the Court did not address the problem of moving the island back to its original location. So today the residents of Ilwaco and the lower reaches of the Columbia River still use and regard it as their own because of its proximity to the Washington shore.

Few places in the world experience such high winds and seas as this part of the Washington coast. "When I was a child," Lucile McDonald writes, "I imagined that all the bad weather in our part of the world began at North Head because that was where the storm reports for the region originated."

According to weather records, she was not far wrong in that assumption. Shortly after the new weather station there was equipped with an anemometer, a triple register, and other modern inventions recently displayed at the Portland Lewis and Clark Exposition in 1905, an early winter storm gave a demonstration of its power. She writes:

> On December 26, the new building and its steel tower were struck by lightning, and the triple register, telephone, and telegraph instruments were destroyed. Windows were blown out and the observer knocked unconscious. When he regained his senses a few minutes later, he found the place on fire. Though he extinguished the blaze, his quarters were a shambles.

On November 17, 1909, a ninety-mile gale picked up the instrument shelter and lifted it over the fence a distance of fifty feet, smashing the building and the four thermometers it contained. It is a matter of record, Lucile McDonald says, that North Head was among the three windiest weather stations in the United States that year.

State 103—Long Beach Peninsula
  25 miles
US 101—Ilwaco to Raymond
  45 miles

How windy does it get there? This windy, McDonald says:

> The worst recorded storm was on January 29, 1921, when the velocity in late afternoon suddenly jumped from 40 to 126 miles an hour, with a single minute of 150 miles. Perry Hill, the weatherman on duty, had driven with his wife in the station car to fetch mail and groceries from Ilwaco. They were on their way home through dense spruce and hemlock when their motor stalled, perhaps from the extremely low air pressure. The delay undoubtedly saved their lives. By the time they entered the heavy timber, large limbs and broken twigs filled the road. A fallen telephone pole brought the car to a halt. Hill and his wife ran for shelter, finding great trees down wherever they turned. A toppling giant missed them by ten feet.

"Not only was this the greatest blow ever known at North Head," McDonald says, "but, judging from the damage done to the forest, it was the greatest disaster in the lifetime of the oldest trees." *That*, we must agree, is windy.

CHINOOK CHIEF COMCOMLY

If the active partners in the Astor party had not disliked Captain Jonathan Thorn of the ship *Tonquin* so intensely that they disagreed with every suggestion he made, the first American fur-trading post on the lower Columbia would have been built on the Washington rather than on the Oregon side of the river. In fact, Captain Thorn had already sent men ashore at Baker Bay, where Fort Canby later stood, to build a pen for the fifty hogs being carried on the ship when his order was countermanded by partners Duncan McDougal and David Stuart—for no better reason than their hatred of the arrogant captain.

Because Captain Thorne thought the best site for the post would be on the north side of the river, the two partners insisted that a location on the south side be examined. Though Chief Comcomly, who knew this part of the country better than anyone else, warned the partners against crossing the river in such heavy weather, they ignored his advice. Lucile McDonald writes:

> Their craft capsized near Point Ellice; and McDougal, who could not swim, was in desperate straits. The Chinooks, anticipating trouble, followed in canoes and picked them up, dried their clothes, and entertained the white men in the tribal houses for three days—until the storm had passed and they could be delivered safely aboard ship.

Insisting that Captain Thorn set the goods of the Pacific Fur Company ashore at what became Astoria, the partners let the ill-tempered martinet sail north on a fur-trading expedition in which his poor judgment and autocratic manner soon earned him the hostility of the natives of Nootka Sound. Killing him and several members of his crew, the massacre was completed for the Indians by a wounded clerk who blew up the ship and a hundred or so of its assailants by dropping a match in the powder magazine. This was the first of many disasters that would overtake the Astor venture during the next year and a half.

Like his Scotch counterparts, Dr. John McLoughlin, Peter Skene Ogden, and Finan McDonald, Duncan McDougal cemented relationships with the local Indians by marrying one of Chief Comcomly's daughters, said to be a beautiful, intelligent young woman. Since the Chinook chief had six wives and a number of children, her exact identity cannot be established. But it is known that McDougal, like the other Scotch traders who married Indian women, remained faithful to her in his way and treated her and the children she bore him with honor and respect as long as he lived.

Another of Chief Comcomley's daughters married a Scotch trader named Archibald McDonald. In 1824, she gave birth to a son, Ranald, who, in time to come, would drastically change the relationship between the United States and Japan. As a boy growing up near the mouth of the Columbia, Ranald MacDonald, (for some reason he changed the spelling of the family name) became fascinated with the three survivors of a Japanese junk which had been blown across the Pacific and wrecked along the nearby coast.

At first thought to be Indians because they so closely resembled his mother's people, they spoke a different language, Ranald learned. In his own *Original Manuscript,* which he wrote later in his life, Ranald MacDonald says he found it easy to learn their language, which he discovered was Japanese. From that day on, he felt a deep kinship with the shipwrecked foreign sailors because of the heritage of his mother's blood.

Because his father wanted the boy to be educated so that he could use his Scotch canniness and his understanding of Indians to become a trader for the Hudson's Bay Company, Archibald McDonald sent his son to Montreal to be schooled and taught the banking business. Though intelligent enough and a quick learner,

Courtesy Ilwaco Heritage Museum
THE CLAMSHELL RAILROAD THAT RAN WITH THE TIDES

young Ranald did not care for city and business life. He later wrote, "I felt ever and uncontrollably in my blood the wild strain for wandering freedom." Quitting his job at the bank, he left Montreal, going "into the darkness of an unsympathetic world alone, telling no one." Feeling that he belonged neither in the white trading world of his father nor in the Indian world of his mother and her people, whose society by then was beginning its slow decay on the banks of the lower Columbia River, he went south to the United States, finding work as a deck hand on a boat on the Mississippi River. A strong, handsome, personable young man, he soon found favor with captains and pilots on the big river, finally signing on with the sea-going ship *Plymouth*, which was bound first for New York, then around Cape Horn for the Orient.

As the ship sailed northwest across the Pacific toward the Sandwich Islands (Hawaii), he told the sympathetic captain the dream that had taken possession of his life. "I want to go to Japan."

Courtesy Ilwaco Heritage Museum
FERRY ACROSS THE COLUMBIA, EARLY 1900s

FIRST AMERICAN TO JAPAN

At that time, Japan was a closed country, with all "foreign devils" landing on its shores risking certain death. But Ranald MacDonald had a plan. Just as the derelict junk and the three helpless Japanese sailors aboard it had been shipwrecked on the the Northwest Coast, so would he appear to be the lone survivor of a maritime disaster that would wash him ashore in a small boat on the coast of Japan.

"All I'll take with me," he told the skeptical captain of the *Plymouth*, "will be my books, writing materials, quadrant, and compass. I speak the language well enough to get by. My Indian blood makes me look like a person whose origins may have been oriental. As a shipwrecked sailor, I'm sure I will be well treated."

"What if my ship is seen still afloat?"

"It need not be. You can stay well out to sea until after dark, make a run in toward the coast, put me and my boat over the side, then beat out to sea. I'll cruise around until daylight, when I'll head inshore and stage my 'shipwreck.' You'll be taking no risk at all."

Courtesy Ilwaco Heritage Museum
FIRST TRAIN FROM ILWACO TO NAHCOTTA

"Well, it's your head to lose," the captain grumbled. "If it's what you want to do, I'll go along with it."

After being put over the side under cover of darkness, near a small, lightly populated island, Ranald MacDonald cruised around aimlessly until he was sure the *Plymouth* was out of sight, then ran the small boat up on the beach, turned it over and smashed it as if it had been wrecked.

Fortunately, his first people-contact was with the Anius, Kurilean fishermen on Hokkaido, whose appearance and culture was very close to that of American North Coast Indians. Ranald MacDonald felt perfectly at home with this half-savage people in their conical hats and grass clothing. In turn, they were drawn to him as a shipwrecked sailor from some region that appeared to be much like their own. But they knew what the law required: when a stranger landed, the military must be notified.

MacDonald was taken to Fukayama, where he was ordered to tell his story to the viceroy. When aboard ship, he was kept below decks. When traveling on land, his sedan chair was closed so that he could neither see nor be seen. When he walked, he was blindfolded. Brought before the viceroy, he was questioned endlessly, with sketches being made of all his possessions and his sea chest sealed.

Through all of this, he stuck to his story: that he had been shipwrecked and was the sole survivor of the craft that had carried him across the Pacific to this distant shore. Now that he was here, he said politely, he would like to be of service and become friends, just as the three shipwrecked sailors from whom he had learned the Japanese language had served and become friends of his own people in America.

Eventually, the viceroy believed his story. Still, he must be sent on to Nagasaki, for that was where the law required that all foreigners be sent for a final disposition of their case, which usually was prison or death. All along the way, he later wrote, curious people came to stare at him, but if he smiled at them or spoke to them in a friendly fashion, they would back away and cry in horror, "No, no! Nagasaki! Nagasaki!" It was death, they knew, to have anything to do with foreigners.

In Nagasaki, he was treated well. Even though it was still a closed country, the learned men and bright young scholars of Japan took advantage of this opportunity to learn something about North America. From all parts of the country, learned men came and talked to him, while fourteen bright, inquisitive students came regularly to a class he taught explaining his own country's customs and ways. It was possible that he might have stayed in Japan for the rest of his life, he said later, if the American government had not sent the warship *Preble* to Nagasaki to rescue a crew that had really been shipwrecked some months before.

Because the two governments had agreed on the ransom and release of the shipwrecked sailors, Japanese authorities felt that Ranald MacDonald's repatriation should be included in the package. MacDonald was shocked by the appearance of the other white men, he said later, for they had not been treated nearly as well as he had been.

Living out the rest of his life in the United States in the Kettle River country northwest of Spokane, Ranald MacDonald died in 1894. His last word, according to his niece, Mrs. Jerry Lynch, who was still alive when Nard Jones's book *Evergreen Land* was published in 1947, was the Japanese expression for farewell: "Sayonara." Jones adds:

> We need not merely speculate on the growth of New World knowledge imparted to those fourteen pupils of Ranald MacDonald. There is in existence a letter written by a Japanese

Bill Gulick Photo

EARLY–DAY CHURCH IN NAHCOTTA

to a Canadian friend in 1888. It says that MacDonald's teaching was "needed very badly" and that the fourteen scholars made themselves valuable when Japan became more involved with the world. They helped the Japanese people, the letter says, "to better prepare ourselves to formulate the future plan of our national course."

FORT COLUMBIA

Purchased as a military reservation in 1867, Chinook Point was said to have been the favorite spot from which Chief Comcomly, who died in 1831, viewed the domain he first called his own, then came to share with the white newcomers, whom he genuinely liked. Over the years, the guns and mines installed as part of the lower river's defense system were updated and modernized, but none were ever fired in anger. Taken over by the Washington State Parks system as a Heritage Site, Fort Columbia today contains a number of items of historic interest.

These include an interpretive center, an Enlisted Men's Barracks set up as it was for the Coast Guard Artillery in 1902, the former commandant's quarters, diagrams of an eight-inch battery and a mining casemate completed in 1898, a replica of the newspaper office of the *Chinook Observer* (which is still being published) as it was at the turn of the century, and the former Coast Artillery Hospital, which is now operated as a Youth Hostel. An AYH approved facility, the Youth Hostel provides traveling members with a place to wash, cook, sleep, and make friends for a nominal fee.

PACIFIC COUNTY MURALOGUE

One of the more pleasant visual delights growing out of the Washington State Centennial observance in 1989 was the idea of turning otherwise unattractive building walls into canvases for historic murals. Not only was the notion enthusiastically adopted in the lower Columbia River area, but the county has enlisted the talents of thirteen different artists whose colorful, eye-catching works now boldly adorn the formerly dull walls of eighteen buildings in half a dozen coastal and river communities.

Depicting such subjects as clam-digging, steamboating, logging, and early–day railroading, the murals have been done by professional regional artists with a high degree of skill. A color brochure showing the murals and their locations is available at the Ilwaco Heritage Museum.

ILWACO HERITAGE MUSEUM

To many people living in eastern Washington, the town of Ilwaco—like Westport fifty miles to the north—is just a point of departure for sports salmon-fishing cruises across the bar or outside the bay. Plenty of that still goes on in Ilwaco, but for the person not eager to rise and shine at four a.m. and risk the perils of weather and choppy seas outside the bar in the pursuit of sometimes fickle Chinook or Coho salmon, a full day beginning at a more reasonable hour may be spent viewing the treasures of the truly excellent local historical museums, interpretive centers, and exhibits of Chinook Indian arts and crafts.

Before contact with European peoples, the original Americans existed here in an area of lush growth and abundant wildlife. In the museum, the Native American Room shows some of the ways the resources were used to furnish clothing, housing, food, medicine, canoes and all the other necessities of life. An overlay map shows the original look of the terrain and the changes brought to it by the construction of the Columbia River jetties.

Further on, the Discovery and Exploration Gallery displays many of the navigational instruments and maps used to chart the first explorations of the Northwest Coast. Flags, maps, and pictures of the four nations involved—Spain, Russia, England, and the United States—emphasize the scope of the competition for fur and territory, raising interesting speculation as to the reasons why the United States was victorious.

The Development Room displays the results of the exploitation of the region's natural resources, which, for the first hundred years, was thought to be synonymous with progress. This includes logging, farming, and methods of fishing no longer used—such as horse-seining, trap fishing, and the use of fishwheels.

For the railroad buff, the gem of the Ilwaco Heritage Museum is a fifty–foot long model of the "Railroad that Ran With the Tides." Playing with the toy train which travels through a replica of the Long Beach Peninsula, built to a scale of 1/16" per foot, is a pleasure not likely to be resisted by any person between the age of three and ninety-three. Push a button and the little train runs the twenty-five simulated miles to Oysterville and back. Since one of its nicknames was the "Irregular, Rambling & Never Get There Railroad," its simulated run no doubt is much faster and more dependable than the original ever was.

CHINOOK TURKEY—TEN CENTS A POUND

If ever a natural food resource could justifiably be called "inexhaustible," the runs of chinook salmon in the lower Columbia River at the turn of the century qualified for the term. Proof of that would be demonstrated to a stranger visiting the area by sight of big draft horses apparently walking on water some distance offshore on the Washington side of the river as they harvested a bountiful harvest of what native white people called "chinook turkey."

Actually, the horses were walking on Desdemona Sands or Sand Island, where the water was only two or three feet deep; the task at which they labored was pulling in long seines filled with huge, fat salmon. From time immemorial, the local Indians had used nets made of fiber to pull in fish. But the white men's drag seines were six times longer, much more efficient, and capable of producing a surplus of fish for distant markets. In Boston, for example, Columbia River salmon sold for ten cents a pound. Even

Courtesy Ilwaco Heritage Museum
WRECK OFF THE LONG BEACH COAST

at that price, a substantial profit was made all along the line, for when a prime fish weighing fifty to seventy pounds first was pulled out of the river and delivered to the cannery, its usual selling price was from thirty to seventy-five cents per fish.

In horse-seining, the fishermen used a boat to lay the net in the channel up which the big salmon ran, then brought the towline to the driver of the horses, which did the rest. Lucile McDonald says, "Each year some animals drowned when the strong current pulled them into the river beyond their depth."

About sixteen percent of the Columbia River's annual salmon catch was harvested by drag-seining. Because there was no damage to gills, the fish sold for high prices in the frozen-fish and "mild-cure" markets.

> The height of seining was reached in 1926, when this type of gear caught 5,802,069 pounds of salmon. The greatest number of drag seines ever to operate at one time was fifty-seven. As soon as the season was over, the surviving horses were moved from the seining grounds and turned out to pasture for the other eight months of the year. Many showed no ill effects from working season after season.

Courtesy Ilwaco Heritage Museum
WRECK OF THE *ALICE*, JANUARY 15, 1909

Gill nets reached the Columbia by way of fishermen from the east coast, who had learned the technique there. Basically, it consisted of adapting the size of the mesh in the net to the type and size of the fish they wished to catch. At slack water, the salmon were most easily caught, so working hours depended upon the tides. McDonald writes:

> Because the best fishing ground was close to the bar, it was customary to take a station out in the river, let the net run out over the stern at ebb, and drift down toward the mouth. The boats returned on the flood tide. Danger lay in reaching the bar too quickly—or in venturing too far out when the salmon were extra plentiful.
>
> To row a heavily laden twenty-four foot boat against a tide rushing seaward at the rate of eight knots taxed the strength of the fishermen, and accidents occurred constantly. The season of 1880 was an especially unfortunate one, with many scattered drownings and the loss of at least nineteen men in a sudden tragic storm which blew up on the night of May 3–4.

Writing about this same storm, marine historian James Gibbs in his book *Shipwrecks of the Pacific Coast*, gives the much larger figure of 250 vessels and 325 lives lost in this freak storm, which lasted only thirty minutes and whose peak wind velocity reached

100 miles an hour. His figures include the entire Washington and Oregon coast, no doubt, as well as the Columbia River bar, while McDonald's are only for the fishing port of Ilwaco. She gives an interesting sidelight with a happy ending:

> A boatpuller, presumed dead, reappeared a year later, having been picked up outside the bar by a vessel bound for Australia. He was carried to the South Pacific and found his way back as a sailor on another ship.

In 1881, five hundred gill-net boats were fishing between Astoria and the bar. With many of them bringing in a hundred big salmon a day, cannery facilities became so overloaded and cans so scarce that the price dropped to a low of thirty cents a fish. Even this bargain could be beaten if the thrifty housewife met a local Indian who had a good day; if he and the people in his village needed no more salmon to eat fresh, dry, or smoke, he would sell a prime fish to an old customer for a dime—if she were a person who had treated him well in time past.

FISH TRAPS

An even greater threat to the salmon run reached the lower river in 1879 when an invention called the fish-trap was imported from the Great Lakes area. By means of wings built out into the river from islands or the shore, upstream–bound fish were induced to swim into an ever-narrowing funnel at whose heart the fish were finally bunched, lifted, and dumped into a cannery pickup boat. Eliminating the hard work and danger of seining and gill-netting, this made the fish do all the work while the cannery reaped the profit.

It also made horse-seiners and gill-netters very mad, for they felt they held prior rights to the fish harvest of the lower river. By 1900, an estimated five hundred fish traps had been installed on the lower river, usurping areas at the choice locations where the gill-netters had formerly worked. Inevitably, this led to violence, with the gill-netters destroying the fish-traps under cover of darkness, the fish-trap owners putting guards near their traps, and the gill-netters then terrorizing the watchmen. McDonald writes:

> Many gill-netters lived in Ilwaco, and the town's rough reputation grew out of their part in the gill-net wars, which lasted from 1884 well into the 1900s. Among the first of the episodes was an attack on a watchman named Miller, who was employed on

Fred Colbert's piledriver. Colbert, a Swede, had arrived on the Lower Columbia in 1866. Miller, recently from Kansas, was terribly frightened one night when the gill-netters boarded the fish-trap, put a rope around his neck, and threatened to hang him from the gins—the big rigs that held the driver.

Miller talked them out of hanging him but they took him in a gill-net boat to a freight scow moored near Sand Island, saying they were shanghaiing him. The scow had two large masts, and in the darkness Miller was convinced it was a ship and that his assailants really were intent on the nefarious business which thrived on Astoria's waterfront.

Dumping him on the scow, the gill-netters returned to destroy the fish-trap Miller had been hired to guard, but by that time he was interested only in his own fate. When the master of the scow came up to see what the commotion was all about, Miller demanded the name and destination of the ship he was on; when told it was only a scow and going nowhere, the Kansas–raised landlubber expressed heartfelt relief at finding he was not destined to take a long sea voyage. But for as long as he lived in the area, he never went out on the water again.

In addition to the conflict between gill-netters and fish-trap owners, a dispute between canneries offering only four cents a pound for prime salmon and commercial fishermen demanding five cents became so serious that the Washington State National Guard was ordered to Ilwaco by Governor McGraw. McDonald writes:

> Three forts were set up on Sand Island, the two outer ones being nicknamed Finstopper and Starvation....Another outpost, dubbed Paradise, was established close to Chinook, where the striking trapmen lived.

Because this was at the time of the ownership dispute over Sand Island, which for several years had been gradually moving from the Oregon to the Washington side of the river, the right of the Washington National Guard to patrol Oregon territory became a ticklish matter. Further complications involved the federal forts established on either shore and the status of the Columbia as a navigable river whose waters could not be denied to vessels of any state or friendly nation. McDonald writes:

> A schooner-rigged boat, the *Pathfinder*, equipped with steel plates, loopholes in the bulwarks, and steam power for drawing piles, was employed several times by the fishermen in commit-

ting depredations along the river...While Ilwaco escaped casualties, it was estimated that at least twenty persons lost their lives
elsewhere on the river during the season's trap war.

Because of real and threatened violence during the strike in
1896, Oregon had to call out a full regiment of infantry and a light
battery on June 16. Long after the strike was finally settled by a
secret union ballot on June 21, the year was remembered as a season of lawlessness on the lower river.

Along the north shore near the small settlement of Chinook,
most of whose seven hundred residents depended on fishing for
a living, traps became so abundant that there was barely room for
steamships to enter the channel.

"On the first day of the big July, 1901, run, an owner of five
traps took ten thousand pounds of salmon," McDonald writes.
"The figure rose to twelve thousand pounds on the fifth day. His
average daily haul brought him five hundred dollars that season.
The fish were likened to free gold; as soon as a salmon was lifted
from the water it turned into coin on the spot."

FISH WHEELS

Still another device used to harvest salmon with little effort was
the fish-wheel. Built on the same principle as the mill-wheel, a
series of buckets scooped up the fish as they swam upstream in
the narrow channel into which they had been guided, then
dumped them into a barge which took them to the cannery.
Because a fish-wheel required river current to turn it, most of
them were located far enough up the Columbia so that they
would not be affected by the ebb and flow of the tides.

That harvesting so many salmon by such efficient means
might eventually affect the annual runs did not seem to occur to
anyone in the business nor to the publishers of newspapers in the
area. In 1900 the editor of the Chinook *Observer* wrote that nothing could stop the salmon from coming into the river.

"As long as salmon run and there are stomachs to feed," he
said, "the Columbia River fishermen will have a mine of wealth
far surpassing in intrinsic value any gold mine on earth."

Ownership of Sand Island finally was settled in 1908, when
the United States Supreme Court awarded it to Oregon. But jurisdiction over the land remained the function of the federal government, which leased trap sites to the highest bidder. Gradually

Courtesy Ilwaco Heritage Museum
THE CLAMSHELL RAILROAD

over the years the use of fish wheels, horse-seines, and fish traps was outlawed, being banned by Washington in 1935 and by Oregon in 1948.

Gill-nets remained legal, though of recent years commercial fishermen are limited as to the number of days they can fish each season in order to help preserve diminishing runs. As any shopper knows, salmon no longer may be purchased in Boston—or anywhere else—for ten cents a pound. Truth is, sports fishing for salmon out of Ilwaco, Westport, or other Pacific Northwest ports has become so popular that a chinook or coho salmon caught off a private or charter boat is considered a bargain at $25 a pound.

Which is a far cry from the day when the thrifty housewife could buy a fifty-pound fish from a friendly Indian for a dime simply because she had treated him well.

WILLAPA BAY: THE GREAT OYSTER RUSH

Just as the promise of gold lured men to California by the thousands beginning in 1849, so did the appeal of other kinds of riches draw men west to Oregon and Washington shortly thereafter. Good farm and range land, plentiful timber, unlimited salmon—these were a few of the treasures offered newcomers in apparently inexhaustible quantities by the Promised Land. Over the years, story, song, stage, and screen have eulogized all these subjects. But to date no writer, songmaker, dramatist, or movie producer has immortalized the epic tale of what was for a time the most colorful story of all—the pursuit of that gem of all seafoods, the oyster.

For whatever it may be worth, we will synopsize that saga here.

The setting is Willapa Bay, a 110–square mile expanse of saltwater into which the Columbia once disgorged its waters when in flood, bounded on the west by a twenty-five-mile-long spit of land rightly called the longest straight stretch of sandy beach in the United States; on the south, east, and north by low hills containing some of the finest stands of timber in the Pacific Northwest; and flushed twice a day by tides of 7.8 feet which take half the water cradled within the bay out to sea on the ebb then bring it back properly blended with Pacific Ocean water on the flood. Called "Shoalwater Bay" by early explorers who despaired of finding a decent anchorage inside its mouth, its shallow, muddy, sandy bottom has from time immemorial been so full of nutrients that the endless acres of delicious oysters it produced made gold-rich San Francisco gourmets salivate at the mere mention of their name.

As a teaser to the main story, a movie-writer might open his script with a scene of an Oregon–bound wagon train being led by a dead man—the embalmed corpse of seventeen-year-old Willie Keil, whose father, Dr. Wilhelm Keil, had promised his son that he would ride in the lead wagon when the Missouri party of emigrants headed west in May, 1855. Unfortunately, the boy died of malaria before the trek began, but his bereaved father kept his promise. Securing a metal coffin, he preserved the body in alcohol, placed it in the lead wagon, and there it stayed during the entire trip.

When the twenty-four wagons in the train arrived on the shores of Willapa Bay, Dr. Keil and his colony of religious followers found the timber too thick and the climate too damp to suit them, so they decided to go back and settle in the Willamette Valley some twenty miles south of Portland. But before they left the bay area, they completed one sad duty—the interment of Willie Keil, whose body they buried after solemn German prayers and hymns on November 26, 1855. By then, the area had become part of

Courtesy Ilwaco Heritage Museum
WORLD'S BIGGEST FRYING PAN, LONG BEACH CLAM FESTIVAL

Washington Territory. Today, Willie Keil's grave may be found near Menlo, Washington, on State 6, a few miles east of Raymond.

FOUNDING OF BRUCEPORT

Though Chief Nahcati and his tribe of Shoalwater Bay Indians had known for generations that the small, tender, delicious oysters growing so abundantly in the bay were such a taste delight that they could be dried, hung on strings, and used as a means of exchange with other Indians, it took the California Gold Rush to teach them and a few white newcomers from the East Coast that the bivalves literally were worth their weight in gold.

In San Francisco from 1850 on, no banquet worthy of the name was complete without a generous serving of fresh oysters. Those available in the Golden Gate area soon were devoured or destroyed by pollution, but newly-rich prospectors, bankers, and merchants had so much gold to spend on imported delicacies that ship after ship went up the coast to ports in northern California, Oregon, and Washington Territory in search of the precious seafood.

Enter the Bruce boys—eight East Coast fishermen who had pooled their resources in 1851, bought an eighty-two-foot schooner of 129 tons named the *Robert Bruce*, and sailed it to San Francisco in hopes of making their fortune. Failing in that effort, they observed the greed of the gold-rich gluttons for oysters, sailed their ship north, and discovered Willapa Bay. At that time, only the local Indians harvested oysters, for, other than a single white man named Bill McCarty, no one but Indians lived in the area. McCarty's interest was in trees, which he laboriously cut down, trimmed, cut into lengths for piling, and sawed into usable lumber to be sold to the infrequent ships looking for cargo that now and then found their way into the hazardous bay.

Whether or not the eight Bruce boys (who were not related and not named Bruce) were looking for oysters or discovered them by accident is a moot point—made "mooter," to coin a word, because the anchorage found by the *Robert Bruce* toward the east side of Willapa Bay proved to be its final resting place. Blame for this lay on an unhappy cook named Jefferson. Whether this was his last or first name, where he came from, and where he went, all are mysteries to which there are no clues. But the statement that he was unhappy seems verifiable enough, judging from his actions. Which were to drug the eight owners of the ship, set it on fire, hop into a boat and row ashore—never to be seen or heard from again.

Exactly why he was unhappy has never been determined, but it seems to have stemmed from the fact that with eight owners aboard to give orders and only one underling to carry them out, Jefferson felt picked on. Growing increasingly resentful during the voyage north from San Francisco, he expressed his feelings by physically attacking the ship's captain, an act of mutiny brought to an abrupt end by the use of a belaying pin in the hands of one of the partners, who knocked him unconscious. Being the only cook aboard, his promise to behave more reasonably in the future was enough to secure his release from irons, following which he resumed his culinary duties.

A couple of days after the ship anchored, the eight Bruce boys went ashore on a hunting expedition, telling the cook they would be back late that afternoon, at which time they expected him to have supper ready. They told him, "Make sure the coffee is hot this time."

"It will be," he mumbled. "Plenty hot."

When the partners returned from their trek ashore and sat down to supper, the coffee was hot, all right. It was also well laced with laudanum—an opium derivative used for painkilling in those days—which the cook had found in the ship's medicine chest. Soon the eight partners lost their appetite for food, laid their heads on the table, and fell into a deep sleep. Loading a carpetbag with a few necessities, cook Jefferson lowered a boat, hopped in, and rowed ashore in the growing dusk, having left behind a bundle of oil-soaked rags which he had set afire.

Switch the scene now to the cabin of the erstwhile logger, piling-fabricator, lumber-miller named Bill McCarty. As he is about to sit down and eat his self-cooked meal, he smells smoke, goes to the door of his cabin, and sees an unusually thick column of smoke rising from the deck of the *Robert Bruce*. Apparently, the cook (who we assume he has met) has left something on the galley stove too long and has scorched it. Well, McCarty muses, the Bruce boys told me they've been having trouble with their cook. Bet they'll peel his hide good for this, once he puts the fire out and serves them a plate of blackened biscuits.

The column of smoke grows larger. Now McCarty can see tongues of flame licking at the deck. Concerned, he gets into his boat, rows out to the *Robert Bruce*, and climbs aboard. Finding the eight drugged men in the smoke-filled cabin, he shakes them awake. When their stupefied efforts to put out the fire are thwarted by the foresight of the arsonist cook, who has thrown all the buckets and other utensils that can hold water overboard before jumping ship, they lower a boat with McCarty's help and row ashore, where they stand and watch helplessly as the ship in which they have invested their all burns to the waterline and sinks.

Shortly thereafter, the eight partners put their mutual heads together and deduce: (1) Willapa Bay raises millions of delicious oysters; (2) San Francisco–based ships sailing into the bay will pay good prices for such a valuable cargo; (3) the local Indians will work cheap harvesting the oysters; and (4) this is a business that the eight partners know well. So with McCarty's help and lumber, they build a couple of oyster-gathering boats and a seafood-producing establishment on the northeast shore of Willapa Bay and begin to make their fortune. Appropriately enough, they call the village "Bruceport."

Courtesy Ilwaco Heritage Museum
SHIP *CAOBO* GROUNDED NEAR OCEAN PARK, FEBRUARY 5, 1945

"In 1853," writes Willard R. Espy, whose grandfather became a fierce rival to the Bruce boys in the oyster business, "a peach basket filled with oysters from Shoalwater Bay brought a dollar in gold on delivery to the schooner, which might hold up to 2,000 baskets. The basket brought $10 on arrival in San Francisco; epicures there would pay a silver dollar for an oyster smaller than the dollar."

FOUNDING OF OYSTERVILLE

Robert Hamilton Espy, the rugged frontiersman who became a stubborn competitor to the Bruce boys in the oyster business, came out the Oregon Trail in a wagon train in 1852. Getting into logging as a way of acquiring a little capital, he at first rounded up stray drift logs, made them into rafts, and "kedged" them across the lower Columbia to Astoria, where he sold them to the sawmill. This was cold, wet, brutally hard work, for it required using currents, tides, and muscle power in a rowboat towing heavy bundles of logs in the direction he wanted them to go.

Meeting and making friends with several of the Bruce boys over the poker table—a game they all enjoyed and played for blood—Espy noted their business success and informed them that he was interested in trading some of his logs for a set of oyster tongs. At that point, friendship ended. The Bruce boys made it clear they wanted no competition.

Courtesy Ilwaco Heritage Museum
TRAIN OFF THE MEGLER FERRY NEAR ILWACO

With typical frontier independence, Espy said it didn't matter a damn to him what they did or did not want, he was going into the oyster business anyway.

Which he did.

Thus began the Great Oyster War of Willapa Bay.

Though the two hundred and fifty Indians living around Willapa Bay were willing to gather oysters for any white man who would pay them ten cents a basket for their labors, Chief Nahcati took a special liking to Robert Espy—for no other reason, his grandson wrote years later, than that Grandfather Espy was content to sit day after day in silence while he waited for the chief to speak whatever words of wisdom he might choose to utter. Watching the sunset one evening, the younger Espy writes:

> At last Nahcati muttered a prime bit of information, one he had withheld from all other whites. The peninsula side of Shoalwater Bay, he confided, was lined with mountainous reefs of oysters—oysters far tastier and fatter than those currently making fortunes for the Bruce boys. If grandpa would agree to hire Nahcati's tribe as crew, Nahcati would personally guide him to this ostreal treasure.

Going back to the lower Columbia where he worked all winter and spring kedging enough logs to Astoria to earn the capital needed to go into the oyster business, Robert Espy struck up a friendship with a man named Isaac Clark, who shared his passion for poker and taught him never to bet against a man holding four treys. Heading north with Clark to Willapa Bay through very wet country, Espy found that the log canoe he had cached and supposedly hid last fall, had been found and stolen. So they found and stole one themselves from an Indian graveyard, patched the hole chopped in its bottom to let the evil spirits run out so that when they launched it saltwater would not run in, then rowed, portaged, and rowed some more until they reached what they hoped was the spit just offshore from their destination, Chief Nahcati's village.

By then, a heavy nor'wester had rolled in, the rain was falling so torrentially that visibility was reduced to zero, and the tide was turning. Consequently, there was a very real danger that their unwieldy canoe would be swept past the upper point of Long Beach, whence it and they would be pulled out into the open sea, where they could not possibly survive.

Chief Nahcati saved them. Catching a glimpse of their canoe well out in the bay just before the storm rolled in, he knew there was only one way to guide them to safety—by sound. Hearing a rhythmic booming first to the left, then to the right, then straight ahead as the chief sat patiently beating a spruce knot against a hollow log, the two white men made grateful use of the first foghorn ever to sound on this stretch of coast. After safely reaching shore, they were warmed and fed in Chief Nahcati's lodge, then, the next morning, waded far out in the offshore muck and examined the finest oyster beds they had ever seen in their lives.

Helped by the chief and his friends, they built a cabin, declared all the oyster beds in sight Espy–Clark property, and began to build their empire. One of the first questions that arose was what to name their village.

"We'll call it Espyville," said Mr. Clark.

"We'll do nothing of the sort," snorted Espy. "We'll call it Oysterville."

Oysterville it remains to this day. Nearby is the village of Nahcotta, located on the spot where the chief once lived, though losing something in the translation.

HOSTILITIES BEGIN

Because the oyster beds of the newcomers and the Bruce boys were separated by only a few hundred feet of water, it was

Courtesy Ilwaco Heritage Museum
ROOTS OF A FALLEN GIANT NEAR LONG BEACH *CA* 1900

inevitable that disputes over territory would ensue. Time after time, holes were punched in the bottoms of canoes owned by the Espy–Clark enterprise—probably by the Bruce boys, though nobody witnessed the acts of vandalism nor could any local authority prevent or punish them, for such an authority did not exist. All the Oysterville entrepreneurs could do was patch their canoes and try again.

One morning in May a San Francisco–based ship eager to pick up a load of oysters rounded Leadbetter Point, sailed into the bay, and dropped anchor. Immediately, hordes of canoes filled with fresh bivalves headed for the ship from both shores. Meeting in the middle of the bay, the dugouts collided, oars were swung, men grappled with one another, and fell overboard—which put them in no great danger, for the water was only waist deep and calm. Meantime, the crew aboard the ship lined its rails and cheered the combatants on to greater effort, enjoying the entertainment.

Having the advantage of superior numbers, the Bruce boys won, dumped the oysters carried by the Espy–Clark contingent into the bay, and sold theirs to the owner of the ship for a good

Courtesy Ilwaco Heritage Museum
THE WORLD'S BIGGEST CLAM FRY, LONG BEACH

price. Next day, the Oysterville people were back again with reinforcements and more oysters. So were the Bruceport battlers.
Again, Bruceport won and Oysterville was forced to retreat.

"At this point, grandpa had three choices," Willard Espy
writes. "He could have abandoned his dream of an oyster empire,
and returned to logging. He could have struck a bargain with the
Bruce boys to serve as their hired man on the peninsula side of the
bay. Or he could have continued to fight."

Not even considering the first two choices, Robert Espy
decided to fight. Expert poker player that he was, he probed for a
weakness in the Bruce boys' armor, found it, and undertook to
exploit it. The weakness was their use of Indian canoes to gather
oysters, as he was doing. If he could obtain a bigger boat built
specifically for oyster-gathering, he and Chief Nahcati's Indians
could collect two baskets of Willapa Bay oysters while the Bruce
boys were gathering one.

Pretending to give up the business, he traveled overland to
Grays Harbor, ten miles north, where he spent a few of his precious gold pieces to hire a man named "Dad" Simmons to build
him a "clinker" or "lapstruck" boat with twice the capacity of the

Bill Gulick Photo

MARINA AT WESTPORT

largest Bruce boys canoes. Twenty-two feet long, flat-bottomed, without a keel, looking more like the side of a clapboard house than a boat, it was just the utilitarian type of vessel he needed to beat the Bruce boys in Willapa Bay at their own game. But after working two months with Dad Simmons to build the boat, he now faced the problem of getting the unwieldy craft from Montesano on the east side of Grays Harbor to Willapa Bay.

Being young, strong, and energetic, he used brute strength and skills learned kedging log rafts on the lower Columbia to solve the problem. Hiring two Shoalwater Bay Indians to help him tow the new boat across Grays Harbor and out to the open sea, he and his helpers waded as far out into the breakers as they dared and literally walked the heavy craft down the coast ten miles to the mouth of Willapa Bay.

"Each time a breaker receded, drawing the boat seaward," Willard Espy writes, "Grandpa and the Indians dogtrotted along the beach, keeping the line taut until the next incoming wave pushed the boat shoreward again. These maneuvers sometimes required that the three men wade a hundred yards offshore, surf

Courtesy Columbia River Maritime Museum, Astoria Oregon
WRECK OF THE FRENCH SHIP *ALICE*
The shipwreck occurred near Ocean Park, January, 1909.

breaking as high as their throats, never sure their next step might not be into a drowning hole between sandspits."

For those people not familiar with this stretch of the Washington coast, it should be pointed out—as it repeatedly is by local tourist promoters—that at no time of day or year is it safe to swim or surfboard off Long Beach. Rolling in across thousands of miles of open ocean, the Pacific strikes and recoils off long reaches of shore with such force that murderous riptides make swimming and surfboarding an extremely dangerous sport. Of course Robert Espy and his two Indian helpers were not engaged in sport; they were in business.

Reaching Leadbetter Bar and rowing the clinker-built boat into the bay on an incoming tide, the three men were surrounded

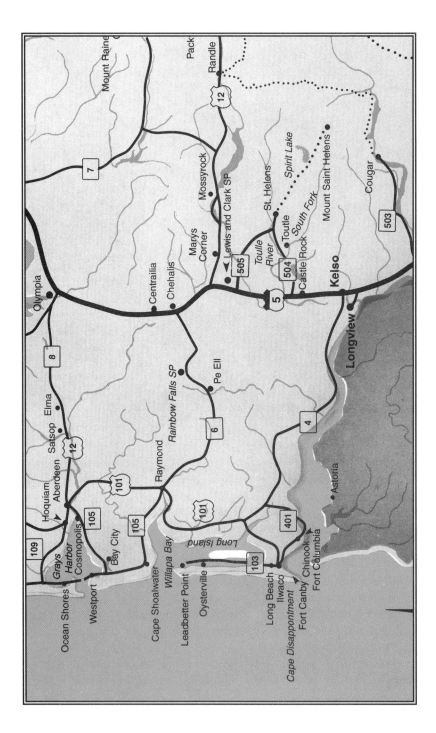

by dozens of Indian canoes, welcomed back as returning heroes. *Now* they would show the Bruce boys how to gather oysters!

Christening the new craft *Stuffy* for some unexplained reason, the Oysterville partners did show the Bruce boys a few things for week or two. Then one dark night *Stuffy* slipped her moorings— only to show up next day as part of the Bruceport oyster fleet. With no law to appeal to and outmanned by their unscrupulous competitors, Robert Espy, Isaac Clark, and Chief Nahcati decided that another temporary retreat was the best strategy.

"Grandpa let it be known that he was giving up and going back to the felling of trees for pilings. Isaac Clark announced that he, too, would depart at the end of the oyster season. Defeatism darker than the daily rain clouds settled over Oysterville. When the white settlers woke up one morning to find Grandpa gone, most of them lost little time in going too."

But Espy had gone only as far as Montesano, where he used the last of his savings to commission the building of a new clinker boat much larger than the *Stuffy*. When he made a triumphant return in it a few months later, the Bruce boys reluctantly accepted the fact that he was not going to give up. Following a series of peace conferences, an agreement was made.

"The Bruce boys would no longer interfere with Grandpa and Clark; Grandpa and Clark would not interfere with the Bruce boys; and both parties would work together to prevent any incursion by other oystermen."

The Great Oyster War was over.

THE CLAMSHELL RAILROAD

Among its many other names—most of which were affectionately derogatory—the narrow-gauge railroad built from Ilwaco north to Nahcotta in 1888 was most often called "The Railroad that Ran With the Tides." The reason for this was that boats carrying people, horses, wagons, and automobiles across the Columbia from Astoria could reach the Ilwaco dock only at mid-flood on the tide. Since this occurred twice a day at intervals that

State 6—Raymond to Chehalis
51 miles

Courtesy Columbia River Maritime Museum, Astoria, Oregon
WRECK OF THE SS *LAUREL*, 1929

grew fifty minutes later each day, train departure schedules had to be changed daily to suit them.

Living by the sea as they did, local people had no problem with this. But to outlanders, it was a strange way to run a railroad.

Despite its name, the railroad was not built on a clam or oyster shells, though it could truthfully be said that clams and oysters did build the railroad. Financed by the Ilwaco Railway & Navigation Co., one of its nicknames used the first letters of those words, calling it "The Irregular, Rambling, and Never-get-there Railroad." It was also called "The Delay, Linger, and Wait Railroad." But by any name, it served its customers well and was so beloved by them that when it finally ceased operations in 1930, a mourning wreath was hung on the locomotive, beach residents filled its coaches for the last run, and then bought the red-plush seats they had sat on to put in places of honor on the front porches of their cottages.

Even big-city people from Portland noted the railroad's impact on resort business and the value of local property, for, in its first year of operation, 1888, the price of beachfront land soared from ten to two hundred dollars an acre.

THE MISUNDERSTOOD OYSTER

Though it may be doubted that the native Americans who had lived in the area for thousands of years consciously practiced conservation, they certainly knew enough about its principles to let Mother Nature alone so that she could reproduce her seafood

Courtesy Columbia River Maritime Museum, Astoria, Oregon
GRAYS HARBOR LIFEBOAT STATION

bounty year after year. This proved to be more than the white man knew, for by 1881 the small, delicious native oyster species called *ostrea lurida* was well on its way toward extinction.

Blame for this was placed by the local oyster shippers on natural causes such as cold winters, pests, red tides, and eelgrass, but it more rightly belonged on the intensive inroads they themselves had made on the beds by stripping them clean year after year, then moving on and finding new areas to deplete. Even worse was their lack of understanding of how oysters were seeded and grew. Lucile McDonald writes:

> Since oysters were sent away in entirety, no shells were returned to the beds to serve as cultch for a new crop...Millions of eggs could be produced by a few parent oysters, but their instinct to attach themselves to solid objects such as mature shells was defeated by the lack of shells.

Even after learning this basic lesson and bringing carloads of seed oysters from the Atlantic coast by rail between 1890 and 1929, the oystermen went through the same cycle of plant, harvest, ship out the whole shell, then watch the beds become depleted again. At last, in 1931, the localities learned their lesson one

Courtesy Columbia River Maritime Museum, Astoria, Oregon
TUG *DANIEL KERN* HAULING ROCKS FOR RIVER MOUTH JETTIES

final time from the Japanese, when large shipments of Oriental seed-oysters were imported. McDonald writes:

> The spat arrives in the form of boxes of broken oyster shells, each of which has a set of ten or more infants which have cemented themselves to the shells. Because nature has given them the ability to acquire a hard, protective coating when no food is available, they sustain little injury on a fast voyage from Japan. Once in the water, they resume normal growth.

Copying many of the methods of the Japanese, such as piercing shells and stringing a hundred or more of them on a wire so that they can catch the free-floating eggs, be fertilized, and begin growing as spat, the Willapa Bay oyster industry began to revive, became healthy again, and remains so today. But the growers keep one basic rule in mind: Mother Nature makes the rules, while human beings just play the game.

Back in 1880, a man named John Pike and his partner James Holman came close to violating those rules when they proposed and actually started digging a canal between the lower end of Willapa Bay and the Columbia River near Ilwaco. Their idea was

Courtesy Columbia River Maritime Museum, Astoria, Oregon
WRECK OF THE *ADMIRAL BENSON* ON PEACOCK SPIT

that such a canal would be an ideal way to transport oysters, logs, lumber, and other products from the saltwater bay to the freshwater river. That ecological disaster might result from this artificial blending of salt and fresh water never entered their minds.

Indeed, even in recent years grandiose projects such as digging a ship canal from the eastern end of Grays Harbor to the southern end of Puget Sound or of taking fresh water out of the lower Columbia and transporting it by means of a massive conduit to thirsty southern California have been proposed by supposedly intelligent men, without proper consideration of the consequences. Fortunately, they—like the earlier canal project—have not gotten beyond the talking stage.

WILDLIFE REFUGES

Since Chief Nahcati and the Shoalwater Indians first welcomed the white oystermen in the early 1850s, many changes have taken place on land and water in the Willapa Bay area. But for people interested in seeing what the region looked like before the white man came, two small, special areas have been preserved.

Courtesy Columbia River Maritime Museum, Astoria, Oregon
COAST GUARD MOTOR LIFEBOAT IN THE SURF

One is on the northernmost extremity of the Long Beach Peninsula, Leadbetter Point, which has been set aside as a state park and a refuge to innumerable waterfowl and animals. Accurately described by a local guide article:

> It's a nature lover's paradise, known to ornithologists as at least a stopover for as many as 100 species of birds. Hiking trails abound and can be reached from parking areas, although the road leading to the park can be bumpy at times. Caution by motorists is advised.

During the April to August nesting season for shorebirds such as the snowy plover, parts of the area are closed to foot traffic. It is wise to bring along mosquito repellent and to wear rubber boots, for the muck loved by nesting seabirds and the brackish pools cherished by mosquitos are not as friendly to non–feathered humans.

The second unique area in Willapa Bay is Long Island, where a 274–acre grove of red cedar has been preserved as one of the last remaining examples of a "climax" forest. In forestry technology, vegetation left alone in a primitive area progresses grass by grass,

Courtesy Columbia River Maritime Museum, Astoria, Oregon
COLUMBIA RIVER JETTY

bush by bush, and then tree by tree over a period of several thousand years, during which one species after another lives, dies, and
is succeeded by the next, until at last the final or "climax" species
has its chance to generate, grow to maturity, and at last die itself—
following which the cycle presumably will start all over again.

The word "presumably" is used because the red cedar now
growing on Willapa Bay's Long Island is the climax species of a
forest that first sprouted during a dramatic West Coast climate
change that occurred approximately 4,000 years ago; so man can
only guess at what will happen next. The cedars in this grove run
from five to eleven feet in diameter and average 150 to 160 feet in
height. Sprouting out of the fallen and decayed trunks of
"younger" trees such as Douglas fir, which died after only 750
years of life, some of the red cedars are estimated to be over one
thousand years old.

Though selective logging is permitted on other parts of Long
Island, the trees in this red cedar grove will never be cut, says the
official guide to the area:

> The grove is just one small part of the 4,700–acre island man-
> aged by the Wildlife Service. Persons wishing to visit the island

Courtesy Ilwaco Heritage Museum
LOGGING CAMP NEAR LONG BEACH, 1920s

must provide their own boat to traverse an approximate 100–yard-wide channel from the boat launch at the refuge head-quarters on US 101, or launch at the Nahcotta Boat Basin for a crossing of approximately one mile.

To reach the grove, visitors must hike 2.5 miles along the island's main road after tying up their boat.

Like most wilderness experiences for those so inclined, the rewards are well worth the effort.

OLD GROWTH PARKS

Though there were a number of open prairies in southwest Washington Territory when the first white settlers arrived, with logging confined to the slopes of the Cascades to the east and the low coastal hills to the west, a few remnants of the ancient forest that once covered this part of the state have been preserved.

One is in Rainbow Falls State Park, sixteen miles west of Chehalis on State 6, where a 120–acre expanse of old-growth trees still stands on the Chehalis River. Five miles of foot-trails wind through the park in a forest wilderness that seems far removed from city and highway traffic, including a 200–foot long cable footbridge suspended over the river near the falls.

Five miles to the west is the once-thriving logging town of Pe Ell, whose intriguing name stemmed from the fact that its first white settler meant to call it "Pierre," but the Indians—who had trouble pronouncing *r* —somehow managed to get its first permanent resident, a man named Omar Maurman, to register their version of the name with the postal authorities. How the Indians would have pronounced his name has not been recorded.

Just south of Mary's Corner off I–5, Lewis and Clark State Park provides a forest area of 518 acres containing tall fir trees over five hundred years old and a number of cool, shaded hiking trails for persons desiring a feel of the country as it once was.

MOUNT SAINT HELENS

For the traveler interested in seeing the site of the mountain that blew apart in 1980 (which will be covered in detail in the next section of this book), Exit 49 leads east off the freeway five miles to the Mount Saint Helens Volcano Visitor Center, where free maps and information regarding the best way to see this truly unique area may be obtained.

Because half a dozen roads lead into it from all sides and there is a great deal to see on all of them, a study of the scale model in the Visitor Center and a few minutes spent viewing movies and slide shows of the eruption will give the traveler a much better understanding of what there is to see and how best to budget one's time to see it.

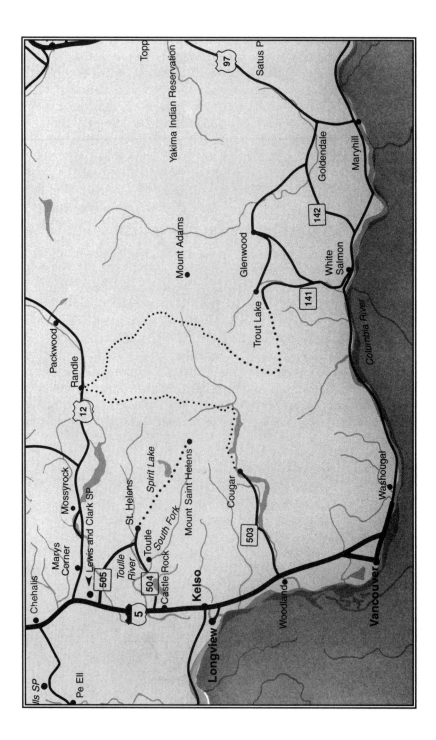

PART FOUR

Cascade Mountains

MOUNT SAINT HELENS

People beginning their tour of the site of the mountain that exploded so dramatically May 18, 1980, usually stop at the Mount Saint Helens Visitor Center, where their most-asked question is, "Will it happen again?"

"Yes," is the quick, firm answer.

This brings on their next question, "When?"

Again, the answer is quick and firm. "We don't know."

Which sums up all the experts know about past and future behavior of volcanoes in the Cascade Range—or anywhere else in the world, for that matter. They know volcanoes have erupted in time past and will do so in the future, but with those two facts their certainty ends.

State 504—Volcano Center
    5 miles
State 504—Coldwater Ridge
    43 miles
State 503—Cougar, Windy Ridge, Randle
    95 miles
State 141—Trout Lake, Windy Ridge, Randle
    110 miles
US 12—Mossyrock, Randle, Windy Ridge
    75 miles

From a painting by John Mix Stanley, Courtesy Penrose Library, Whitman College
THE DALLES AND MOUNT SAINT HELENS

To laymen without a geological background, understanding the role played by volcanoes in changing the surface of the earth is difficult for two reasons: time and human perspective. Only geologists can perceive time in terms of millions of years; only they can imagine this earth of ours when no human beings were present to witness and record what was happening on it.

During the brief course of man's history on the planet, no more than a dozen major volcanic eruptions have occurred when people were around to witness them. Only half a dozen took place in this century.

But the Mount Saint Helens eruption was exceptional in that, from beginning to end, it was a media event with a huge audience. Human beings whom we all had come to know were at risk—and some of them died. Rumblings that began months before the final explosion were so well recorded and publicized that few people in the civilized world were not made aware of what happened before, during, and after the climactic blowout, which the experts have rated as being the equivalent of from 21,000 to 27,000 atomic bombs.

Courtesy Penrose Library, Whitman College
PORTAGE RAILROAD AROUND THE CASCADES, ABOUT 1865

Today, the best way to learn how and why it happened is to take Exit 49 off I–5 at Castle Rock, drive east five miles on State 504, and spend some time at the Visitor Center. Here, you may examine a scale model of the affected region, see slide shows and movies of what happened, ask questions of helpful experts, and acquire free maps showing how best to see the area today.

HISTORY OF MOUNT SAINT HELENS

The Cascade Mountains are part of what is aptly called the "Pacific Rim of Fire," the chain of mountains running from the tip of South America north to Alaska, across Bering Strait, then down through Japan, Java, and Indonesia.

Before the white man came, the Klickitat Indians, who knew this section of the Cascade Range better than any other tribe, called the youthful volcano *Tah-one-lath-clah*—or "Fire Mountain." According to Indian legend, two handsome young chiefs living on opposite sides of the Columbia River fell in love with a beautiful, shapely young maiden, whose duty was to tend the fire in the middle of a natural bridge of rock spanning the river. But as young chiefs will do, the two men got to quarreling over the

Courtesy Penrose Library, Whitman College
"OREGON PONY," 1862
The locomotive pulled portage cars at the Cascades.

maiden, tore up and threw increasingly bigger rocks at each other, until their father grew tired of their squabble, heaved the biggest rock of all, and collapsed the natural bridge across the Columbia into the depths of the river.

As a lasting memorial to the three lovers, he turned the chief on the south side of the river into Mount Hood, the chief on the north side into Mount Adams, and the beautiful maiden who had tended the flame in the middle of the bridge into Mount Saint Helens. Proof of the legend, the Indians said, was that at certain stages of water a person could gaze down into the depths and see trees growing out of the top of the sunken bridge ten or twenty feet under water.

This was before Captain George Vancouver came along in 1792 and named Hood and Saint Helens after high-ranking British naval officers. In the naming game, Mount Adams was part of a grandiose scheme devised by a New England promoter named Hall Jackson Kelley, whose plan to call the Cascades the

BPA Photo, Courtesy Corps of Engineers
BONNEVILLE DAM NEAR SITE OF THE LOWER CASCADES

"Presidents Range" and to name all of its mountains after American presidents got as far as Adams north of the Columbia, Washington and Jefferson south of the river, and then—like so many of his schemes—petered out to the extent that some really respectable mountains in Oregon ended up with quite ordinary names like "North, Middle, and South Sister," "Broken Top," and "Three Fingered Jack."

Ranking twelfth in stature among the Cascade peaks at 9,677 feet, Mount Saint Helens before 1980 was a symmetrical mountain with a perfect cone and a graceful appearance from every direction, often being called the "Fujiyama of America" because of its resemblance to that peak in Japan. Even so, because of its activity since white men first viewed it two hundred years ago, it was at the top of most Pacific Rim volcanologists' lists as the "Mountain Most Likely to Blow Its Top."

Regional environmental writer Rob Carson, whose book *Mount Saint Helens: The Eruption and Recovery of a Volcano* gives an intriguing account of the eruption in 1980 and a perceptive look at the region ten years later in 1990, says that the local Indians were afraid of the mountain and seldom ventured above timberline on its slopes.

Courtesy Ilwaco Heritage Museum

LOGGING THE BIG TREES IN THE EARLY 1900s

Courtesy Ilwaco Heritage Museum

Apparently, the only time tribal members would even go near the mountain was on the occasions of spirit quests. Young men would venture to the tree line, and there, knees shaking and hearts pounding, they would absorb mana from the Great Spirit within.

He says one Klickitat Indian named John Staps was bold enough to lead a party of whites to the summit in 1860 "...and lived the rest of his life in shame for having done so..."

Though geological evidence testifies that Saint Helens has erupted many times during the past, with its last major performance as little as two thousand years, the wandering Canadian artist, Paul Kane, was the first to make a visual record of it when he paused at The Dalles, across the river in Oregon, long enough in 1847 to do a water color showing an Indian village, the river, and the perfect, snow-covered cone of the mountain in the background, with a thin plume of smoke or steam rising above it.

Early–day missionaries such as Samuel Parker and Elkanah Walker, as well as the government explorer, Captain John C. Fremont, also noted that Saint Helens had emitted ash, steam, or smoke between 1831 and 1843, but none of them seemed to realize that the volcanoes in the Pacific Northwest were potentially just as violent as southern Europe's Vesuvius and Etna.

An imaginative writer named Frederick Balch wrote a romantic novel titled *Bridge of the Gods*, published in 1890 and a best-seller for the next ten years, in which he used the Indian legend of the natural bridge across the Columbia and its collapse during a volcanic eruption and earthquake as the central theme of his story. In its climactic scene, an Indian runner, who has covered thirty miles since dawn, arrives in the village of Chief Multnomah in the Willamette Valley and breathlessly announces the tragic news. In the italicized words of the author, *"The Great Spirit has shaken the earth, and the Bridge of the Gods has fallen!"*

To make sure the reader does not miss the importance of those words, the author writes that after a moment of silence, the message is repeated in the tongues of all tribes present. "The Bridge of the Gods has fallen! The Bridge of the Gods has fallen!"

Just as Frederick Balch's romantic novel caught the fancy of the readers ninety years ago, so did the real-life collapse of thirteen hundred feet off the top of Mount Saint Helens capture the attention of a much larger audience, which literally saw it happen, when the earth shook May 18, 1980.

PEOPLE ON THE MOUNTAIN

As noted earlier, only a geologist can appreciate the drama of an earthquake, an eruption, or the shifting of the continental plates which support the surface of the planet. The layman reader of newspaper accounts or the viewer of TV news needs human beings with whom he can identify to understand the impact of a natural catastrophe. In time past, the human beings involved with volcanic eruptions such as Vesuvius or Krakatoa were the nameless dead mummies found in the lava-covered ruins of Pompeii or the equally anonymous 36,000 victims drowned in a tidal wave caused by the explosion of a mountain half a world away.

But in the case of Saint Helens, the victims were people all the readers and viewers felt they knew, for they had several months to get acquainted. Some were loggers working in the "Red Zone" of imminent danger; one was a personable young geologist who risked and lost his life, Dave Johnston; another was an amateur photographer who risked his life and survived, Gary Rosenquist; while others were the fifty or so campers and sightseers who were closest to ground-zero when the mountain exploded, most of whom were identified later.

Best known of all, of course, was Harry R. Truman, the crusty, eighty-three–year-old namesake of the country's equally crusty president during the Korean War, Harry S. Truman.

Born in West Virginia in 1896, the Mount Saint Helens' Harry R. Truman had come to Washington State in 1907, where his mountain-loving parents acquired 160 acres of stump-filled farm land in eastern Lewis County on the Cowlitz River. Claiming he never knew what his middle initial *R* stood for, Truman went to high school in Mossyrock, was trained as an aero-mechanic in World War I, served two years in France, then returned to Chehalis and worked for a few years in a gas and service station "Harry's Sudden Service."

Disliking civilization, he suddenly folded that enterprise in 1926, leased a fifty-acre site on Spirit Lake just below Mount Saint Helens from the Northern Pacific Railroad Company, which owned both the land there and the crest of Saint Helens itself, and started a business renting boats and cabins to sportsmen and vacationers. There he remained for the rest of his life.

Of the many accounts written about Truman, by far the best is the book *Truman of Saint Helens: the Man and His Mountain*, by

SPIRIT LAKE AND MOUNT ST HELENS BEFORE THE 1980 ERUPTION

Shirley Rosen, which was published by Rosebud Press, Bothell, Washington, in 1981. A niece of Truman's wife, Shirley was fourteen years old when she began to work at the Spirit Lake resort in 1948. Returning summer after summer until she married and keeping in close touch with him until the end, she tells us about "Truman" (as he insisted on being called) warts and all.

And warts he certainly had, as his niece reveals with both candor and affection. Like many hill-raised people, Truman lived by his own peculiar code of conduct, resentful of all law and authority, carrying on a perpetual feud with fish and game wardens, the Forest Service, and the "revenooers" who kept trying to catch him distilling and selling illegal moonshine. Exasperated as these same local officials were when they failed to catch him breaking the laws he hated (which they never did), they were among his staunchest friends, for they knew that he poached fish and game only to eat, cut down trees only to use for building purposes, kept his bootlegging within reasonable bounds, and never refused to lend a neighbor in need a helping hand.

When he first came to the area, the only road in from Castle Rock required a spine-shattering drive over forty-six miles of rocky, stump-filled road, bad at any time of year and impassable during winter months because of deep drifts of snow. Typical of the way the few people who lived in the remote area helped one another, Shirley Rosen writes, was what happened following Emil Lange's death in 1933.

Owning a sawmill two miles from Truman's lodge, Lange was a big man, weighing 250 pounds. When he dropped dead of a heart attack, his friends decided that they must carry his body out of the wilderness so that it could be properly buried in a cemetery in the lowlands. Shirley Rosen writes:

> It was a time of another torrential rainstorm and the Toutle at Dry Gulch had turned into a raging river...Four men—Truman, Spirit Lake ranger Harold Samuelson, and Lige Coalman from the nearby Y.M.C.A. camp, and his son, Elrod—carried the corpse across the Toutle, over the hills and down steep trails. "When we returned to Spirit Lake—tired, wet and weary," Coalman wrote in his diary, "we had hiked 40 miles that day, half of it carrying the 250–pound weight of a dead man. But we all felt it was a good service to a fine neighbor and friend."

JUSTICE DOUGLAS TURNED DOWN

As the highway to Spirit Lake improved and more vacationers and sportsmen came in, Truman added a number of cabins, expanded the resort, and did a thriving business renting boats and selling fishing licenses and gear. But whether business was good or bad, he often judged people by their looks, Shirley Rosen writes, sometimes turning down a person who wanted to rent a cabin even when he had a vacancy. Now and then he made a mistake.

> My sister Elaine was on duty in the lodge when the middle-aged man walked in. He was wearing a rumpled suit, his tie was askew, and he had a squashed hat on his head. He looked like just another fisherman to Elaine. Truman, who was sitting by the door in the kitchen, eyed the man with obvious disapproval as he walked around the interior of the lodge.
>
> Truman motioned to Elaine. "Hey, kid," he said, "go out there and tell that old coot that if he wants a cabin, we don't

have any. Tell him we're all full up." Elaine did as she was told. She walked over to the counter and when the man inquired about renting a cabin, she told him all the cabins were taken. She suggested he head down the road to Spirit Lake Lodge. A half-dozen men were sitting at the counter drinking beers and after a few minutes one of them yelled over to Truman, "Hey, Truman, do you know who that was that you just turned away? That was Supreme Court Justice William O. Douglas!"

"I'll be goddamn go to hell!" Truman shouted. He shot out the back door, jumped in his pickup, and sped down the road. By the time he caught up with Douglas, the justice was inside the Spirit Lake Lodge...

Catching him just before he registered, Truman said there had been a mistake, that he did have a room, and that he also had some great horses, in case Douglas wanted to go for a ride. Furthermore, he added, he himself would go along as guide. Loving horses and back-country trails as he did, Justice William O. Douglas accepted the belated offer—and from that day on the two men were the best of friends.

Which surprised no one who knew them, for both men were unique characters. Born and raised in Yakima, Washington, Douglas had graduated from Whitman College in Walla Walla, then had shocked its conservative faculty and alumni by becoming one of the most liberal-minded justices in the Supreme Court. Like Truman, he loved wilderness, solitude, horses, and bourbon, cared nothing for appearances or conventions, and, during the time he served on the high bench, wrote some landmark opinions whose effect was to preserve important wilderness areas. One of these (which I will detail later in this book) preserved a ninety-mile sector of the Snake River in Hells Canyon as a National Recreation Area instead of losing it to a huge hydroelectric dam that would have stilled the free-flowing river forever.

On their first trip up the slopes of Saint Helens, Truman told Douglas with no false modesty, "There ain't no one livin' who knows that ol' mountain and the trails around it better than ol' Truman from the hills of West Virginia."

Many years later when the danger of an eruption became so great that all the people living, working, or camping in the vicinity of Mount Saint Helens were ordered to leave, Justice Douglas probably would have understood better than anyone else why Truman refused to go, saying:

If anything did happen to me, if the mountain did do something, I'd rather go right here with it. If I was down and out of here and lost my home, I wouldn't last a week at my age. I'd have nothing left to live for at all and I'd just double up and die. I couldn't make her and everybody knows that. My old heart would stop—if I've got one. A lot of people say I ain't got no heart.

THE MOUNTAIN BEGINS TO TREMBLE

In late March of 1980, the moving and shaking of Mount Saint Helens made it clear that some sort of eruption was imminent. Like all dramas building up toward a climactic moment, this one had a number of developing crises which would be resolved by a cataclysm of nature. Racing against time, a crew of loggers working for the Weyerhauser Timber Company was struggling with the elements, the state and federal bureaucracies, and a number of increasingly militant environmentalists as they attempted to harvest the last patch of marketable trees on the mountain before their operation was closed down permanently. Their camp was on the South Fork of the Toutle River, twenty-two miles away.

In the Spirit Lake area, over a hundred cabin owners who had been advised to leave were resisting the order with considerable vehemence, for they feared that as soon as they pulled out, vandals would move in. At the nearby Forest Service campground, early spring campers ordered to evacuate were doing so grudgingly. As for Truman himself, he claimed he had half a million dollars invested in his lodge, cabins, boats, and equipment, which ranged from a pink Cadillac to a pickup truck, a Sno-Cat, chainsaws, bulldozers, motorcycles, and a large collection of firearms (including a Thompson sub-machine gun), not to mention an antique player piano, two pinball machines, and sixteen cats. Furthermore, this was his home, holding treasured memories of his beloved wife, who had died five years ago. To him, leaving was out of the question.

Because the threatened eruption would be a rare opportunity to see a volcano in action, experts were moving in on Saint Helens from all parts of the United States, planting their instruments and observation posts as close as possible to the anticipated center of the action. One of these was Dave Johnston, a young USGS geochemist and self-proclaimed volcano junkie, who had been working in the University of Washington geophysics lab interpreting seismic readings. Now he moved into a trailer on the shoulder of the mountain itself, where he could both record and see what was happening.

In Olympia, Governor Dixy Lee Ray, herself a scientist as former head of the nation's Nuclear Energy Commission, admitted to the press that she was excited.

"I've always said for many years that I hoped to live long enough to see one of our volcanoes erupt."

RED ZONE ESTABLISHED

Her duty as governor was to protect the people, of course, so after consultation with the experts she established what was called the "Red Zone" around Mount Saint Helens, beyond whose boundaries unauthorized persons were not permitted to go. But when the mountain spewed steam and ash from a black hole in the snow March 27, 1980, the people went wild.

Sightseers rushed to the mountain. Nearby towns were flooded with volcano-watchers. On Sunday, March 30, 93 small eruptions of steam and ash spurted from the summit during the day. Traffic on Interstate 5 stopped, jamming the main route between Portland and Seattle.

Overhead, the sky buzzed with private planes and helicopters. On March 30, the Federal Aviation Administration counted 70 violations of the five-mile restricted zone it had established around the mountain.

Contrasted to the holiday attitude of sightseers, the comment made by volcano junkie Dave Johnston struck a grim note. "This is like standing next to a dynamite keg and the fuse is lit, but you don't know how long the fuse is. If it exploded, we would die."

Many people regarded the idea of an eruption as a joke. "I wish it would do a big Pompeii bit on us," one excited volcano-watcher in Cougar told a newspaper reporter.

"People went over, under, through, and around every time we tried to restrict access to what we believed were dangerous areas," Skamania County Sheriff William Closner said. "There were even maps sold showing how to get around our blockades on the mountains. People were climbing right up to the rim of the crater. It would have taken the US Army to control those people."

THE MOUNTAIN EXPLODES

Instruments planted on Mount Saint Helens during the the month of April indicated that molten lava was rising inside as pressure

pushed it up through cracks and fissures. By early May, measure-
ments showed that a bulge was forming on the north side of the
mountain, changing its shape. Growing at the rate of five or six
feet a day, sections of that bulge were 450 feet higher than they
had been weeks earlier, showing that the magma still was rising.
Sooner or later, something had to give.

Angry owners of cabins around Spirit Lake demanded that
they be allowed to go into the Red Zone in order to retrieve
belongings and rescue starving pets. Staging a protest at the road-
block, some of them threatened to use guns to force their way in.
Faced with near rebellion, Governor Ray permitted a party of
property owners to go in and retrieve their belongings, after first
insisting that they sign waivers absolving the state from any liability for their safety.

They were accompanied by a phalanx of reporters and pho-
tographers and led by a Washington State Patrol plane. Four
hours later, the property owners drove back down the valley, their
cars loaded with all they could carry. A second caravan was
scheduled for ten o'clock the following morning—May 18.

That same Saturday night, Geologist David Johnston camped
at the Coldwater II observation station, six miles north of the
mountain. Though Johnston was authorized to be close to Saint
Helens, Gary Rosenquist, an amateur photographer, was not.
Even so, Rosenquist was camped at Bear Meadow, ten miles
northeast of the peak, with a party of friends. They had evaded
the roadblocks south of Randle and followed logging roads to a
spot from which they could get an unimpeded view of the peak.

An unemployed taxi driver from Tacoma, Rosenquist was
hoping to get some good shots of the smoking mountain which he
could print and sell to tourists. Finding a spot with a clear view of
Saint Helens, he set up his camera on a tripod and used what was
left of the warm spring day to shoot some pictures. Though not
much was happening that afternoon, he planned to rise early the
next day, when the mountain might be more active.

As he ate breakfast at 8:26 a.m. Sunday morning, an unnatur-
al quiet lay over the Bear Meadow camp. Suddenly William
Dilley, a member of the party, yelled, "Something's happening!"

Rosenquist ran to his camera, nervously bumping the tripod
with his leg as he fired the first shot. Something definitely was
happening. He took another picture, then stared in disbelief. Half

the mountain had turned to a brown, churning liquid. He squeezed the shutter again. Below the black plume spilling into the sky, a dirty brown cloud boiled up.

As the five members of the party watched the dark cloud grow, Joel Harvey, in whose station wagon they had driven to Bear Meadow, suddenly was more concerned about the safety of his wife, Linda, their ten-year–old son, Jo-Jo, and himself than he was about pictures for tourists.

"Let's get out of here!" he yelled.

Rosenquist snapped another picture, then turned and ran for the station wagon with the others, who piled in willy-nilly, with Harvey behind the wheel and Rosenquist in the front seat beside him. An immense black cloud of ash shot out of the mountain ten miles away and rolled toward them at tremendous speed as the car started to move. Rosenquist fumbled in the glove compartment for more film.

"No, no, man!" Harvey yelled. "Help me drive!"

Even with the headlights on, it was difficult to see the road. Marble-sized rocks rattled down on the roof. Lightning flashed, trees whipped back and forth, hot mud and ash poured out of the sky. Sure that they all were going to die, Joel Harvey stopped the car and waited for the end to come.

Apparently protected by an intervening ridge between them and the eruption, they sat in total blackness for a time, then the light began to return and they could again see the road. As he drove on toward Randle, Harvey reached out, patted the camera, and smiled at Rosenquist, saying, "I think we got it."

Indeed, they did have it, for the series of photos Rosenquist had taken became famous. Showing the step-by-step disintegration of the mountain beginning at 8:32:33 a.m. May 18, 1980, and continuing for thirty seconds, they recorded the pulverizing of more than half a cubic mile of rock and the beginning of a process that in a few brief moments turned 234 square miles of prime forest into a gray, bleak desert, as lifeless as the surface of the moon.

THE CASUALTIES

Sudden death or miraculous survival depended upon where people were at the moment of the explosion. Two of the lucky ones were geologists Keith and Dorothy Stoffel, who were flying over the mountain's summit in a four-seat Cessna.

Bill Gulick Photo
MOUNT SAINT HELENS FROM THE EAST IN 1992
The photo shows the mountain twelve years after the explosion.

"Within a matter of seconds, perhaps fifteen seconds, the whole north side of the summit crater began to move instantaneously," Keith Stoffel reported later. "The nature of movement was eerie. The entire mass began to ripple and churn up, without moving laterally. Then the entire north side of the summit began sliding to the north along a deep-seated slide plane. We were amazed and excited with the realization that we were watching this landslide of unbelievable proportions. We took pictures of this slide sequence occurring, but before we could snap off more than a few pictures, a huge explosion blasted out..."

Sensing the force of the explosion, the pilot of the Cessna put the plane into steep dive and gave it full throttle in an effort to escape the effects of the blast. In this he was successful, barely outrunning the cloud and landing safely at the Portland Airport a few minutes later.

On the ground at the Coldwater II observation station, Geologist Dave Johnston was not as fortunate. When the mountain exploded, he barely had time to radio one last message.

"Vancouver, Vancouver, this is it!" he shouted into his microphone.

His Jeep, his trailer, and his monitoring equipment were swept away, never to be found.

Harry Truman was dead, too—buried under 300 feet of avalanche debris. So was Reid Blackburn, a Vancouver *Columbian* photographer under contract to the USGS and *National Geographic*, stationed at Coldwater I observation station, two miles northwest of Johnston's station.

Though it would be two years before the list of casualties was called complete, the official total of people killed by the initial blast was fifty-seven. Because it happened on a Sunday, when the Weyerhauser crew was not at work and the hundred property owners and visitors to the area were not in the Red Zone, the number of deaths was not nearly as high as it might have been otherwise.

CAUSES AND RESULTS

Why was the explosion so sudden and so violent? The main factor was steam pressure, geologists later wrote, estimating the force of the blast to have been the equivalent of 21,000 to 27,000 bombs like the one that devastated Hiroshima.

A chain reaction of catastrophic events followed. Moving at an estimated speed of 175 miles an hour, the collapsing mountain slid down Saint Helens north side, swept across the west arm of Spirit Lake, and ran up a ridge six miles to the north, carrying material up and over the 1,200 foot high crest, while the main body of the slide filled seventeen miles of the North Fork of the Toutle River bank to bank with debris six hundred feet deep.

In the immediate blast area of 234 square miles, tens of thousands of trees were laid flat, looking from the air like toothpicks spilled out of a box in a pattern that clearly showed the direction from which the impelling force had come. But these were not toothpicks; they were mature Douglas fir trees, six or seven feet in diameter and two hundred feet tall. As far as eight miles away, all the trees were shredded and felled, while the earth beneath them was sandblasted to bedrock. A little further away, trees left standing were scorched and killed, with an estimated 4.7 billion board feet of timber damaged, though much of it later was salvaged.

When the hot magma hit Spirit Lake, it created a second explosion far greater than the first one, which was heard as far away as Vancouver, B.C., two hundred miles to the north. The plume from the summit crater began to expand into a mushroom cloud that rose to an altitude of twelve miles. For the next ten hours this vertical column swept millions of tons of ash into the stratosphere, where strong winds bore it northeastward in a narrow plume. The ash canopy cast an eerie pall across the ground beneath. At 10:10 a.m. ash fell in Yakima, ninety miles away; by 2:00 p.m. the plume hung over Spokane, over 300 miles distant. By 10:15 p.m. it reached West Yellowstone, Montana. Ash fell in quantity as far east as central Montana. On May 19, a light dusting settled on Denver; later, ash fell visibly in Minnesota and Oklahoma.

Falling over a wide area of eastern Washington, the talcum-powder-like ash covered Yakima to a depth of four or five inches. The fall was particularly heavy in Ritzville, where it choked the air filters of autos, buses, and trucks, causing state patrol and county sheriff's vehicles to stall. In Spokane, where visibility was reduced to ten feet, the airport was forced to close.

While the ash was floating eastward on the prevailing wind, pyroclastic flows were moving westward down the valleys of the North Fork of the Toutle River. Made up of incandescent rocks and hot gases that traveled downslope like heavy fluids at a rapid rate, they raced past Spirit Lake at speeds exceeding sixty miles an hour, damming its western outlet, then moved on down the Toutle valley.

Filling the lower Toutle River with a mudflow the consistency of wet concrete where it emptied into the Cowlitz, which was backed up for two and a half miles, the latter river then carried its load of mud, logs, and other debris seventeen miles on down to the Columbia. An estimated 3,900,000 cubic yards of sediment reduced the depth of the Columbia from 38 to 13 feet for a distance of four miles, making it unnavigable for deep-draft ships.

Dredging by the Corps of Engineers eventually reopened the river to ocean-going freighters, but the city of Portland estimated it lost $5,000,000 during the temporary closure.

Though Saint Helens continued to erupt on a smaller scale during the next few months, nothing approaching the May 18 explosion occurred during that time or later.

When the air cleared, the physical appearance of Mount Saint Helens had changed from that of a perfectly formed young lady to a broken-down old hag. An estimated thirteen percent of the former cone collapsed into the crater, flowing down the slopes as molten rock, or blew into the air as ash, reducing its height by

Bill Gulick Photo
DEBRIS IN SPIRIT LAKE, TWELVE YEARS AFTER THE EXPLOSION

1,313 feet, leaving an open scar two miles in diameter and half a mile deep on the north slope.

For those who loved the mountain as it once was, geologists give a slim ray of hope when they write that a dome-building process began on the floor inside the crater as soon as the eruption was over and continues today. They say:

> By 1994 the dome measured more than 3000 feet in diameter and rose 800 feet above the crater floor. At its present rate of growth, geologists estimate that it will take 150 to 200 years to replace the volcano's former summit.

AFTERMATH:
NATIONAL MONUMENT ESTABLISHED

Urged by diverse groups to preserve the area in some manner, Congress passed legislation in August, 1982 creating the 109,900–acre Mount Saint Helens National Monument. As might be expected, a brief, bitter struggle between environmentalists and timber interests took place before the final legislation was enacted, so the resulting bill did not please everybody. But it was the best that could be passed under the circumstances. Administered by the United States Forest Service, it appropriated funds for the building of roads and visitor centers, rehabilitation of the blast area, protection of the environment, and scientific research.

The main Visitor Center is located five miles east of Castle Rock (Exit 49 off I–5) and is the starting point for most people who want to see the area. Here are a scale model of the mountain, photo displays showing Saint Helens before, during, and after the eruption, movie and slide shows, publications dealing with geology, volcanos, wildlife, and ecology of the Cascades, and free maps on which well-informed National Monument employees are glad to block out routes showing you how best to see the blast area in the time you have available.

Other entrances from the west are at Woodland (Exit 21 off I–5) to Cougar; Mary's Corner (Exit 68 on US 12) to Mossyrock and Randle; from the south at White Salmon off State Highway 14 to Trout Lake; and from the northeast at Randle off US 12. Along any of these routes, there are Visitor Information and Ranger Stations which are staffed with helpful persons during the height of the tourist season, while the larger Ranger Stations such as those at Packwood, Randle, and Trout Lake are open the year around.

At any time of year, pausing to inquire about road conditions, camping, hiking, climbing restrictions, or fire season dangers is always a good idea, for these can change overnight locally, and the ranger stations always have up-to-the-minute information. Because all of the roads are crooked and some are narrow, driving time cannot be judged by mileage, but the visitor and ranger station people can give you good estimates of how long it will take to get where you want to go.

OUT OF THE ASHES

Following any fictional catastrophe as big as the Saint Helens blast, a hero of super–human proportions who surveys the destroyed landscape with perceptive eyes and devises a plan by which it can be rejuvenated probably would appear. But since this was a real-life disaster occurring on a scale never experienced by human beings, a hero capable of repairing its damage was difficult for the most imaginative of writers to visualize.

But a hero did show up shortly after the Saint Helens blast. Not a bigger-than-life human hero, but a small, insignificant-looking animal hero. Perhaps "climb up" would be a better way of putting it, for the little animal that surfaced out of its network of tunnels deep beneath the surface of the ground was a pocket gopher.

Estimates of the wildlife killed by the blast (made by the Washington State Game Department) listed 1,500 elk, 5,000 black-tailed deer, 200 black bears, 11,000 hares, 15 mountain lions, 300 bobcats, 27,000 grouse, and 1,400 coyotes. Hot ash falling miles away wiped out millions of birds and insects, damaged twenty-six lakes, and heated the rivers to such a high degree that at least eleven million fish perished.

No doubt the heat was so intense on the ground that a number of animals hibernating or living in shallow burrows just under the ground were roasted to death, too. But here and there beneath deep drifts of snow and many feet of earth, a few pocket gophers dozing in their burrows survived. Though no human witness was around when it occurred, a few hours or days after the blast, a dazed, near-sighted gopher must have surfaced, looked around, and muttered aloud to the scorched-earth landscape, "What happened?"

All over the United States since the first atomic bomb went off fifty years ago, survivalist cults have attracted followers, the cornerstone of their philosophy being that sooner or later the leaders who are mismanaging the world are going to make a mistake and set off a nuclear war that will destroy all civilization above the ground. These cults have been particularly active in the West, with several of them spending large amounts of money to dig and stock underground shelters with food, water, bandages, medicines, and computer-stored scientific wisdom with which they plan to rebuild the world—presumably better—as soon as it cools off following the Big Blast.

Pocket gophers lack the intelligence to organize survival cults and run computers, of course, but they do possess a very good substitute. This is the instinct to gather seeds, roots, nuts, and food materials of many kinds, which they take down and store in burrows deep underground. This food supply carries them through cold winters, forest fires, droughts, and other lean times when there is not much nourishment available on the surface of the earth. So wherever this nameless, unobserved gopher surfaced and looked around in amazement following the blast, we may be sure he was munching on some kind of food he had stored and brought up from underground. We may also assume that he had cleaned out his tunnel a bit as he climbed, storing the dirt in his cheek pockets, then disgorging it along with some undigested seeds in the middle of the sterile, still warm ash lying all around him.

Without the rich, fertile soil he had brought up in his cheeks and disgorged, the seeds could not have sprouted and grown. With it—and a bit of natural fertilizer—the seeds flourished.

And life in the blast area began anew.

A VIRGIN LANDSCAPE

Two and a half weeks after the blast, a group of scientists was flown into the area in a helicopter. In the party was a plant ecologist, a research geologist, and two other Forest Service scientists. Ecologist Jerry Franklin later described their feelings:

> We were all a little nervous, but excited, too. We didn't know what to expect. Our first stop was Ryan Lake [12 miles northeast of the crater]. We got out of the helicopter and stepped across a ditch on the edge of the road and right away we saw fireweed sprouts coming up through the ash. I looked a little farther and saw ants working, then signs of gophers digging and coyote tracks. After that we went over to the Clearwater [Valley] and there, right in the middle of all this unbelievable destruction, with grey, shattered trunks and branches everywhere and the air filled with smoke from smoldering logs, there was a trillium growing. I couldn't believe it. Every time we turned around we saw another way something had lived through the eruption. I said, "Oh, my God, this place is covered with survivors."

In the days and weeks that followed, the scientists realized that the 234 square miles of the blast area had given them a unique opportunity to do something never done by earth scientists before. Here lay a piece of the world as it must have existed in the first days of its creation—before its newly-formed peaks and valleys shaped by volcanic action had been altered by erosion, with most of its life above ground wiped out. Now that the slate was clean, this was a priceless chance to see how the forces of erosion worked and how life renewed itself in a sterile area.

If the purists among the scientists had had their way, no human hand would have contributed to the natural healing process. Man would simply have watched and recorded the greatest natural ecology experiment that had ever taken place. This did not happen, of course, for economic factors affecting human life in the area immediately applied pressure to the scientists, who were forced to let various private and public interests give nature a helping hand. The best the scientists could do was set aside a few "control" areas in which nature would be left alone to begin the healing process in her own way, while in adjacent plots man applied his remedies, with the two different processes being carefully watched and compared.

It would be an oversimplification to say that all the measures taken by man failed while those taken by nature succeeded. As more than one scientist commented, nature takes all the time it needs to heal its wounds, so, in the end, always repairs the damage. But man's time is limited by many factors—such as cities and freeways built in flood plains downstream from natural or artificial dams that may burst—thus man often is required to take preventive measures *now* or risk disasters costly in human life and material wealth.

Even so, some of the immediate measures taken by humans to mitigate the effects of the eruption turned out to be ludicrously ineffective. For example, there was the dilemma of the migrating elk. Though all the elk that had been in the blast zone had been killed, those living outside had not been harmed. With the Soil Conservation Service planting grass seed to prevent erosion and hunting prohibited on the avalanche debris along the North Fork of the Toutle River, hundreds of outside elk soon learned that there was good browse and no hunters in the area, so they migrated into it from all directions.

This proved to be a mixed blessing. Because their hooves broke up the crust of ash on the surface, which mixed it with the topsoil, this helped sprout the grass. But as soon as a plant appeared above ground—whether a blade of grass, a sprig of lupine, or a seedling tree—the elk ate it, leaving the churned-up earth as barren as before. They also played havoc with an experiment initiated by research professor John Edwards of the University of Washington Department of Zoology. Wanting to find out how many insects were flying into the blast zone, he filled some plastic cups with a highly toxic antifreeze, which should kill and preserve any insect that happened to fly, crawl, or hop into the cup. By collecting and counting the dead insects every couple of weeks, he could estimate the number of new arrivals.

"The results were skewed at first," Rob Carson writes, "because thirsty elk and other animals kept drinking the antifreeze. Edwards tried electric fences around the cups, but the pumice was too dry to ground the batteries. The researchers eventually ended up surrounding their traps with barbed wire..."

What effect the antifreeze had on the elk was not noted by the researchers.

Before the blast, the Weyerhauser Timber Company had owned substantial plots of timber in the Saint Helens area, with 45,000 acres of trees knocked down or damaged by the blast. Though the company soon got busy salvaging all the downed timber it could save before bark beetles and other insects made it worthless, the company also planned an emergency reforestation project. As forester Dick Ford put it, "A forest not growing trees is like having money in your checking account, not your savings account."

Before the company could undertake its tree-planting project, a government agency, the Soil Conservation Service, came up with a grandiose reseeding plan of its own. Rob Carson writes:

> To the horror of environmentalists, the Soil Conservation Service was given $20 million in federal emergency-relief funds to seed and chemically fertilize most of the blast zone and avalanche flow. In July 1980 the Conservation Service announced the specifics of its plan: It would use helicopters to seed the area with 13 species of grass—including clover, Kentucky bluegrass, birdsfoot trefoil, and creeping red fescue— of which only one (pine lupine) was native to the Pacific Northwest. Scientists, who wanted to see the blast zone recover naturally, were incensed. They howled in protest, and in large part because of their objections, the Conservation Service scaled back its plan from the 200 square miles to 33 square miles. In September and October of 1980, helicopters swung back and forth over the devastated area, dropping tons of grass seed and fertilizer onto the blast zone and avalanche debris flow.

Because the surface was so barren and dry, the fertilizer blew away; the grass seed washed downhill with the first rainfall and never sprouted. The seed did not go to waste, though, for the birds loved it and so did the mice, whose population increased rapidly. Meanwhile, Weyerhauser, which was beginning its ambitions and costly tree-planting program, was horrified to discover that with twenty-five times the normal mice population per acre, its seedlings were being devoured by the still-hungry rodents, which had finished off the grass seed.

What to do? Why, the mice must be poisoned of course, else no new trees would grow. Rob Carson writes:

> The timber giant fought back by dropping more seeds—this time oats tainted with a coating of zinc-phosphide. The mice gobbled up the oats. Inside their stomachs, the zinc-phosphide reacted with the gastric juices and turned to gas that required a great deal of room to expand. The mice blew up like balloons and died.
>
> The pneumatic mice illustrate a recurring feature of human attempts to alter the course of nature in the blast zone. In the decade after the eruption, virtually every intrusive action prompted chains of reaction, many of which were utterly unexpected and irrevocable. The moral is similar to one from the tale of Br'er Rabbit and the Tar-Baby: when you're not sure what you're doing, you can get into some very sticky situations with Mother Nature.

ENGINEERING DIFFICULTIES

While much of the natural renewal of the blast area could be left to nature, there was too much risk involved in letting clogged lakes and rivers find new channels through heavily populated areas downstream to permit the law of gravity, erosion, and time to solve the problems. One of the most urgent of these was the blockage of shipping lanes in the Columbia River below the mouth of the Cowlitz, which were so filled with debris that they had shallowed from forty to thirteen feet.

Using three vacuum–style dredging ships twenty-four hours a day, the US Army Corps of Engineers required seven months to fully restore the shipping channels to their former depth. Including work on the Cowlitz, where the Corps signed twenty-eight contracts with private companies to dredge or clean out sections of the river channel, $600 million was spent over a period of ten years to repair the damage the eruption had done in a matter of minutes.

Another problem demanding a quick solution was that of sedimentation below the slopes of Mount Saint Helens, which was filling both the North and South Forks of the Toutle Rivers as fast as the Corps of Engineers could clean them out. To hold back the sediment long enough to allow it to settle on the bottom of artificial lakes, the Corps dynamited a rock knoll, producing enough material to build a forty-three-foot high wall a mile long from one side of the valley to the other, forming an impoundment on the North Fork of the Toutle. On the South Fork, where the problem was less severe, the Corps built a 600–foot long dam to hold back the water.

Together, the two dams cost $21 million. But both of them failed on Christmas day 1980, when a heavy rain brought a torrent of gravel, shattered tree trunks, and debris down off the mountain, bursting the two dams and carrying 9.5 million cubic yards of new sediment down the Toutle River.

On the South Fork, the dam was repaired and maintained until the spring of 1982, when it was removed to allow the migration of steelhead and salmon upstream to spawn. On the North Fork, the Corps built a much bigger and more expensive dam—four times higher and three times costlier at $60 million. Officially referred to not as a dam but as a "Sediment Retention Structure," it was completed in 1989 and as of this writing is still standing. Its designers say it will handle mudflows at least as large as the one caused by the May 18, 1980 eruption.

Eventually it will fill up with an estimated 258 million cubic yards of sediment. Though this will not happen until the year 2035, disposing of the accumulated material will pose a problem, for if hauled away in ten-yard dump trucks, 25.8 million of them would be needed. Bumper to bumper, the trucks would circle the globe six times. Where they would be emptied, no one will venture to say.

PUMPING SPIRIT LAKE

What appeared to be an even more urgent problem was the rising level of Spirit Lake, which, two years after the eruption, rose sixty feet and doubled the amount of impounded water it retained. If the rubble blocking the outlet to the lake were suddenly to give way, the experts warned, the flow of water coming down the narrow valley of the North Fork of the Toutle River would exceed two million cubic feet per second—more than twice the flow of the Columbia River—and far more than any dam could withstand.

If this happened, the cities of Kelso, Longview, the Port District facilities, Interstate 5, and the Burlington Northern Railroad would be buried under twenty feet of mud and water.

Cowlitz County regarded this threat so seriously that it installed $750,000 worth of flood-warning sirens along the river. Granted $7 million in emergency funds in August 1982, the Corps of Engineers began pumping water out of Spirit Lake in order to lower it to a less threatening level. Rob Carson writes:

> Water from the lake was pumped through 3,450 feet of pipe across the debris flow to the North Fork of the Toutle at the rate of 5,400 gallons a second. Pumping continued for three years, 24 hours a day, burning 3,000 gallons of fuel each day and three million dollars each year to keep the lake at what engineers considered a safe level.

Efforts to lower the lake had several curious ecological side effects, Carson says. Though the camp of the workmen was in what was supposed to be a protected area so far as imported animals and plants were concerned, men wanting fresh eggs for breakfast brought in live chickens which they fed grain. Later, the grain sprouted, attracting mice. So the workmen brought in cats...

And there went the protected neighborhood.

Seeking a permanent solution to keep the Spirit Lake water level low, the Corps of Engineers decided to bore a tunnel through the base of Coldwater Ridge, which would serve as a permanent drain to the lake. Working from July, 1984 to May, 1985 the digging crew used a machine called the "Mole" to bore a twelve-foot diameter tunnel through 1.6 miles of solid rock at the rate of eighty feet a day.

When completed, the new drain brought Spirit Lake down to 3,440 feet above sea level,—still two hundred feet higher than it had been on May 18, 1980, but considered to be safe so far as downstream flooding was concerned.

REFORESTATION

While an army of one thousand loggers moved into the blast zone in September, 1980 and started salvaging what trees they could, Weyerhauser and the Forest Service experimented with techniques to replant the area. They encountered several problems. As much as two feet of ash—called "tephra"—covered the ground, and, contrary to common belief, it did not contain the nutrients seedlings needed. When the top layer got wet, a crust formed that was nearly impenetrable by water. To make matters even more difficult, there was no precedent to go by. Gene Sloniker, chief forester for the Saint Helens District of the Gifford Pinchot National Forest, later said:

> We had some doubts about whether it was even going to be possible to grow trees at all. We went out in four-wheel drive vehicles after the eruption and there were so many, many unknowns. I remember my first thought was "What a catastrophe." My second thought was, "God, what a challenge—to turn this area back into a productive forest." We went back and made a search of the literature to see what we could learn from past experience. There was no literature. We basically found out nobody had ever reforested a volcano before, at least not in this environment.

In less than a month following the eruption, Weyerhauser and the Forest Service established test plots of seedlings to see which species of trees would grow and what special care they needed. They quickly discovered that if the trees were planted so that the roots went down through the ash to the mineral–filled soil below, they did quite well. But the planting required some special techniques. Rob Carson writes:

> On National Forest land, much of the planting was done with augers attached to chain-saw motors. The augers, 3 feet long and 4 inches wide, were used to drill holes in the ash and mix it with mineral soil underneath. On Weyerhauser land, much of which was flatter, vast acreages actually were plowed with bulldozers that used front-mounted blades to peel away the ash in long, parallel rows, 10 feet apart. Tree planters followed along the furrows with shovels and planted the seedlings one by one. On sunny slopes, the light-colored ash acted like a reflector oven, raising surface temperatures as high as 160 degrees. In those places, workers put a low-grade cedar shingle next to each tree as a sunshade.

In seven years time, Weyerhauser planted 18.4 million trees on 45,500 acres of blasted land at a cost of $10 million, while the Forest Service planted 9 million trees on 18,000 acres. At this writing fourteen years after the eruption, some of these trees are thirty feet high and growing, making a much better showing than trees within the "control" area of the Mount Saint Helens National Volcanic Monument, where natural regeneration is proceeding at a much slower pace.

Ecological purists may argue that a tree farm planted by man is not the same as an old growth forest developed by nature, which is true. But at least trees are growing on the slopes of Saint

Helens, which eventually could become an old growth forest in another five hundred to a thousand years, if left alone. Considering the fact that man is a beginner in this renewal business, while nature has been at it for millions of years, the new greenery on Saint Helens makes the mountain slope look much better than it did fourteen years ago. Given enough time—and barring another eruption—it will all look beautiful again.

MOUNT SAINT HELENS TODAY

Like a patient who has survived a life-threatening coronary but is still in the intensive-care ward of the hospital, Mount Saint Helens is wired with sensing devices to give warning in case it threatens to erupt again. As the most closely watched volcano in the Cascade Range, this include eighteen seismometers and half a dozen tiltmeters, plus a tie-in with a network of 120 seismometers set up at locations throughout Washington and Oregon, monitored by the Northwest's central seismic-monitoring laboratory at the University of Washington.

Even with all this equipment, the scientists refuse to make firm predictions. Will the mountain erupt again? Yes, sooner or later. When? Not before sundown today, probably. Beyond those two qualified statements, they refuse to go.

If pressed to speculate further, they point out that when Mount Vesuvius erupted in 79 A.D. the citizens of Pompeii were surprised, even though the surrounding area had been occupied for several thousand years. When the same mountain erupted in 1631 A.D., the local residents were surprised again, saying, "We knew it was a volcano, but we thought it was extinct."

Completed in the summer of 1992, the new $165 million Spirit Lake Memorial Highway takes tourists to a high point on the ridge where geologist David Johnston was killed by the blast Sunday morning, May 18, 1980. In order to accommodate the millions of tourists expected to drive to the Coldwater Ridge Visitor Center built forty-three miles east of the I–5 exit at Mile 49, the new highway has been designed to be as safe as possible and as environmentally compatible as the difficult mountain terrain will permit.

"It *should* be a good highway," Duane Chatham, director of the Coldwater Ridge Center told us wryly when we visited the Center shortly after it opened in early summer, 1993. "It cost $1,000 a linear foot."

From the observatory deck five miles away from the gaping mouth of the crater, a person may look directly into its mouth, which now and then still emits steam and smoke. Like all mountains in the Cascade Range, clear weather in which to hike the many miles of trails originating at the Center or to view and photograph the core of the mountain itself cannot be guaranteed at any time of the year, no matter how cloudless the lowland country at its base may be. During the three visits we have made to the Coldwater Ridge Visitor Center in mid–June, late July, and late September, the fog was so thick on one occasion that we could see no more than fifty feet, while, on the other two visits, rain clouds which at first restricted vision suddenly lifted to reveal distant vistas.

But whether the weather is clear or cloudy outside, the Coldwater Ridge Visitor Center inside is a marvel of visual volcano-watching history. Built at a cost of $12 million, the Center is expected to attract 1.5 million visitors a year, Duane Chatham told us, adding, "We have 280 parking places, but it's not uncommon on a nice weekend to see traffic backed up on the highway waiting for space."

At 3,200 feet, the Center overlooks Coldwater Lake, which Mike Nitsch, Chief of Security for the Mount Saint Helens National Monument District of the Forest Service, told us is 160 feet deep and a couple of miles long. An avid fisherman, he says that the lake has been restocked with rainbow trout following the eruption, which now have grown to sufficient size that fishing is permitted on a limited basis.

"I came up on opening day and got one of the hundred permits issued daily," he said. "You have to fish with flies or lures and can keep only one fish over sixteen inches in length. I caught one seventeen inches, another fourteen inches, then released them both."

As Chief Security officer for the 284 square mile National Monument, Mike Nitsch coordinates what is called "concurrent jurisdiction" of the various state and federal agencies which enforce laws in the area.

"The scientific community is very protective of this area," he says. "There is a strong international effort to research its growth. That's why a number of our regulations are very strict so far as staying on the trails and not going into restricted areas are concerned. In the experiments they're doing, the scientists see this as a unique opportunity to study how the earth regenerates itself after volcanic destruction."

Because the Coldwater Ridge Visitor Center will be open the year 'round, its construction was very rugged, Duane Chatham says, meant to withstand a load of snow or volcanic ash ten feet deep. He states:

> The most important part of the exhibits' message is caring for the land. The exhibits show the destruction caused by the eruption, then the recovery of the area. They use state-of-the-art technology developed and applied by the same people that created Disneyland. To use a trendy term, they're all "high tech."

"Everything in this building," he adds, "is virtually computer-controlled. For instance, we have a device you can rent that will translate the English narration of the exhibits into four foreign languages, so that as you walk around you can hold it up to your ear and listen in Japanese, French, German, or Spanish. It also has a channel for the hearing-impaired."

No matter what language the children speak, they are fascinated with a life-like lady ranger mannequin who talks to them about the environment in such an appealing way that they never tire of asking her questions and enjoying her company. Since the Center opened in late May, 1993, visitors have come to it from all over the world, Duane Chatham says, with foreigners making up ten percent of its total attendance.

As noted earlier, one of the first victims of the Mount Saint Helens explosion was the young geologist, David Johnston, whose trailer was parked on the very brink of the crater when the mountain exploded. When asked if any remains of this brave young man or his equipment ever was found, Duane Chatham shakes his head and answers sadly, "I don't think so. From what I've heard, he was so close and the heat was so intense that everything was just vaporized.

As a memorial to the dedicated volcano-watcher who lost his life on the shoulder of Mount Saint Helens, May 18, 1980, a Johnston Ridge Center will be built and is scheduled to open in 1996.

Perhaps visitors to it will eye the nearby crater and remember...

MOUNT ADAMS, THE LOST PEAK

Though Mount Adams is the second highest peak in the Pacific Northwest at 12,276 feet, it is not nearly as well known as Mount Hood across the river in Oregon, Mount Saint Helens thirty-five miles directly west, and Mount Rainier a hundred miles to the

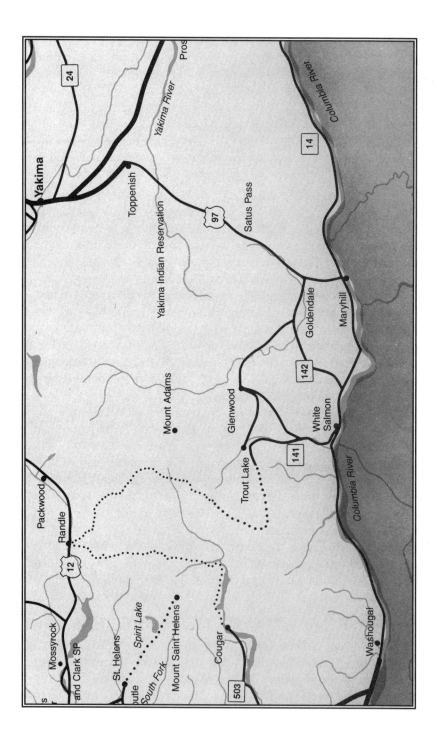

north. A broad, sprawling peak whose summit is neither shapely nor spectacular, it is a big mountain whose base covers an area of 250 square miles.

Because no paved highways cross its lower slopes and only one surfaced road from Trout Lake approaches it from the south, it does not attract many casual sight-seers. This means that hikers, campers, huckleberry pickers, and back-packers who like their wilderness areas left relatively untouched find Mount Adams a wonderful place to explore.

Adjacent to the Mount Adams Wilderness Area, which includes the summit and 32,365 acres, the Yakima Indian Nation in 1972 was awarded a 10,000–acre timbered area on the northeast side of the mountain over which the Yakimas have jurisdiction and control logging, grazing, hunting, fishing, and water-use rights.

Persons wishing permission to hike or camp in this area should first check at the Yakima Indian Reservation in Toppenish, Washington. Those wishing to enter public lands from the south should inquire about roads, trails, camping, and climbing permits at the Trout Lake Ranger Station.

Seeking a camping or fishing spot on the lake for which the town was named is fruitless, for the lake that was once there is now only a grass-filled marsh, having been filled up over the years by mudflows washing down off the slopes of Mount Adams. Though the Saint Helens eruption may have added a few inches of ash to the marsh, the filling-in process started many years ago.

PEAK OUT OF PLACE

As noted earlier, an Oregon Country promoter named Hall J. Kelley proposed back in the 1830s that all the Cascade peaks hon-

State 141—White Salmon to Trout Lake
   25 miles
Forest Roads 80, 8040—Trout Lake to Mt. Adams
   25 miles
State 142—Trout Lake to Glenwood, Goldendale
   47 miles

Bill Gulick Photo
MOUNT ADAMS FROM THE SOUTHWEST NEAR TROUT LAKE

oring Britishers be patriotically renamed after American presidents, with the mountains to be called the "Presidents Range." A later explorer, Thomas J. Farnham, went along with the idea to the extent that on the maps he copied or made he placed the peaks where he thought they were located and gave them the names Kelley had suggested.

What neither he nor Kelley knew was that the British explorer Captain George Vancouver, whose lieutenants had gone around discovering and naming mountains and bays in 1792, had never even seen what came to be called Mount Adams, thus had left it nameless. But on the map Farnham drew, he missed the location of Mount Saint Helens by thirty-five miles, so when he renamed Saint Helens "Adams" he accidentally got the location of Adams right, though neither he nor Kelley ever saw it. So Mount Adams it became—and remained when the maps finally were corrected—with Saint Helens, Rainier, Baker, and Hood retaining their British titles.

Because of its height and bulk, Mount Adams receives a heavy rain and snowfall on its upper western slopes, so supports ten spectacular glaciers and related ice fields. To see them requires traveling afoot.

VOLCANIC ACTIVITY
So far as eruptions are concerned, Mount Adams has behaved much more quietly than its smaller neighbor to the west. Though there is evidence of seven lava flows above the 6500 foot level during the past 10,000 years, they do not appear to have been very violent. Other than the Indian legend related earlier regarding the Mount Hood, Mount Saint Helens, Bridge of the Gods feud, the local Indians have only vague tribal traditions of eruptions during the time they have lived in the region. Geologists say that the volcano erupted four times between 275,000 and 100,000 years ago. During dormant intervals, glaciers destroyed much of the cone, each time reducing it to an elevation below 9,000 feet.

MINE ON A MOUNTAIN PEAK
Mount Adams has the dubious distinction of being the only peak in the Cascade range ever to have a mining claim filed and worked commercially on its crest. In accordance with the mining laws passed in 1872 (which are still in effect), any prospector finding a trace of gold, silver, lead, copper, or any other useful mineral on public land may file a claim and retain possession of that land indefinitely, as long as he does a reasonable amount of development work on it each year.

Because sulphur was found on Mount Adams, a promoter named Wade Dean from the nearby town of White Salmon filed a claim on the 210–acre summit plateau in 1929 and 1931, built a primitive horse and mule trail up the relatively easy south slope, and began trying to develop it commercially. Since the law as then written (and little improved today) let the claim owner dig, waste, destroy, and pollute in any way he so desired, without an iota of responsibility for restoring the area to its original condition, the amount of ecological damage that could have been done to the sensitive high-altitude environment is horrible to contemplate.

Fortunately, it was not a profitable venture. After digging up a seventy–acre area north of the summit with no great success, the miners drilled test holes through 305 feet of ice and thirty-four feet of rock, finding a few sulfates and a small amount of sulphur in the drill holes. The promoter's attempts to sell stock and raise the capital needed for fuller development did not succeed, for by then it had become clear that the potential of the sulfur resource had been grossly exaggerated, while the cost and difficulty of recovering it had not been properly assessed.

In 1959, when the last required assessment work was done, the operation was seen as unprofitable, so the project was abandoned. Mining rights to the mountain peak reverted to the original owners—the federal government and the American public. It is not likely that a future claim will be granted.

ROADS AROUND MOUNT ADAMS

For reasons noted earlier, it is not possible to circle Mount Adams by surfaced road at close range, but the mountain can be encompassed at a distance by driving east from Trout Lake on an unnumbered blacktop road to Glenwood, then southeast up the spectacular canyon of the Klickitat River to its junction with State 142 twelve miles west of Goldendale.

From Goldendale, US 97 goes north over the timbered foothills of Satus Pass, to Toppenish and Yakima, a distance of seventy-five miles. Heading west from Yakima, US 12 climbs the scenic valley of the Naches and Tieton Rivers past Rimrock Lake, tops the White Pass ski area at 4,500 feet, then drops down to Packwood on the western slope of the Cascades, some eighty miles from Yakima.

Here, the traveler wishing to complete the circuit of Mount Adams should stop at the Ranger Station and inquire about road conditions, for, twelve miles to the west at Randle, two roads head south between Adams and Saint Helens toward Trout Lake some seventy-five crooked miles further on. Both of these roads are closed in winter and are not recommended for the average driver except under ideal conditions.

If the late Supreme Court Justice William O. Douglas, who was a long-time resident of the Mount Adams area, had had his way fifty years ago, most of the region would have remained roadless wilderness, with the only access to it by means of hiking or horse. Born and raised in Yakima, Justice Douglas returned to Washington State every summer, first to a cabin on the shoulder of the mountain in Glenwood, later to another in Goose Prairie a few miles to the north. A strong supporter during his long term on the Supreme Court from 1939 to 1975 of laws protecting the wilderness, he felt that there ought to be a few places a person could reach only by walking or riding a horse. For example when he revisited a favorite spot in 1960 and found that it now could be reached by car, he wrote indignantly in his book *My Wilderness:*

Courtesy Yakima Valley Regional Library
PICKING HUCKLEBERRIES
Yakima women find a plentiful supply in Mount Adams' Goat Rocks area.

I had not seen Bird Creek Meadows for over thirty years. I left Glenwood by jeep, planning to park it at road's end and hike in, as I used to do. As the jeep climbed on and on, I discovered to my dismay that the good dirt road went all the way. When I arrived, I counted twenty-seven cars ahead of me. My heart sank. An alpine meadow that I used to reach only after days of hiking was now accessible to everyone without effort. It had been desecrated by the automobile. This high shoulder of Mount Adams now had all the amenities of Rock Creek Park in Washington, D.C., and Central Park in New York City.

More than once during his career on the bench he went hiking with bird-watching or wilderness trail groups and showed up at a lodge or eating establishment looking so bedraggled and disreputable that the inn-keeper turned him away—as did Harry Truman at Spirit Lake. But eventually he got his revenge. Some of the landmark decisions he made regarding preservation of the wilderness kept the inn-keepers down in the low country where he felt they belonged, while making sure enough wilderness was left to offer solace to kindred souls who wanted to enjoy it their way in the years to come.

Click Relander Collection, Courtesy Yakima Valley Regional Library
ENTRANCE TO THE YAKIMA NATION RESERVATION AREA

MOUNT RAINIER

By far the biggest mountain by bulk in the lower 48 states, Mount Rainier at 14,410 feet is topped in height only by California's Mount Whitney, 14,494 feet, and Colorado's Mount Elbert, 14,433 feet. Because it is so close to Puget Sound, it begins its rise from sea level, while the two higher mountains rest on already elevated plateaus; thus, Mount Rainier is the most visually impressive peak south of Alaska—a fact frequently alluded to by the residents of Seattle, Tacoma, and Olympia, who rightly boast of its scenic wonders.

Moisture-laden winds sweeping across the Pacific from the southwest nine months out of the year unload immense amounts of rain and snow on Rainier's western slopes, most of which are within the boundaries of a large National Park, so the region is heavily forested with magnificent, uncut trees, while twenty-six major glaciers feed half a dozen good-sized rivers flowing downslope in all directions.

Because the large population centers are on the west side of the mountain, most visitors come from that direction, creating a heavy traffic and use of the Paradise Valley Visitor Center at the

Courtesy Washington State Library
WILDFLOWERS IN PARADISE VALLEY, MOUNT RAINIER NATIONAL PARK

mile–high level. Since this is a mountain that deserves to be seen from all directions (and we concluded our Mount Adams exploration in the Packwood area), we might as well get our first view of Rainier from the eastern side, which many people feel offers the best view anyway.

From Packwood on US 12, go east fifteen miles to the Cayuse Pass highway, State 123, which goes through a town only slightly larger than its name, Ohanapecosh, then proceeds north sixteen miles to connect with State 410 from Yakima. After climbing steeply to the 5,430 foot crest of Chinook Pass, which is closed in winter because of heavy snowfall, this route reveals a stunning closeup view of the "Mountain that Was God" (as the Indians supposedly called it) when the sun shines. After winding down a series of hairpin turns for five miles or so, an unnumbered surfaced road turns south to Sunrise Ridge and Lodge twenty miles away. Here, facilities are open during the summer months, offering a fine starting point for hikers of back-country trails, while for day visitors its viewpoints offer magnificent panoramas of the mountain, its glaciers, its canyons, and its avalanche areas.

Though Snoqualmie Pass a few miles to the north carries most of heavy traffic across the state on I–90, while Chinook and White Pass are popular with tourists in search of more scenic routes, old-timers who know Mount Rainier have claimed for many years that the best pass across the Cascades was never properly examined as a potential route for wagons, cars, or trains. They called it "Naches Pass." As a matter of historic interest, let us examine their argument here.

NACHES PASS ROAD

While Governor Stevens and his party were heading west from St. Paul in late spring, 1853, with the purpose of selecting a northern route for a transcontinental railroad on the way out to Washington Territory, Lieutenant George McClellan, who had been a classmate and friend of Governor Stevens at West Point, traveled to Puget Sound via the sea route from New York City to Panama, crossed the Isthmus by land, then sailed north to Seattle by steamer. Because he, like Stevens, was a qualified engineer, his task was to start from saltwater and find a feasible route east across the Cascade Mountains over a grade that a railroad could climb. Hopefully, he would meet the westward-moving Stevens party somewhere in the eastern portion of the new Territory.

Because Jefferson Davis, Secretary of War, was a Southerner and thus would be bound to favor a southern route across the United States for a transcontinental railroad, (a central route was also being surveyed) there was little chance that a railroad would be built on the northern route for some time to come. But if the Stevens–McClellan parties could lay out a route of relatively easy grades that would not be drifted too deep with snow during the winter, the Congressmen from the northern states would at least have some bargaining chips with which to play the railroad-building game.

At the very least, the $20,000 appropriation which had been approved for the construction of a military road from Fort Steilacoom on the lower reaches of Puget Sound to Fort Walla Walla in the eastern part of the Territory might be made available so that work could begin on a road that would divert part of the emigrant traffic. At the present moment, all the emigrants were going first to Portland through the Columbia River Gorge, then, if they wanted to go north to Puget Sound, they must traverse the horrible "mud-wagon" road through the lowlands between the Columbia River and the new capital, Olympia.

Even though the distance was only a hundred miles, this route during most of the year was so wet and muddy that the complaint "...a wagon can get stuck going downhill..." was no exaggeration.

But "Little Mac," (as he was called ten years later when President Lincoln made the mistaken assumption that a military general who was a good organizer would be just the man to give the Union Army a badly needed victory) proved to be as inept at selecting a railroad pass through the mountains as he was at giving his troops the order to attack. In a feeble effort to find a relatively snow-free pass across the Cascades, he tried to explain to the local Indians—who knew nothing about railroads—what he was looking for. When they guided him up to what would become Snoqualmie Pass and told him by grunts and signs that even at this 3,500 foot level the snow sometimes got twenty feet deep, he threw up his hands in defeat, said a railroad route across the Cascades was an impossibility, and went back to the shores of Puget Sound, where he gloomily awaited the arrival of Governor Stevens and his party. Apparently, he was just as pessimistic about the proposed Steilacoom–Walla Walla Military Road.

But the American settlers newly arrived on Puget Sound, most of whom had come by wagon two thousand miles across the continent and knew what people could do when they put their hearts, minds, and backs into a project, did not give up so easily. Because federal funds for a road across the Cascades probably would not be available for a year or two, they decided to begin to build the road themselves. Seeking contributions in cash and pledges of labor, they collected $1,195 from some seventy sources, with individuals giving a minimum of $5 each, while contributions of $100 came from commercial groups such as Weed & Hurd and the Puget Sound Agricultural Company. Though no record was kept regarding the contributions of labor, the loan of oxen and horses, or the employment of Indians who worked on the road, Ezra Meeker says that their total value was several times that of the cash contributions.

All through late spring, summer, and early fall months, the amateur road-building crew labored, chopping, sawing, grading, and filling a wagon road up the western slope of the Cascades through incredibly difficult terrain toward the crest of Naches Pass. Though Ezra Meeker, who with his brother Oliver, had just arrived in Washington Territory and was busy establishing a claim and building a cabin on McNeil Island, did not work on the road-building project that first summer, he was aware of it, for his father, mother, and the rest of the family back in Iowa had sent word that they would come out to Washington Territory next year if Oliver would come home and be their guide.

Sure that the Naches Wagon Road would be finished by then (the summer of 1854), Oliver Meeker planned to leave the Oregon Trail on the way west in the vicinity of Fort Walla Walla, ascend the Columbia River twenty-five miles to the mouth of the Yakima, then turn northwest up that river to the eastern slope of the Cascades, climbing it to the crest of the range and then descending to Puget Sound by way of the Naches Pass Road.

Today, this is near the route followed by State Highway 12 across White Pass. The fact that the highway was not completed and opened to automobile traffic until 1951 because of the difficulty in building a road across this sector of the Cascades is an indication of the problems faced by the pioneer road-builders one hundred years earlier.

Beginning their work July 30, 1853, a crew of twenty men managed to hack out a road of sorts sixty miles up the western slope in two months time. On the rainy side of the mountains, the trees were so huge that they were seldom felled; the road simply wound in and out among them. Where the trees grew too close together to permit the passage of a wagon, their lower trunks were sawed or chopped out just enough to let a wagon get through. In places where a two hundred foot giant had fallen and lay parallel to the route of the road, its twelve-foot diameter would be transformed into a road, with three parallel notches being chopped along its length, the outside grooves for the wheels of the wagon, the center one for its tongue.

The exposed roots of these prone, slow-rotting monsters sometimes were as thick as a man's body and fifteen feet off the ground, making it necessary for the workers to dig a tunnel so that the wagons could go underneath them. With the coming of the rainy season in early October, the thick growth of head-high ferns that covered the forest floor constantly dripped moisture, soaking the chilled laborers to the bone. On the few days when the rain stopped for a couple of hours and the sun shone feebly, its rays never penetrated to the ground.

Though the road-builders had hoped that a wagon train or two would try their route this first year and had sent word over to the the Grande Ronde Valley in northeastern Oregon that a new route leading directly to Puget Sound was being opened up, news relayed from one tribe to another via the Indian grapevine brought the information that the last of this year's emigration had passed through, choosing to go down the Columbia to Portland and the Willamette Valley by the usual route. So the cold, wet, weary road-builders abandoned their camps and went home.

THE RAWHIDE WAGON TRAIN

Unknown to the Indians, one late-traveling party of twenty-nine wagons and 128 individuals *was* still on the trail. Unknown to the disappointed road-builders, they had heard of the new Naches Pass Road and chosen to give it a try. Arriving at Summit Prairie, seventy miles southeast of the future site of Tacoma, they found neither the road-builders nor any sign of a road. Without even an Indian guide to show them the way, they attempted to cross the mountain range through the trackless wilderness on their own. Quite suddenly, they came to what one horrified woman in the train aptly described as, "The Jumping-Off Place." Ezra Meeker writes:

> This lady felt they had come to the end of the world. . . . Go around this hill they could not; go down it with logs trailed to the wagons (lashed behind the wheels to brake the descent), as they had done before, they could not, for the hill was so steep the logs would go end over end and be a danger instead of a help.

The only thing that could be done, the leader of the party realized, was to tie ropes to the wagons, belay them around stout trees, then carefully lower the wagons down the near-vertical slope cautiously foot by foot. But when all the usable lengths of rope possessed by the party were assembled and spliced together, a seemingly unsurmountable problem arose. The available lengths of rope were too short by several hundred feet. What to do?

It is at this point that the fiction writer with a vivid imagination would use a device known in the trade as the "common sense beats book knowledge" gambit. After letting the stuffed-shirt captain of the wagon train berate his people for their stupidity in not bringing along enough strong lengths of rope to serve in this emergency, the ignorant old mountain man who has been put down and sneered at for two thousand miles because he cannot read an emigrant guide book or a map, steps forward and says quietly, "You got all the rope you need, captain. Trouble is, you jest don't recognize it when it's alive and walkin' around." Following which, he pats the lean, sturdy back of the nearest ox, and drawls. "Ain't you never heerd of a leather lariat?"

As a fiction writer who used this tried and true gambit in the first story he sold the *Saturday Evening Post* many years ago, without realizing how many times it had been used before, I can vouch for its authenticity. But in the 1850s, when everybody who lived on the frontier knew that rawhide could be used to fix practically anything, there could not possibly have existed a wagon train captain so ignorant that he would not know what to do when in need of rope. Ezra Meeker writes, "`Kill a steer,'" the leader said. "They killed a steer, cut his hide into strips, and spliced it to the rope. It was found to be too short to reach to the bottom. `Kill two more steers!' And two more steers were killed, their hides cut into strips, and spliced to the rope, which then reached to the bottom of the hill; and by the aid of that rope and strips of the hides of those three steers, twenty-nine wagons were lowered down the mountain side to the bottom of the steep hill."

Thus the name, *The Rawhide Wagon Train*.

The following year, 1854, Ezra Meeker got word that his brother Oliver would be coming through the Grande Ronde Valley with the rest of the Meeker family some time in September. Leaving his wife and their newly-born second baby in the care of a neighbor woman, who came and said she would stay with them in the cabin until he returned, Ezra borrowed a small, but sturdy horse from a settler friend who lived on White River near the beginning of the Naches Pass Road, and went to meet them. Encouraged by the arrival of the first wagon train the year before, a working party was camped in the thick timber of the western slope, trying to improve the road, for whose building federal funds still had not arrived.

By the time Ezra met his brother and the rest of the family, he had crossed the Cascades and the dry, sagebrush-covered plain beyond as far as the big bend of the Columbia where it turned westward toward the sea. Here at Wallula Gap, where the Hudson's Bay Company post first called Fort Nez Perces, then Fort Walla Walla, and now about to be abandoned as the British Company gave up its holdings in the United States, Ezra was reunited with his family. Sad to say, some of its members were missing.

> I inquired for my mother first thing. She was not there; had been buried in the sands of the Platte Valley months before; also a younger brother lay buried near Independence Rock. The scene that followed is of too sacred memory to write about, and we will draw the veil of privacy over it.

So shall we...

FIRST ATTEMPT

Though the the first American explorers of the Puget Sound region attributed the Indian fear of Mount Rainier to superstition, it probably was based on the more solid ground of practicality and racial memory. Above the 6,500 foot level, no vegetation grew, thus the only game to be found on the immense fields of ice and snow were mountain goats and marmots, the first hard to kill and the second tough to eat. Why waste time hunting poor game in that hostile environment when plenty of deer and elk were to be found at lower levels?

According to the grandfather tales by which the native Americans passed down their tribal history, "Takhoma," as the Indians called it, had once violently erupted in an explosion remarkably like that of Mount Saint Helens, killing hundreds of their people. Just as millions of present–day Washingtonians were impressed by the blast in 1980, the Indians remembered that ancient tragedy and avoided the mountain's upper region as a bad-luck place. Though their oral-memory calendar did not date the eruption, today's geologists say it happened about 5,700 years ago.

In any case, the Indians feared it might happen again, so instead of erecting an information center nearby and inviting distant Indians to visit the spot, they avoided the summit with dread and fear. When Naval Commander Charles Wilkes toured the region with his United States Exploring Expedition in 1841, he had great difficulty hiring an Indian guide willing to venture even part way up the lower slopes of the peak, let alone all the way to its crest.

A party led by Lieutenant Robert E. Johnson did cross the lower ridges of the mountain from west to east over what later became the Naches Pass route, but got no higher than 5,500 feet and no nearer the summit than ten miles.

It was not until the summer of 1857 that a serious attempt was made to ascend Mount Rainier, historian Edmund S. Meany writes in *Mount Rainier: a Record of Exploration*. Led by Lieutenant August Valentine Kautz, a US Army officer stationed at Fort Steilacoom, Washington Territory, the party's intentions were serious enough, but because of a lack of experience in mountain-climbing it encountered almost fatal difficulties.

To begin with, Lieutenant Kautz had never climbed a mountain before. As he himself admitted later, his only reason for making the attempt was that he was "...young, and fond of visiting unexplored sections of the country, and possessed of a very prevailing passion for going to the tops of high places." A number of his fellow officers expressed interest in making the climb when he was just talking about going, but none of them volunteered to join him when he actually decided to climb it in July, 1857. Though he managed to persuade a couple of enlisted men named Dogue and Carroll to "volunteer" for the trip, he was resigned to undertaking it with no other officer companion until a military doctor visiting from Fort Bellingham got intrigued with the project and decided to join him.

After reading accounts of the ascent of Mount Blanc and a few other peaks in Europe, Lieutenant Kautz writes:

> We made for each member of the party an alpenstock of dry ash with an iron point. We sewed upon our shoes an extra sole, through which were first driven four-penny nails with the points broken off and the heads inside. We took with us a rope about fifty feet long, a hatchet, a thermometer, plenty of hard biscuit, and dried beef such as the Indians prepare.

In order to lighten the packs as much as possible, each member of the party carried only his own provisions and bedding, along with a single tin canteen of water apiece. The doctor (who is not named) decided to lighten his load still further by filling his canteen with whisky instead of water. This proved to be a mistake, for by the middle of the first day—which was hot—his continued nips failed to quench his thirst, requiring him frequently to "borrow" a sip of water as a chaser from someone else's canteen, then finally to pour out what was left of the whisky and refill his canteen with water at the next stream. What his condition was by then can only be judged by what happened next.

Described by Lieutenant Kautz as a big, rawboned man, six feet tall and close to two hundred pounds, he became so "exhausted" that he could no longer carry his pack. When he developed severe leg cramps and was about to be left behind, he made a deal with the Indian guide, Wah-pow-e-ty, who agreed to carry his pack for ten dollars. Noting that the Indian, who now was carrying double, was twice as old and half as big as the doctor, Lieutenant Kautz made the sage observation that the doctor "...was habituated to a sedentary life..."

Of elbow-bending in the post canteen, no doubt.

For a week, the ill-prepared party of amateur mountain climbers struggled—"straggled" would be a better word—up the slopes and ice fields of a mountain so high and difficult to ascend that even experienced climbers take it very seriously today. Well below the summit, Private Carroll and the Indian gave out, saying they could go no further. Even with no pack to carry, the doctor began to lag behind. After pleading time and again for the Lieutenant to turn back, which Kautz refused to do, Private Dogue threw himself down on the ground and said he could go no further.

Though the top of the mountain was in sight, it was now late in the day and growing very cold; even in mid-summer Mount Rainier makes its own winter climate on the summit.

"I went on to explore by myself," Kautz writes, "but I returned in a quarter of an hour without my hat, fully satisfied that nothing more could be done. It was after six o'clock, the air was very cold, and the wind blew fiercely, so that in a second my hat which it carried away was far beyond recovery. The ice was forming in my canteen, and to stay on the mountain at such a temperature was to freeze to death."

Collecting the members of his party as he descended, Lieutenant Kautz dutifully recorded the doctor's scientific comment—which attributed his own "fatigue" to the "rarity of the atmosphere,"—though Kautz also noted non–scientifically, "My breathing did not seem to be in the least affected."

With the party's stock of provisions down to a total of four crackers, Lieutenant Kautz hoped that their Indian guide, Wah-pow-e-ty, who had brought along a rifle and was a good hunter, would kill a deer and provide some badly needed fresh meat. Meany writes:

> But this dependence, too, was cut off; the Indian was snow-blind, and needed our help to guide him. His groans disturbed us during the night, and what was our astonishment in the morning to find his eyelids closed with inflammation, and so swollen that he looked as if he had been in a free fight and got the worst of it. He could not have told a deer from a stump the length of his little old rifle.

During a night spent near the foot of a glacier, they heard the mountain working at one of its favorite pastimes, the mortar-and-pestle process of grinding granite rocks into the white powder which colors glacial rivers. "It was a fearful crashing and grinding that was going on, where the granite was powdered that whitened the river below, and where the boulders were polished and partially rounded."

After an absence of two weeks, the party returned to Fort Steilacoom so exhausted and emaciated that their fellow soldiers hardly recognized them.

"We found that the doctor had lost twenty-one pounds in weight in fourteen days," Lieutenant Kautz writes, "and I had lost fourteen pounds in the same time. The doctor, while we were in the village, was taken with violent pains in his stomach, and returned to his post quite sick. He did not recover his health again for three months."

Both Privates Carroll and Dogue reported to the hospital immediately, and for the rest of their military careers were in the hospital much of the time. The Indian guide suffered an acute attack of gastritis, Lieutenant Kautz writes, and was sick for a long time before he recovered. Only the young lieutenant himself came through the ordeal in good condition, a happy circumstance he attributes to sensible eating habits. Surviving to reach the rank of brigadier–general during the Civil War, August V. Kautz became Commander of the Department of the Columbia at Fort Vancouver, later retiring, living, and dying in 1895 in Seattle, from which on a clear day he could see the crest of the mountain he had almost been the first to climb.

In recording that attempt for historian Edmund Meany, he made a prediction that turned out to be at least half right when he said:

> When the locomotive is heard in that region some day, when American enterprise has established an ice cream saloon at the

Courtesy Washington State Library
ADMIRAL PETER RAINIER OF THE BRITISH NAVY, *CA* 1780

foot of the glacier, and sherry-cobblers may be had at twenty-five cents half-way to the top of the mountain, attempts to ascend that magnificent snow-peak will be quite frequent.

Quite frequent, the attempts have been. But not the twenty-five cent sherry-cobblers...

FIRST SUCCESSFUL ASCENT, 1870

Traveling with Governor Isaac Stevens on his hasty treaty-making tour of Washington Territory in 1855, was his thirteen-year old son, Hazard Stevens. If ever an outdoors-loving boy led an idyllic life, young Hazard certainly did. For example, he was at his father's side at the great council in the Walla Walla Valley when five thousand Indians representing the Nez Perce, Yakima, Cayuse, Walla Walla, and Umatilla tribes met Governor Stevens and his meager escort of one hundred soldiers in a nineteen-day

Courtesy Penrose Library, Whitman College
ICE CREVASSE NEAR SUMMIT OF MOUNT RAINIER IN 1900

treaty negotiating session. An expert horseman, an excellent hunter, and eager to learn all the survival skills the mountain men guides and Indian interpreters could teach him, he earned his father's trust to such a degree that Governor Stevens often used him as a courier to carry messages from one place to another, making swift round-trip rides of a hundred miles or more across wild country, accompanied only by an Indian boy his own age.

Twenty years old when the Civil War began, he became an officer in the Union Army, fighting at the side of his father, who was killed leading his regiment at the Battle of Chantilly in 1863. Returning to Washington Territory after the war, Hazard Stevens was residing on a farm near Olympia in 1870, when he and a friend named Philemon Beecher Van Trump decided that they

Courtesy Penrose Library, Whitman College
ICE CAVE NEAR SUMMIT OF MOUNT RAINIER IN 1900

would be the first to climb the as yet unscaled mountain in whose shadow they lived.

Like most local white people and all the local native Americans, they preferred some variant of the Indian name Takhoma, Tahoma, or Tacoma to the British title Rainier. But even after the prestigious eastern magazine *Atlantic Monthly* published "The Ascent of Mount Takhoma" by Hazard Stevens in November, 1876 the Bureau of Geographic Names refused to make the change. In several local Indian tongues, "Tacoma" and its variants simply means "The Mountain." An interesting white variant sometimes used by ex–trappers was "Old He." But by any name, the mountain was there, and, during the summer of 1870, was about to be climbed.

Hearing about the proposed expedition, a Canadian resident suggested giving it an international flavor by letting him join the party. At first, this struck Hazard Stevens as a good idea. He wrote, "Mr. Edward T. Coleman, an English gentleman of Victoria, a landscape artist and an Alpine tourist, whose reputed experience in Switzerland had raised a high opinion of his ability above the snow-line, completed the party."

By then, a passable wagon road had been completed from Olympia across Yelm Prairie thirty miles up into the foothills to the home of a settler named James Longmire, who had homesteaded there and explored more of the lower reaches of the mountain than any other white man. Spending the night and being served a good supper and breakfast by Mrs. Longmire, who rose from her sick bed to prepare the meals, Stevens and Van Trump tried to persuade James Longmire to go with them as a guide. Reluctant to leave his wife for an extended length of time, he at first declined, then said that he would put them on the trail—which was hard to find—and travel with them for as long as it took to hire a competent Indian guide. That settled, Stevens and Van Trump accepted the invitation of their new British friend to come to his room and inspect the equipment he had brought along for the climb, each and every item of which he regarded as indispensable.

Merely listing the articles—which ranged from a large gum blanket that would serve as a ground-sheet, tent, or a portable bathtub, to "creepers" to prevent slipping on the ice, through "...several medical prescriptions, two boards for pressing flowers, and sketching materials..."—required half a page of print in Hazard Stevens' article. How and by whom all this equipment was going to be carried to the top of the mountain was a minor detail with which Mr. Coleman did not concern himself.

Somewhat caustically, Hazard Stevens noted an earlier incident when an old mountain man named Packwood had been employed to guide a railroad survey party across the lower reaches of the Cascades. Before leaving the settlements, Stevens wrote, Packwood asked the chief of the party if he could have a cash advance with which to buy his outfit for the trip.

"How much do you want?"

"Well, about two dollars and a half."

Given the money, he went to the nearest trading post, bought what he needed, then returned to camp. When asked that evening to show what he had purchased, he reached into his pocket and hauled out his newly purchased supplies—a jack-knife and a plug of tobacco.

How much equipment Coleman finally was allowed to bring along, Hazard Stevens does not say, but quite a bit of it must have been left behind, for when the party set out, next morning, it consisted of only four rather small mules, the first ridden by Stevens, the second by both Van Trump and Coleman riding double, while Longmire followed behind on one laden pack mule, whose lead rope Coleman supposedly was holding in his hand, while a second pack mule trailed behind. Stevens writes:

> The cavalcade, linked together in this order, had but just entered the stream when Coleman dropped the neckrope he was holding. The mule, bewildered by the rush and roar of the waters, turned directly down-stream, and in another instant our two pack animals, with their riders, would have been swept away in the furious rapids, had not Longmire with great presence of mind turned their erratic course in the right direction and safely brought them to the opposite shore.

Experienced mountain-climber though he may have been by European standards, it was beginning to be apparent that the British artist was not very dependable when such a mundane matter as holding onto the end of a rope in the Cascade wilderness was concerned. More of his shortcomings soon would be revealed.

In a timber and grass area called Bear Prairie, the party found the camp of a Yakima Indian named Saluskin, who agreed to act as their guide at least part way to the top. In Chinook Jargon, he told them that he had frequently hunted mountain sheep on the snow fields of the upper slopes, though he had never ascended to the summit itself. Stevens wrote that he said, "It was impossible to do so, and he put aside as idle talk our expressed intention of making the ascent."

Satisfied that he had put them in good hands, Longmire set out for home. Because from here on they would climb afoot, they reduced their stock of food and equipment to absolute essentials, which they divided into forty-pound packs. Next morning:

> Saluskin led the way...Leaving the last vestige of trail, we toiled in single file slowly and and laboriously up the mountain all afternoon. The steepness of the ascent in many places required the use of both hand and foot in climbing, and the exercise of great caution to keep the heavy packs from dragging us over backwards. Coleman lagged behind from the start, and at intervals his voice could be heard halloing and calling upon us to wait.

Toward evening, Stevens, Van Trump, and their Indian guide reached a level terrace, where they decided to camp, threw off their packs and waited for Coleman, who they thought was just below. When he failed to appear, Saluskin went back down the slope looking for him. After an hour or so, the Indian returned and told them that he finally had found Coleman some distance down the mountain. Stevens writes:

> He was near the foot of the mountain, had thrown away his pack, blankets and all, and was evidently returning to camp...What was to be done? Coleman carried in his pack all our bacon, our only supply of meat except a few pounds of dried beef. He also had the barometer, the only instrument that had survived the jolts and tumbles of our rough trip. But, on the other hand, he had been a clog on our march from the outset. He was evidently too infirm to endure the toil before us, and would not only be unable to reach, still less ascend Takhoma, but might even impede and frustrate our own efforts. Knowing that he would be safe in camp until our return, we hastily concluded to proceed without him, trusting to our rifles for a supply of meat.

After a rugged day of climbing across ice fields, then descending fifteen hundred feet down steep slopes into timbered meadows, the party made camp on the divide between the headwaters of the Nisqually and Cowlitz Rivers. Saluskin killed a grouse, which they broiled for supper to go with their coffee and dry bread. Convinced now that these crazy white men really intended to attempt climbing to the top of the mountain, Saluskin did his best to talk them out of it.

> Takhoma, he said, was an enchanted mountain, inhabited by an evil spirit, who dwelt in a fiery lake on its summit. No human being could ascend it or even attempt its ascent, and survive...
> Finding that his words did not produce the desired effect, he assured us that, if we persisted in attempting the ascent, he would wait three days for our return, and would then proceed to Olympia and inform our friends of our death; and he begged us to give him a paper (a written note) to take to them, so that they might believe his story.

For a long while after the two white men rolled into their blankets, their Indian guide sat by the fire, chanting what sounded to them like a dirge or a requiem for their souls, appropriately accompanied by the low, distant rumble of avalanches roaring down the steep, icy slopes they would be climbing tomorrow.

Leaving Saluskin behind next morning, the two men moved on up the mountain to the ice fields, where they donned snow-spikes and used alpenstocks as they planned their route for a final assault on the summit.

"In honor of our guide we named the cascade at our feet Saluskin Falls; the stream we named Glacier Creek, and the mass of ice whence it derives its source we styled the Little Nisqually Glacier."

Before daylight the next morning, Wednesday, August 17, 1870, they got up, had breakfast, and by six o'clock were on their way. After a long, exhausting, dangerous climb of eleven hours, they reached what they judged to be one summit of the mountain, which they called Peak Success. Though it was now so late in the day that they faced the bleak prospect of spending a night without shelter, they decided to cross a rocky ridge to another peak about a mile distant, which appeared to be two hundred feet higher. Reaching it after strenuous effort, they were rewarded with a pleasant surprise.

"As we were crossing the crater on the snow, Van Trump detected the odor of sulphur, and the next instant numerous jets of steam and smoke were observed issuing from the crevices of the rocks which formed the rim on the northern side. Never was a discovery more welcome! Hastening forward, we both exclaimed, as we warmed our chilled and benumbed extremities over one of Pluto's fires, that here we would pass the night, secure against freezing to death, at least."

Hazard Stevens then goes on to describe in detail a phenomenon still to be seen on the crest of Mount Rainier today—the steam-heated ice caves.

> A deep cavern, extending into and under the ice, and formed by the action of heat, was found. Its roof was a dome of brilliant green ice with long icicles pendent [sic] from it, while its floor, composed of the rocks and debris which formed the side of the crater, descended at an angle of thirty degrees. Forty feet within its mouth we built a wall of stones, inclosing a space five by six feet around a strong jet of steam and heat...The heat at the orifice was too great to bear for more than an instant, but the steam wet us, the smell of sulphur was nauseating, and the cold was so severe that our clothes, saturated with the steam, froze stiff when we turned away from the heated jet. The wind outside roared and whistled, but it did not much affect us, secure within our cavern....

Descending the mountain the next day much more rapidly than they had climbed it, Van Trump slipped while crossing a snow field, skidded forty feet down a steep incline into a pile of rocks, and suffered extensive cuts and bruises. But camp was nearby, and soon they had a fire going, made coffee, and roasted the four marmots Saluskin had killed and dressed for them, in the unlikely event that they did survive their climb to the top of the sacred, evil mountain. Despite its tough, muscular taste and "doggy" odor, the two men were hungry enough to relish it. As they finished, Saluskin returned to camp, saw them, and was astonished to find them still alive.

"*Skookum tilicum, skookum tumtum*," he kept repeating. "We were strong men with brave hearts. He expected never to see us again, he said, and had resolved to start the next morning for Olympia to report our destruction."

Since that time, Mount Rainier has been climbed many times, but it still is a peak that must be respected, whose ascent should be undertaken only by people in good physical condition under the direction of experienced guides.

MOUNT RAINIER NATIONAL PARK

Designated a National Park in 1899 and covering some 235,404 acres, Mount Rainier is an easily accessible mountain in its lower reaches, with the most popular access reached from Tacoma by driving sixty miles southeast on State Highways 7 and 706 to Longmire and Paradise Valley at the five thousand foot level. All sorts of tourist facilities are available here, though at times during the height of the season the most wanted amenity—a parking place—is not to be found.

With a total of twenty-six glaciers covering the mountain and hundreds of miles of logging roads criss-crossing the lower slopes and the Pacific Crest Trail nearby, solitude may still be found by those who seek it. If a closeup look at a working glacier is desired, the Nisqually Glacier Vista Trail provides views of a three-mile–long river of ice. It may be reached from the Paradise Visitor Center by means of an easy, one-mile, round-trip walk through a beautiful flowering meadow, though the foot traffic is so heavy the path has been black-topped in order to save the wild grasses and flowers.

The last violent eruption of Mount Rainier took place 5,700 years ago, when the peak's 16,000–foot top blew off and the Puget Sound lowland country now occupied by Olympia, Tacoma, and suburbs southeast of Seattle was inundated with a hundred or so feet of hot rock and ash. But the volcano's internal fires have by no means gone out. As recently as 1961, steam blasted a hole near Gibraltar Rock, sending a column of pressurized vapor two hundred feet into the air and scattering debris over the nearby Cowlitz Glacier.

What may have been the largest avalanche in modern times was initiated on December 14, 1963, when forest rangers heard a loud boom from the direction of Mount Rainier. The rangers later learned that approximately 14 million cubic yards of lava and gravel had fallen from the north face of Little Tahoma Peak. Plummeting straight down for 1,700 feet, the avalanche struck the glacier with tremendous force, shooting across it at speeds up to 100 miles an hour. One of the boulders it carried weighed 50,000 tons.

In view of these verified facts in the present, can we doubt an Indian legend of the past relating how a father displeased with his quarreling sons threw a rock so big that it crushed a natural bridge spanning the Columbia River?

Like all the peaks in the Washington Cascades, Mount Rainier now is "wired" and carefully monitored so that the experts can keep a volcano watch on it. Some day, they know, "Old He" may decide to show little sister, Saint Helens, what big brother can do when he really puts his mind to it.

THREE PEAKS:
GLACIER, SHUKSAN, BAKER

In our travels over the State of Washington for many years, I have collected a number of treasures that cannot be put in scrapbooks or hung on walls. Ferry rides, mountain passes, and vistas of snow-capped peaks from viewpoints as close as we can get without resorting to jeep, horse, or foot trails are included in this collection, for in no other state south of Alaska may such a variety be seen. Because most of the readers of this book will be seeing the Cascades without straying too far off surfaced roads, as we have done for the past two years, I have tried to direct them over high-

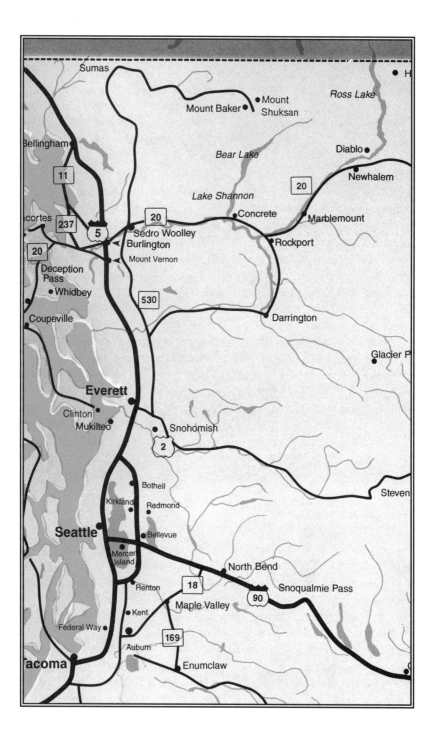

ways on which they will find a minimum of traffic and a maximum of scenery.

What follows is a suggested route covering both the west and east sides of the Cascades from Mount Rainier north to the Canadian border. Since this is a matter of only two hundred miles on I-5, the distance can be covered in half a day, if one is in a hurry, but the route detailed here is quite a bit longer and slower. Assuming that the traveler has ended up his visit to Mount Rainier at Enumclaw headed west on US 410 and would like to try the scenic route in total or in part, here it is:

State 169—Enumclaw to Maple Valley
  15 miles
State 18—Maple Valley to North Bend
  16 miles
I-90—North Bend to Cle Elum
  68 miles
State 970—Cle Elum to Jct. US 97
  7 miles
US 97—Jct. to Leavenworth
  46 miles
US 2—Leavenworth to Stevens Pass
  36 miles
US 2—Stevens Pass to Snohomish
  58 miles
State 9—Snohomish to Sumas
  92 miles
State 547, 542—Sumas to Mount Baker
  45 miles

Because the Cascade Mountains split Washington State down the middle from north to south, its residents have long since come to use the term "East and West of the Mountains" to describe their differences. Not only are the climates of the two regions dramatic opposites, so are the living conditions, the economics, and the politics of the two areas. From 1853 when Washington was first organized as a Territory down to the present day, the contrast has been sharp. Despite the homogenizing effects of improved communication and transportation, marked distinctions between the two parts of the state still are visible in both the scenery and the attitudes of the people. Taken for granted by most Washington residents are assumptions that:

West of the mountains, it rains nine months out of the year, never gets too hot or too cold, traffic is in perpetual gridlock, everybody living near Puget Sound owns a boat, and the economy is fueled by Boeing, Weyerhauser, trade with Alaska, salmon-fishing, and clam-digging.

East of the mountains, both winter and summer are six months long, with lots of snow and sub–zero cold in winter and no rain and hundred–degree heat in summer, relieved only now and then by a dust-storm. Here one can look further and see less than anywhere else in the country, the land is populated by more cows than people, has practically no traffic or culture, and is made habitable only by the Columbia River, whose Grand Coulee Dam stores a massive amount of irrigation water and generates electricity for more civilized places such as Seattle.

That both concepts are cliches with many exceptions changes nobody's basic attitude. Firmly believing the slogan, "Divided we stand," the five million people living in unbalanced numbers on the wet and dry side of the Cascades somehow manage to get along together, even though they agree on only one thing: that theirs is the best state in the union.

NORTH BEND TO CLE ELUM AND STEVENS PASS

Boosters of Interstate 90, which crosses the northern United States, recently made a great ceremony over the removal of the single traffic light between Boston and Seattle, which happened to be in Wallace, Idaho. Motorists who so desire now may drive from coast to coast without stopping. But when crossing the Cascades, at least, most of them will look at the scenery, which is truly spectacular.

Rising gradually in long, easy curves through green, timbered foothills to the crest of Snoqualmie Pass at 3,022 feet, the Interstate carries a heavy amount of commercial and tourist traffic. But many of the drivers on winter weekends are snow-loving Puget Sound dwellers who can go from "sea level to ski level" in only a couple of hours.

Because most of the moisture is drained from the clouds by the western slope, the trees become thinner and more widely spaced as the highway descends to Cle Elum, changing imperceptibly from Douglas fir to Ponderosa pine, with the undergrowth going from lacy fern to small scattered bushes.

Where US 97 turns north from Cle Elum toward Leavenworth, the main spine of the Cascades averages eight thousand feet, with only here and there a higher peak standing alone. Receiving a heavy winter snowfall because of their proximity to the crest of the Cascades, the high ridges were not easily traversed by north–south trails in pack-train, horse-and-wagon, and early automobile days, though of recent years highway standards have improved to such an extent that even the steepest mountain passes can be crossed without the driver being sure if the grade is rising or falling.

For example, Swauk Pass on US 97, which crosses a spur of the Cascades, is so well-graded and gradual at 4,102 feet, that it bears no resemblance to the crooked, narrow, steep highway that it replaced, Blewett Pass, which was a few feet lower at 4,071 feet. Now closed in winter, Blewett is still on the map as a blue-line highway in case a nostalgic driver wishes to compare the old with the new. Since I already have several winter crossings of Blewett in my collection, I usually resist the temptation to try it again.

As noted earlier, the first governor of Washington Territory, Isaac Stevens, was instructed to survey a northern route for a transcontinental railroad on his way out from St. Paul to Puget Sound in 1853–54. From the beginning, he knew that his greatest problem would be to find a feasible pass that a railroad could climb across the Cascade Mountains. Searching for such as a pass from saltwater east, Lieutenant George McClellan was no help, for when the local Indians told him that snow in the Cascades often reached a depth of twenty feet, he gave up the task as impossible.

But the word "impossible" was not in the newly-appointed governor's vocabulary. Though it took him a while longer than he originally planned, he did discover a route that a railroad could climb across the Cascades of northwest Washington. When the Great Northern was completed into Everett in 1893 by "Empire Builder" James J. Hill, the line required some spectacular feats of engineering, tunneling, switchback and snowshed building before the trains could run. But it used the trail Governor Stevens had blazed.

Today's highway US 2, which crosses the Cascades from Leavenworth to Everett, closely follows the route Stevens laid out. Appropriately, Stevens Pass, 4,061 feet, is named after the governor. As a main artery of travel, it is kept open the year round and is second only to Snoqualmie Pass in the amount of traffic carried. The snowdrifts still get twenty feet deep, just as the Indians told McClellan they did, making tough work for rotary plows on both the railroad and the highway, but most of the time the two arteries of travel are kept open.

SNOHOMISH TO SUMAS

In the ninety-two miles from Snohomish north to Sumas, State 9 stays down in green, level, lowland country, with Puget Sound a few miles to the west and the vast rugged wilderness of the North Cascades to the east. Here, the range of mountains is at its widest and least populated, for most of the region is designated National Forest, National Park, or National Wilderness. Between US 2 and the Canadian border—a distance of one hundred miles—it is crossed only by the North Cascades Highway, which, because of extremely heavy snowfall, is closed in winter. In the next chapter, we will cross the Cascades by that route, but first we want to take a look at the region's three principal mountains—Glacier Peak, Mount Shuksan, and Mount Baker.

Though the terms "shy" and "virgin" hardly seem appropriate when applied to mountains, Glacier Peak, 10,451 feet high, often is called that by geologists and wilderness lovers, for it is seen and climbed only by those relatively few people who know it is there and are willing to make a strenuous effort to reach it.

Located halfway between Darrington on the west and Lake Chelan on the east, Glacier looms above an eight thousand foot high jumble of slightly lower peaks whose very names are rugged—Fortress Mountain, Mount Formidable, Forbidden Peak,

Mount Fury, Mount Terror. For such a shy mountain, it certainly has a violent past. During eruptions 12,000 to 200 years ago, it disgorged large quantities of pumice and ash. Today, geologists regard Glacier Peak as one of the half dozen most active volcanoes in the Cascade Range.

Because at least two of its eruptions left distinctive ash layers over a wide area, scientists use these deposits to help date other geological formations or archaeological remains, he says.

Though there are no active fumaroles at the present time, several hot springs on the flanks of the cone indicate that the magma underneath is still warm. Potentially, Glacier Peak ranks high on the list of volcanoes to be watched for future eruptions.

MOUNT BAKER AND SHUKSAN

Despite its impressive height of 10,775 feet, Mount Baker was not named for British Lords of the Admiralty who never saw the peaks, as were Hood and Saint Helens. Instead, Captain George Vancouver named it for an officer on his ship, Third Lieutenant Joseph Baker, who first sighted it in 1792 and described it as "a very high, conspicuous, craggy mountain...."

Strictly speaking, it had been discovered and named two years earlier by the Spanish explorer Manuel Quimper, who had christened it *La Gran Montana del Carmelo* (The Great Mountain of the Carmelite), in honor of a feast day of the Carmelite Order. But as often happened in those days, the simpler, more pronounceable name stuck.

Because of its extensive snowfields and glaciers, its steep slopes are sheathed in white much of the year, so its Nooksack Indian name, *Quck-Sam-ik* (White Rock Mountain) also would have been appropriate. Another local Indian tribe, the Lummis, had observed its volcanic activity over many generations, so they called it *Komo Kulshan*, (Shot at the Point), which referred to the legend that the peak had been struck and scarred by a lightning bolt cast by the gods, making it smolder and smoke ever after. But the simpler name Mount Baker outlasted the more complicated competitors.

Located only twelve miles east and slightly north, steep, rugged Mount Shuksan, 9,127 feet, is a fit mate for Mount Baker; both are sentinels in the North Cascade Wilderness, offering a challenge to people who like their mountains untamed. According to the *WPA Guide*, the Indian name means "steep, rocky, precipitous," which Mount Shuksan certainly is. It defied attempts by mountain climbers to scale it until 1906, though its taller neighbor, Mount Baker, was successfully climbed half a century earlier, in 1868. Together, the two peaks and adjacent areas are so rugged that when movie makers were looking for a location resembling Alaska for films such as *Call of the Wild* by Jack London and *The Barrier* by Rex Beach, they found Heather Meadows, between the two mountains, ideal for their scenic purposes.

Today, a paved, steep, crooked road goes east from Sumas and Maple Valley to Mount Baker Lodge and Heather Meadows Viewpoint, where a dramatic vista of the two peaks and the adjacent wilderness area is obtained. Despite the tremendous amount of snowfall in the vicinity, the road to the Lodge and the ski-lifts is kept open most of the time; winter sports have a long season here because of the altitude.

Though four thousand feet lower than Rainier, Mount Baker still was a difficult peak to climb. Because Edmund T. Coleman, the man credited with its first ascent in 1868, also was involved in the Stevens–Van Trump attempt to climb Mount Rainier in 1870, it is interesting to compare the two "first climbs" as recorded by the men who accomplished them—and to examine some discrepancies in their stories.

FIRST ASCENT OF MOUNT BAKER

To the layman interested in geology and native American history, an attempt to relate the record in the rocks with Indian legends is both intriguing and baffling. For example, "an old Indian" told Edmund Coleman in 1866 that when he was a boy around 1810 a Mount Baker eruption deposited so much ash in the Skagit River that all its fish were killed for the next two years. Coleman also was told by local Indians that in 1864 the upper one thousand or fifteen hundred feet of Mount Baker had collapsed into its crater, "so that the appearance of the peak was decidedly altered as seen from Victoria, Vancouver Island, it being no longer conical and sharp, but truncated."

Despite the fact that exactly those two things happened when Mount Saint Helens exploded in 1980, geologists say they have found no confirming evidence in the rocks that similar events happened on Mount Baker. Would the experts have believed the awesome cataclysms that occurred on Mount Saint Helens, we

Courtesy Washington State Library
MOUNT SHUKSAN
The view is from Picture Lake, near Mount Baker Lodge.

wonder, if no one but native Americans had been around to witness and report them years later?

In any case, Edmund Thomas Coleman was a Britisher living
in Victoria, B.C., who became a member of the Stevens–Van
Trump party in their assault on Mount Rainier in 1870. Somewhat
superciliously, Hazard Stevens wrote that Coleman "claimed to be
an artist and an experienced mountain climber." Despite these not
very subtle efforts to disparage Coleman's abilities, his credentials
on both counts were impeccable. A charter member of the English
Alpine Club, which had been established in 1857, he was a trained
librarian, an amateur botanist, and an accomplished artist with
sufficient talent that his paintings had been placed on exhibition
in the Royal Academy in London in 1849, 1853, and 1854.

Having climbed all the peaks in the Alps and in search of new
challenges, he came to Victoria in 1862, bringing with him a tool
never used in mountain-climbing in America before, the ice axe. A
lifelong bachelor, he apparently had inherited a fortune, which he

went through pursuing expensive hobbies such as traveling, mountain-climbing, and painting. By 1866, he was supporting himself by working as the librarian of the Mechanics' Institute in Victoria.

On a clear day, Mount Baker was visible from the waterfront, where he often gazed longingly at it, recalling the Alps, becoming, as he wrote, "jaded and depressed, sick of the monotonous round of my ordinary occupation." So in the summer of 1866, he decided he would attempt to climb it.

Accompanied by Dr. Robert Brown of Edinburgh and Federal Judge Charles Benjamin Darwin of Washington Territory, he loaded supplies and climbing gear into an Indian canoe and headed up the Skagit River toward the base of Mount Baker, July 21, 1866. Six miles up the river, a massive log jam required three exhausting portages through mosquito-filled lowlands. Beyond these hazards, the local Koma Indians, whom the three men tried to hire as guides, proved hostile, refusing either to work for the white men or let them pass through their country. So the attempt had to be abandoned for the time being.

Returning to Victoria, Edmund Coleman stayed there less than a week before trying again with different companions and another approach to the base of the mountain. This time, he ascended the Nooksack River in the company of two American settlers, John Bennett and John Tennant, who were friendly with both the Lummi and Nooksack Indians. Hiring two members of the Nooksack tribe as guides, the party got as far up the mountain as snow-line, where Tennant became ill, remaining behind with the two Indians, while Coleman and Bennett attempted to complete the climb.

Bringing all his climbing skills into play, Coleman got himself and his companion within fifty feet of the final summit, where an overhanging cornice of ice brought them to a halt too late in the day to make a try for the top. Retreating to a nearly vertical wall of ice which they named Coleman Saddle, they spent a miserable night without blankets in temperatures so cold they had to keep moving or freeze to death. In his book *Mount Baker: a Chronicle of Its Historic Eruptions and First Ascent*, historian Harry M. Majors writes, "The next morning, Coleman and Bennett made another attempt to get over the barrier but failed. Not only was the route unfeasible at this time, it was also very dangerous on account of

Courtesy Washington State Library
HIKING THE HIGHLANDS OF MOUNT BAKER NATIONAL FOREST

avalanches and sliding ice. . . At the Coleman Saddle, Bennett left a flag he had hoped to carry to the summit of Mount Baker, along with a `pain killer' bottle. Both items were found here untouched two years later..."

SUCCESSFUL ASCENT, AUGUST 17, 1868

In a long article published in *Harper's Monthly*, November, 1869, titled "Mountaineering on the Pacific," Edmund Coleman related his experiences on Mount Blanc in the Alps, and on the Olympic Peninsula of Washington Territory, then related the successful climb of Mount Baker which he led in 1868. This article must have been read by Hazard Stevens by 1870, so his statement that Coleman was "...an Alpine tourist, whose reputed experience in Switzerland had raised a high opinion of his ability above the snow-line..." may have been shaded by a touch of jealousy. At the very least, it seems strange that Stevens does not mention the fact that Coleman was the conqueror of Mount Baker.

In any event, after twice failing to reach the summit of Mount Baker in 1866, Coleman put together another party in the summer of 1868. This one included John Tennant, who had climbed with him on the second attempt; Thomas Stratton, Inspector of Customs at Port Townsend, and David Ogilvy of Victoria.

Again, the route chosen was up the Nooksack River. Making their final base camp where they would leave their Indian packers just downslope from the ice fields, they killed a ptarmigan, a snowy partridge, and four marmots, with which Stratton, the "chef de cuisine" of the party, cooked what was pronounced to be an excellent stew, made more palatable by "half a bottle of sauce" whose ingredients he did not reveal. As the most experienced mountain-climber in the party, Coleman had brought along some special footwear, which now was tested.

> Tennant and Stratton went to try some creepers (crampons) which had been made for the occasion, being doubtful that they would answer; they also reconnoitered the proposed route. They returned in high spirits from their preliminary essay, declaring that with the creepers they could walk up the slopes of the snow as firmly as on a hill-side.

Packing provisions for twenty-four hours so that they could spend the night on the summit, if need be, they blacked their faces against sun-glare and began their climb up the steep, icy ridge. A few days earlier, Stratton, who was very handsome and something of a ladies' man, had asked a member of the gentler sex he had encountered at a social gathering in Bellingham to pray for his success in climbing the unscaled peak. She refused, saying, "Oh, no; you'll be so much closer to Heaven that you better do the praying."

Roping themselves together at twenty-five foot intervals so that if one fell because of the collapse of a snow bridge or slid into a crevice, the others could hold him, they crossed twenty-seven "great crevasses" in a distance of three miles. On one of his earlier trips, Coleman noted, he had made good use of his ice axe in crossing a two-foot wide gap when:

> I made a leap, ice-axe in hand, with the pick pointed downward, so that I might easily anchor on the snow. As I made the spring Mr. (John) Bennett pushed me with his pole, and I managed to alight and catch on to the slope. Fixing myself firmly in the snow with the aid of my pole, Mr. Bennett made a leap, and at the same time I gave him a good tug with the rope, and he managed it also in safety.

Again, the ice axe was put to good use, for fresh snow had fallen on the steep, sixty-degree slope, but it had not had time to bind with the older ice beneath, and could not be trusted.

We had thus to cut steps. The axe was passed on to Stratton, who plied it with vigor and skill. While thus engaged he got a great fright. Having heard a dull, grating sound, he looked up, and saw a mass of frozen snow, about twelve feet square, moving down toward him. Paralyzed with terror, he was about to warn us, when it fortunately stopped. Even at this height there were crevasses. Into one of these Tennant sank, but he managed to extricate himself. The work of cutting the steps is very severe, and our progress was necessarily slow, for some 350 were required to be cut.

Bypassing the overhanging cornice that had defeated them two years earlier by cutting steps and then moving transversely around it, the party reached the summit at four o'clock in the afternoon. In words, Edmund Coleman described what he would later recreate in sketches:

The plateau on which we stood was about a quarter of a mile in diameter, and embraced an extent of about eighty acres. The scene was grand in the nakedness of its desolation. The white surface of the snow was unrelieved by a single rock. The forests had been on fire for weeks, and a dense pall of smoke veiled the surrounding scenery from our view. It lay like a reddish cloud beneath us. We felt cut off from the world we had left. Overhead the sun poured down his bright beams from a sky which formed a dome of purplish blue, unsullied by a cloud. We felt at Heaven's gate, and in the immediate presence of the Almighty.

After singing a chorus of the *Doxology* and sharing a sip of brandy from a flask, the party planted a flagstaff in the snow and christened the peak General Grant. Noting another summit five hundred yards away, which they thought might be higher, they crossed to it and planted another flag there, dubbing it General Sherman. Later, they learned that the two peaks were the same height, but there could be no question that they had reached the summit.

While Edmund Coleman sketched furiously, his companions explored a nearby depression that appeared to be a volcanic crater whose black walls were streaked with yellow, green, and red rocks. Ribbons of steam were seen issuing from vents; the fact that there was no snow on the lava indicated that fire was slumbering in the rocks below.

"My companions returned about five," Coleman complained, "and hurried me off before I had an opportunity of inspecting it personally. Indeed, as there was no time, unless we spent the night on the summit, they concluded not to tell me of their good fortune."

As they started their descent, enough daylight remained so that they could pick their way down through the treacherous ice fields while visibility still was good. By nine o'clock, they reached the lower limits of the snow-line, then stumbled for two hours through the darkness until they saw the welcoming campfires their Indian guides had built for them.

Since they had started their climb at 6:30 a.m., it had been a long day.

STEAM CAVES ON MOUNT BAKER

The assumption made by Edmund Coleman that the steam and the lack of snow on the crater summit indicated that the mountain was still alive proved accurate in the years to come. The steam caves in Sherman Crater remain an interesting feature of the summit today. Like those on Mount Rainier, the caves were formed as heat melted a series of passageways and chambers between the crater floor and the overlying snowpack.

Following his successful ascent of Mount Baker, Edmund Coleman, looking for new peaks to conquer, turned his gaze southward toward Mount Rainier. In an earlier chapter, Hazard Stevens has given his account of that venture, as well as his opinion of Edmund Coleman. But historian Harry M. Majors tells a different story.

In August, 1870, Coleman did join Hazard Stevens and Philemon Van Trump in their attempt to ascend Mount Rainier, he writes. But as an artist and experienced mountaineer, Coleman wanted to do some sketching along the way and was not in as much of a hurry as they were. Not only did he instruct them in the use of the crampons, he also loaned them his ice axe, a tool they had never seen before; in fact, when they complained of his slow pace and parted company with him, they took along his ice axe and carried it with them to the crest of Mount Rainier. Majors writes:

> When Coleman's pack tumbled down a mountainside, his two companions summarily abandoned him and left the English

botanist to fend for himself. Stevens and Van Trump headed upward toward imagined visions of fame and glory, their chief regret being that Coleman's lost pack had contained their provision of bacon.

In Hazard Stevens' account of the climb, which was published in the *Atlantic Monthly* in November, 1876, he mentions the missing bacon. But he says nothing about Edmund Coleman's ice axe, which went along on the climb and proved to be a very useful tool. This being the case, it seems to have received shabby treatment. Majors writes:

> When Stevens and Van Trump descended from Rainier, they left it embedded in a tree at the base of the mountain instead of returning it to Coleman. In 1892, Len Longmire found the ice axe, removed the metal head from the rotting haft, and placed this on a new shaft of wood. Longmire carried the historic ice axe to the summit of Mount Rainier on September 3, 1892, but lost it in a snow drift on the summit. It has never been found, and probably has since settled with its snow layer to the rock of the summit crater.

So symbolically, at least, Edmund Coleman did make the climb. The assumption that the ice axe lost on the summit will remain there forever is not necessarily true, for glaciers, though they move very slowly, have been known to give up well-preserved bodies of woolly mammoths, Stone Age men, and artifacts thousands of years after they fell into a crevasses.

Perhaps a few dozen centuries from now a child walking with his parents at the foot of Nisqually Glacier will find an ice axe in the rock debris of the terminal moraine and wonder who lost such an intriguing tool.

NORTH CASCADES NATIONAL PARK

To reach the North Cascades Park, you must backtrack from the Mount Baker area on State 542 and 9 to Sedro Woolley, from which US 20 goes east for 109 scenic miles to Winthrop. It is a paved, well-graded highway capable of accommodating all kinds of passenger and recreational vehicles, but is closed because of heavy snowfall during the winter—usually between mid–November and early April.

Because the one hundred mile sector of the Cascades between Highway US 2 and the Canadian border is designated National

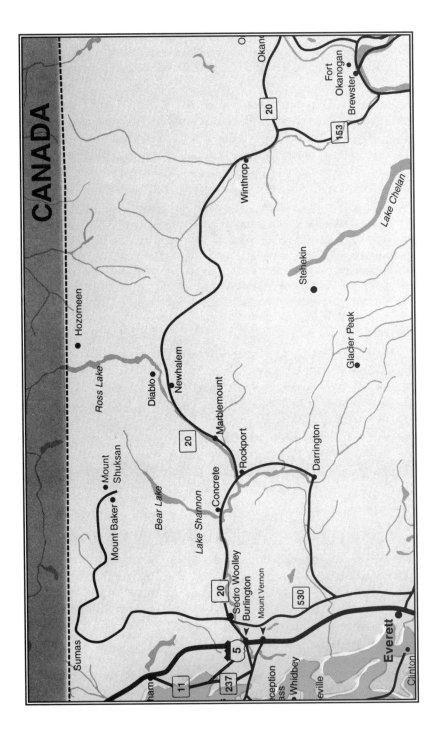

Park, Wilderness, or Recreation Area land, only one highway crosses it from west to east. From its opening in 1972, the North Cascades Highway has been called "The Most Beautiful Mountain Highway in the State of Washington." It lives up to its name.

Along a narrow corridor through the Park, a number of small towns such as Concrete, Rockport, Marblemount, and Newhalem offer commercial services and information regarding the roads leading into the lakes and scenic areas, which give access to trailheads, campgrounds, and boat-launching facilities.

In 1884 when settlement began in the Skagit River Valley, women had not yet been given the vote, but they certainly could and did exercise the veto power. In a region covered with such heavy stands of red cedar that the trees were considered an obstacle to be cleared away so that the land could be farmed, the village begun by a male pioneer named Mortimer Cook first was called "Bug." But the ladies—with no intentions of being squashed—would not stand for that, insisting on the more genteel name "Sedro"—which is Spanish for "cedar."

With its name now painted on the rough boards of a storefront, the town at the head of navigation on the Skagit River soon attracted a shingle mill, then briefly prospered as an outfitting center for a short-lived gold rush to the Mount Baker area.

"When, in 1889, the Great Northern and Northern Pacific railroads established a junction north of Sedro," says the *WPA Guide*, "P.A. Woolley, an enterprising individual, platted a townsite at the crossing. Jealousy arose between the towns, but a reconciliation soon followed, and in 1890 the two cities combined their names and incorporated as one."

Because of its rugged remoteness, few explorers or travelers penetrated the wilderness of the North Cascades. In 1814, a Canadian fur trader, Alexander Ross, crossed the lower part of what would become the Park. Between 1880 and 1910, a few miners prospecting for gold, lead, zinc, and platinum did make some minor strikes, but transportation was so difficult and the returns so meager that the area never did develop as a profitable mining region. Working as an assistant on the International Boundary

US 20—Sedro Woolley to Winthrop
109 miles

Commission in 1859, a surveyor named Henry Custer made an accurate assessment of the region when he wrote, "Nowhere do the mountain masses and peaks present such strange, fantastic, dauntless and startling outlines as here." After saying which, he summed up his feelings by saying that "words failed him."

In the low-lying areas where the trees were more accessible, extensive logging operations were carried on well into the present century. The hydroelectric potential of the Skagit River was recognized at an early day, as was the need for storage dams to control the flow of the river, which in times of flood wrecked the settlements and farms in the low country with massive crests of mud and debris.

Between 1924 and 1961, Seattle City Light built three dams on the river, supplying cheap hydro power to its customers and taking the top off disastrous floods in the lowlands, though there was no way to control them completely. Built in a chain upstream from one another on the river, Gorge Lake covers 210 acres, Diablo Lake 910 acres, while Ross Lake, which is two miles wide and twenty-four miles long, covers 12,000 acres and backs water across the border into Canada.

To the west of the Park north of Concrete, there are two more reservoirs, Lake Shannon and Baker Lake. Covering an area of 505,000 acres, the North Cascades National Park encompasses 318 glaciers—more than half of all the glaciers in the United States south of Alaska. Because this huge, rugged area can only be seen and appreciated by hikers and backpackers, it has rightly been called, "The best-kept wilderness secret in the country."

For example, the shore of Ross Lake in its upper part is reached by road through a small settlement named Hozomeen, Washington, which can be gotten to only after driving forty miles on a dirt road from Hope, British Columbia, which (if you haven't gotten lost by now) is in Canada a few miles east of Vancouver. For the information of those interested, there are campgrounds on both sides of the border, with the ranger station serving as a makeshift border crossing.

At one stage early in his writing career, local people say, Jack Kerouac once spent a summer as a fire lookout at a place called Desolation Peak.

As Washington State's newest national park, North Cascades is a place few people visit and even fewer come to know, Superintendent John Earnst said recently, "The park is really a wilderness environment...We're in the business of making it available, but only on its own terms."

Bill Gulick Photo
LAKE CHELAN FROM THE SOUTH SHORE

In 1990, only 457,000 visitors were logged at the North Cascades complex, ranking it forty-second among the fifty national parks. Of these, most were motorists passing through on the North Cascades Highway who did not leave the pavement. In attendance, it is just behind Theodore Roosevelt National Park in North Dakota and just ahead of Crater Lake in Oregon.

As a matter of comparison, the most-visited park, Great Smoky Mountains, drew 8.1 million visitors this same year.

Though no more roads into the Park are planned, a few changes and improvements are in the works. One is a full-scale visitor center at Newhalem, to be completed in 1993. Another is a $5 million project for urgently needed new housing for the 58 year-round and sixty-seven seasonal employees of the Park, who now live in dilapidated cabins, trailers, and sub–standard housing. But the Park Service is determined to keep the park as a refuge for wilderness lovers.

On the eastern slope of the Cascades, the southern corner of the Park touches the upper reaches of the Lake Chelan National Recreation Area, which contains the village of Stehekin. Since this is on the "dry" side of the Cascades in an area we will cover in PART FIVE, COLUMBIA BASIN, we will now move on into that part of the state and see how the natives there live...

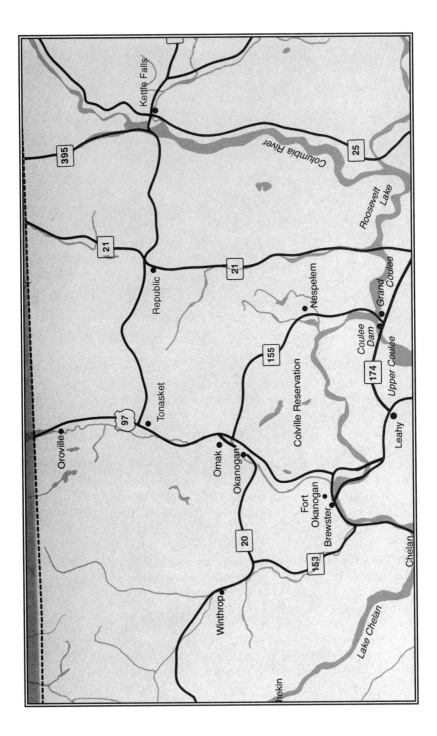

PART FIVE

Columbia Basin

OKANOGAN RIVER COUNTRY

Though most residents of Washington think of the Columbia River as belonging to the United States, the truth is it originates in Canada, five hundred of its 1,240 miles flow through British Columbia, and one-third of the 198 million acre-feet of water which it annually pours into the Pacific Ocean comes from and is controlled by Canada. One large tributary, the Kootenai, does begin south of the border in Montana before flowing north to join the Columbia in Canada, so the United States does originate some of the water it eventually gets back. But basically the Columbia is an international river.

In all, the Columbia River and its tributaries drain a basin larger than France, a watershed which covers some 259,000 square miles.

During the two hundred years that we have lived in peace with our northern neighbor, one of the many things we have not quarreled about is Columbia River water, the mutual attitude being that we both have so much there is no point in squabbling

US 20—Winthrop to Okanogan
  40 miles
US 97— Okanogan north to Oroville
  50 miles
US 97—Okanogan south to Fort Okanogan
  21 miles

A TRAVELER'S HISTORY OF WASHINGTON

over it. But now that both nations have come to realize that our once-thought "unlimited" resources are finite, the water, power, timber, and fish which are so vital to our economies and lifestyles are being measured much more carefully.

Ranked second only to the Mississippi in the amount of water carried, the Columbia leads the nation as a source of hydroelectric power, contributes irrigation water to millions of acres of fertile farm land, supports an extremely valuable fishery, and carries tug and barge traffic whose importance to the Pacific Northwest is as great as that of the Mississippi River system to the country's heartland.

Already a sizable river where it enters the United States after being born in the Canadian Rockies and circling around the Selkirk Mountains by way of Lake Louise and Banff, the Columbia has been brought under control by three Canadian dams—Duncan, Arrow, and Mica—whose building and benefits required the kind of intricate diplomacy that could only have been conceived and agreed to by good neighbors and friends.

THE FUR TRADERS

In the bloodless battle between Great Britain and the United States over who would gain title to the Pacific Northwest, fur traders played a leading role. Duplicating the Lewis and Clark journey of exploration up the Missouri River and then down the Snake and Columbia to the Pacific were trips by David Thompson, Alexander McKenzie, and Simon Fraser across Canada from Montreal to the West Coast, which they reached only a few months after the Americans floated down the Columbia to the Pacific in 1805.

In each case, the explorers were followed by the managers of fur trading posts whose employees planted flags, built forts, then went into the business of trading with the local Indians or sending out their own men in small parties to trap the wilderness streams. By far the largest percentage of pelts gathered were beaver.

Though many people think of this water-loving animal as dwelling only in cold-water streams in high mountain country, its range is far wider than that, for beaver are found in both high and low country from the Arctic to the Gulf of California, in small streams and in big rivers, in cold and in hot country—in a word, wherever water flows.

Between 1811–14, trading posts were established by the Americans at Fort Astoria near the mouth of the Columbia, Fort Nez Perces on the Snake River near the mouth of the Clearwater, and Fort Okanogan at that river's juncture with the Columbia in what is now north–central Washington State. At this same time, the British North West Company, which soon would be taken over by the Hudson's Bay Company, was establishing posts in western Canada, on the lower Fraser, and on the upper Columbia.

As the first trading post built in the area, Fort Okanogan was the first permanent American settlement in the State of Washington. Though ownership passed to the British between 1814 and 1846, after which it again became an American post, Fort Okanogan played an important role in the development of the interior country. It is now marked as a Historic Site five miles north of Brewster on US 97.

THE CARIBOO TRAIL

Because the force Americans called "Manifest Destiny" developed in an east–west direction, important north–south trails which were made at the same time often are overlooked. One of these was the Cariboo Trail, a route which ran one thousand miles from The Dalles, Oregon, through the dry-land country of eastern Washington and British Columbia north into the heart of the gold country in Canada's colorful Cariboo district. Following the route now taken by US 97, the trail made over this rugged country was heavily traveled from its beginning in 1858 until the railroads came in the 1890s.

In the 1850s, all a person had to do was whisper the word "gold" and hordes of frantic men headed pell-mell for the new bonanza. Even if the find proved to be a good one, very few men managed to become wealthy. But the smart men and women knew that every last soul taking part in the gold rush must eat, be housed, entertained, and supplied with tools and transportation. So stores, saloons, ranches, and "entertainment" establishments sprang up along the routes the gold seekers traveled and in the settlements near which they lived.

For example, in the spring of 1861 a glut of Oregon cattle drove the price of beef on the hoof down to five cents a pound. In the booming Cariboo gold country one thousand miles to the north, live beef was selling for a dollar a pound; so it was inevitable that cattle should be driven north to that market, just as cheap Texas longhorns would go north to the railhead at Abilene, Kansas, following the Civil War.

Trail drives across Washington Territory into British Columbia never have been immortalized in Western novels and movies as was the trek in Larry McMurtrey's *Lonesome Dove*. But the thousand miles of desert, mountains, rivers, and other natural hazards encountered by cattle herds between The Dalles and the Cariboo country made crossing the plains of Texas, Indian Territory, and Kansas look like a Sunday ride in the park.

Following the gold-seekers north up the Cariboo Trail, the cattle drivers got a good look at the seventy-five mile long Okanogan Valley and learned that it contained all the elements needed to sustain a cattle industry: grass, water, sunshine, space, and enough timber in the nearby mountains to construct needed buildings. Furthermore, shows of "color" found by prospectors in the higher country nearby started local gold rushes which assured a market for meat and agricultural crops no matter whether they succeeded or failed. Invariably, far more gold stuck to the hands of the people who supplied the goods and services than to the blistered palms of those who dug it.

Most gold strikes along the Cariboo Trail were made in the narrow valleys of small mountain streams, rather than along the flats adjacent to the slow-flowing Okanogan River. As a lure for prospectors and merchants, a settlement just south of the Canadian border called itself "Oro," which is Spanish for gold. But the Post Office objected, saying there already was a town named "Oso," which is Spanish for "bear," registered in the state, which might confuse people. So they added a "ville"—thus the present–day name "Oroville."

The Okanogan country did get a brief shot at immortality in the Western genre when Owen Wister, author of the 1902 best-selling novel *The Virginian*, visited the Methow Valley for a brief time, then later used some of the people he met as characters in his classic tale of cowboys, rustlers, and "schoolmarms." Changing the setting to Wyoming and inventing fictional names for his characters, he gave that state a certain amount of notoriety, which it did not particularly need. Without passing a personal judgment on the novel's quality as literature, I am inclined to agree with what Andy Adams, whose *Log of a Cowboy* was a classic of its day, said

Click Relander Collection, Courtesy Yakima Valley Regional Library
PICTOGRAPHS ON THE COLUMBIA RIVER
Just north of Vantage, the ancient markings are now submerged by waters of Priest Rapids Dam.

after reading *The Virginian*, "Four hundred and fifty pages about cowboys—and they never punched a cow."

In any case, during Owen Wister's stay in the Okanogan Valley around 1900, he met the most famous Western artist of the day, Frederic Remington. When Remington painted a group of Indians sitting astride their horses on the banks of the languid Okanogan River as they gazed stolidly at the fences of the white settlers and mused their secret thoughts, Owen Wister wrote a poem describing what he guessed were their feelings:

> Of old, when Okanogan ran
> Good medicine for horse and man,
> The winged shaft was wont to fly
> In peace or war, beneath the sky.
> Gone is the arrow, and instead
> The message of the white man's lead,
> The poison of the white man's drink—
> These lessons by the river-brink

Are learned, where Okanogan ran
Good medicine for horse and man.

Both painting and verse were certainly appropriate to the place and time, for just to the east of the Okanogan Valley lay the immense Colville Indian Reservation on which had been placed the remnants of a number of inland tribes—among them Chief Joseph and the non–Christian survivors of the tragic Nez Perce War of 1877. By then, the Indian conflicts were over, farming and fruit-raising were beginning to develop in the Okanogan Valley, and settlers were learning that in this land of few white people and little rain two elements were needed to make a living: water for irrigation and seasonal labor to harvest the crops. By organizing water districts and employing Indians, the needs were filled.

Though Hudson's Bay Company employees and Oregon Trail emigrants had been planting apple seeds and root-stock for many years and knew that the fruit did well in the Pacific Northwest, settlers in the Okanogan Valley now discovered that nowhere else in the country was the climate, soil, and growing season as ideal for the raising of top quality apples as was this area. By the time statehood came to Washington in 1889, the Okanogan Valley was well on its way toward becoming the apple capital of the world.

Leading the region in the production of the best of all apples—the Red Delicious—was the nearby Lake Chelan area— which could also lay claim to being the region's most scenic spot.

LAKE CHELAN

Fifty miles long, three miles wide, and fifteen hundred feet deep, mountain-girt Lake Chelan contains the clearest, purest water in the world, a quality maintained largely by the fact that roads and settlements extend only ten miles up the lake into the wilderness that surrounds it, with access only by boat, plane, or on foot. All activities in the area are strictly controlled by the US Forest Service, which regulates the uses of the Lake Chelan National Recreation Area.

Though early explorers such as David Thompson, Alexander Ross, and Lieutenant George McClellan did report the presence of the lake and record its location on their maps, none of them actually saw or explored it. In 1870, a white man named D.C. Linsley hired an Indian guide to paddle him the length of the lake in a canoe; he was told by the native that his people sometimes

Click Relander Collection, Courtesy Yakima Valley Regional Library
TOPPENISH YAKIMA INDIAN CELEBRATION IN 1953
Left to right: Mary Ann Selatsee, Lila Ambrose Walawawaitsa, and Geraldine Pinkham.

crossed the mountains over a poor trail to the Skagit River and Puget Sound. In 1879, Lieutenant Thomas Symons, Lieutenant Colonel Henry C. Merriam, and a party of three Indians went by canoe 24 miles up the lake, reporting, "The water is of diamond-like clearness and yet in places no sight can penetrate to the bottom of its liquid depths."

Where the lake's outlet flowed over a natural precipice called Chelan Falls, the drop was augmented in 1927 by a forty-foot high, 490–foot long dam which channeled water down a 2.2–mile underground penstock through a powerhouse just above the Columbia River. Built by the Chelan Public Utility District for the purpose of generating cheap electrical power, the dam allows regulation of Lake Chelan between 1,079 and 1,100 feet above sea level, providing a usable storage area of 640,000 acre-feet. Since the deepest point in the lake is 1,479 feet, this means that its bottom is almost five hundred feet below sea level.

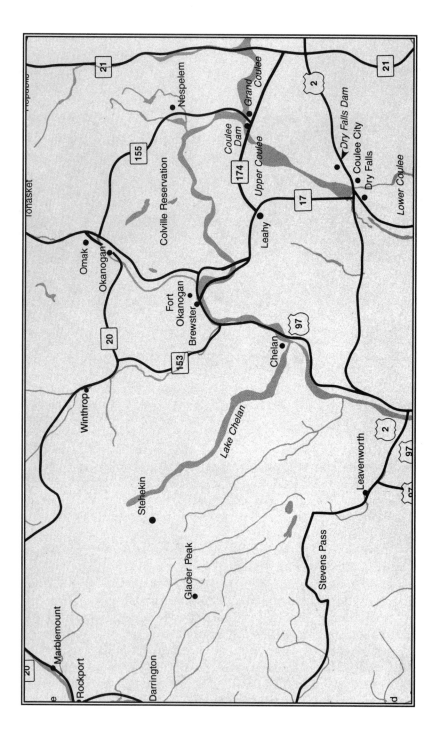

After prolonged hearings and condemnation proceedings, the PUD eventually took over the Chelan electrical distribution system, then consolidated its holdings in the field of power generation by building Rocky Reach and Rock Island Dams on the Columbia River. For the statistically curious, the Columbia River and its tributaries now contain a total of 161 dams. On Lake Chelan itself, both day-trippers and permanent residents of Stehekin at the upper end of the lake agree that the scenery cannot be excelled. For over one hundred years, passenger boats of one sort or another have hauled mail, freight, visitors, and residents up the lake. Since 1929 the Lake Chelan Boat Company has operated the boats from a dock near downtown Chelan.

Currently, the company runs the *Lady of the Lake II* and the *Lady Express*. Operating daily from April 15 to October 15, the 100–foot long *Lady of the Lake II* carries 350 passengers, takes four hours to make the trip each way, staying at the upper end of the lake an hour and a half before starting the return trip.

With less than half the passenger capacity, the 65–foot *Lady Express* runs daily from June 16 to September 15, with weekend trips before and after those dates, making the run up and back in half the time and with fewer stops along the way than the larger, slower boat. For the person who is really in a hurry, flights on float planes are also available.

To its seventy-five permanent residents, Stehekin is a very special place. Said to be an Indian word meaning "the way through," the narrow, glacier-formed valley at the head of the lake was a traditional route through the mountains for natives wishing to trade with the coastal tribes. Today's backpackers and hikers use it as a takeoff point into the North Cascades National Park and the Lake Chelan National Recreation Area.

Much as some of the year-round local residents would like to maintain local control of the area, pressures for change frequently

US 97—Brewster to Chelan
   20 miles
US 97—Chelan to Omak
   51 miles
State 155—Omak to Nespelem
   54 miles

Courtesy Penrose Library, Whitman College
CHIEF JOSEPH JUST AFTER THE NEZ PERCE WAR IN 1877

conflict with what they regard as traditional rights. Part of the problem derives from the 1882 discovery of mineral outcroppings by a US Army expedition led by Lieutenant Henry Hubbard Pierce, which created a stampede of miners to the area after his report was published. According to a local historian writing for the the *Chelan Mirror:*

> By the turn of the century, an estimated 2,000 seasonal residents were either prospecting or servicing the prospectors with packing operations, lodging, small sawmills or trade.
>   Stehekin attracted few year round residents, but some families did take root over time. Prospectors were largely gone by

1910, but sightseers flocked into the area, attracted by the incredible scenery and pleasant climate.

Stehekin boasted one of the premier hotels in the Pacific Northwest from about 1890 until the Chelan Dam was built, inundating the site in the late 1920s. The Hotel Field, with its sixty rooms and deluxe accomodations, was dismantled, with salvaged portions used to build the Golden West Lodge, now a National Park Service museum and visitor center.

Most of the seventy-five permanent residents live along a narrow twenty-mile road originally built by the county to provide access to early century mining operations. Following the establishment of the National Recreation Area, Chelan County gave the road to the federal government in 1970. Now the county wants it back, for some of the residents want to use it for tourist activities, which are tightly regulated.

Nine miles up the valley, Stehekin Valley Ranch offers a rustic, back-to-nature experience in wood-frame, canvas-roofed cabins and meals served family-style in a dining hall. Horseback riding and river rafting are also offered.

Along the twenty–mile road outside this private holding, there are campgrounds where permits are required from the National Park Service office in Stehekin or from the Ranger Station in Marblemount, Washington. Some of the year-round local residents feel that the area is over-regulated. Given a $50 parking ticket, one man was so incensed that he carried an appeal all the way up to the Ninth US Circuit Court of Appeals in San Francisco, where he lost. Next time, he vows, he will go all the way up to the Supreme Court.

Criticized by some of the residents for being too strict in their use regulations, the federal government also is under fire from environmental groups, some of which threaten to sue unless the rules are enforced more strictly. Gradually, the federal government is gaining control of the area, for of the 1,700 acres in private hands when the 62,000–acre Recreation Area was established only 477 acres now are privately owned.

But whoever owns the Lake Chelan region, its wilderness beauty remains largely unspoiled.

THE NOBLE EXPERIMENT THAT FAILED

Before leaving the town of Chelan, we must relate its unique claim to historic immortality by telling a story recorded for posterity by the jewel of all public histories, the *WPA Guide*. Back in the 1930s during the depths of the Depression, all sorts of schemes were proposed to jump-start the economy by stimulating the movement of the money supply so that prosperity would return for people in general, the able-bodied unemployed in particular, and especially for that special bloc of older retired men and women we now call "Senior Citizens."

An idea proposed by a man named Townsend had such wide appeal that for a brief time he became a very popular public figure whose supporters wanted to run him for President. Before agreeing to become a candidate, he proposed to field-test the scheme upon which his popularity was based: namely, that each and every old person would be given fifty dollars a week by the federal government—whether he needed it or not—with the stipulation that he must put it back into circulation by spending it before being given next week's check.

"Fifty Dollars Every Friday" was the Townsend Plan slogan. The place chosen for the test was Chelan, Washington. The *Guide* tells us:

> Chelan received wide attention from the press in 1936 when a pension plan was tested by the Townsendites. One thousand dollars in dollar bills were circulated, with the provision that a two-cent stamp should be attached each time a bill changed hands. The plan was abandoned after a period of trial.

What happened to the stamp-filled dollar bills or to Townsend himself, we do not know. All we know is, he did not get elected President.

THE INDIAN MOSES

From the time of the first English settlement at the Roanoke, Virginia Colony in 1601, the dealings of the European white newcomers with the native Indians were inconsistent. Following the establishment of the United States and the movement of its people westward, government policy first was to regard the natives as hostiles to be fought and conquered, then as heathen to be converted to Christianity and "civilized," and finally as members of sovereign nations with whom treaties should be made, giving them special status as government wards.

The only thing these varied policies had in common was that none of them worked. By 1872, the government had adopted the practice of establishing reservations by Presidential Executive

Click Relander Collection, Courtesy Yakima Valley Regional Library
GENUINE BUFFALO TEPEE
Over 100 years old when this picture was taken in the 1950s, the tepee was never exhibited again.

Order rather than by negotiating treaties, which must be ratifield by the US Senate and could only be repealed by a two-thirds vote. Though an Executive Order also required Congressional approval, a simple majority vote was sufficient to affirm or cancel it, thus it did not have the status of a treaty made with a sovereign nation. So the boundaries of reservations created by Executive Order often were changed for practical or political reasons.

Called Columbia Indians, the scattered, loosely related tribes of the Chelan, Okanogan, and upper Columbia River area were both horse and river Indians who lived on roots, salmon, deer, elk, and occasionally made treks to the buffalo country east of the Rockies in Montana were they fought or mingled with the Blackfeet, Crow, Sioux, Nez Perce, and Shoshone. Though some of

their neighboring tribes such as the Yakimas, Walla Wallas, and
Spokanes had made treaties with Washington Territorial
Governor Isaac Stevens in 1855 and agreed to go on reservations,
their part of the country was so big and settlements so few that
pressures by the whites to restrict them to limited areas did not
become substantial until the mid–1870s.

By then, the acknowledged leader and spokesman for most of
the tribes of the region was a colorful, outspoken-by-no-one
Columbia Indian known as Chief Moses. As a bright-eyed boy of
nine, he so impressed the missionary Henry Spalding in 1838 that
the Congregational minister undertook to educate him in his
Lapwai Mission school in the Nez Perce country, giving him the
Christian name Moses, by which he would be known for the rest
of his life as he tried to lead his people through the aboriginal
wilderness into the promised land of the white man's world.

Like all young Indian boys between the ages of nine and thirteen, Moses got the urge to go on his *Wyakin* (Vision-Seeking)
quest shortly after his ninth birthday, traveling alone into the
mountains to commune with his guardian spirit for advice as to
how he should live from then on. In their excellent book *Half-Sun
on the Columbia: a Biography of Chief Moses,* historians Robert A.
Ruby and John A. Brown write:

> One morning the Indian Moses was missing. Heavy with home-
> sickness, he had ridden out on a spirit quest to quiet his soul. In
> a dream trance the spirit had told him to return to his mother's
> tipi. Since this was the revelation he was seeking, he mounted
> his Appaloosa and rode home to his people without going back
> to the mission for the formality of farewells.

Despite the fact that he left the Spalding Mission and never
did officially become a Christian, he remained friendly with
Spalding, Americans, the Congregational religion, and white
politicians for the rest of his life. Adroitly playing the game of getting as much out of the federal government for himself and his
people as he possibly could by being a "good" Indian, he always
counseled his fellow tribesmen to follow the straight and narrow
path of peace rather than the broad and bloody trail of war.

In the preceding chapter, mention was made of the importance of the Cariboo Trail leading north from The Dalles to the
gold fields of British Columbia. Employed as a cowboy driving
the first herd north in 1861, a sixteen-year old youth named Jack

Splawn, who later became Mayor of Yakima and a substantial rancher in the region east of the mountains, met Chief Moses at a crucial time during the drive and was greatly impressed by him.

When asked his name, Splawn said, the big, colorful Indian would tap his chest and proclaim, *"Nika Moses"* ("I am Moses"). No one who met him ever forgot him.

To some of the rash young braves in the Entiat band, a thousand fat cattle guarded by only a handful of white men was a temptation difficult to resist. Concocting a plan to strike the herd and its drovers that night, the group was overheard by Moses, who immediately rode between the hostiles and the party of white drovers, waving the would-be attackers back until the hill was cleared. Not only did Chief Moses save the lives of the little group by his dramatic action, he also strengthened his leadership among his own people as well.

SMOHALLA THE DREAMER

Because the various bands of Columbia Indians had no reservation of their own, leadership of the scattered tribes was delegated to Chief Moses only by those people who felt that they could benefit by having him speak for them when dealing with white men—an art at which he excelled. In some cases, Indian leaders who disliked him became his bitter rivals.

This was the case with the hunchbacked prophet, Smohalla. Spiritual leader of the Wanapum band, whose home was near Priest Rapids on the Columbia just to the south of the Colville country, Smohalla the Dreamer led a cult with a large following among the Plateau Indian tribes.

Details of how Moses and Smohalla became enemies are lost in the realm of legend; but the basic cause stemmed from the fact that each leader advocated opposite ways of dealing with the white invaders of their lands. Having attended the Spalding Mission School where he learned English as well as the white man's religion and ways, Chief Moses had become fond of the gadgets and goods of the white world, not the least of which was whiskey. Having seen what happened to hostile Indians who fought the white man, Moses chose what he regarded as the wiser course—keeping the peace and being paid to be a "good" Indian.

Smohalla, on the other hand, warned his followers to have nothing to do with the white man, rejecting white religion, white gifts, white treaties, and all the white man's material goods. If the

Click Relander Collection, Courtesy Yakima Valley Regional Library
INDIAN WOMEN PREPARING A FEAST
They work on the floor of the Longhouse at Nespelem.

Indian people would turn their backs on the white man's world, dance the mystic "Ghost" dance, and dream of how their people lived before the white man came, then all their ancestors and all the animals that had ever lived would return to inhabit the Indian world as it used to be—and white men would return to their world, never to be seen again. Basically, Smohalla advocated a passive, non–violent faith, though it was not seen as such by apprehensive white men at the time.

On one occasion, the rivalry between the two Indian leaders became so intense that Chief Moses journeyed to Priest Rapids and attacked the Prophet (as he was called), beating him to within an inch of his life.

Dragging himself to a canoe, the badly injured Smohalla floated downriver out of danger, then began a period of wandering through the wilderness for several years, dreaming dreams and having visions, before returning to the upper Columbia River country to set himself up as a prophet and spiritual leader.

In view of the fact that Chief Moses long had felt he could get more out of the government by talk than by violence, he did not agree with the Dreamer philosophy. Nor did he support Chief Joseph and the Nez Perces in their tragic 1877 war against federal troops. But in a time and place when settlers living in isolated homes in the eastern part of Washington Teritory panicked at every rumor of threatened Indian attack, he built up a great deal of good will by playing the role of an Indian leader advocating peace.

Following the well-circulated dispatches of white correspondents who were covering the Nez Perce War and recording one defeat after another of supposedly well-trained federal troops, few white people living in the upper Columbia River region doubted what would happen if Chief Moses decided to turn the thousands of warriors supposedly under his command loose against the white community in support of Joseph and his gallant followers.

Blood would flow ankle-deep down every hill and through every hollow.

Well aware of this fact, Chief Moses never once threatened to support Chief Joseph and his people by going to war. To the contrary, he repeated time and again, "I have kept the peace. I tell the young men they must not go to war. I will not let them kill innocent white women and children."

To make sure his message reached the right places, he had letters written and telegrams sent to important people such as Father James Wilbur, Yakima Indian Agent, Governor John McGraw, and General Oliver Otis Howard, commander of the federal troops pursuing the Joseph band. In each and every case, local and regional newspapers picked up and printed the dispatches as reassuring, front-page news for worried readers, "Chief Moses says he will keep the peace."

Typical of his letters was one he sent General Howard shortly after the end of the Nez Perce War:

> I, Moses, chief, want you to know what my *tum-tum* [heart] is in regard to my tribe and the whites. Almost every day reports come to me that soldiers from Walla Walla are coming to take me away from this part of the country. My people are excited and I

want to know from you the truth, so that I can tell them, and keep everything quiet once more among us. Since the last war [the Nez Perce] we have had up here rumors that I am going to fight if the soldiers come. This makes my heart sick. I have said I will not fight and I say it to you again...I am getting old and I do not want to see my blood shed on my part of the country. Chief Joseph wanted me and my people to help him. His orders were many. I told him, "No, never!" I watched my people faithfully during the war and kept them at home.

CHIEF MOSES GOES TO WASHINGTON

Though the Colville Reservation was established by Executive Order in 1872, Chief Moses refused to go either to it or the Yakima Reservation, as he was being urged to do. Instead, he and the widely scattered Columbia bands for whom he was the principal spokesman continued to live and roam across the upper Okanogan and Columbia River country, professing peace but a threat for war. As a reward for controlling his people, Chief Moses at last got what he wanted—an invitation in 1879 to travel to the nation's capital in Washington City to meet with the Great White Father, President Rutherford B. Hayes.

Traveling in style at government expense, Chief Moses and several lesser chiefs went down the Columbia River by boat to Portland and by ocean-going ship to San Francisco. Spending a couple of nights there, the chiefs were taken to the theatre, where, before a full-house audience, they appeared briefly onstage in costume to thrill the crowd with a glimpse of real, live Indians in all their pagan glory. A born actor, Chief Moses made such an impression that more than one reporter suggested he should join the troupe of Buffalo Bill Cody, who was starring in his own production, *Knight of the Plains,* in another jam-packed San Franciso theatre just a few blocks away.

But Chief Moses had more important things to do, journeying with his delegation overland via the Union Pacific to Washington, where, with proper ceremony, he signed a paper giving him and the tribes he represented a reservation of their own.

And a huge reservation it was, running north from the juncture of the Chelan and Columbia Rivers to Canada, bordered by the Okanogan River on the east, the crest of the Cascades on the west, and exceeding in size even the Yakima Reservation, which until then had been the largest Indian Reservation in Washington Territory. Placed on what at first was called the Moses then the

Click Relander Collection, Courtesy Yakima Valley Regional Library
THE LONGHOUSE, OR CEREMONIAL TEPEE OF THE YAKIMAS
This one was erected for a root festival.

Columbia Reservation, were the Wenatchees, Entiats, Chelans, Methows, Okanogans and any other regional bands that might wish to live there. As far as Moses himself was concerned, he felt he also was chief of bands living on the Colville Reservation to the east, such as the San Poils, Nespelems, and Colvilles, though some of their chiefs disputed his claims.

By this time, the tragic remnants of Chief Joseph's defeated Nez Perces had been transported to Indian Territory in what would become northeastern Oklahoma, where their plight as exiles had begun to raise a great deal of sympathy among religious people and the Eastern press. Consumate politician that he was, Moses talked to Joseph—who also visited Washington City in the spring of 1879—and they agreed to merge their pleas for justice in appeals to their mutual friend, General Howard, to Eastern religious leaders, and to the national press.

From the first establishment of the reservation system, it had been government policy to put all the bands living in a certain area together in close proximity to one another on single reservation, whether they got along with one another or not. In the white world, this would be equivalent to merging towns, counties, or congressional districts regardless of the wishes of the residents, with no overall authority to enforce local and regional laws. Add the fact that Moses had been granted a $1,000 annuity, while salaries paid to some of the other headmen ranged downward to $500, $100, or in some cases nothing at all, the causes of dissension were numerous indeed.

Often the politically-appointed agents in charge of the reservations were lazy, greedy, or downright dishonest. For example, the white man in charge of the Colville Agency at first claimed that the annuity due Chief Moses was to be just a house worth $1,000, not cash. When he could not make that stick and Moses insisted he be given the annuity in $20 gold pieces, the agent grudgingly cashed the government check but withheld five $20 gold pieces for handling the transaction. When after much foot-dragging a house was built for Moses, it was so ramshackle that its worth was closer to $100 than the required $1,000.

RETURN OF THE NEZ PERCE EXILES

In the spring of 1885, Chief Joseph and his people, who had been held as conquered exiles in Indian Territory since their surrender following the Battle of the Bear's Paw Mountains in 1877, were at last allowed to return to the Pacific Northwest. According to Yellow Wolf, a nephew of Chief Joseph who had fought gallantly through the long, bitter campaign, when their train reached Wallula Junction in the southeastern part of Washington Territory, the returning Nez Perces were given a choice. Yellow Wolf said:

> When we reached Wallula, the interpreter asked us, "Where you want to go? Lapwai and be Christian, or Colville and just be yourself?"

While no written instructions as to which was to be considered a good and which a bad Indian have ever been found by historians, Yellow Wolf seems to have told it about right. By then, the Nez Perce Reservation at Lapwai was under the control of Charles E. Monteith, a strait-laced Presbyterian, who wanted no rebels on his reservation. Long hair and spirited horses were symbols of dissent which he would not accept. Those Indians who would agree to cut their hair and become Christians could come to Lapwai, he decreed. Those who kept their hair and their belief in the old ways must go to the Colville Reservation.

Click Relander Collection, Courtesy Yakima Valley Regional Library
INDIAN ENCAMPMENT AT NESPELEM IN THE EARLY 1900S

In bidding good-bye to ninety-two adults, twelve youngsters, and fourteen infants, Chief Joseph spoke briefly to them as a group. Many years later Josiah Red Wolf, who was seven years old at the time, told Robert Ruby what he remembered of Joseph's words, "I'm not going back to my own country. My own people will fight me. I'm going where Chuckatas [Chief Moses] is."

From Wallula Junction the Lapwai group went by train to Riparia, fifty miles up the Snake River, then to Lewiston by boat, thence overland twelve miles to the reservation and what from then on would be their home.

The Colville band continued on by train to Spokane Falls, then by wagons sixty-five miles west to Fort Spokane, which was adjacent to the Colville Reservation. In the group were 120 adults, including Chief Joseph and Yellow Bull, who was second in command, sixteen children, and fourteen infants. Their eight-year oddessey was over.

MOSES AND JOSEPH: A STRANGE FRIENDSHIP

Some ten years older than Joseph, Chief Moses was officially recognized as the leader of five Salish tribes: the Wenatchees, Entiats,

Click Relander Collection, Yakima Valley Regional Library
INDIAN RIDERS ON THE MEMORY TRAIL
The photo was taken just before the 1953 Ellensburg Rodeo.

Chelans, Methows, and Okanogans. He also claimed he was head chief of the San Poils, Nespelems, and Colvilles, though certain leaders among those tribes—such as the badly crippled San Poil Chief Skolaskin—violently rejected his authority. First established by Executive Order in 1872, with its boundaries modified in 1879, 1880, and again in 1884, the Colville Reservation lay between the Columbia and Okanogan rivers, extending north to the Canadian line. It was a large reserve, with plenty of good water, grass, and timber. Eventually, fragments of seventeen tribes of Plateau Indians were placed on the reservation. Chief Moses was their principal spokesman. Though circumstances dictated that they be friends, Joseph and Moses had totally different personalities. Joseph was soft-spoken and dignified, drank nothing stronger than sugared coffee, and was content with only two wives. Moses was loud and talkative, loved his toddy, and usually had at least five wives. On one occasion when asked how many children he had, he thought for a few moments, then shook his head and admitted he had lost track.

When a Catholic priest sent word to him that he must put aside all but one of his wives, Moses asked Agent Gwydir if the priest had a wife. Gwydir told him that the priest was not allowed to have a wife. Moses thought that over, then said. "Tell the Blackrobe that I will give him one of my wives if he will keep his mouth shut."

At first the Nez Perces were placed across the Columbia from Fort Spokane, Ruby and Brown write, "So that they could be protected from the soldiers, who it was feared would ravish their women, and from Moses, whose drinking and gambling propensities would do them no good."

Poorly clad, badly sheltered, and provided with insufficient food, the returned exiles were confronted with the hostility of the San Poils, into whose living space they had intruded. Calling Moses's and Joseph's people "murderers and horse thieves," Skolaskin launched such a violent attack on the government for placing the Nez Perces in San Poil territory that Joseph asked that they be permitted to move fifty miles west to the Nespelem valley.

Moses was delighted with the decision. But when Joseph and 132 Nez Perces rode into their valley, the Nespelems greeted them with unconcealed hostility. As had happened in Indian Territory down in Oklahoma, the Nez Perces once again were being imposed upon a band of Indians who did not want to share their living space with strangers. Because indifferent agents let two years pass before supplying seed grain and farming tools, they were wholly dependent upon the federal government for rations. Some of the impoverished exiles desperately tried to replace the horses they had been forced to sell in Indian Territory by betting blankets issued them against Nespelem ponies in gambling games.

Even if they had wanted to become farmers—which they did not—they would have found it impossible. What tillable land existed in the area already was occupied by the Nespelems, who refused to share it. In an effort to keep the Nez Perces at home and force them to farm land they did not have, with tools that had not yet arrived, the agent issued an order requiring all Indians to have permits before leaving the reservation—an order completely ignored by the Nez Perces. Yet so dependent had they become upon the government for food that when several of them went to Lapwai for an extended visit with relatives, Chief Joseph sent his nephew with a message urging them to come back to Nespelem in time to get their share of a beef issue.

Click Relander Collection, Courtesy Yakima Valley Regional Library
YAKIMA SUMMER TEPEE MADE OF REED MATS, NOW VERY RARE

As time passed, the friendship between Joseph and Moses cooled somewhat, with Joseph blaming Moses for encouraging the local whiskey trade and Moses blaming Joseph for his people's aversion to work. But they were brought together again by an invitation to come to Portland and share the limelght at the Exposition of 1891, which would give them both national publicity as two of the best-known Indians of the day.

By a curious turn of events, General Howard's aide, Lieutenant Charles Erskine Scott Wood, had become Chief Joseph's best white friend. A brilliant man and a born rebel at heart, Lieutenant Wood had served with Howard through the Bannock War in 1878, had gone east with him when Howard was appointed superintendent of West Point, then, having long been interested in law, had studied at nearby Columbia and earned a degree. Although he was a West Point graduate, a decade of military discipline and two Indian wars had given him his fill of the army, so in 1883 he resigned his commission, came west to Portland, and began practicing law.

Following the surrender at Bear's Paw, Lieutenant Wood had been assigned the task of watching over Chief Joseph, seeing to his creature comforts, and protecting him from the curious. It had been Wood who recorded Chief Joseph's surrender speech. Although he respected Howard as a man, he had been sharply critical of the general for his failure to return the Nez Perces to Idaho, as promised, and had done everything he could to persuade the government to return the exiles from Indian Territory to the Pacific Northwest.

In 1889 he had brought Chief Joseph to Portland to pose for the New York sculptor, Olin Warner, who was doing a series of large medallions of famous Indian chiefs. Now, in addition to appearing as stars at the 1891 Exposition, the two chiefs were honored guests in Wood's home. When wine was served at dinner one evening, Joseph did not touch his glass. But Moses kept it from going to waste by emptying first his own glass, then the one placed in front of his abstemious friend.

ERSKINE WOOD VISITS CHIEF JOSEPH

Wood's twelve-year old son, Erskine, who loved hunting, fishing, horses, and the outdoor life, was so fascinated by the two Indian chiefs that his father asked Joseph if the boy could visit him the next summer. Joseph graciously invited him to do so. In July 1892 young Erskine went to Nespelem and was taken into Chief Joseph's tepee as a member of the family. He liked it so well, and was so well liked in return, that he did not go home until Christmas. The following year, 1893, he returned for a second visit during the fall, this one shortened to a mere three months.

Though he kept a diary both years, the first one was lost. The one written during his 1893 stay has been preserved and published by the Oregon Historical Society under the title *Days With Chief Joseph*. Erskine Wood writes:

> He was the kindest of fathers to me, looking after me, providing for me, caring for me, and, it must be said, sometimes gently rebuking me when necessary...I have been asked whether he was somber. No, he was not. Neither was he merry or boisterous or prone to loud laughter. But he was not morose, nor over-

Click Relander Collection, Courtesy Yakima Valley Regional Library
LINCOLN ROCK LOG CABIN, ON THE COLUMBIA EAST OF VANTAGE

whelmed by his misfortunes. He bore them like the great man he was. Within the limits of the reservation he lived his life quietly with a calm and dignified acceptance of his fate.

Preoccupied with going to high school and college and a three-year battle with tuberculosis, Erskine Wood never saw Chief Joseph again after their parting in December 1893. Many years later he wrote:

> But the regret that has lived with me longest occurred at our saying goodbye. We had ridden from the camp at Nespelem down to the Columbia River, where I was to cross in a dugout canoe to Barry, the trading post on the other side, and there to be met by a team to drive me to the railroad. Joseph and I sat on our horses on the bluffs of the Columbia overlooking the river. It was time to part.
>
> My father had written me to tell Joseph that if there was anything my father could do for him he was, through me, to let my father know. I gave this message to Joseph, and he said that he would like a good stallion to improve the breed of his pony herd. I looked on Joseph as such a great man, a noble chief driven out of his ancestral home, I revered him so, that I thought

his request for a stallion was too puny—was beneath him. I thought he ought to ask if my father could do anything to repair the great wrong done him, perhaps get him back a portion of his Wallowa Valley or something like that, so that when Joseph asked for a mere stallion, I shook my head and said, "No, that was not what my father meant!"

Joseph accepted this calmly and we said no more. But I always regretted my utter stupidity. A fine stallion which would have upbred Joseph's herd of ponies would have been a wonderful thing for him. Just the kind of thing in his Indian life that he needed, and of course well within the ablility of my father to get for him. But just because I exalted him so high I deprived him of it, and it is something I shall always regret.

TWILIGHT YEARS OF CHIEF JOSEPH

Refusing to take an allotment of land on the Lapwai Reservation because he hoped to return to the Wallowa Valley or go to the Umatilla Reservation nearby, Chief Joseph made a trip to Washington, DC during the summer of 1897 and presented his request to the authorities. Though his appeal was strongly supported by General Howard and General Miles, it was denied. During the trip he visited New York City, where he rode beside General Howard in a parade celebrating the dedication of President Grant's tomb. While there he was offered a starring role in Buffalo Bill's Wild West Show, which he declined.

In 1899 his friend, Chief Moses, died at the age of seventy-one. Following the funeral, a great potlatch was held during which a buckskin suit and war bonnet given Chief Moses by Sitting Bull was passed on to Chief Joseph with a moving speech amid chanting and weeping.

Pressured by Joseph's friends in high places, US Indian Inspector James McLaughlin came to Nespelem in June 1900 and made a tour of the Wallowa country with Joseph to investigate the feasibility of purchasing tracts of land there for Joseph and those of his people who wished to return to their ancestral land. His conclusion, in which the Nespelem agent, the Indian Bureau, and the whites living in northeastern Oregon concurred, was that it would not be practical to return Joseph to the Wallowa country.

In the winter of 1903 Joseph made yet another trip to Washington, D.C., repeating the request he had made many times before:

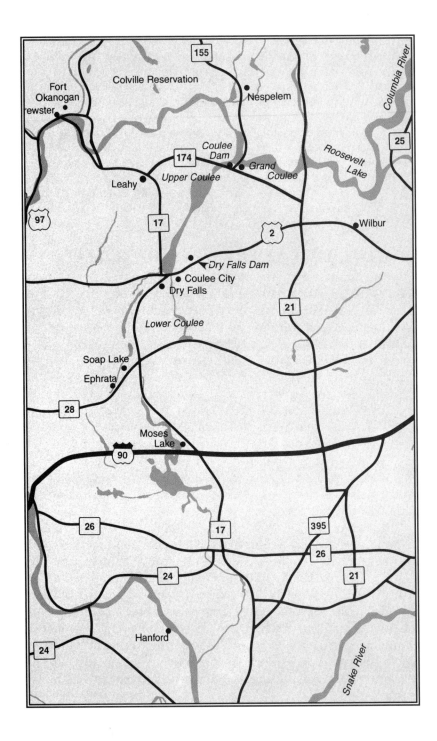

My home is in the Wallowa Valley, and I want to go back there to live. My father and mother are buried there. If the government would only give me a small piece of land for my people in the Wallowa Valley, with a teacher, that is all I would ask.

On this trip he visited the Carlisle Indian School in Pennsylvania, saw his old friends Howard and Miles, and met the railroad magnate, James J. Hill, and President Theodore Roosevelt. All of them treated him with respect and sympathy but could do nothing for him. On September 21, 1904, at the age of sixty-four, Joseph died in his lodge at Nespelem, still an exile from the land of the winding waters. Dr. Edwin Latham, the agency physician who had become Joseph's friend, probably gave an accurate if not very scientific cause of death when he said, "He died of a broken heart."

GRAND COULEE PROJECT

Just fifteen miles south of the Colville Indian Agency Headquarters, Grand Coulee Dam blocks the flow of the Columbia River. The biggest concrete structure ever poured by man, it generates more electricity than any dam in North America, while the 150–mile reservoir backed up behind it supplies water for a million acres of once-desert land, which it turns green as the largest irrigation development in the nation.

By following the route detailed above, you may see the dam, the pumping facilities, the awesome coulee, the man-made lakes, and the expanse of irrigated acres downstream, which will give

---

State 155—Nespelem to Grand Coulee
    15 miles
State 155—Grand Coulee to Coulee City
    26 miles
State 17—Coulee City to Soap Lake
    21 miles
State 28—Soap Lake to Ephrata
    6 miles
State 282, 17—Ephrata to Moses Lake
    19 miles

you some idea of the scope of the project as it exists today. What cannot be seen is the vision, stubbornness, and persistence of the handful of men who conceived the incredibly ambitious scheme seventy-five years ago and finally made it a reality despite the tremendous obstacles they were forced to overcome.

First among these men was a small town newspaper editor, Rufus Woods, whose *Wenatchee World* at the time he published his epic story had a circulation of less than one thousand subscribers who, when pressed, paid four dollars a year for the weekly paper, and twenty or so advertisers, who were equally slow in paying their bills.

Second was an Ephrata lawyer named Billy Clapp, a man long on ideas and dreams, but, like most attorneys in that not very prosperous section of the state, perpetually short on cash.

Third was a small-time construction contractor, James O'Sullivan, who for a while had taught law at a college in western Washington, then had been drawn to the Moses Lake area by his purchase of a farm he had bought sight unseen. When he discovered that even the man who had sold it to him considered him a "sucker" for buying a quarter-section of land with no water on it now and little prospect of getting water on it in the forseeable future, his Irish temper flared, making him swear he would force this barren desert to blossom like a rose, if it took him the rest of his life to do it—which it did.

WATER ON THE LAND

As man learned thousands of years ago, given sunshine and fertile soil, land in a temperate clime can be made to produce prodigiously if it receives sufficient moisture from the sky in the form of rain or enough water on the roots of its crops by ditch irrigation. In eastern Washington, if a district receives less than fifteen inches of rainfall a year, it is considered marginally productive—that is, by conserving two years' moisture by letting the land lie fallow, its yield will be satisfactory when it is cropped the third year. During drier than normal years, such land will produce little or nothing; in wetter years, fairly good crops can be grown.

Over the Columbia Basin as a whole during the early 1900s, there were millions of acres of land whose annual rainfall ranged between five and fifteen inches. Adjacent to much of that land

Major Lee Moorhouse photo, Courtesy Smithsonian Institution National Anthropological Archives, Bureau of American Ethnology Collection
CHIEF JOSEPH IN 1901

flowed the biggest river west of the Mississippi—the Columbia—whose abundant waters could turn the land green and productive if only some way were found to put that water on the land.

Hand pumps, windmills, and gravity ditch irrigation from small streams served a scattering of small farms and settlements in the Basin country, where the climate had proved excellent for the development of fruit orchards. But large scale irrigation required dams, canals, ditches, and laterals created by systems and agencies far beyond the scope of anything a small group of farmers could finance and build.

Normally, water runs only one way—downhill. But in this strange, tortured land through which the mighty Columbia flowed, the geologic pages of history, which lay open for even a layman to read, showed a massive scar revealing the intriguing fact that a million or so years ago the Columbia had dramatically changed its course.

The scar was called Grand Coulee.

A thousand feet deep, two to three miles wide, and fifty miles long, the deep slash cut diagonally from northeast to southwest across an ancient dry bed of the Columbia River, which now flowed west and then south again by a much longer, lower route. What apparently had happened, geologists explained, was that during an age when the world turned cold, glaciers moving down from the north had blocked the flow of the Columbia River to the west and south, forcing it to form a new, higher channel. When the ice finally melted and the river returned to its former course, it left Grand Coulee high and dry, its floor two hundred and fifty feet above the present level of the river.

"What would happen?" Billy Clapp mused, "if a dam high enough to lift the Columbia River up and into its old channel were built?"

Though neither he nor the small-town newspaper editor, Rufus Woods, were engineers, a bit of rudimentary sight-lining and arithmetic led them to an interesting conclusion. What would happen would be that a huge pool of water lying well above the present river level would be brought into being. From this pool, an immense amount of desert land in the Columbia Basin could be irrigated by gravity flow. The dam would have to be 550 feet high and a modest amount of electricty would be required to lift the water over the intervening ridge, but since only a small por-tion of the river's flow need be diverted for irrigation purposes, the force of the falling water that remained could be used to spin massive turbines that would generate a tremendous amount of electrical energy.

On July 18, 1918, the entire front page of the *Wenatchee World* carried the Rufus Woods article headlined:

Two Million Wild Horses

The last, the newest, the most ambitious idea in the way of reclamation and the development of water power ever formulated is now in the process of development. It contemplates turning the Columbia River into its old bed in Grand Coulee, by the construction of a giant dam, the reclamation of between one and two million acres of land in Grant, Adams and Franklin counties and the development of water power approximating Niagara Falls. It was first conceived by William Clapp of Ephrata who kept it under his hat for a several months owing to the fact that it appeared too much at first an evanescent dream. But as the idea began to develop he talked it over with some of his friends. It so appealed to the Grant county commissioners that they have sent the county engineer to look the matter up from an engineer's standpoint.

At that time, the Bureau of Reclamation had begun to irrigate a few thousand acres of Idaho and Arizona desert land under the Reclamation Act of 1905; the generation of electrical energy was completely in private hands. Following the tremendous expenditures forced on the United States by the recently ended World War, the annual federal budget was approaching $5 billion, while the national debt had soared to $1 billion. So the very idea of committing the government to a project of this size was simply out of the question.

"Dam the Columbia?" Superior Court Judge R.S. Steiner wrote the *Wenatchee World.* "Verily, Baron Munchausen, Thou Art a Piker!"

"It can't be done because it has never been done," another writer protested. "Too much water! Too swift!"

"It's a great idea, boys," wrote a sympathetic Tacoma contractor, "but you will find that you are up against all the money in the world."

This warning proved to be true, for within a matter of months a Spokane association financed by a private utility and given strong backing by the largest-circulation newspaper in eastern Washington came up with an entirely different reclamation plan of their own. What this plan proposed was to take water from northwestern Idaho, which eventually flowed into the Columbia via the Spokane River, and by a 134–mile series of canals, ditches, and tunnels bring it by gravity flow to the desert lands of the Columbia Basin.

Because no electricity would be required for pumping purposes, this plan included no generating facilities. However, written into the plan was a scheme to divert water not needed following the end of the four month long irrigating season into the Spokane River a few miles above that city, where the private utility backing the scheme just happened to have some water-generation turbines.

In other words, for eight months out of the year the private utility would be receiving extra water it had not paid for and was taking away from Idaho users to generate electricity which it then could sell to its customers at whatever rate it chose to set. This, at least, was what the dam proponents claimed.

So the battle was joined, with the dam proponents being called "Pumpers" while the canal-ditch-tunnel advocates were dubbed "Gravity Flows."

The no-holds-barred battle raged for twenty-three years before a bucket of concrete was poured.

Because of the limited space available in this book, only the highlights of the struggle can be detailed here. But the principles involved were so basic to the development of the Pacific Northwest and the country as a whole, that they must be covered.

Involved were such questions as the ownership of natural resources such as water, land, energy, food production, transportation, minerals, and timber, and whether private or public investment should pay for their development and use. Should irrigated farms be subsidized by power revenues or was this a form of socialism? Should public land be given to private utility companies, as was done for the railroads, who then would control the distribution of water and allow speculators to make private profit on the increased value of that land? Should the people or the capitalists run the country?

During the 1920s when the economy of the United States was riding the crest of a boom that appeared to have no end, private enterprise had been in control. When the crash of 1929 ended the boom and brought on the Great Depression of the 1930s, the political philosophy of the country changed drastically. The Harding, Coolidge, Hoover era was over. For the next twenty-five years, Franklin Delano Roosevelt, Harry Truman, and the liberal-minded Democratic party would control the economy of the country, trying one experiment after another to fix what ailed it.

One of the most visible and dynamic experiments during those years was the building of Grand Coulee Dam and the development of the million desert acres downstream into fertile farm land and sites for new industries.

OBJECTIONS TO THE DAM

The first objection to the dam site was that the rock in the river bed was rotten and would not support the great weight of concrete that must be poured above it. Quoted in the Spokane *Spokesman–Review* in 1920, an engineer said:

> It is very clear that in the stretch of the river at the head of Grand Coulee, the Columbia has the old glacial deposit and not the granite rock for its bed. Judging from the outcrops of granite on the sides of the valley at opposite ends of the dam, the maximum depth of the bedrock in the center of the channel is estimated to be between 150 and 250 feet. The probabilities are that the depth would be in excess of 200 feet, rather than less.

Boring for rock samples, commented the editor, would be "a waste of money."

Needless to say, the Pumpers disagreed. After considerable scrounging from private and public sources, they managed to raise enough funds to do extensive core-drilling on the site. Their findings, they gleefully announced, were that solid granite not only underlay the river bed dam site at a depth of less than fifty feet, but also was available in the canyon walls as anchors for the ends of the dam. Loftily ignoring the pronouncement of the Pumpers, the Gravity Flow people still insisted that the rock was rotten to a depth of at least two hundred feet.

To the argument of the Pumpers that income from the sale of electricity produced by the dam would pay for the development of the irrigable lands, the Gravity Flows replied: (1) Since excess crops now were being raised in other parts of the country, more irrigated land was not needed; and (2) No market existed now or in the forseeable future for electric power in the region; when and if such a market did develop, the private utilities could easily supply it.

Each group brought in outside experts to make studies and voice opinions supporting its side of the argument. One of the most prestigious of those imported by the Gravity Flow people was General George Goethals, who eight years earlier had been in charge of building the Panama Canal. At the suggestion of C.C. Dill, a young Spokane attorney who, though a Democrat in a Republican district, had managed to get elected to Congress, the Pumpers imported Colonel Hugh L. Cooper, who, Dill later said:

> . . . was known as the greatest dam builder in the world. He had built the Niagara Falls and Keokuk dams. They (the Pumpers) raised enough money to pay him to investigate the proposal. Cooper spent the whole day at the damsite, and he approved it with a 150 mile reservoir extending to the Canadian border.

After being guaranteed a $20,000 fee for his expert opinion, General Goethals came to Spokane, studied the Gravity Flow plans, then paid a brief visit to the proposed site of the dam under the watchful eye of the people paying his fee and a reporter for the *Spokesman–Review*. In a curious mixture of factual reporting and mind-reading, the reporter wrote:

> General Goethals made no remarks as he studied this great challenge, but his face admitted the magnitude of the task. He gazed at the Columbia River today rolling along placidly and visualized the river at high water time, when the mountain snows would melt, realized huge flows would crash into the superdam which might stand as a threatening menace to life and property on the flat lands below.

Though General Goethals' final report expressed approval for the Gravity Flow proposal, he also was quoted by the Pumpers as having said, "Given the time and the money, the dam can be built...", which the Pumpers took to mean he was on *their* side. Though he left behind a bunch of cost estimates related to developing the irrigated land under the Gravity Flow plan, they were so ridiculously low when compared to known sums spent for reclamation projects elsewhere in the West that even his sponsors were too embarrassed to publicize them.

But on one cost estimate he was right on the money—his $20,000 fee. After collecting it, he returned to New York City and was heard from no more.

ROOSEVELT LEARNS ABOUT THE DAM

At about this same time, a young Assistant Secretary of the Navy named Frankin Delano Roosevelt, who was a candidate for vice-president in 1920, toured Washington State. Accompanying him

JAMES O'SULLIVAN AND INTERIOR SECRETARY J.A. KRUG
The photo was taken on September 28, 1948.

was C.C. Dill, who was about the only sympathetic Democrat FDR could find in the state. The two men became friends.

By a strange set of coincidences, Dill was serving in Congress ten years later when the General Electric Company invited him to come up to Schenectady, New York, to look at a new gadget they were playing with, a prototype television set. Aware of the fact that Franklin Roosevelt now was Governor of New York, whose capital was only eighteen miles away, Dill called him, and was invited to dinner at the executive mansion January 3, 1931. "My missus will be away," Roosevelt said, "and we can discuss politics all evening."

Following dinner and two hours of discussing the nation's ills, Dill told Governor Roosevelt that he had a Northwest problem he wanted talk about. FDR asked him what it was. Dill explained.

> I began by telling him of the great need for water to irrigate the dry lands of the Columbia Basin and that we were proposing to build an immense dam on the Columbia river to provide the water and at the same time produce a large amount of low cost power for the whole Northwest.

Among the many questions asked by Roosevelt was the attitude of President Hoover toward the project.

"All I can say say is he's against it now," Dill answered. "But we want to build it now. That's why I came to talk to you about it."

"I don't suppose I'll ever be president," Roosevelt said, "but if I am, I'll build that dam."

"That's what I came here to get you to say, but we'll have a long hard fight to persuade Congress to authorize it. It's so big they'll be afraid we can't sell the power to pay for it."

"Ah, if I were president," Roosevelt answered quickly, "I'd start it and Congress would have to finish it."

"If you stick to that promise," Dill said, "I'm going to help nominate and elect you president."

Both men kept their word.

POOREST LOBBYIST IN WASHINGTON

Between 1931 when the first serious efforts to get federal backing for the Grand Coulee Dam project were made and 1948 when the first water was put on the land, James O'Sullivan made twelve trips to Washington, DC as an advocate and expert witness for the Columbia River Development League—formerly known as the Pumpers. Since funds to pay his expenses were extremely limited, forcing him to stay in dollar-a-day hotels or boarding houses, he could truthfully be called a "poor" lobbyist, so far as finances were concerned. But he had no equal in the extent and quality of his knowledge regarding the project, his enduring belief in it, and the political know-how with which he steered enabling and appropriation bills through often hostile committees, executive-branch offices, and the halls of Congress.

Then as now, the squeaky wheel got the grease. Backed by far more resources than the Pumpers possessed, the Gravity Flow people fought tooth and nail against such Socialistic ideas as pub-

Courtesy Bureau of Reclamation
GRAND COULEE DAM SITE, BEFORE CONSTRUCTION BEGAN IN 1934

lic power and federal involvement in putting water on the land. But in James O'Sullivan's silver tongue, stubborn persistence, and Irish sincerity, the Pumpers had a resource beyond price.

Ready, willing, and able to preach the virtues of the project at any time or place, Jim O'Sullivan became a Prophet in the Wilderness, a man with a holy cause, an evangelist without a peer. Though a good Catholic, he once preached a Thanksgiving Day sermon in an Presbyterian church, which began as a paean of gratitude and then turned with no great subtlety into a pitch for the Grand Coulee project. Asked by an Ephrata church member to fill in for the minister, who was out of town, he gladly accepted, then began his Thanksgiving Day sermon thusly:

> Who shall say that he is not thankful for having been born into a paradise of freedom of religion, of politics, of economic opportunity, of power harnessed to do the work of man, of surpluses instead of famines, of love instead of brutality, of bewildering advances in science and invention? And we can be thankful for living not only in this great republic, but in that part that is still undiscovered—the new West—the West of opportunity and a future...

It seems that at last the star of destiny points toward the Northwest. All factors point this way—the President's waterway development, the growing use of electric power, the shortage on the Sound, the Boulder Canyon precedent, the crash on Wall Street, the very atmosphere seems to be charged with hope and faith. Grand Coulee is next.

How many people joined the Presbyterian Church following the service is not known. But it is a matter of record that the next day five members of the congregation joined the the Columbia River Development League.

ARMY ENGINEERS 308 REPORT

Because of pressures being exerted from many directions, the Army Corps of Engineers was authorized in 1929 to make an study of 425 miles of the Columbia east and north of Portland, then give recommendations as to how the river should be developed and used in the forseeable future. Put in charge of the project was Major John S. Butler, who, before beginning the work, told a meeting of the Washington Irrigation Institute in Yakima, "The problems to be solved in connection with any comprehensive plan of improvement of this river are so many and so intricate that no interest except the Federal Government can arrive at a satisfactory solution."

His words proved to be prophetic, just as the report he eventually turned in became the starting point for all future studies of the river.

Meanwhile, the use of electricity in the Puget Sound area was outstripping the supply available, despite the boasts of private utilities that they could take care of all future demand. The city of Tacoma ran so low on power that political pressure was exerted in Washington DC to force the aircraft carrier *Lexington*, which had a huge generator aboard, to leave its base in Bremerton, anchor in Commencement Bay, and hook onto the municipal power system to supply electricity for essential services. Learning of this, Jim O'Sullivan put together a statement syndicated in thirty-four Northwest newspapers: "As a source of year round power, Grand Coulee Dam could be built for the cost of a single aircraft carrier."

By now, a dam built to the full height of 550 feet, with all its generating and pumping facilities, was estimated at $450 million. On the lower Colorado River, a high dam first called Hoover, then

Boulder, and finally Hoover again, had been authorized for a mind-boggling $165 million. With the national debt now approaching the $3 billion level, the chances of the federal goverment's committing $450 million to the Coulee project lay somewhere between zilch and zero.

Still, people living in the Columbia Basin were suffering so severely that it was becoming increasingly obvious something must be done. After several especially dry years, the land itself was rising up and leaving the country. Historian George Sundborg relates in his excellent book *Hail Columbia: the 30–year struggle for Grand Coulee Dam:*

> Six hundred miles at sea, en route from Seattle to Honolulu, passengers aboard the Matson liner *Maui* were surprised one day to see the sun suddenly obscured by a great black cloud and then to see, feel, and taste descending gritty particles which could only be soil blown there from the mainland. The Pacific Northwest was having the most spectacular dust storm in its history . . .
>
> Much of the soil was being blown from the waterless lands of the Big Bend. One day during the storm the county agent at Wenatchee joined O'Sullivan for a drive over the Columba Basin project area. They found that the stretch of beautiful farming land from Wilson Creek to Hartline, and containing 200,000 acres of some of the finest soil in America, now seemed to be largely an area of drifting sand.

In a dramatic show of support for the Grand Coulee project, a crowd estimated at 8,000 people showed up for a picnic in Coulee Park featuring plane rides in a Ford Trimotor taking off from an 1,800–foot dirt runway scraped out of the sagebrush, lots of home-cooked food, and speeches by Rufus Woods, Jim O'Sullivan, and Senator C.C. Dill. The temptation to call the assembly a show of "grass-roots" support was resisted by the newspaper reporters who covered the mass meeting, for neither grass nor roots were visible under the ankle-deep dust. One newsman did quote a farmer who told him, "It's so dry around here we have to prime our cows before we can milk 'em."

After long months of waiting and speculation, Major Butler's 308 Report was finally released. Since both the Gravity Flow people and the Pumpers had guardedly said that they would abide by its conclusions, they perused it with eager eyes. To their mutual surprise, they found its conclusions to be far more sweeping than they ever had dreamed they would be.

Covering the entire drainage area of the Columbia and its tributaries in both the United States and Canada, the report analyzed dam sites, power, irrigation, and navigation possibilities, proposing potential development that would require the expenditure of billions of dollars over a period of fifty to seventy-five years.

Beginning 145 miles upriver from the mouth of the Columbia at a dam site called Bonneville, it identified a dozen more sites up the Columbia to Grand Coulee and beyond into Canada. Yes, Grand Coulee was feasible, the report said, as was the irrigation proposal of the Pumpers. But since each dam located on the upper reaches of the river would store water to be reused and produce electricity by the next dam downstream, the total energy available in the river would be doubled dam by dam; therefore, this factor should be considered before any dams at all were built.

Being an engineer, Major Butler stressed the fact that his report stated only what *could* be done. Privately, he admitted to Jim O'Sullivan that what *would* be done lay in the realm of politics and economics, which he was happy to say was outside his field of expertise.

By this time, President Roosevelt had been elected by a landslide vote and was being besieged with proposals to spend money and put people back to work. Boulder Dam was already underway and would be carried through to completion. In the Mississippi watershed, Muscle Shoals on the Tennessee River—the first step in a massive public power system that would develop into TVA (Tennessee Valley Authority)—would be approved and funded. While on a campaign swing through the Pacific Northwest, FDR had responded to Oregon Senator Charles McNary's plea that the federal government build a dam east of the Cascades by making a vague promise that a dam would be built somewhere on the Columbia in Oregon. Portland, which was west of the Cascades, took that to mean that the promised dam would be built in their area.

Astute politician that he was, FDR favored the region with the most unemployment and the most votes, dipping into emergency Public Works Administration (PWA) funds to authorize the building of Bonneville Dam forty-five miles east of Portland for a modest $43 million as the first dam to be built on the Columbia River under the 308 Report.

As might be expected, Senator C.C. Dill wasted no time in calling on President Roosevelt and reminding him of his promise to build Grand Coulee Dam if he were elected. Senator Dill later reported that their coversation went something like this:

FDR. "How much will it cost?"

DILL. "$450 million."

FDR. "Out of the question. Money is tight and the government already has taken on a lot of Public Works projects."

DILL. "You promised to build it."

FDR. "I know I did and I will. But can't it wait for a while?"

DILL. "We need it now."

FDR. "Would you settle for a low dam now, with a high dam to be built later on?"

DILL. "How low?"

FDR. "Say a hundred feet or so—just high enough to generate a little power we could sell and get the project going, with a high dam to come.

DILL. "How much money will you commit?"

FDR. "Say $40 million."

DILL. "Why, that won't even get concrete poured across the river, let alone build a dam. How about $100 million?"

Eventually, they settled for $60 million and a 145–foot high dam, which Dill later admitted was probably what the president had in mind in the first place.

Typical of his behavior once he had made a commitment, President Roosevelt plunged full speed head. In March, 1933 Senator Dill introduced a bill requesting the appropriation of $60 million; a permit was applied for on May 19; FDR tapped already-approved PWA funds to get the project started immediately; job applicatioins poured in at the rate of 150 a day; and on July 16, 1933, a ground-breaking ceremony was held at the dam site with 5,000 people in attendance.

Try to match that feat today.

In the East, politicians and newspaper editors howled in protest. The *Washington Post* editorialized, "Muscle Shoals, Hoover Dam, and the Columbia River projectsare all misuses of federal authority, and now Roosevelt adds the immensely costly Columbia River project to the list of squanderings..."

"The Bureau of Reclamation is public enemy No. 1," declared New York Representative Francis D. Culkin. "Not a single reclamation project has been sound....The proposition of the Grand Coulee in my judgment is the most colossal fraud in the history of America."

"Of all the outrages on agriculture, not stumbled into by accident, but deliberately to be riveted on our necks," raged the *Farm Journal*, which was published in Philadelphia, "we are beginning to think the Columbia Basin project takes the cake...Who wants it? Nobody. Well, perhaps not quite nobody, but nobody whose wishes have the slightest weight with Congress and the nation..."

BUILDING THE DAM

As the cofferdams to divert the flow of the river were built and the foundation was excavated to bedrock, Senator Dill and advocates of the project grew more and more concerned that completion of the low dam would preclude the building of a high dam later on. From an engineering and financial standpoint, it certainly would be a waste of money to pour a foundation for a 550–foot-high dam and build only a 145–foot dam on its base. Installing penstocks, gates, and generators that would be used for only a few years on a low dam, then would have to be removed and replaced by those for a high dam, would be a blatant squandering of money, while problems involved with making concrete sections poured for a low dam bond with those later poured for a high dam, would be difficult to overcome.

But as President Roosevelt often did during his long administration, he overcame the problem with ease. When Senator Dill told him of his concern, FDR flashed his famous smile and said calmly, "Don't worry, Clarence. The important thing is that we have our foot in the door."

Shortly thereafter, the president asked Secretary of Interior, Harold Ickes, to come over to the White House. When Ickes arrived, FDR told him that the Grand Coulee project was to be approved and completed as a high dam. "If that is what you want," Ickes replied simply, "it will be done."

It was.

As a staunch Democrat in a solidly Republican district, Senator Dill had never been much of a hero in Spokane. But he certainly got a hero's welcome when he came home a few days after telegraphing the good news.

A band was on hand to tootle the conquering hero off the train at the Great Northern station in Spokane, [George Sundborg writes]...Dill spoke from the station over a radio hookup which carried his words not only to Spokane, Seattle, Tacoma, Wenatchee, Bellingham, Walla Walla, Everett, and Aberdeen but across the state line to Portland...The first Sunday after the big news it was reported that more than one thousand people drove to the damsite to see what it was all about. The *Spokane Chronicle* reported, "One of the beneficial aspects of the mass visitations to the damsite is that the rattlesnakes have retreated from the area. A party from Spokane on a rattlesnake hunt succeeded only in taking one small one after an all day's search.

POWER FOR INDUSTRY AND WAR

Although the primary purpose for building Grand Coulee Dam was to put water on the land, making the desert blossom was the last objective accomplished before the project was completed. There were several good reasons for this. First, the nation's farmers already were producing more food than could be consumed, so new farmland was a low priority. Second, liberals in the administration were trying to break the grip of the private electric monopolies with cheap public power supplied by entities such as TVA. Third, events in Europe foreshadowed a World War for which the country was ill-prepared, insofar as armaments and the capacity to produce them were concerned.

On the private–public power issue, Senator Dill reports traveling in February, 1933, with President Roosevelt and a group of Southern senators to Muscle Shoals, a key area in the developing TVA project. He writes:

Muscle Shoals was built during the first world war to make war munitions, but the war ended too soon. Instead the War Department sold the power to private power companies for distribution in surrounding towns...As we stood there, Roosevelt said, "You see all those church spires of Florence," pointing to the town. "The private power company buys this power from the War Department for eight mills per kilowatt hour and sells it at 8 cents per kilowatt hour to the people of Florence, Sheffield and other towns near here. That must be stopped."

Despite the strong protests of private utilities in the Pacific Northwest, the federal government established a new agency, Bonneville Power Administration, to distribute and sell power generated by Bonneville, Grand Coulee, and all other dams to be built in the Northwest. The high-voltage transmission lines connecting these dams would be built and controlled by BPA, with public power companies and rural electrification co–ops given first preference as energy purchasers, while the rest would be sold to private utilities.

For a time, a lively debate took place on the question of rates. If the "bus bar" scale were used, this would mean that the further away the user was located from the source of the power, the higher the rate he would pay. If the "postage stamp" scale were used, rates would be the same all over the area—just as a letter at that time could be sent anyplace in the United States for a three-cent stamp.

Eventually the "postage stamp" rate concept won out and has remained in effect ever since.

Meanwhile, the threat of war made it necessary that the nation rearm. Both the aviation and the ship-building industries required metals such as aluminum and steel, but there was not a single fabricating plant or shipyard of any size in the Pacific Northwest. Within the next few years, this deficiency was corrected by building five alumimum mills in the Columbia Basin, while in Portland the massive Kaiser shipyard came into being.

Facilities operating twenty-four hours a day there built and launched ten-thousand ton Liberty ships at an incredible rate. In one case in 1942, only fourteen days elapsed between the time a keel was laid and the freighter slid into the water.

By the time Bonneville Dam's power came on the line in 1938, its entire output was committed to the war effort, as was that of the first set of generators installed at Grand Coulee, which began spinning March 22, 1941.

THE HANFORD PROJECT

With ninety-six percent of the power produced in the Pacific Northwest committed to the war effort, reclamation projects obviously would have to be postponed until the end of the war. But in 1943, for some mysterious reason, the federal government set aside a 200,000–acre tract of dry, mostly uninhabited desert land

Courtesy Bureau of Reclamation
PRESIDENT ROOSEVELT AND CROWD AT DEDICATION, AUGUST 4, 1934

in the lower Columbia Basin for a purpose which it refused to divulge. Though speculation was discouraged, the project was too big to be ignored. Historian George Sundborg writes:

> The plant at Hanford was still an absorbing mystery. Some, noting that another election year had rolled around, suggested that the secret works might be manufacturing Roosevelt buttons. Ed Southard had written to O'Sullivan in Washington: "The most astounding thing in this whole state is the Du Pont project building between Kennewick and Priest Rapids. I had a talk with the supervisor of supplies for the Milwaukee [Railroad] and he said they were sending from 120 to 180 carloads down from Beverly to the project every day. They are building a city that will accomodate from 30,000 to 50,000 people.

What they were also building, the world learned two years later, was the atomic bomb that would end the war with Japan in August, 1945, a project that required a vast amount of electricty and cooling water available only in this part of the nation.

RECLAMATION COSTS

It had long been the policy of the federal government to discourage speculation on desert land, which could be claimed for little or no cost under a number of government programs, but then became extremely valuable when water was brought to it. Usually a farm family was limited to 160 acres and must eventually pay a portion of the cost of irrigating the land.

Because of its size, the costs, revenues, and benefits of the Grand Coulee project were extremely difficult to estimate. In trying to explain what was going on in Washington DC to the people back home, Jim O'Sullivan used a football analogy:

> The ball was being carried by the Bureau of Reclamation, BPA, and the Power Division of the Interior Department, he wrote, "and I have to pry open the lid, if I can, to ascertain progress. I think they are using the T–formation to keep the location of the ball hidden, or they have not made enough progress themselves to be able to say definitely what progress they have made."

In 1932, the Bureau of Reclamation had estimated the Grand Coulee Dam and power plant would cost $186 million. Late in 1943 they submitted a new estimate of $220 million, which they soon raised to $240 million. When they reduced the size of the project from 1.2 million to 1 million acres, this upped the per–acre cost for reclamation from $173 to $240. Of course power revenue would repay the plant cost and navigation benefits would be set at $3.5 million, so the direct irrigation investment would be $155 million, with the farmer paying one-third of that, or about $85 an acre. To both settlers and Congressmen, it was all very confusing.

But O'Sullian was quick to point out to the taxpayers and voters that cheap power from Grand Coulee and Bonneville Dams already had brought the Pacific Northwest war industries valued at more than $1 billion.

"Grand Coulee," he said with no false modesty, "already has proved itself to be the largest, most useful, and the most daring engineering conception in the history of mankind."

Named Roosevelt Lake, the 150–mile long reservoir behind Grand Coulee Dam, which extended into Canada, reached its full 550–foot level on June 1, 1942. An anti–speculation bill was passed by Congress and signed by FDR March 11, 1943. Soon after the war ended, irrigation districts formed and preparations began to

Courtesy Bureau of Reclamation
WORKERS LINED UP FOR PAYDAY, 1937

lift water up and over the intervening ridge by means of massive pumps powered by electricity from the dam's turbines.

Sucking water up through 14–foot diameter pipes, each pump was rated at 65,000 horsepower, with a lift from the reservoir of 280 feet. Discharging the water, the twelve pumps would create an instant river on the floor of the coulee, which, when filled, would irrigate a million thirsty acres downstream. Plans called for the first water to be delivered in June, 1948. But before that happy event could take place, the Columbia River put on an unscheduled show of its own.

During the winter just past, snowfall in the mountains of the Pacific Northwest had been unusually heavy. With the coming of May, a large amount of rain fell over the region; when it ceased,

386   A TRAVELER'S HISTORY OF WASHINGTON

an early hot spell began to melt the deep drifts of snow at a rapid rate.

In an average year, the Columbia River spilled 198 million acre–feet of water into the the Pacific Ocean. Of this amount, 36 million acre–feet was contributed by the Snake River, which joined the Columbia near Pasco, Washington. Because its watershed was two hundred miles south of the headwaters of the Columbia, the peak runoff period of the Snake usually came two or three weeks prior to that of the Columbia. But on May 10, 1948, the Portland Weather Bureau warned that the two great rivers would peak at the same time. The highest crest on the lower Columbia since the record flood of 1894 was expected.

Since that time, of course, many cities and industries had been built in the river basin, so a disaster of major proportions seemed inevitable. The most vulnerable of the downstream communities was Vanport, on the outskirts of Portland, where a jerry-built project housing 40,000 people had been erected during the war years as living quarters for the massive Kaiser shipyards. Though its population had dropped to 18,700, many ex–GIs and their families were living here because of the community's cheap housing and proximity to what then was called Vanport City College.

Dubbed "wartime box" because the units had been built quickly and cheaply, the community had been sited on fill land, which lay fifteen to twenty-five feet below the bed of the nearby Columbia River. Hastily erected earth dikes protected it on all sides, giving its residents the feeling of living in a hole. As the river rose day by day to flood stage and beyond, the residents became concerned.

"Will the dikes hold?" they asked the housing authority.

Checking with the Corps of Engineers, who had completed the diking system and had previous experience in flood control, HAP (Housing Authority of Portland) was assured that the dikes were solid, so told the residents they had nothing to worry about. On May 30, 1948—Memorial Day—a message was shoved under each resident's door at 4 a.m. by the furnace firemen. It stated:

> ...the flood situation has not changed...barring unforseen developments Vanport is safe. However, if it should become necessary to evacuate, the Housing Authority will give warning at the earliest possible moment."

Courtesy Bureau of Reclamation
SHEEP CROSSING THE TOP OF GRAND COULEE DAM IN 1945

At 4 p.m. that afternoon, the river gauge on the north bank at Vancouver read 28.3 feet, 13 feet above flood stage. Near what was regarded as the strongest link in the chain of dikes protecting Vanport—the railroad fill to the west—the water level was still seventeen feet below the top. This dike, 125 feet wide at its base and 75 feet wide at its top, was considered indestructible. But deep within its seemingly solid exterior lay a hidden, fatal weak spot. This was an old wooden railroad trestle which, covered up with earth for many years, had gradually rotted away.

At 4:17 p.m., without warning, the railroad fill gave way. Suddenly the break was six feet, then sixty, then five hundred feet wide. In a matter of minutes, Vanport City was gone.

Though this was the worst flood damage done in the Columbia Basin in 1948, with twenty-five people known to have drowned, tremendous property losses were incurred all over the watershed. This turned the attention of river-use planners to a facet of the 308 Report that had not been seriously addressed before—flood control.

Along the 1,250 miles of the Columbia and the 1,036 miles of the Snake, there were only a handful of dams, most of which had little if any storage capacity. When used to generate power, a dam had to be full so that its turbines could spin at maximum capacity. Even if the entire 150–mile-long reservoir behind Grand Coulee had been empty in early May, the heavy rain and melting snow would have filled it within five days, taking little off the crest of the flood. What was needed was clearly spelled out in the 308 Report—a series of dams on the Columbia, the Snake, and their major tributaries that would control the rivers and put them to their maximum beneficial use.

DAM BUILDING ERA

Though the first water was put desert land below Grand Coulee in 1948, much of the emphasis during the next thirty years was on the building of dams for power, flood control, and the development of navigation. By 1974, dams and locks on the Columbia and Snake had made seaports of towns as far inland as Lewiston, Idaho, 470 miles from mouth of the Columbia River. During this period, the following dams were built:

RIVER MILE:	NAME:	COMPLETED:
145	Bonneville	1938
196	The Dalles	1957
230	John Day	1968
307	McNary	1953
412	Priest Rapids	1959
430	Wanapum	1963
468	Rock Island	1933
483	Rocky Reach	1961
526	Wells	1967
552	Chief Joseph	1965
596	Grand Coulee	1941

Because a substantial portion of Columbia River water originates in Canada, it was felt necessary to bring that nation into the planning process. Since Grand Coulee blocked the return of anadromous fish to Canadian waters and much of the flood control and electric energy benefits would help the economy of the United States rather than of Canada, some touchy negotiations were required before all the problems could be solved. But eventually they were, with the treaty being signed by President Lyndon Johnson and Canadian Prime Minister Lester Pearson on September 16, 1964.

Appropriately enough, the signing ceremony took place beneath the Peace Arch near Blaine, Washington, where a bronze plaque on the Canadian side states, "Brothers Dwelling Together in Unity," while another on the American side says, "Children of a Common Mother."

Beneficial to both nations, the pact provides 14 million acre–feet of water storage behind five Canadian dams, with Canada entitled to fifty percent of the extra power generated downriver for the next fifty years. Added to the capacity of other dams in Montana, Idaho, and the Snake River in eastern Washington, this gives a total of 40 million acre–feet of storage capacity over the watershed as a whole, thus assuring that devastating floods such as the one of 1948 can never happen again.

Like all projects that drastically alter the natural environment, the end effects of having what engineers call "a fully plumbed river system" do not please everybody. One of the unhappy results—which will be considered in the final section of this book—has to do with the loss of anadromous fish.

But for the present, Grand Coulee Dam, where a third powerhouse was recently completed, now generates 9.2 million kilowatts of electricty and is North America's leader in that field, while downstream the one million irrigated acres now in production top any other project on the face of the earth.

Rufus Woods, Billy Clapp, James O'Sullivan, C.C. Dill, and all the other men who dreamed, moved earth, and built, are long since gone. But what they built remains...

DRY FALLS

After seeing Grand Coulee Dam, its pumping facilities, and the extensive irrigation development below, you likely have had enough statistics dealing with large concepts to last for quite a while. But as long as your imagination is being stretched, you might as well take in one more sight in the area whose facts and figures will completely boggle your mind.

As noted earlier, Grand Coulee was created during an ice age that ended about 100,000 years ago. When the climate changed

Courtesy Bureau of Reclamation
PEAK OF FLOODWATERS AT GRAND COULEE DAM, MAY 30, 1948
This was the day the dike broke at Vanport on the outskirts of Portland.

and the melting period began, a silt-and-boulder-filled river that grew bigger and more powerful each day began to flow from the lower end of the coulee. Because the gradient was steep, it became an excavating mechanism of tremendous power as it eroded a channel vertically into the basalt overlay, while at the same time working its way north toward the original course of the river.

Over a period of six thousand years, geologists estimate, forty cubic miles of rock were eroded from the floor of the coulee by this water action. Two-thirds of the way down the coulee, the most magnificent waterfall ever to exist on the earth came into being. Four hundred feet high, a mile and a half wide, and fifty feet deep, the sheet of water plunging over the brink of the horse-shoe- shaped falls far surpassed the size of Victoria Falls in Africa, which is 256 feet high and a mile wide.

Though only a trickle of water now passes over the brink, the tremendous voice of that ancient waterfall must have made the earth tremble for miles around.

Today, at Dry Falls State Park near Coulee City, a viewpoint overlooks the now silent falls. But if you close your eyes, stand there a while, and give your imagination free rein, you may hear its roar...

H.S. Holmes Photo, Courtesy Bureau of Reclamation
OVERALL VIEW OF GRAND COULEE DAM AND IRRIGATION PROJECT
Notice in the center of the photo the pipes lifting water from the reservoir into
the main Coulee Canal. They are fourteen feet in diameter and there are twelve
of them.

SPOKANE AND THE INLAND EMPIRE

For some years now regional historians have carried on a lively
debate over the meaning of the term "Inland Empire" and
whether or not Spokane is entitled to call itself ruler of that far-

Courtesy Corps of Engineers
BONNEVILLE LOCK AND DAM
The first of many dams built on the C o l u m b i a , Bonneville was completed in 1938. This view looks south, with Oregon on the far side of the river.

Courtesy Corps of Engineers
THE DALLES LOCK AND DAM
Looking west down the river, the fish-ladder is in the foreground, the power bays in the middle, and the navigation lock on the upper right.

Courtesy Corps of Engineers
JOHN DAY LOCK AND DAM
Ninety miles downriver from McNary Dam, John Day Dam shares its name with John Day River and the eastern Oregon city of John Day.

Courtesy Corps of Engineers
MCNARY LOCK
AND DAM
Three miles east of Umatilla, McNary Dam was completed in 1952. It is one of four dams on the Columbia between eastern Oregon and Portland.

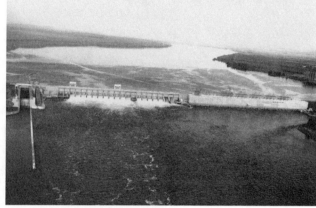

BPA Photo, Courtesy Corps of Engineers
CHIEF JOSEPH
DAM, COLUMBIA
RIVER

BPA Photo, Courtesy Chelan County PUD
ROCKY REACH
DAM, COLUMBIA
RIVER

BPA Photo, Courtesy Grant County PUD
ROCK ISLAND DAM, COLUMBIA RIVER

PUMP LIFT INTAKE AT GRAND COULEE
Each pump has a 65,000 horsepower rating.

Courtesy Bureau of Reclamation

PRIEST RAPIDS
DAM,
COLUMBIA
RIVER

WELLS DAM,
COLUMBIA
RIVER

WANAPUM DAM,
COLUMBIA
RIVER

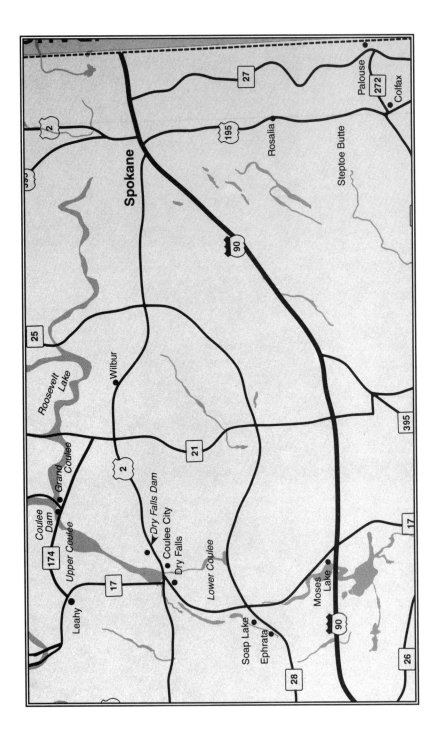

flung domain. The simple truth is that all the country east of the Cascade Mountains drained by the Columbia River may be called the Inland Empire, with Spokane the dominant metropolis of the region. How much the city controls this highly diverse kingdom is open to endless argument.

From the lovely valley in which the second largest city in Washington State sets, Spokane looks in four directions, seeing a different view from each cardinal point of the compass.

North lies British Columbia and the two-hundred-and-fifty mile sector of the great river nominally under Canadian control, though much of its water and trade flows into the United States and the Spokane area. East lies the Idaho Panhandle, whose immense stands of timber, beautiful lakes, and productive mines have channeled wealth into the economy of Spokane for over a hundred years. South lies the fabled Palouse Hills country, whose favorable climate and incredibly fertile soil have made it the bread-basket of the world since large-scale farming began. West lies the Grand Coulee country, whose unique treasures of sunshine, soil, water, and hydroelectic energy were described in the preceding chapters.

To some degree, the character of Spokane has been shaped by all these diverse elements, though the city by no means exercises complete control over any of them. In his book *The Inland Empire*, historian John Fahey says it best when he writes, "The Inland Empire is a state of mind as well as a place; it expands and contracts, depending on who is defining it."

US 2—Grand Coulee to Spokane
    89 miles
US 2, State 211, 20, 31—Spokane to Canada
    107 miles
I–90—Spokane to Coeur d'Alene, Idaho
    30 miles
US 195—Spokane to Colfax, Pullman, Palouse
    70 miles
I–90—Spokane to Ellensburg
    174 miles

Courtesy Penrose Library, Whitman College
FALLS OF THE SPOKANE RIVER IN 1847

Like the rest of the Pacific Northwest, Spokane's recorded history began when British and American fur companies such as the North West Company, the Hudson's Bay Company, and Astor's Pacific Fur Company sent brigades westward across the continent from Montreal and St. Louis in 1812. Reaching the Columbia Basin only months apart, the American company established a fur-trading post called Fort Astoria at the mouth of the Columbia, while the British, who planted a flag at the juncture of Snake River with the Columbia a short while later and proclaimed all the region the property of His Royal Majesty, built a post called Spokane House near the site of the present city.

Willing to compete head to head with the British for furs, the American company erected a post called Fort Spokane within a mile of the rival station, not in an attempt to preempt a good location but as mutual protection against possible Indian hostilities.

As matters turned out, the local Spokane Indians remained peaceful and friendly, while the breadth of a continent and an ocean away, the United States and Great Britain went to war again, taking two years to finally reach the conclusion that fighting was a poor way to settle disputes over territory and freedom of the seas. Under duress, the Astor Company sold Astoria, Fort Colville, and Fort Spokane to the British, then later agreed to the terms of the Joint Occupancy Treaty signed at Ghent in 1818, which decreed that the two nations would have equal rights in the Pacific Northwest for the next decade or two, when its ownership would be settled by the people who wanted to live in the region.

Until this event happened in 1846 and the boundary line was drawn at the 49th parallel, Fort Walla Walla near the mouth of the Snake, Spokane House, and Flathead Post in the lake country to the east, were Hudson's Bay Company posts, and the region's fur trade was controlled by British interests. Feeling that the best way to keep Americans out of the Pacific Northwest was to deplete its most valuable asset, beaver, Sir George Simpson, director of operations for the Company in North America, ordered his trapping brigades to "strip the country bare" by decimating its beaver population. But brilliant as Sir George may have been as a fur company executive, he was a poor judge of the force that in that place and time inspired religious people to carry their message into the far places of the world.

That force was missionary zeal.

"GO YE THEREFORE..."

In compiling his comprehensive history of western North America—which was published in the 1890s—the testy, often biased historian, Hubert Howe Bancroft, summed up the manner in which he thought religious white people should have treated native Americans by saying, "The best thing the missionaries could have done for the Indians was to leave them alone."

Of recent years, a school called "Revisionist Historians" has achieved a certain amount of notoriety by telling us how badly our ancestors handled westward expansion and the terrible crimes they committed against the environment and the native population. After admitting that there is some truth in these criticisms, what also must be said is that deploring what happened does not alter the fact that it did happen and was generally approved at the time. Certainly the movement to send preachers and priests into the wilderness to "convert the heathen" cannot be ignored as an important factor in the development of the Pacific Northwest.

Sir George Simpson, a practical as well as a religious man, felt that it would be helpful to the local Indians if some of their future leaders were educated in a white man's eastern school so that they could return and become teachers to their people. On one of his visits to Spokane House, he told Factor Alexander Ross, "Pick for me a promising boy of the Middle Spokanes and another of the Kootenais (a nearby tribe) to be sent to the Protestant mission school conducted at the Red River settlement (Winnipeg)."

The two boys sent east in 1825 were given the names Spokane Garry and Kootenai Pelly. Both were fourteen years old, intelligent, malleable, and eager to learn the white man's language and ways, as their fathers had instructed them to do. Within a year, Kootenai Pelly became infected with a white man's disease against which he had no immunity, and died. But Spokane Garry thrived and remained in the school for five years, learning his lessons well and becoming an enthusiastic advocate of the white man's way of life.

When he returned to the Spokane area at the age of nineteen, he was given the title of "Chief" despite his youth, and at once began to teach his people what he had learned. At first, they were impressed, working under his direction as he showed them how to plant and tend an extensive vegetable garden and erect a twenty-by-fifty-foot wooden school building and church, listening attentively as he taught them the Ten Commandments and how to pray to the white man's God.

Hearing about his return and the marvelous things he had learned and was sharing with his people, delegations of Indians from friendly tribes such as the Nez Perces and Flatheads came and listened, then decided that they, too, would make the long trek east to the white man's world in search of wisdom and spiritual guidance. Because the Nez Perces and their cousins the Flatheads still remembered the visit of the Lewis and Clark party to their country in 1805–06 and had been told by American trappers that William Clark was now Superintendent of Indian Affairs for the Oregon Country, their delegation decided to go to St. Louis instead of Winnipeg. Instead of sending their boys east to be educated in the white man's school, they would ask that *taitamnats*—religious teachers—be sent to their country, where the white missionaries would live and teach in the Indians' own environment.

In response to the delegation to St. Louis in 1831, first the Methodists, then the Congregational–Presbyterians, and finally the Catholics sent out parties of missionaries to live with the Indians and attempt to teach them a way of life so different from the one they knew that it proved impossible for the native people to adopt it in the few years given them before their country was overrun by white expansion.

Further complicating relationships between the Indians and the whites were the intense rivalries that existed between Catholics and Protestants for the winning of heathen souls; and between British and American traders over furs. Though an Indian might not understand what the rivalry was all about, he certainly was perceptive enough to see that it existed. Consequently, when asked to join a church or sell a beaver pelt, he usually did business with the preacher or trader who offered him what he judged to be the best bargain.

THE TRAGEDY OF SPOKANE GARRY

The first American missionaries to settle at Tshimakain among the Spokanes were Elkanah and Mary Walker, who were sponsored by the same Presbyterian–Congregatonal American Board for Foreign Missions that had sent Marcus and Narcissa Whitman to the Cayuse Indians in the Walla Walla Valley and Henry and Eliza Spalding to the Nez Perces at Lapwai in what would become Idaho. Shortly thereafter, the Catholics arrived and established a mission on Lake Couer d'Alene thirty miles east of Spokane.

Reading the diaries, journals, and letters of these missionaries, the unbiased historian cannot doubt that these were sincere, dedicated people who believed that their holy mission in life was to educate the heathen and teach them about the white man's God. At the same time, the unbiased historian cannot doubt that the Catholic priests—who were Jesuits—and their Protestant rivals—whose Presbyterian–Congregational credos were equally dogmatic—had little understanding and less sympathy for the spiritual beliefs of the Indians they were trying to convert.

Spokane Garry, who had spent five years in the white man's world and now was trying to improve the lives of his people by teaching them new ways, found himself criticized and resented for more reasons than his youth. Native *shamans* (priests) and *tewats* (medicine men) who did not want to lose their power over the people told them that Garry's teachings were sacrilegious. Since the earth was their mother, they said, scarring her breast with a fence or a plough, as he advocated doing, was a desecration that might well invite the wrath of the native gods.

The creed learned and preached by Spokane Garry was a stern one. If people were good and obeyed the Ten Commandments, he said, when they died they would go to Heaven and see God. But if they disobeyed the laws written in the Holy Book, they would go down and face the fires of Hell. What kind of a religion was that, the *shamans* asked scornfully.

When the missionaries arrived at Tshimakain in 1838, Garry greeted them politely, helping them master the Spokane tongue and translating the sermons they preached accurately but with no great warmth. Undoubtedly he resented the fact that he no longer was the center of attention as a preacher and teacher. In need of help because of Indian backsliding and disaffection, he got little backing from the Protestants and was ridiculed by local Indian converts made by the Catholics, who claimed the kind of religion he taught was heretical.

Visiting the area in 1841, Sir George Simpson expressed disappointment in his protegé when he found Garry "...unkempt and unclean, his hands full of filthy cards with which he was gambling with others of his tribe."

When asked why he had quit teaching in the Indian school, Garry grunted "because they jawed at me too much."

Following the closing of the Tshimakain mission after the Whitman Massacre in 1847, the Walkers departed, leaving Garry alone to carry on the religious instruction of his people. Though his power as a chief was limited, he did wield enough influence to resist the efforts of the Jesuit priests to move in and take over, maintaining at least a token Protestant control over the church and school. Further, he continued his efforts to aid his people in an economic sense. In *Spokane Story*, historian Lucile Fargo writes:

> On the agricultural side, Garry's efforts also produced lasting results. When Governor Stevens arrived in the Spokane country in 1853 [on his way west to Olympia], he was pleased and astonished at the progress some of the Spokanes had made under Garry's tutelage...He had recently contracted for a flour mill on the Little Spokane, and had flour, sugar, and coffee on hand in sufficient quantity to supply the Governor's party.

When Stevens returned to eastern Washington Territory in 1855 to meet in the Walla Walla Valley and make treaties with the

Nez Perce, Yakima, Cayuse, Walla Walla, and Umatilla tribes, Garry attended the nineteen–day negotiation session and spoke in behalf of his people in words of simple eloqence, saying, "When you look at the red men, *you* think you have more heart, more sense, than these poor Indians. I think that the difference between us and you Americans is in the clothing; the blood and the body are the same. Do you think because your mother is white and theirs dark, that you are higher and better? We are dark, yet if we cut ourselves the blood is red, so with the whites it is the same though their skin is white. I do not think we are poor though we belong to another nation. If you take the Indians for men, treat them so now."

After negotiating treaties and setting aside reservations for the tribes in the Walla Walla area, the Stevens party traveled northeast to the Spokane, Couer d'Alene, and Blackfoot country. Under duress, the Couer d'Alenes and Blackfeet signed treaties and agreed to go on reservations. Despite his long history of friendship with the whites, Garry was offered such a small, unattractive piece of land for the Spokanes that he and the scattered bands for whom he was the spokesman refused to sign the proferred treaty. Experienced in dealing with the whites, Garry was sure he could get a better bargain by holding out for a while. But before further talks could take place, a series of tragic events for which he was in no way responsible occurred.

First, small parties of white prospectors seeking gold in the Colville area trespassed on lands reserved for the Indians, quarrels ensued, and several white men were killed. In an ill-conceived show of force, an Army contingent under Major Granville O. Haller rode north into the Yakima country, tangled with several hundred angry warriors under the leadership of Chief Kamiakin, and were soundly whipped. A short while later, another Army unit under Colonel Edward J. Steptoe marched into the Spokane country "to show the flag," were attacked by a large body of dissident Indians also under Kamiakin's leadership, and were defeated in a humiliating manner.

Keenly aware of the fact that unless federal troops whipped the Indians in a decisive fashion, the entire interior country must be abandoned by whites, the United States Army turned that unpleasant task over to Colonel George W. Wright—a martinet, if ever there was one—who carried out the job given him with stark brutality.

Though Chief Garry had counseled peace from the very beginning, rebellious young men among his people refused to listen, went to war, and paid a bitter price for their bad judgment. Three of Garry's own brothers and a brother-in-law were killed in the fighting. When Garry met with Colonel Wright and protested that all the Spokanes should not be made to suffer because of the mistakes of a few hot-headed young men, Colonel Wright refused to listen.

Ordering that eight hundred horses owned by the hostiles and captured during the fighting be killed so that the Indians would be set afoot, he then told Garry the terms on which he would make peace.

> You must deliver to me, to take to the General, the men who struck the first blow in the affair with Colonel Steptoe. You must deliver to me to take to Walla Walla, one chief and four warriors with their families. You must deliver to me all property taken in the affair with Colonel Steptoe. You must allow all troops and other white men to pass unmolested through your country.

In addition to this stern ultimatum, Colonel Wright ordered his troops to burn all captured Indian lodges, stores, and grain that could not be used by the troops, then brought to summary military trial a number of warriors accused of having killed white people. Of these, ten were were convicted and ordered hanged on the spot. In late September, 1858, the multiple executions were carried out in the pine trees bordering what then was called Latah Creek in what would become southeast Spokane.

Shortly thereafter, the stream was renamed "Hangman Creek"—a name it bears today.

Still hoping to find justice and a permanent home for his people in the Spokane area, Garry patiently pleaded for a reservation, an agent, and a contingent of soldiers to be stationed nearby in order to protect the Spokanes from the greediness and brutality of the whites. Army officers such as General William S. Harney and religious leaders such as Father Pierre Jan DeSmet endorsed his efforts, writing letters and signing petitions to the federal government urging that Spokane Garry's long history of friendship toward the whites be rewarded. But year after year nothing happened. Fargo writes:

Poverty-stricken, disinherited, with no spot officially theirs, the Spokanes did the best they could living from hand to mouth—and rapidly deteriorating.

During the Nez Perce War in 1877, Chief Garry did get some attention from the military when General Sherman, who was visiting in the area, sternly warned him against letting his people join Chief Joseph in his rebellion and admonished him "to be good," the implication being that if he were a "good" Indian, he would be rewarded. Unlike Chief Moses, who was shrewd enough to win concessions from the whites by playing upon their fears that he might let his people join the hostiles, Garry had such a long-established reputation for being a peaceable Indian, that he was given nothing for his "good" behavior.

In 1880, the Spokanes were finally given a choice of taking up land claims in severalty or moving to a reservation west of the Columbia River, in a land they had never called their own, with other tribes to whom they were at the best strangers, at the worst traditional enemies. A few accepted, but most, including Garry, refused.

Under an agreement finally entered into in 1887, Garry undertook to gain title to a piece of land he had been living on for a number of years. But despite the fact that he had fenced the tract, erected buildings on it, and planted an extensive garden year after year, the claim was "jumped" by a white settler when Garry left it for a few days to go on a salmon-fishing trip. Fargo writes:

> When he hurried back to his home and land he was ordered by the white men in possession to get off and stay off. All his efforts to regain possession were fruitless. Legal procedures proved as futile as argument. The newcomers had filed on the land and their claims were allowed to stand in spite of the evidence inherent in Garry's improvements, his fence, his growing crops. What was one more Indian more or less, even though he happened to be a "good" Indian.

Dispossessed, impoverished, and forced to sell off what had once been his large herd of horses and cattle in order to live, Spokane Garry lived out his twilight years with two or three other Indian families in the Hangman Creek area until white neighbors made the place too uncomfortable for them, then moved to what now is called the Indian Canyon district, where the white man who "owned" it gave them space enough to pitch their tepees.

There, in 1892, at the age of eighty-one, Spokane Garry, who had learned the white man's ways at the age of fourteen and tried to follow them ever after, died.

"A Presbyterian minister preached the funeral sermon," Lucile Fargo writes, "and friends laid him to rest under a little wooden cross in a white man's cemetery."

In a footnote, she adds that on June 15, 1935, a monument bearing a proper inscription was unveiled by the Spokane Chapter of the D.A.R. at Garry's grave in Greenwood Cemetery.

BEGINNINGS OF SPOKANE

When the Washington Territorial Legislature first met in 1853, the boundaries of both the Territory and the political districts designated as Counties were extremely vague. With the eastern border of the Territory at the "summit of the Rocky Mountains" and the southern line at "the extension of the northern border of Oregon Territory"—wherever *that* was—the limits of Spokane County could be set pretty much where its representatives chose to place them.

With the Indian troubles settled in the early 1860s, a trickle of white and Chinese prospectors drifted into a region measuring roughly two hundred miles from east to west and four hundred miles from north to south, an area which might reasonably be named Spokane County—which it was. No funds were available to pay for such badly needed services as law enforcement. Since titles to property had not been established, there appeared to be nothing to tax for needed revenue.

Then some nameless genius had a brilliant idea. Why not tax the two items in most visible supply—saloons and Chinamen? This was immediately done, the law being applied by the unpaid County Sheriff and his deputies, who garnered their own salaries by retaining a twenty percent commission on all taxes collected. Needless to say, the law was strictly enforced.

From its first discovery, the finest asset of the Spokane area was the scenic waterfall on the rushing, sparkling river that ran through the heart of the valley. In fact, beginning in 1873 and for many years thereafter, the settlement adjacent to the water-pow-

Click Relander Collection, Courtesy Yakima Valley Regional Library
FORT SPOKANE ADMINISTRATION BUILDING, 1870
The building is near the juncture of the Spokane and Columbia Rivers.

ered sawmill built by James Glover and his partners was known as "Spokane Falls."

Rightly called "The Father of Spokane," Glover soon was joined by the Reverend Henry T. Cowley, a Presbyterian minister who had worked for a time with Spalding and the Nez Perces, then brought his wife to the Spokane area, where he would eventually raise six children, become prominent in teaching, business, and financial matters, and give the the Northern Pacific Railroad an expensive lesson in legal matters.

Like all Western communities, Spokane Falls yearned for a railroad and was willing to offer practically anything to entice the rails to pass through their town. Free right-of-way along whatever route the railroad chose to follow was the main lure, so when first the Northern Pacific, then the Great Northern, and finally the Chicago, Milwaukee and St. Paul lines decided to come through the city, their joint rails and Union Station preempted the best view of the Spokane River and its scenic Falls. By the mid–1890s, the growing metropolis could and did boast that with three transcontinental and four branch lines fanning out in all directions, Spokane Falls was the railroad capital of the inland Pacific Northwest.

By then, the publicity departments of the railroads—euphemistically called "Literary Bureaus"—had done yeoman work telling landless people in Europe and the eastern United States how easy it was to claim a quarter-section or more of land in the Far West, broadcast a few bushels of seed wheat or set out a few thousand fruit trees, then wait for the harvest that would make them rich. Of course the fact that the railroads had been given alternate sections of land across a belt extending forty miles north and south of their right-of-way as an inducement to build their lines was merely coincidental to the fact they were encouraging settlement and traffic. They just liked to make people happy.

What was interesting about these alternate sections was that they were not blocked out on the map until the railroad magnates evaluated them as potential town sites, timber claims, or other uses. For example, when the federal government offered to let the Spokane Indians take title to land in severalty and Enoch Siliquowya laid claim to 160 acres surrounding the falls of the Spokane River in 1875, he was informed that the land fell within the odd-numbered sections granted the Northern Pacific, whose rails would not reach Spokane until six years later.

However, "some adjustment would be made..." the government assured Enoch, later awarding him a piece of dry, rocky land, well away from the noise of the waterfall and the train whistles. The original piece of land he had claimed would have been of no use to him or his descendants for pasture or farming, of course, because eventually downtown Spokane would be built on it.

Like all western cities, Spokane Falls had its great fire in 1889, destroying most of its wooden buildings, which were replaced by solid, imposing structures of stone. By then, the big timber companies moving west from St. Paul had discovered that the magnificent forests of northern Idaho were second only to those bordering Puget Sound. Under its new charter, the booming city—feeling grown up—dropped the "Falls" from its name and became plain Spokane—a change many of its residents deplore to the present day.

More important, the biggest silver strike north of Mexico was made in the Idaho Panhandle in 1883 when a wandering burro lead his master to the richest mine ever discovered by a jackass. It happened in this manner:

A grubstake given an elderly prospector named Noah S. Kellogg had included a burro, more familiarly known to Inland Empire history as a jackass. With summer gone and no precious metal found, Kellogg decided to return to the small mining settlement of Murray empty-handed. But the pesky jackass, he said, which was always wandering away, was missing. Exasperated, Kellogg went stumbling heedlessly across hills and hollows looking for the contrary animal, and, in the process, stubbed the toe of a well-scuffed boot on an outcropping of galena laced with silver, over which the missing jackass was standing with ears pointed foward as if to say, "Is this what you're looking for?"

Such was the beginning of the Bunker Hill and Sullivan Mine, whose fabled riches have not yet been exhausted today.

THE HERCULES MINE

A few years later, the second richest mine in the Coeur d'Alene area was discovered without the help of a four-footed animal, though the human beings involved were just as colorful and contrary as the fabled jackass.

To put it as delicately as possible, May Arkwright was a big, homely woman from the coal-mining country of Ohio, who had come to Idaho to make her living as a camp cook. She was said to be the "unrecorded child of an itinerant backwoods preacher, who had elbowed her way to belligerent womanhood."

Levi William Hutton was an unwanted orphan who had finally left his uncle's farm in Iowa, wandered out to Idaho, and becomed a railway engineer. Other than the fact that she was a fine cook and had a heart as big as all outdoors, May possessed no attractive physical features whatever. But apparently she was just what Levi Hutton was looking for. In any case, they met and married in the boarding house May was running, with Levi bringing a load of guests in the cab of the locomotive he was driving, while May cooked the wedding feast for the crowd in her own kitchen.

After the wedding, the Huttons moved to Wallace, a little further up the Couer d'Alene River. Lucile Fargo writes:

> Wallace was a step upward on the social scale; but such efforts
> as Levi Hutton's wife made to live up to her new social status
> were not successful. Her very looks were against her. She was

huge, she was homely. She was strident, uncouth, and given to strong language. From the first, May was "that woman"—not to say "that awful woman!"

Truth was, the only strata of society that May and Levi wanted to impress were representatives of the "radical" labor class. During the 1890s, the battle between capital and labor became so bitter that federal troops were called in by the mine owners to break strikes, while the workingmen retaliated by bombing property and public figures. Though May won the hearts of her boarders with both her blueberry pies and her strong verbal support, Levi, in his quiet way, proved equally supportive of the Radical cause when he permitted a freight train he was driving to be kidnapped at gunpoint, then drove it and the load of dynamite it carried to Wardner, where it was parked and blown up under the buildings at the Bunker Hill and Sullivan Mine.

For his part in the violence, Levi and nine hundred other men were rounded up and thrown into a stockade called "the bullpen"—an experience May immortalized in book she wrote shortly afterwards titled *The Coeur d'Alenes, a Tale of the Modern Inquisition in Idaho*. For its place and time, the book was an instant bestseller, with eight thousand copies going like hotcakes. Now a collector's item, the book was a confused jumble of invective, dime novel narrative, wit and oratory, earning its author a reputation hard to live down when she and her husband later got rich and moved to Spokane.

Like everybody else in the area, the Huttons now and then invested a few spare dollars in what they called "prospects." The particular gopher hole in which they and a boarder named Gus Paulsen were sinking their extra money in 1901 was named the "Hercules," for no better reason than that they happened to see a can of blasting powder bearing that brand name. Every week or so, Gus Paulsen—who delivered milk for a living—would dump a pocketful of ore samples he had chipped off the roof and walls of the mine's tunnel on a sheet thrown over the bed, and the investors would paw through them, looking for color. At last, they found it. Fargo writes:

> By 1902 the Hercules began to pay. For the Huttons, a modest first dividend of seven hundred and fifty dollars rose sixteen years later to a peak of five hundred thousand. They moved from their two-room cabin on the Wallace hillside to a comfortable

house on a corner lot in the town itself. May acquired a hired girl, became an avid student of Shakespeare, and papered her "study" with personal notes and critical comments on her book.

MAY, LEVI, AND FREE SPEECH

Though their fortune eventually grew to six million dollars, they managed it with remarkable shrewdness, while at the same time spending a portion of it to do exactly what they wanted to do. Nationally known figures such as Clarence Darrow, Senator William Borah, and writer Ella Wheeler Wilcox often were their guests in Wallace. But their idea of a big evening was to go to a dance sponsored by the local Elks or Masons or to join in a shell game on the dining room table which had been cleared after the evening meal.

Interested in free speech, votes for women, and the temperance movement, May attended the Idaho State Elks Convention held in Wallace, contributing a few lines of poetry which she had written for the occasion:

At eve the antlered elk came down
    From each surrounding hill,
And from the purling mountain streams
    Each one would drink his fill.
And though the forest now is dead
    And muddied each pure rill,
The Elk of this, our latter day,
    Still often drink their fill!

Pleased that Idaho had at last given women the vote, May sought a nomination on the Democratic ticket for State Legislator. Asking her fellow delegates at the Shoshone County convention to vote for her, just to show that woman counted for something politically, she surprised everyone—including herself—by winning the nomination and then running an amazingly close race, which she barely lost, for the state post. When asked how she had conducted her campaign to do so well, she shrugged and said, "Just like any man. I gave away cigars—and hustled."

With their money still accumulating, the Huttons moved to Spokane. Good-natured as always, Levi advised his cherished partner May, "Don't make a holy show of yourself," then watched with good-humored approval as she did exactly that. Possessed of a basic shrewdness and good business sense, Levi directed the management of the Hercules Mine, then supervised the erection of what became known as the Hutton Block in downtown Spokane, while May went East to visit with the Clarence Darrow family in Chicago and pick out furnishings for the luxury apartment on the top floor of the building in which she and Levi planned to live.

Buying a fire-engine-red Thomas Flyer in which a uniformed chauffeur drove her around town to shop and do charity work, she invariably wore a scarlet dress, a yellow satin shirtwaist, and a tiger-striped coat, with tidal waves of ostrich plumes billowing from hat to shoulder. Efforts of more genteel lady social leaders to put her in her place by reminding her of her humble beginnings, proved as ineffective as trying to block Spokane Falls with a handful of sand.

"Oh, my dear," gurgled a socially aspiring acquaintance of mining camp days, "do you remember how once you used to do our washing for us?"

"Sure," May replied, "and that you never paid me for it."

Touring Washington State in support of Suffragist causes, May gave generously of both her money and time. For one occasion, she rolled up her sleeves, floured her hands, went into the kitchen and baked her specialty—eighty blueberry pies. Visiting the East Coast and learning that Boston women regarded themselves as too cultured to vote, she made the comment that "criminals and idiots can't vote, and neither can women."

Though initially she had been a strong supporter of Theodore Roosevelt, who espoused some liberal ideas for his day, she deserted his camp and never voted for him again when he thoughtlessly made the remark that a lady's name should appear in print only twice: "When she married and when she died."

Appointed as a member of the Charities Commission in Spokane, she proved to be as competent as a well-trained detective, though not as subtle.

Attending a national convention in Baltimore one humid summer, May gave her home state considerable newspaper publicity when she decided to do her laundry in her room. When she hung her intimate garmets out the window of the swank hotel room to dry, the manager objected, starting to say, "It's not customary to expose—"

"Customary nothing!" May interupted. "I rented the room, didn't I? Windows go with the room, don't they? I'll leave my washing right where it is or know the reason why."

Calculating her personal wealth at two million dollars, the Baltimore reporter who wrote the story noted that her laundry was permitted to hang out the window until it was dry. One lady journalist wrote that May had put a plump, bejeweled hand on her arm and said gently, "I'm not militant, you know. We Western women don't have to be militant. The men out West are too nice. All we have to say is we want something and we get it. Why, if I told you all about the West you'd want to take the next train and go out there yourself."

In failing health and confined to an invalid's chair, May's final weeks in 1915 were devoted to the cause of world peace. After she and Levi had bought the Liberty Theatre in downtown Spokane, she imported the nationally known actress, Mrs. Leslie Carter, to star in the hit play *The Heart of Maryland*. Seated in their special box, she and her husband listened with moist eyes to a male quartette singing an entre-acte song whose lyrics May had recently penned, "The Song of the Soldier Boy," sung to the music of "Just Before the Battle, Mother."

The song, a plea for world peace, would be on sale in the theatre at twenty-five cents per copy, with the proceeds to go to the Children's Tuberculosis Sanitarium.

May Arkwright Hutton's last public appearance was to welcome a thousand members of the Washington State Federation of Women's Clubs to a "Women For Peace" fete in Spokane, where a resoluton was signed commending President Wilson for his neutral stand in a world at war.

Following the death of his beloved wife, Levi Hutton lived alone and lonely in the big house he had built, still managing his money shrewdly but now seeking a way to put his millions to good use after he was gone. Having been an orphan himself, he was not long in working out a plan. Fargo writes:

> A few miles up the Spokane Valley between the irrigated orchards and the foothills he purchased a farm. On its three hundred and twenty rolling acres he built barns, granary, and a group of friendly, gabled cottages arranged about an ample lawn, the whole to be known as the Hutton Settlement. On a white painted post he swung the bell of his old locomotive...

For its time and place, the Settlement was unique—one of the early substitutes for the old-fashioned lock-step, institutionalized orphanage. Levi's cottages were to be homes. In each was to live a small group of children mothered and directed by a kindly woman, as in a real home where everybody helped and everyone old enough had his job in kitchen, dairy, or field. No starched "Matrons" for Levi's orphans. The women were "Mothers." The lack of a father he made it his job to supply personally. From the hour when in his own arms he carried the first child across a Settlement threshold he was "Dad" to all of them.

Levi Hutton died in 1928 and was buried beside his wife in the Fairmont cemetery near the Spokane River.

Today, the Hutton Settlement still thrives, operating as it was meant to do as a refuge for children who have neither parents nor homes. In celebration of its 75th anniversary in 1994, hundreds of the 2,000 people raised in the home returned to Spokane to witness the removal of the 1919 cornerstone and the opening of a copper box placed there by the soft-spoken mine owner, Levi Hutton, whose silver fortune was given to the Settlement so that future children could have a home and parents, which he and his beloved wife never had.

"With what proved to be amazing foresight," says an article in the *Spokesman–Review* July 10, 1994, "he stipulated none of the 319 acres could ever be sold or subdivided. The board of directors would consist entirely of women, appointed for life. Today the board, a primer of Spokane's Who's Who, includes twenty-one women who do everything from overseeing the cottages to working with the schools the children attend in West Valley to plant the flower beds.

"Hutton also arranged a financial advisory board that still includes the mayor of Spokane and a Spokane County commissioner. Finally, he built buildings to last 200 years."

EXPO '74—SPOKANE WORLD'S FAIR

Long and hard though Spokane had worked to get railroads to come through the city, ninety years later the citizens were beginning to resent what had become a downtown eyesore. Lost in an unsightly tangle of trestles, stations, freight sidings, and industrial junkyards, their beautiful river and spectacular falls, if visible at all, no longer were sights to be proud of.

Though Spokane residents and downtown businessmen long had talked about converting the river and falls area into a park, whenever the idea came up it was blocked by the ugly fact that the railroads had preempted the most scenic sections of the river, giving passengers passing through on trains of the Northern Pacific, Great Northern, or Chicago, Milwaukee, and St. Paul far better vistas of the Spokane River than residents of the city could obtain.

In 1963, with the one-hundredth birthday of the the city's founding just ten years away, Spokane's population numbered 180,000, with a total of perhaps 250,000 if the outlying communities were included. Hoping to put on some kind of modest affair to celebrate the centennial, a businessmen's organization called "Spokane Unlimited" raised $150,000 to finance a study of what could and should be done. As its executive secretary, it hired a tall, husky, enthusiastic Irishman named King F. Cole.

A man who had worked with city redevelopment projects in several California municipalities, King Cole agreed that whatever kind of celebration was staged, its site ought to be centered along the downtown section of the river. This meant that the mess of tracks, trestles, bridges, depots, and freight warehouses would have to be cleaned up. The heart of the jumble was Havermale Island, an area just below Spokane Falls where tracks blossomed like weeds. As a modest beginning, Spokane Unlimited spent $2,000 to buy an option on the island, got the City Planning Commission to designate it "open space," then applied to the federal and state governments for funds with which to make the purchase. When these were approved, the celebration was off and running—though nobody knew where.

After exploring several possibilities, a Los Angeles Company hired to do a feasibilty study came up with an idea that stunned everybody. Instead of putting on a regional celebration, whose economic and permanent effects would be limited, the consulting company suggested that the city celebrate its birthday in the biggest way possible—by staging a *World's Fair* whose overall theme would be the environment.

By this time an international organization called the Bureau of International Expositions, whose purpose was to put its stamp of approval on all proposed world's fairs, had come into existence. Headquartered in Paris, it probably would ask, "Where is Spokane?", then, when told, "In the state of Washington," would say it had just approved the staging of a world's fair in a nearby village called Seattle in 1962.

Thus, the purpose of King Cole's first trip to Paris was to diplomatically explain that Seattle and Spokane were some distance apart and that the date Spokane requested was 1974, some nine years in the future. This was the first of a total of 21 trips King Cole would make to Paris on Expo business, not to mention his flights to numerous other cities around the world. In fact, he was on planes so often, he said, that once when he sat down in barber's chair to get a long-delayed haircut, he automatically reached down to fasten his seat belt.

As the smallest city ever to host a world's fair, Spokane had a number of obstacles to overcome. When local businessmen signed enough pledges to permit the borrowing of $1.3 million in "seed money," it looked like the project was off to a good start. When a $6 million city bond election failed because it gained only a 56.7 percent affirmative vote when the law required that it get 60 percent, it looked like the fair was dead. In response, a majority of hard-headed businessmen, backed by the City Council and the Chamber of Commerce, passed a Business and Occupation tax that raised $5.7 million—and the show was on the road again.

When the private sector of the economy was asked to invest in $4.3 million of debenture bonds—and did—the project kept rolling.

Just as Seattle's 1962 Exposition had been "A World's Fair in a Jewel Box," so was was Spokane's Fair set on a limited piece of ground. Eliminating the tangle of rails, yards, freight houses, and stations, the Expo '74 architects persuaded the railroads to combine their lines through Spokane so that they avoided the 100–acres of river and falls to be designated Riverfront Park—with one unique exception. This was the tall brick clock tower of the Great Northern Station, which was retained as a landmark while the Expo buildings rose around it, with the four faces of its clock now set to show the number of days and hours left before the opening of the Exposition.

Appropriately enough, the big railroad companies, whose federal land grants had helped populate this part of the country, now deeded back to the City of Spokane enough of their land so that the long dreamed-of park could be built.

It was fitting that Canada, Spokane's nearby neighbor, with whom the waters of the Columbia River long had been shared, be the first nation to commit itself to building a pavilion. The Soviet Union, the Republic of China, Korea, Germany, the Phillipines, Japan, Australia, and Iran soon followed. In all, fifty nations built pavilions, with a total of 104 exhibits.

By opening day May 4, 1974, the park area and adjacent downtown business area had invested $300 million in a facelift. Not bad, Fair boosters said, for "...a village on the outskirts of Seattle."

FIRST ENVIRONMENT WORLD'S FAIR

Opening under sunny skies on May 4, 1974 with a capacity crowd of 85,151, the Spokane Exposition ran for six months, closing on November 3rd with a performance by the Spokane Symphony in the new Opera House, one of several buildings and features that would remain as a permanent legacy after the Fair was over. Others would be the refurbished Carousel with its painted wooden ponies, which children between the ages of two and ninety-two loved to ride again and again. Another would be the framework of the US Pavilion, whose 200–ton vinyl covering had not been meant to last more than a year or two and did not, but had become such a distinctive landmark that when rips and tears began to appear in it a couple of years later it was preserved simply by stripping off the covering, then leaving the unique framework standing in place as a symbol of its former glory. Since then during the holiday season, it has become the best-lighted Christmas tree in town.

As an environmental fair, Expo '74 could not have been a staged at a better time, for that was the year when the oil-producing countries of the Middle East tried to throttle the industrial world by declaring a world-wide embargo on the export of oil until OPEC'S exorbitant price was met.

This act of banditry caused the United States to take a hard look at its use of energy and the price it was paying for gas-guzzling cars, wasteful use of electricity, and heedless pollution of the environment. Though Spokane could take credit for encouraging a few mine smelters, factories, and other industries to clean up their act, the lasting effect of Expo '74 was the visual heritage it left behind in the form of beautiful downtown Riverfront Park, a sparkling river, and a waterfall once again as scenic as it had been when Spokane Garry and his people first welcomed white settlers to Spokane Falls a hundred and fifty years earlier.

THE YAKIMA VALLEY

By following I–90 from Spokane to Ellensburg in an east–west direction, three hours of high-speed driving will give you some notion of the vastness of the lower Columbia Basin region. Included in it are the million acres irrigated by the Grand Coulee project near cities such as Moses Lake. But uphill from areas turned green by abundant water lie eye-stretching miles of dry-land country, whose only cover so far as vegetation is concerned is bunchgrass and sagebrush.

In early spring, the bunchgrass is faintly green, then turns brown and dry-looking during the usually rainless months of summer and fall. But you should not be deceived into believing—as some early–day stockmen did—that there is no nourishment in this semi–desert grass. As the Indians native to the region learned hundreds of years ago, horses turned loose on bunchgrass range flourished and grew strong, for the dead-looking grass was as full of minerals and vitamins as well-cured hay.

Though the regional Indians probably acquired the horse as did the Shoshones, Nez Perces, and other inland tribes—by picking up animals strayed or stolen from the Spaniards around 1730—lower Columbia Basin tribes tell a colorful legend which relates the manner in which they became a mounted people. Like all oral Indian history, this legend was passed down from generation to generation by what the natives called "Grandfather tales."

GRANDFATHER CUTS LOOSE THE PONIES

Just a few miles east of the Vantage bridge across the Columbia River, Indian artist David Govedare recently completed a visualization of the tale by erecting a structure on the high point of a ridge overlooking the Columbia south of the freeway. In a dramatic silhouette against a wide expanse of sky, an unseen hand tips a basket out of which fourteen ponies are spilling. Fabricated of inch–thick, bullet-proof, tempered steel, the basket is thirty feet in diameter, while each of the ponies is life size. According to the grandfather tale, Speelyi, the Coyote Spirit who created the Indian world, decided one day that his people in this part of the country had walked long enough. Summoning one of his favorite shamans to a cave, he gave the medicine man a basketful of ponies and told him to turn them loose as a gift to his people.

In the massive sculpture, which measures 36 feet high by 250 feet long, the ponies appear to light running as their hoofs strike the earth. From that point on the bluff, the legend relates, they spread to all the inland tribes as Speelyi's special gift. At the present time, access to the sculpture is only by footpath off the eastbound lane of I–90, though the dramatic memorial may be seen from a long distance from any direction.

On the west side of the Columbia just to the north of the town of Vantage is Gingko State Park, where more verifiable items of historic interest such as petrified trees and archaeological displays may be seen.

ELLENSBURG AND EARLY–DAY IRRIGATION

From its source on the east slope of the Cascades near Snoqualmie Pass, the Yakima River supplies water for irrigated districts downstream that predate the Grand Coulee project by many years. In trying to get these projects underway, developers encountered the problem that long had stalled irrigation in the arid West. As Dorothy O. Johansen and Charles M. Gates write in *History of the Columbia*:

> The paradox of irrigation was that while it stimulated individuals and fed upon private speculation, it was actually ill-suited to either one....Reclamation demanded for its success a collective institutional approach. Individualism and capitalism might flourish and prosper once the land was watered, but the task of watering it was one that called for social action...

Because laws intended to make land in the arid West available to the public were drawn up in the verdant East, they were full of contradictions. Basically, what they said was that a person could claim a piece of unoccupied desert land wherever he liked, but he could not gain title to it until he put water on it and made it bloom. Few prospective farmers had the kind of money required to build a gravity flow irrigation system of any size, which meant that only big companies with deep pockets could afford to speculate on such projects.

In the Yakima River country, a few small-scale capitalists did try to develop irrigation districts and towns. Coming north across the desert from The Dalles to the Kittitas Valley, one of them, John A.

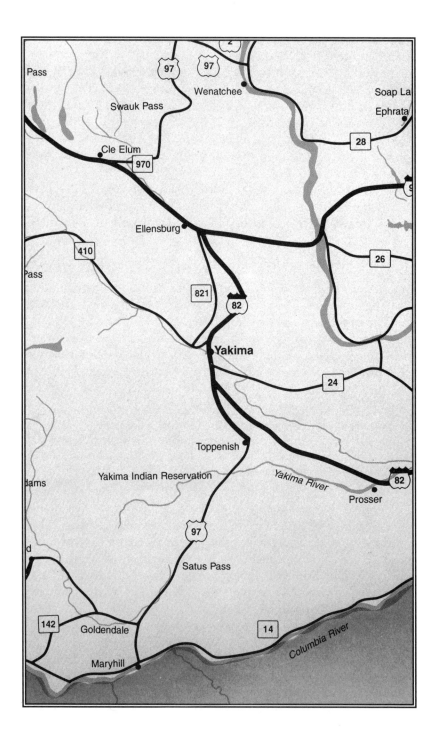

Shoudy, founded a settlement named in honor of his wife, calling it Ellen's burg. Thirty-five miles to the south, Charles and Joseph Schanno scraped out a ditch and erected a few frame buildings to begin a town that became Yakima. But even after the railroad came and a land office was opened, there were more cattle than people living in the area, for in 1879 the Yakima County assessor counted only 318 familes while the cattle numbered 22,665.

For a time, the little hamlet of Moxee, six miles north of Yakima, became a showplace of corporate development when a company owned by the founder of the National Geographic Society, Gardiner G. Hubbard, and his son-in-law, Alexander Graham Bell, inventor of the telephone, developed 6,400 acres of range and experimental crops, including hops, alfalfa, fruit, tobacco, and cotton. Historian John Fahey writes:

> After the Smithsonian Instition (of which Hubbard was a regent) pronounced a soil sample ideal for tobacco, the Moxee company tried Havana, Sumatra, and Virginia varieties and sold cigars (the Moxee Belle and Fleur de Yakima) for several years until frost destroyed the plants.

Other corporate speculators in cheap desert land were the Chicago merchant, Marshall Field, who bought 15,000 acres in Spokane and Whitman Counties, and the California Land Company, whose investment in 32,000 acres for a time paid its stockholders a 233 percent dividend. While such speculation made money for corporate managers and stockholders, it put lit-

---

State 821—Ellensburg to Yakima
*   35 miles*
US 12—Yakima to Prosser
*   59 miles*
US 97—Toppenish to Goldendale
*   50 miles*
US 97—Goldendale to Maryhill
*   10 miles*

tle water on the land, leaving the farmer who was trying to make a living on it still struggling and still dry. When the financial Panic of 1893 became the great leveler, wiping out big and little investors alike, it proved to be constructive eventually, for in its aftermath real solutions for real problems were found.

With the federal government now getting into irrigation development under such programs as the Bureau of Reclamation Act and railroads such as the Northern Pacific selling 500,000 acres of dry land for as little as twenty-eight cents an acre, communities along the Yakima River watershed began to form irrigation districts of manageable size which could put water on the land at a reasonable price. Tobacco and cotton proved to be too tender for this northern region, but fruit such as apples, peaches, and pears did extremely well, as did alfalfa and hops, the first as feed for the growing dairy industry west of the Cascades, the second as a vital flavoring agent for beer.

Though pioneers like Ezra Meeker had cultivated hops in the Puyallup area from the time of the first settlements on Puget Sound, a disease that flourished west of the Cascades but did not occur in the Yakima Valley area made it profitable to transfer that

"GRANDFATHER CUTS LOOSE THE PONIES"
David Govedare Sculpture

DETAIL OF "GRANDFATHER CUTS LOOSE THE PONIES"

BLUFFTOP LOCATION OF PONIES SCULPTURE

Bill Gulick Photo

Bill Gulick Photo

VANTAGE BRIDGE ACROSS THE COLUMBIA
The view is from Ponies Sculpture side of the river.

labor-intensive crop across the mountains. The fact that Yakima Nation Indians were seasonably available, liked to pick hops as an annual social-festival-money-making fete, and were good at hop–harvesting, made the crop ideal for the area—as it still is today. Though the price of wheat and other crops might fluctuate wildly, the three thousand acres of hops grown in the Yakima area provided so many small farmers a steady if small income, they called it their "survival crop."

WALTER N. GRANGER, IRRIGATION SPECIALIST

As the biggest land owner in the area, Northern Pacific brought in an expert named Walter N. Granger in 1892 and made him a sporting proposition. They would give him an option on 90,000 acres of railroad land, they said, at $1.25 cents an acre if he would build an irrigation system on it. After looking over the region, he agreed, joining Thomas F. Oakes, President of the N.P., in forming The Northern Pacific, Yakima and Kittitas Irrigation Company, which appropriated 1,000 cubic feet per second of Yakima River flow.

With the Northern Pacific furnishing construction funds through a bond issue and Granger supervising the project, the first twenty-five miles of canals were scraped out with horse-drawn scoops. Smashing a bottle of champagne on the headgate to start the water flowing while the town band played lively airs, Granger opened the irrigation season on March 26, 1892, an event which the Yakima *Herald* immodestly called "the beginning of the most important system of canals in America."

The truth was, the *Herald* was right. Pointing out that at that place and time most so-called irrigation experts were astoundingly ignorant, knowing next to nothing of hydrology, climate, soil chemistry, or peculation, historian John Fahey then lists some of the project's accomplishments:

> Walter Granger's system diverted flowing water from the Yakima into a projected sixty-mile canal with planned laterals and branches of 550 miles covering 40,000 acres. He platted two townsites, one aptly named Sunnyside on a treeless slope above the river and the other Zillah, named for Oakes's daughter. The railroad trumpeted Sunnyside as if it were already in bloom; it passed out booklets at the Chicago World's fair of 1893, hoping to beguile prospective settlers at $45 to $65 an acre, 5 percent down and a second installment in two years. The settlers' purchase contracts guaranteed them water forever. Most who came planted alfalfa for sale to stockmen and set out fruit trees for themselves.

Though the Panic of 1893 made some companies fold or reorganize under different names, Walter Granger stayed on as manager of what became the Washington Irrigation Company, which by 1905 was putting water on 36,000 acres of land as far down the Yakima Valley as Sunnyside. Because most farmers were new to irrigation, they operated under the theory that if a little water was good, a lot would be better, literally drowning their crops and themselves if not held in check by the experts.

Under the Carey Act of 1894, 55,000 acres of potentially irrigable land in the Yakima Valley was set aside, with so many water claims immediately filed on it that O.L. Waller, an irrigation engineer at the Washington State Experiment Station, snorted that if all the claims could be honored, Yakima water would cover the United States seventeen feet deep.

Whatever claims may have been made, one fact became crystal clear by 1918. Whether an acre of irrigable land in the Yakima Valley was purchased for twenty-eight cents, $2.50, or $65, once water and crops were put on it, $1,000 was not an unreasonable price. John Fahey quotes some amazing figures:

> By the 1920s, every one of Washington's nineteen counties east of the Cascades contained irrigation systems, although the others combined did not match the quarter-million acres under federal ditch in Yakima and Benton County...
> A singular contribution of the Reclamation Service was financing large reservoirs. Of 205 reservoirs in the state containing 447,789 acre feet of water, the service controlled 440,000 feet in seven reservoirs. Private systems continued to rely chiefly on stream diversion.

It is also a singular fact that many Easterners regarded the Grand Coulee project—which did not get started until twenty years later—as a massive booondoggle by a ponderous agency that had no idea of how such a vast investment could ever pay off.

But in the Yakima River Valley, the farmers and orchardists knew...

BACK ROADS DOWN THE VALLEY

The best way to see the Yakima Valley is to stay off I–82 between Ellensburg and Prosser, for the freeway goes up and over the ridge across dry sagebrush highlands and avoids irrigated country. But if you take the old river level highway State 821 south to Yakima, then US 12 east to Prosser, you will get a closeup view of irrigation canals, headgates, fishscreens, orchards, and cultivated fields of corn, grapes, alfalfa, hops and other crops which make the Yakima Valley one of the richest agricultural regions in the world.

Because the freeway takes big trucks and high-speed drivers off these lower roads, they are a real pleasure to drive for the person not in a hurry.

Near Toppenish, US 97 heads south toward Goldendale and across the Yakima Indian Reservation which is the largest in the state. Just off US 12 at the southwest edge of town stands a unique building that resembles an oversize Indian longhouse. This is the Yakima Nation Cultural Center, a multi–million dollar museum financed, built, and managed by the Yakima people themselves.

BPA Photo, Courtesy Bureau of Reclamation

ROZA DAM, YAKIMA RIVER—TWO VIEWS

BPA Photo, Courtesy Bureau of Reclamation

Courtesy Ellensburg Public Library
EARLY–DAY IRRIGATION FLUME ON THE YAKIMA, NEAR ELLENSBURG

In its excellent dioramas, displays, exhibits, and library, the Cultural Center—which opened in June, 1982—tells tribal history in the voices of the Indians themselves. Because the road south to Goldendale and the Columbia River crosses much of the country occupied by the Yakima Reservation, a few hours spent touring the museum are good preparation for what you will see further on.

KAMIAKIN AND THE YAKIMA NATION

Until Governor Isaac Stevens met and negiotiated treaties with the Indians east of the Cascades in June, 1855, the Yakima Nation did not exist. Ranging north from Celilo Falls on the Columbia to the region near what would become Ellensburg, some fourteen different related bands such as the Wishrams, Klickitats, Entiats and others spoke the same language, shared hunting and fishing grounds, traded, and intermarried with one another. But they did not call themselves a tribe and they recognized no overall chief.

Insisting that someone must speak for the fourteen bands, Governor Stevens asked Father Pandosy, a Catholic priest who had worked among the scattered bands and had come along as an interpreter, who their most important leaders were.

Courtesy Ellensburg Public Library
BIG PLOWS BREAKING THE VIRGIN SOD
The photograph, taken near Ellensburg, dates from the early 1900s.

"Kamiakin, Owhi, and Skloom," the priest answered. "Of the three, Kamiakin is the one they all look up to."

That was good enough for Governor Stevens. Declaring Kamiakin "Head Chief" and Owhi and Skloom (who were his younger brothers) "sub-chiefs," Stevens created the Yakima Nation when he stated that whatever treaty papers were signed by these and the eleven other Yakima area Indians he later appointed as sub-chiefs would be binding on all the people of the fourteen bands.

A proud, moody, uncommunicative man, Kamiakin had been extremely reluctant to come to the council, let alone speak for a tribe second only in numbers and power to the Nez Perces. According to the verbatim record kept by Secretary Hiram Doty during the nineteen days the talks lasted, Kamiakin had very little to say beyond an enigmatic statement he made when the subject of a reservation for the Yakima Nation was brought up.

> The forest knows me; he knows my heart. He knows I do not desire a great many goods. All that I wish for is an Agent, a good Agent, who will pity the good and bad of us and take care of us.

Click Relander Collection, Courtesy Yakima Valley Regional Library
YAKIMA INDIANS FISHING
They are using dip nets on the Yakima River, near Ellensburg.

I have nothing to talk long about. I am tired. I am anxious to get back to my garden. That is all I have to say.

There is ample evidence that the claim made by many present-day Yakima historians that the treaty was signed under duress is true. Andrew Dominque Pambrun, who was there as an interpreter and who must be considered a reliable witness, stated in an autobiography written in 1890 but not published until many years later:

> The Indians were called in council...finally the Governor, getting out of patience, recapitulated all that had been said and offered and concluded by saying, If you do not accept and sign this paper [holding up the paper] you will walk in blood knee deep.

The Priest [either Father Chirouse or Pandosy] remarked that this is an error, he should not make such a threat. There were several interpreters. I was one of them and know whereof I speak. All the chiefs signed, Kamiakin was the last, and as he turned to take his seat the priest hunched me and whispered, look at Kamiakin, we will all get killed, he was in such a rage that he bit his lips [so] that they bled profusely.

Within weeks of the treaty's signing, several white men trespassing on lands reserved to the Indians were killed by angry Yakima braves. When a detachment of federal army troops rode north from The Dalles, Kamiakin led his fighting men in an engagement that inflicted a humiliating defeat on the white soldiers. For two years, a brutal Indian–white war raged over the interior country, with Kamiakin playing the role of the Indian leader in defense of his people and their way of life—a war that he seems to have known from the beginning they could not win.

When peace finally was made, he was offered amnesty and given a chance to return to the Yakima Reservation and live out his years as Chief Moses later did on the Colville Reservation in the northern part of the Columbia Basin—as a "good" Indian paid an annuity to keep the peace.

But he never did, spending the rest of his life as an exile in remote parts of Washington Territory and Canada, finally dying unhonored and alone. But the people of the Yakima Nation still cherish his memory.

Curiously enough, whatever pressure forced him to touch the end of the writing stick above "Kamiakin—`X'–His Mark" on the 1855 Treaty, the paper became the most important document ever signed by a leader of the Yakima people. First, it recognized them as a Nation with whom a Treaty ratified by the United States Senate and signed by the President had been made. Second, it gave them title to and control over a large piece of valuable land whose timber, crops, minerals, water, fish, and game they could use as they saw fit. Third, it gave them sovereignty rights as a nation.

In cases disputing those rights, some of which have been carried up to the United States Supreme Court, the Yakima Nation has not lost a single one.

After topping Satus Pass in pine-dotted country at 3,107 feet, US 97 drops down into Goldendale, the seat of Klickitat County.

Courtesy Ellensburg Public Library
HAYING NEAR ELLENSBURG, EARLY 1900S

The most lightly populated county in the state, the region is unique for several reasons, among which are such a large number of sunny days each year that an astronomical observatory has been built atop a nearby hill, so many windy days that three immense wind generators were erected on the bluffs overlooking the Columbia River a few miles to the south, and—most surprising of all—a former resident so patriotic that he built an exact replica of England's 4,000–year-old Stonehenge as a memorial to a handful of Klickitat County soldiers who lost their lives in World War I.

WIND ENERGY

Between 1981 and 1987, the lonely Goodnoe Hills area a few miles southeast of Goldendale was the site of a unique experiment in the generation of electrical energy by using the strong winds that often blow in this region. Concerned during the Carter administration in the late 1970s that our oil imports might be cut off, that sites for hydroelectric dams were dwindling, and that coal or nuclear-fueled thermal plants could not be built because of envi-

A BIG HARVEST CREW NEAR ELLENSBURG, EARLY 1900S

ronmental constraints, energy experts turned their attention to non–polluting sources such as solar and wind power.

Sponsored by the US Department of Energy (DOE), an impressive amount of brain-power drawn from a prestigious list of agencies and companies such as the National Aeronautics and Space Administration (NASA), the Boeing Company, Battelle–Pacific Northwest, and the Bonneville Power Adminstration (BPA) combined on a $48 million project to build, install, and test three immense propellor type generators whose operation hopefully would answer a number of questions.

Erected on 200–foot towers placed in a triangular configuration, each propellor measured 300 feet from tip to tip, produced up to 2500 kilowatts of power, and was configured to operate in wind velocities ranging from fifteen to forty-seven miles-per-hour. The electricity generated during the experiment was fed into the Klickitat County PUD system, which was tied into the BPA grid.

In addition to the three MOD–2 WT units (as they were called) erected at the Goodnoe Hills site, a fourth was built by Boeing for the Bureau of Reclamation and installed at a windy spot near Medicine Bow, Wyoming.

As might be expected in a project of this scope, mechanical, electrical, control systems, and lubrication problems occurred during the early period of the tests, but all were corrected by design modifications. Among the research tests conducted were: studies of television interference and acoustical noise; wind turbine wake interaction (the influence of one generator upon the others); and performance under varying velocities of wind.

"No adverse noise was detected," the engineers reported. "Local TV interference exists but can be mitigated with a good antenna system." Additional test data was gathered during the 1985 summer wind season to "map" the wind flow over the site, and to better understand the WT performance in that wind flow.

In November 1982 a large crack appeared in the low speed shaft of unit # 1. The steel, hollow-shell designed shaft which supported the weight of the turbine rotor was removed and shipped to Seattle for study. When smaller cracks appeared in the low speed shafts of units #2 and #3, they were placed in a shutdown mode. Eventually all three shafts were replaced and the wind turbines resumed unattended operation by May, 1985. Through September 30, 1986, the average power generated by the three units over a period of 16,182 hours was 1,320 kilowatts.

As so often happens with experimental projects such as this, the news media magnified relatively minor correctable problems such as cracks, lubrication blockages, and temporary equipment shutdowns to such an extent that the Goodnoe Hills venture into the field of wind generation got an undeserved bad rap. According to the experts, the cost of electricity generated by the wind during the 1981–87 period was around ten cents a kilowatt hour. Compared to the regional retail rate of four-and-a-half cents, this was not competitive, of course. So when this rate differential was publicized and the project was closed down by the Reagan administration, the "instant experts" of the media pronounced the six-year test a bust.

But so far as Ron Holeman, the Bonneville Power Administration engineer who was in charge of the Goodnoe Hills project is concerned, the experiment accomplished exactly what it was designed to do—which was to test new concepts in wind generation under field conditions in order to gain more extensive knowledge that might be needed some day. Holeman says:

> Even though the current research program has produced information on many issues, before wide acceptance of wind turbine generation by utilities can occur several technical and economic questions remain. These questions include: determining the estimated resource requirements needed to maintain and operate wind turbine generation complexes; and determining what operational compatibility problems exist in merging wind generation with conventional hydro/thermal generation. The answers to such questions should be resolved as several thousand hours of operation are accumulated on new and existing wind turbines.

As a writer who has seen the use, cost, availabilty, and attitude toward electric power in the Pacific Nothwest change many times during the past thirty years, I must comment that regional energy decisions often depend as much on political and economic factors as they do on engineering expertise. As noted earlier in this book, the building of Grand Coulee Dam once was derided as a waste of taxpayer money. Later, electrical demand was projected to double every ten years—which it did not do. Still later, nuclear power was promoted as the economic salvation of the region—which it has not proved to be. So wisdom requires that we keep our alternate energy options open.

At the present moment, both our domestic and imported supply of oil is plentiful and reasonably priced. But that situation could change overnight. Though currently the winds blowing across the Goodnoe Hills no longer are generating power, the day may come when we will be only too eager to put them back to work.

When the Goodnoe Hills project was still operating, a group of Bonneville Power Administration employees with a whimsical sense of humor put together a visual display that became a conversation piece at the site's Visitor Center. Since then, the display has been preserved in the Vern Markee Park on East Broadway at North Third Avenue near the entrance to Goldendale. Designed by Joe Brockway and constructed by Leonard Lynch and Robert Anderson, the weathered steel sculpture shows a mounted Don Quixote about to tilt with a windmill.

Click Relander Collection, Courtesy Yakima Valley Regional Library
FORT SIMCOE
Built in 1856 on the Yakima Reservation near White Swan, the site was
Agency Headquarters until moved to Toppenish. The area is now a State
Park.

Whatever philosophy may have inspired the sculpture is left
unstated; but because of the noble purpose of the wind-genera-
tion project—as well as the many high-powered government
agencies involved—it may be assumed that the symbolism is apt.

FUTURE POSSIBILITIES

According to Mary Jean Lord, Energy Resource Specialist for the
Klickitat County PUD, at least two private companies currently
are interested in the wind generation possibilities of the Goodnoe
Hills area.

"To be economically feasible, you need to have two hundred
or so units operating on the same site," she says, "as is being done
on 'wind farms' in California. At the present time, wind just can't
compete with our cheap hydro power. But the day may come..."

Click Relander Collection, Courtesy Yakima Valley Regional Library
FORT SIMCOE, ANOTHER VIEW

Though all of the MOD–2 generators have been dismantled, an even larger 330–foot MOD–5 wind generator now is operating on the island of Oahu in Hawaii, apparently successfully.

STONEHENGE AND MARYHILL

Though the wind-generators are gone, the observatory and the war memorial are still there, both well anchored to the ground. In fact, this Stonehenge replica will probably last much longer than the original did, for its facsimile stones are of steel reinforced concrete, while the real ones in the crumbling ruin in England are of softer natural rock.

The man who conceived and built both Stonehenge and what is now Maryhill Museum two miles to the west was named Samuel Hill. Closely associated with the early–day railroad magnate, James J. Hill, Sam Hill was not related, though he further confused future historians and readers by marrying James Hill's daughter, Mary Hill.

As an ambitious, energetic young attorney back in Wisconsin during the 1880s, Sam Hill often took on farmer or dairymen clients who wanted to sue the Great Northern Railroad, of which James J. Hill was president, because of a right-of-way disagreement or a locomotive-killed cow. By insisting on a jury made up of farmers and dairymen, all Sam Hill needed to do was present a well-reasoned case—which he always did. Consequently, he always won. Growing tired of paying off, James Hill called Sam Hill into his office one day and asked him how he would like to go to work for the Great Northern.

"No, I won't work *for* you," Sam answered. "But if you'll teach me the railroad business, I'll work *with* you."

Thus, the bargain was struck, with Sam later taking Mary Hill as his bride.

By any name and in any position, Sam Hill was a unique individual, who soon knew as much about the railroad business as his father-in-law did. He was a man with a great deal of energy and intellectual curiosity, whose power, wealth, and political connections permitted him to roam worldwide.

Taking an interest in that newfangled gadget, the automobile, he studied hard-surfaced European roads dating back to Roman days, hired an engineer, and built the first stretch of macadam-paved highway in the Pacific Northwest called the "Maryhill Loops," winding up from the north shore of the Columbia River to the bluff above.

His offer to build a highway through the Columbia Gorge if the Washington State Legislature would permit him to use convict labor and make a small appropriation to get it underway was approved—then abruptly canceled when the legislators learned that the dynamite expert he was using had been thrown in prison because his last employer had been the I.W.W., for whom he had planted a bomb on the doorstep of a judge.

With his funds and labor supply cut off, Sam Hill told the legislators, "If you won't back me, maybe Oregon will."

Which Oregon did, the result being the engineering marvel and scenic wonder of its day—the seventy-five–mile-long Columbia River Gorge Highway, sections of which may still be driven today.

WIND ENERGY GENERATORS
Erected on the Goodnoe Hills southeast of Goldendale, these Mod 2 turbines
had blades 300 feet long supported on 200–foot-high towers. Notice the size-
of the man working atop the single tower in relation to the surroundings.

As related in Part One of this book, Sam Hill also was responsible for the building of Peace Portal Park on the outskirts of
Blaine, Washington, where two centuries of peace between the
United States and Canada are commemorated with a beautiful
white marble arch and a gate locked open forever.

The Stonehenge memorial was inspired by a visit Sam Hill
made to the ancient ruins on Salisbury Downs in England during
the early years of World War I. At that time, British historians
thought the massive blocks of fallen stones were somehow connected to the Druids, who, to celebrate the arrival of the spring
solstice, sacrificed human captives on the central altar in order to
placate their heathen gods of war. After his guide, Lord Earl

Department of Energy Photo, Courtesy Klickitat County PUD
THREE WIND GENERATORS
Erected and operated from 1981 to 1987, they have since been dismantled and removed.

Kitchener, told him this, Sam Hill stood in silent contemplation for a few moments, then he said softly, "Four thousand years. We have come that far. And still we are sacrificing the blood of our youth to the gods of war."

At the time the Stonehenge Memorial was begun and first dedicated on July 4, 1918, three servicemen from Klickitat County had died. By the time it was completed and rededicated on Memorial Day, 1930, nine more names were added to the bronze plaques on the walls.

MARYHILL MUSEUM

Among his friends in high places around the world were Prince Leopold of Belgium and Princess Marie of Rumania. In their salad days, the trio was rumored to have had some great times and romantic adventures during the carefree years prior to World War I. With the war ended and their countries destitute, the now King Leopold and Queen Marie appealed to the European Relief Commission, which was headed by Herbert Hoover, for help.

Bill Gulick Photo
SCULPTURE OF DON QUIXOTE TILTING WITH THE WINDMILL
The sculpture is in Vern Markee Park, Goldendale.

Because their close friend Sam Hill had become Hoover's aide in Europe, he saw to it that their countries got all the assistance the law allowed.

During the 1920s, tabloid reporters—then called "yellow journalists"—made much of Sam's friendship with Leopold and his romance with Marie. However close their relationships may have been, all that was ever proved was that they were good friends. This was evidenced by King Leopold when Prohibition became a law in the United States. Aware of how well Sam liked his toddy, King Leopold tried to solve his friend's thirst problem by appointing Sam Hill the Belgian Ambassador to the State of Washington—which would give him diplomatic immunity and let him drink what and when he chose.

Learning of the appointment, a lady assistant in the Washington DC Secretary of State office decreed that it was illegal for an American citizen to become an Ambassador for a foreign country, stripping Sam of his title, immunity, and booze. For the rest of his life, legend has it, every morning before he washed his teeth he would shake his fist in the direction of the nation's capital, say the lady's name in an angry voice, and add, "May I live to spit on your grave!"

As for Queen Marie, when the mansion sometimes called "Castle Nowhere" was finally completed and furnished as a Fine Arts Museum a year before Sam Hill's death, she not only contributed a number of her nation's treasures to stock it, but she also came to America in a well-publicized tour, the high point of which was her speech dedicating the museum. Parts of that speech tell as much as we'll ever know about her relations with Sam Hill:

> Sam Hill is my friend. He is not only a dreamer but he is a worker. Samuel Hill once gave me his hand and said that if there were anything on earth that I needed, I had only to ask. Some may even scoff, for they do not understand. But I have understood...

STONEHENGE REPLICA NEAR MARYHILL

Bill Gulick Photo

COLUMBIA BASIN 443

There is much more than concrete in this structure. There is a dream built into this place—a dream for today and especially for tomorrow.

Some years before his death, Sam Hill expressed the wish that his remains be cremated and buried in a small crypt to be erected a short distance down the hill from Stonehenge. When he died in 1931, this was done. Ironically, though most all the other structures he designed and had erected during his lifetime still survive, the crypt deteriorated so rapidly that it had to be torn down in 1955. Replacing it was a small stone monument under which his ashes now lie buried. The text on the bronze tablet was written shortly before his death by Sam himself:

Samuel Hill: among nature's great unrest, he sought rest.

MARYHILL MUSEUM ON THE COLUMBIA RIVER
Bill Gulick Photo

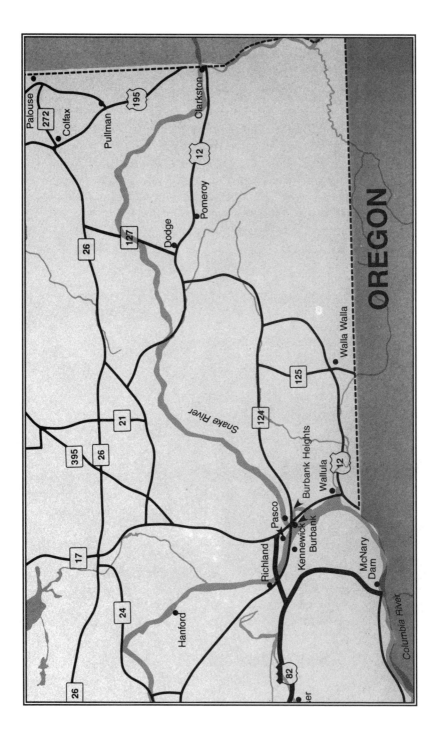

PART SIX

Southeast Washington

TRI–CITIES, WHERE THREE RIVERS MEET

When the Lewis and Clark party reached the junction of the Snake River with the Columbia six miles south of Pasco, October 16, 1805, they learned that this was a central meeting place for a number of inland tribes. Clark wrote:

> We halted above the point on the river *Ki-moo-e-nim* [Snake] to smoke with the Indians who had collected there in great numbers. Here we met our two Chiefs who had left us two days ago and proceeded on to this place to inform those bands of our approach and friendly intentions towards all nations.

So far as future relations between white Americans and Columbia Plateau Indians were concerned, the "smokes" held at this point would be important for many years to come. This was an age-old gathering place for tribes allied by blood, tongue, and tradition, later to be classified as belonging to the Sahaptian group of Northwest Indians: Nez Perce, Palouse, Walla Walla, Cayuse, Umatilla, and Yakima—a loose association of far-roaming Indians whose access to the fish resources of the great Columbia River system and the game resources of the buffalo country east of the

---

US 12—Richland to Walla Walla
50 miles

State 124, US 12—Burbank to Clarkston
140 miles

Bitterroot Mountains gave them a strength and knowledge of the interior found in few other groups.

Sacajawea, the child bride of Touissant Charbonneau, knew nothing about this country, which was far to the west of the land of the Shoshones where she had been born and raised, so was of no value as a guide. But the very fact that she was present assured the local Indians that this party of whites came in peace. Naming the green, lovely recreation area and historic center Sacajawea State Park—which was done a hundred and fifty years later—was an honor she richly deserved.

But in 1805, this was a bleak, barren desert of sand, heat, little rainfall, and no vegetation other than sagebrush and bunchgrass. Furthermore, the party of white men had gotten so sick of a steady diet of overripe salmon, that they eagerly traded for forty Indian dogs, which all members of the party except Meriwether Lewis ate with relish.

This personal aversion to dog meat later caused the hot temper of Captain Lewis to flare when a boisterous Nez Perce brave tossed a live puppy in his lap while the captain was was eating dinner and made a remark expressing his contempt for white dog-eaters. Had he not been restrained by cooler heads, Lewis might have taught the Indian some table manners in an undiplomatic way.

Sweeping down through the lower Basin country after passing through Grand Coulee and the millon acres of desert land that eventually would be irrigated, the Columbia is joined by the Yakima River near Richland, turns east for a few miles past Kennewick and Pasco, then flows south, to pick up the Snake. A few miles further on, it turns west one final time before making the rest of its 340–mile journey from the mouth of the Snake to the Pacific Ocean. Because the Columbia River system ranks just behind that of the Mississsippi in the volume of water carried, its potential for power and irrigation is unequalled in the West. When this fact is added to the abundant sunshine, excellent soil, and equable climate of the region, the area where the three rivers meet long has been one of the most promising in the country, so far as development is concerned.

Until recent years, that development has come very slowly. In pioneer days, Puget Sound, the lower Columbia, and the wetter, greener country west of the Cascades seemed far more desirable as a place to settle than did the interior desert lands east of the mountains. In the competition between Great Britain and the United States as to who would gain title to the area, the British made a claim of sorts when a representative of the North West Company planted a flag on a sandbar at the mouth of the Snake in 1811, three months after the Astorians had passed through, declaring the entire region to be the property of His Royal Britannic Majesty because "...no citizen of a civilized nation has ever visited it before..."

Even though this portion of the future State of Washington was included when the boundary between the United States and Canada was drawn well to the north at the 49th parallel in 1846, almost a century passed before any substantial growth occurred. In 1940, Pasco, a railroad division point, had a population of 3,913; Kennewick, just across the Columbia River to the west, claimed 1,918 residents; while the village of Richland, seven miles further west, tallied a modest 327 people.

Then came World War II and the decision of the US government to create an entirely new scientific and manufacturing community called the Hanford Reservation on which the atomic bomb would be designed and built. Acting with great speed and secrecy, the government prempted the land, water, and electrical energy it needed for the project, hired thousands of workers to build and fence the facility so tightly that not even a jack rabbit could slip past the perimeter sensors without triggering an alarm, and then imported an awesome number of scientists and highly-skilled technicians to do the work.

Before the first bomb exploded in August, 1945, security was so strict that none of the people working on the project knew its purpose. Even speculating upon the type of object to be fabricated at the facility was frowned on, with the least sort of leak sure to bring a swarm of FBI investigators to the household of the offending person. Inevitably, leaks did occur—one of them by a fourth-grade child who volunteered in class one day, "I know what they're making. Daddy brings some of it home in his lunch pail every day—light bulbs and toilet paper."

BOOM AND BUST AFTER THE WAR

By 1947, the population of Pasco had risen to 16,000; that of Kennewick to 15,000; while Richland had zoomed to 25,000. Few

Bill Gulick Photo
SNAKE RIVER BELOW ICE HARBOR DAM
This is near the juncture of the Snake and Columbia Rivers.

people had planted trees or grass, so the hastily built wartime housing let bushels of sand drift through inch-wide gaps in the siding every time the wind blew. The general feeling among the well-paid technicians and scientists was that now that peace had come what essentially was a company town run by the Atomic Energy Commission and managed by the General Electric Company would fold up and vanish.

But the hostility between the United States, Russia, and China, the Korean War, and Cold War tensions that would continue for many years made it prudent to maintain our defensive armaments, many of which required such nuclear fuels as plutonium. Because the Hanford Project employed a large number of physicists and other people with technical skills, the region's economic well-being depended in a large measure on the rise and fall of international temperatures. This made the lives of the area's residents unique in many ways, which were little understood by outsiders then and not much better today.

The most interesting book I have read dealing with what happened in the Tri–Cities area between 1945 and 1975 is *Tiger by the Tail*, by Frances Taylor Pugnetti (Mercury Press, Tacoma, Wash.

Courtesy Oregon Historical Society
FORT NEZ PERCES (LATER FORT WALLA WALLA) IN THE 1830s

1975). With her husband, Don, who was editor of the daily paper called the *Tri–Cities Herald* for its first thirty years, the author moved to the Tri–Cities and raised five children with him there, so she tells the story of Hanford's boom-and-bust years with the insight and feeling of a person who was there "when the guns went off," so to speak.

Saying that her husband affectionately dubbed the area "Sagebrush Flats" when they first arrived, she points out that the community was unusual in many ways besides its hectic wartime birth. For instance, instead of phasing out the nuclear facility after the war, the federal government expanded it. She writes:

> The decision to reactivate the Hanford plant and to double its size touched off a great building boom. It also projected Hanford and its geographical region into the limelight and held it there. But the region's great nuclear project almost became its tombstone in the 1960s when the decision was made to close its giant plutonium reactors and to lock up the huge reservation.

From the beginning, Hanford had been a one-industry town, and neither the Atomic Energy Commission nor the General

Electric Company saw any reason to change that. But to the residents—many of whom had come to like the area and did not want to leave it—diversification, self-government, freedom of the press, and the eradication of stifling federal rules and regulations were goals devoutly to be sought, for no matter what a businessman, a farmer, a rancher, or even a weekend hunter-fisherman attempted to do some federal agency had a rule against his doing it.

For example, Frances Pugnetti points out, the weekly newspaper *Village Voice,* whose office was in the government-controlled town of Richland, published only releases given to its editor by the Atomic Energy Commission or the General Electric Company. Since the paper was issued on Thursday, news of an event happening on a Sunday or Monday could not appear in print until several days later. When the *Tri–Cities Herald* challenged the AEC officials, they responded with the unique ruling that news could not be reported when it happened but only when they released it. In a land only a generation removed from the frontier, when most editors kept a loaded pistol on their desk as a defense against the intrusion of an indignant reader carrying a horsewhip because his honor or integrity had been questioned in print, this was a serious infringement of freedom of the press.

Led by the outspoken, aggressive, and often-sued *Tri–Cities Herald,* the movers and shakers of the area inagurated a nationwide search for industries that would make use of the region's abundant water, sunshine, cheap land, low electric rates, and—most important of all—the impressive amount of brain-power that would be available once the bomb-making ended and the manufacturing of peacemaking products began. In this they were remarkably successful, setting an example for other communities in the nation who were dependent on federal payrolls and seeking ways to survive, earning for Richland the title, "The City That Wouldn't Die."

FIGHT TO SAVE THE "N" REACTOR

The first battle fought by the committee, which had raised $800,000 in private funds to aid in the conversion from a federal to a private economy, was preventing Congress from wasting money it had already appropriated for using the waste heat of a nuclear reactor to generate electric power. In the plutonium-making process, one of the by-products is a vast amount of heat,

Bill Gulick Photo

PALOUSE FALLS, 198 FEET HIGH

which must be dispersed in some manner—usually by running river water through cooling pipes which carry it away and disperse it over a wide area. Scientists had proposed that at least one of the reactors on the Hanford Project be designed so that its heat would create steam pressure that would spin turbines. Convinced that the scheme would work, Congress had authorized spending between $25 and $46 million to give the reactor the convertibility feature to become the Free World's first dual purpose reactor.

In 1960, a schedule to close down the reactors one by one was set up as the future needs for plutonium were satisfied: the first in 1964, the second and third in 1965, the fourth in 1967, the fifth in 1968, and so on. Though no date was set for closing what was called the "N"–Reactor—the one designed with the convertibility factor—no plans had been made to use the $25 to $46 million already appropriated for its generation of electricity using heat that would otherwise be wasted.

When the committee trying to save jobs in the Tri–Cities area protested what appeared to be an oversight in the long-range power program, they ran into formidable economic and political opposition. First, the giant privately-owned utilities objected because this would be a public power project. Second, coal states such as Pennsylvania and West Virgina—where the coal industry was in a bad way—protested vehemently. Though technically this was not nuclear power, the use of waste heat from a reactor was only one step away from the development and use of nuclear energy, which, its advocates claimed, would make electricity so cheap that it eventually would replace all other kinds of thermal generation. Third, the railroads, which owned extensive deposits of coal all over the country and earned substantial freight revenues from hauling it, added their powerful objections to the project.

Three times in 1961, legislation approving use of the already appropriated funds passed in the Senate but failed in the House. Finally, during a committee hearing attended by the head of the private power association, Washington State Senator Henry "Scoop" Jackson made a suggestion that he later admitted came "...right off the top of my head..."

"Suppose there is a provision that not less than half of the power output at Hanford would be available to the private utilities upon their request on a long-term basis. How would you feel about that?"

Put in the uncomfortable position of fighting a project which would benefit both their customers and their stockholders, Owen Hurd, the private power representative, answered cautiously, "I personally, without any consultation with my board, would feel that there would be no serious objections to such an arrangement."

Thus, the deadlock was broken, with Congress approving the use of waste heat from the "N" reactor to generate electricity at the Hanford site. Though the battle between public and private power over who would be licensed to build dams on the Columbia River system and control the sale of electric power would continue for several years, the principle of sharing the power from federally funded projects on an equal basis was established. With all plants and transmission lines eventually intercon-nected from British Columbia to southern California, electric power now flows where it is needed most at the lowest rate pos-sible, with automated control equipment at the BPA Celilo Intertie Station keeping track hourly of who owes who for what and whether payment shall be made or received in cash or a return of energy.

In September, 1963, President John F. Kennedy flew west to wave a "nuclear wand" lifting the first shovel of dirt to start con-struction of the Hanford steam plant. In honor of the occasion, the reservation was opened to the public for the first time in its histo-ry, symbolizing the change in the facility from bomb-making to peaceful use.

After flying on *Air Force One* to Ephrata and then by heli-copter to the Hanford site over miles and miles of empty sage-brush desert, Eastern newsmen stared down in amazement at the a crowd of 40,000 people gathered below for the ceremony. One of them exclaimed, "My God! Where did they all come from!"

When the desert is made to blossom like a rose, someone probably told him, one of its first products is people.

DIVERSIFICATION AND IRRIGATION
By the time the Atomic Energy Commission reliquished its con-trol and the General Electric Company withdrew, the attempt to lure new industry to the area was bearing fruit. Frances Pugnetti writes:

> United States Testing was the first company to win a contract. Battelle Memorial Institute was the second, arriving shortly after the withdrawal of General Electric....The third company was Douglas United Nuclear....Battelle had "spinoff" compa-nies. Among them were a subsidiary called "Nortec" which manufactures instruments; and Automata Corp., a small elec-tronics manufacturer. Battelle also constructed an Oceanographic Laboratory at Sequim, Washington, an office in Seattle, and a "think factory" called Battelle Research, also locat-ed in Seattle.

As still another part of the diversification process in the 1960s, the Tri–Cities area began to develop its agriculture through inten-sive irrigation of the lower Yakima Valley and the Columbia

Basin. But in both endeavors, the planners ran into governmental roadblocks.

The most serious of these was the old, seldom-invoked, often-evaded Bureau of Reclamation 160–acre limitation law, which decreed that a farmer using water developed under a Bureau project could own no more than 160 acres of land. When first written into law in 1902, a lone farmer using a horse-drawn grader, ditch irrigation, gum boots, and a shovel could handle no more than a quarter-section of irrigated land. If married, he could obtain an additional 160 acres and put his strong-backed wife and the kids to work. But those days were long gone. Today, an irrigated farm required machinery, high-pressure pumps, sprinkling systems, chemical fertilizers, and all the other expensive gadgetry of this new scientific farming age; thus, the successful farmer might need to invest $100,000 and own or lease one thousand acres of land even to begin operations.

In addition to its outmoded, 160–acre limitation law, the Bureau of Reclamation declared that all water impounded behind a federal dam—even those built by the Corps of Engineers for power and navigation purposes—belonged not to the states, which traditionally allocated water rights, but to the federal government. This stirred up a hornet's nest of objections.

In the early West, Bret Harte once wrote, more men were killed in disputes over water than in quarrels over gold, women, livestock, and land combined. More recently, President Kennedy had made the comment, "Anyone who can solve the problem of water will be worthy of two Nobel prizes—one for science and one for peace."

When the Bureau of Reclamation was the prime mover in the development of an irrigation project, the usual procedure was for potential beneficiaries to form water districts, allocate the amount of water to be granted each piece of land, then pay modest fees in the form of taxes or repayment charges for the use of the water, so that eventually the reclamation project would pay for itself. Obviously, the Bureau could not develop all their water projects at once, for this would not only break their budget but would also worsen an already bad farm surplus problem.

In the late 1960s, it was estimated that the Bureau of Reclamation had enough approved projects on its plate to keep busy for the next forty years. But impatient private developers

John Mix Stanley Painting, Courtesy Penrose Library, Whitman College
PALOUSE FALLS

saw no reason why they should not purchase land and put water on it at their own expense to raise crops for which there was a market. A few miles southeast of Pasco, for instance, the Universal Land Company bought several thousand arid acres on the south side of Snake River upstream from recently completed Ice Harbor Dam, built a pumping plant on the river, leveled the land, seeded it with potatoes, grapes, and other crops, and began watering it with automatic circle sprinklers, each unit of which could cover 128 acres of land several times in a twenty-four hour period without requiring human care. The company's initial capital investment was five million dollars.

Then came the big blow.

> The Department of Interior issued an administrative order that the National Reclamation Act applied to private irrigation projects if they pumped from a Federal Reservoir—no more than 160 acres per single ownership.

Before the *Tri–Cities Herald* exploded in editorial protest, Senator Jackson warned that it would be unwise to pick a fight with the Interior Department until he found out what had inspired the ruling. Its genesis, he discovered, had been a question by the Bureau of Management and Budget asking why it was that irrigators were taking water from Federal reservoirs without paying for it. Frances Pugnetti writes:

> The matter had arisen in the upper Missouri River Basin where South Dakota irrigators had a Corps of Engineers easement to cross Federal land to reach the river for their pumping operation. When they sought to have it renewed, the Corps told them that the National Reclamation Act of 160 acres would apply. That, of course, ended the development.

Now the protest against the ruling took on national significance, for several basic principles were in question. In an editorial titled "Let's Develop Our Own Assets," which appeared in the *Herald* November 18, 1969, Don Pugnetti wrote:

> A Federal dam may create a reservoir, but God created the river. The states and the water were there long before the dams. Impoundment or not, the basic water flow of the river continues to exist. Doesn't any of that flowage belong to the states?

The director of the Washington State Department of Water Resources certainly believed that it did, saying, "The position of the state is that there has been a historic flow in the rivers and we grant rights to withdraw water from this historic flow."

As push came to shove, positions hardened on both sides. In a legal opinion written for the Interior Department, attorney J. Lane Morthland declared:

John Mix Stanley Painting, Courtesy Penrose Library, Whitman College
MOUTH OF THE PALOUSE RIVER, IN 1847

1. There is no natural flow in the rivers. All water is managed and controlled and stored.
2. Water stored behind a Corps of Engineers dam is Federal water and anyone who pumps such water is subject to the Reclamation Act, which limits irrigators to 160 acres.

This opinion came as a great surprise for the Pacific Northwest. The position taken by the states of Idaho, Oregon, and Washington was:

1. There is a natural flow in the rivers. The rivers may be managed and controlled but the natural flow remains.
2. There is no "stored" water within the concept stated by Interior. The dams were constructed as power dams, not storage dams, and the reservoirs they created were not designed for irrigation but to insure a head of water for power production.

Certainly this was true of the mainstem dams on the Columbia and the Snake, whose reservoirs by law were not permitted to fluctuate more than one foot per hour or a total of twelve feet in a day. Since the rivers were used chiefly for tug and barge traffic, fish passage, and power generation, water storage for irrigation purposes was a minor consideration. Irrigators pumping out of the reservoirs backed up by the dams simply were using the water that was there in such a large supply that withdrawal by pumps had little effect on the level of the river.

In an editorial titled "Who Owns Our Rivers?," Don Pugnetti stated the essence of the argument:

Should only Uncle Sam develop the land? If the government's position is sustained, that will be the result. The government's legal representatives say they are obeying the law and that this is the will of Congress.

Is this really what Congress means and intends? It appears that Congress should begin looking into this situation itself, for what is occurring has cast a suspicion over every major water right in the West.

If such an explosive question ever had reached the discussion stage on the floor of Congress, it would have torn the nation apart as no subject had done since the Civil War—this time on an East versus West axis. But the tremendous outpourng of protest and the pressure generated upon the federal agency, caused the Interior Department to back off. On April 28, 1970, Assistant Secretary James Smith announced:

It has been determined that the provisions of Federal reclamation law do not apply to a private irrigator when the water to be diverted is covered by a valid natural-flow water right under state law, and whose water supply is not dependent at any time during the irrigation season upon the existence or operation of Federal project facilities.

Thus, common sense and the laws of nature in the arid West—where water is life—prevailed, with the great rivers of the Pacific Northwest permitted to go on flowing downhill without interference from federal edict.

For the time being, at least, the West would not secede from the Union.

THE WALLA WALLA VALLEY: HISTORIC FORT WALLA WALLA

A few miles south of the Snake River bridge on US 12, you will see a sign on the west side of the highway reading "Site of Old Fort Walla Walla." Originally named "Fort Nez Perces," the site now is buried beneath the backwaters from McNary Dam twenty-five miles downriver. This was the spot where the British Empire, the

Courtesy Oregon Historical Society
OLD FORT WALLA WALLA

Manifest Destiny policy of the United States, and the native American culture of a number of inland tribes came in contact—blending or conflicting with varying degrees of violence from the time of Lewis and Clark down through the end of the Indian wars in 1858.

Like other trading posts built with the dual purpose of protecting its people while at the same time allowing trade with the Indians, the fort established at the mouth of the Walla Walla River went by many names and moved to many locations over the years. The first post was erected by Astorian partner Donald MacKenzie at the juncture of the Clearwater with the Snake 130 miles to the east in 1812. The big, red-bearded trader liked the Nez Perces, and they liked him. But when England and the United States went to war, the Astor enterprise appeared to have no future in the Pacific Northwest, so Donald MacKenzie agreed with the other partners at Astoria in 1813 to make the best bargain they could by selling out to the British-owned North West Company.

Carrying a draft for $80,500 back to John Jacob Astor in New York, MacKenzie expected to be praised for having salvaged at

Gustaf Sohon Sketch, Courtesy Washington State Historical Society
PEO-PEO-MOX-MOX, WALLA WALLA CHIEF, 1855

least a portion of the doomed venture. Instead, Astor castigated him bitterly, accusing him of selling out for ten cents on the dollar and conniving with the enemy in an act of treason to his country. Since Donald MacKenzie weighed 312 pounds—not an ounce of which was fat—and had a temper that matched his hair, it is a wonder that he did not break the pudgy little German merchant into small pieces. But he did not. He simply walked out, went to Montreal, and offered his services to Astor's most bitter rival, the North West Company. Returning to the Pacific Northwest, where the Joint Occupancy Treaty now was in effect, he was given the men and money to establish a major trading post near the spot where the Columbia River turned westward toward the sea.

Because his superiors feared the Indians of the inland country, MacKenzie was ordered to build the new post on the west side of the Columbia so that his clerks would be protected by having the width of the river between them and possibly hostile Indians. This he flatly refused to do, declaring it would be a slap in the face to a tribe that always had been friendly to him. If he must build the post on the Columbia, he said, he would place it on the east side of the river and he would name it Fort Nez Perces as a tribute to his friends. Since the North West Company insisted, he did build defensive towers at diagonal corners, strong wooden gates that could be closed, and a small sally-port behind which timid clerks could remain when they traded with the natives. But whenever he was at the fort, no gate ever was closed against his Indian friends.

Despite the comment made by some latter-day historians that the trading post was misnamed, its name was appropriate, for, as Lewis and Clark had learned many years ago, the Nez Perces were the dominant tribe between the Bitterroot Mountains and Celilo Falls. Bands so closely related to the Nez Perces that they called one another "brothers" or "cousins" did live in the immediate area: the Walla Wallas nearest the Columbia, the Cayuses twenty miles or so to the east, and the Umatillas just to the southeast of them near the foot of the Blue Mountains. All of these bands used the Nez Perce language in communicating with one another, with the isolated Cayuse variant dialect so difficult that only a few hundred local Indians spoke or understood it.

For no other reason than its proximity to the mouth of the small river by that name, Fort Nez Perces became Fort Walla Walla after the North West Company was absorbed by the Hudson's Bay Company in 1821. Still later, when Washington Territory became part of the United States, the federal government built a new military post twenty-nine miles east of the Columbia River on Mill Creek in the heart of the Walla Walla Valley. Wanting to remove the soldiers from the temptations of the grog shops that immediately sprang up surrounding it, the government claimed a square mile of land a mile or so to the west and built a permanent, unstockaded military post there, with officers' quarters, enlisted men's barracks, and a hospital surrounding an extensive parade ground.

Following this, of course, the grog shops moved as close as they could get to the limits of the military reserve, while the site of the first post became downtown Walla Walla. At first, the settlement was called Steptoeville in honor of the post's commander,

Gustaf Sohon Sketch, Courtesy Washington State Historical Society
OW-HI, YAKIMA CHIEF, 1855

Lieutenant Colonel Edward J. Steptoe, but when troops under his command suffered a stinging defeat, the name was hastily changed, with the local Indian name Waiilatpu being considered for a time, then because nobody could spell or pronounce it, abandoned in favor of the name Walla Walla.

In the local Indian tongue, *Walla* meant "water," which, when repeated, meant "many waters" or "many little streams" because eleven of them descended the slopes of the nearby Blue Mountains and crossed the fertile valley. Having lived for more years than we care to admit between two of these little streams a mile or so southeast of town on a piece of land claimed by ex–mountain man Ransom Clark, who was a guide for Major John C. Fremont in 1843, we can vouch for the fact that at least two of the "many waters" still run the year round.

Gustaf Sohon Sketch, Courtesy Washington State Historical Society
KAMIAKIN, HEAD CHIEF OF THE YAKIMAS

In existence as a military post between 1856 and 1910, the latter-day United States Fort Walla Walla was deactivated and converted into a Veterans Hospital in the early part of the century, in which capacity it still serves today. On its one-hundredth birthday in 1956, most of the original square mile of land taken over by the federal government was deeded to the City of Walla Walla on the condition that it be converted into a park. This was eventually done by stages, with the old military cemetery, a Pioneer Village and Farm Implement Museum, a 1,200–seat outdoor amphitheatre, a campground, a day-park, and a walk-in-the-wild area gradually being developed on the former military reserve.

THE WHITMAN MISSION

Despite the tendency of today's "revisionist historians" to denigrate their efforts, no single group of people exercised a greater

Gustaf Sohon Sketch, Courtesy Washington State Historical Society
YOUNG CHIEF, CAYUSE CHIEF, 1855

influence on the history of the Pacific Northwest than the mis-sionaries. Any person who doubts this fact should read the jour-nals, letters, and newspapers of the 1830s—copies of which are available in major regional libraries—before accepting the judg-ment of a minority of today's so-called scholars who for some strange reason insist on rewriting history so that it will be "polit-ically correct" in their view.

Earlier in this book I mentioned the comment made by the highly-biased historian Hubert Howe Bancroft back in the 1890s that "...the best thing the missionaries could have done for the Indians would have been to leave them alone..."

Perhaps so. Perhaps it would have been better for the Indians if Columbus had not discovered America, if the Spaniards never had brought over the horse, if gunpowder, firearms, and the inter-nal combustion engine had never been invented, and the natives had been left in their state of unsullied innocence—which proba-bly never did exist except in the academic minds of the revision-ist historians.

Gustaf Sohon Sketch, Courtesy Washington State Historical Society
FIVE CROWS, CAYUSE CHIEF, 1855

But like it or not, these unsettling events did happen. And the Indian—native American, if you will—simply has had to live with that fact, as have the rest of us in this multi–racial nation.

While on the subject, I would like to point out a fact often overlooked or ignored by "politically correct" writers. Any person born in the United States, whatever his or her ancestry, is a "native American." Note the small *n*, which incidentally may be found in the generally accepted bible of print usage *The Chicago Manual of Style*. The term cannot be claimed exclusively by or for the Indian. What can and should be claimed by the original inhabitants of the United States is that they are the only people in this country who need not hyphenate their name. If they wish to write or say: "Indian," "Native," or "American," the classification is accurate, for they fit any of these one-word categories. Only those of us who are Dutch, English, Irish, Swedish, or whatever-else-combination Americans need hyphenate our names if we wish to qualify our ancestry.

During my close association with individuals belonging to a number of regional Indian tribes over the past forty years, I have found them to be quite comfortable with this fact—as I have been—and now will mention it no more.

Due largely to the visit of Lewis and Clark in 1805–06, the Nez Perces were far more friendly to Americans than to the British. Learning that Spokane Garry had been educated and taught religion in Canada under the sponsorship of the Hudson's Bay Company, the Nez Perces sent a delegation of chiefs to St. Louis in 1831, where they asked their old friend, William Clark, who by then was Superintendent of Indian Affairs for the Northwest, to send *taitamnats*—religious teachers—who would live among them in their own country and teach them the white man's ways. When this appeal was broadcast in somewhat garbled form, it literally set the religious world ablaze with excitement.

Just as President Kennedy's idea of a Peace Corps inspired young people to volunteer for service in foreign fields during the early 1960s, so did the thought of becoming missionaries appeal to spiritual-minded people during the 1830s. Catholic, Protestant, Mormon, or whatever their faith, the Great Command recorded in Matthew 28:19, "Go ye therefore, and teach all nations, baptizing them in the name of the Father and of the Son, and of the Holy Ghost," became a powerful order which many religious people felt they must obey.

Among the first to respond to the Nez Perce appeal were Marcus and Narcissa Whitman, who in 1836 established a mission in the Walla Walla Valley twenty-three miles east of the Hudson's Bay Company post on the Columbia River. A medical doctor by training, thirty-two-year-old Marcus Whitman had been given a rude introduction to life on the western plains when traveling with a fur brigade under the leadership of Lucien Fontenelle on an exploratory trip in the company of the Presbyterian minister, Samuel Parker, the year before.

Fontenelle was not happy with the escort chore. Like the rough-hewn trappers in his employ, he equated men of the cloth with a loss of freedom and sensed that a cherished way of life was coming to an end. While in St. Louis he dared not violate company policy of friendship to the missionaries, but once the brigade left Liberty (near present–day Kansas City) and headed out across the open plains he did his best to discourage Whitman and Parker from tagging along.

How long the hostility between the trapping brigade and the missionaries might have lasted became a moot question when the caravan reached Bellevue, two weeks out from Liberty, and an epidemic of Asian cholera struck the party. Whitman later wrote:

> At this place the Lord had a great change for us, for the Cholera appearing in camp, my aid was greatly sought. Mr. Fontenelle himself being one of the subjects of the disease and recovering (as also most of his men), he showed his gratitude, as well as all other persons in the company, by bestowing upon us every favor in his power.

Since it was not unusual for a cholera epidemic to kill half the community through which it raged, the fact that they lost only three members of the brigade—which numbered more than fifty—says a great deal for the skill with which Dr. Whitman treated the sick men. Having been trained and licensed thirteen years earlier as both a surgeon and a general practicioner, he was as knowledgeable as any doctor of his day.

Meeting with the Nez Perces at fur rendezvous on Green River and finding them eager to welcome white missionaries, Marcus Whitman returned to Angelica, New York, where an attractive, strong-minded, twenty-eight year-old young lady named Narcissa Prentiss had promised to marry him, while the Reverend Parker continued his journey to the Nez Perce country to select sites for several missions which the American Board for Foreign Missions planned to establish there.

Within the next three years, Henry and Eliza Spalding built a mission at Lapwai twelve miles east of present–day Lewiston; Elkanah and Mary Walker built at Tshimakain in the Spokane country; while Marcus and Narcissa Whitman settled at Waiilatpu—"Place of the Rye Grass"—six miles west of what would become the city of Walla Walla among the Cayuse Indians.

During their eleven-year stay at the mission (as the revisionist historians are quick to point out), the Whitmans officially took no Indian converts into the church. Neither did the Walkers at Tshimakain. In contrast to these apparent failures to win the heathen to Christianty, the Reverend Spalding baptised and renamed a number of Nez Perce Indian leaders such as Timothy, James, and Joseph, while the Catholics also took a sizable number of natives into churches they established in the Spokane and Coeur d'Alene country. But in playing their numbers game, the revisionist historians overlook several important facts.

First, Marcus Whitman was a doctor, not a minister, so was not qualified to accept converts. Second, according to the Presbyterian–Congregationalist credo under which the Protestant missions were operating, a potential convert was required to study the tenets of the religion intensively, then undergo an examination by a qualified board of elders, which would decide whether or not to admit him to church membership. In this part of the country, such a board seldom could be assembled—a rule the headstrong, dogmatic Reverend Henry Spalding repeatedly ignored (and later was reprimanded for). Finally, the Catholics conferred church membership on potential converts first, then undertook to teach them the nature of the religion they had accepted. So mere numbers are meaningless.

In any case, Marcus and Narcissa Whitman felt that their first obligation toward the Cayuse Indians among whom they had settled was to care for their physical rather than their spiritual needs. Toward this end, their efforts were eminently successful.

Plowing and fencing an extensive plot of land between two streams, Dr. Whitman and his white helpers planted wheat, corn, potatoes, melons, and fruit trees, which flourished in the fertile soil. They built a water-powered gristmill, a sawmill, and a blacksmith shop. Carefully tending the cattle, sheep, and swine they had either brought along or purchased from the nearby Hudson's Bay Company post, they soon developed a supply of domestic meat to supplement the locally slaughtered wild game.

While attempting the hitherto untried task of bringing a four-wheeled wagon west from fur rendezvous grounds to the Columbia River, Marcus Whitman had labored so prodigiously over rock-strewn mountain and sandy desert trails to keep the wagon moving that Narcissa feared he would injure himself. When an axle broke and could not be replaced just east of Fort Hall (near present–day Pocatello), she secretly rejoiced, thinking that would end his herculean endeavor. To her dismay, he sawed off the broken end of the wagon, turning it into a two-wheeled cart, which he muscled two hundred miles further west to Fort Boise.

Because time was running short and Hudson's Bay Company personnel at Fort Boise declared that taking a wheeled vehicle of any kind across the Blue Mountains was impossible, he abandoned the cart there for the time being, swearing—or perhaps vowing—that he would come back and get it in a year or two. He never found time to do so; but, inspired by his example, a trio of ex–mountain men—Doc Newell, Joe Meek, and William Craig— did bring a wagon from Fort Hall across the desert then up and over the Blue Mountains and into the yard at the Whitman Mission four years later in 1840.

Admittedly, the wagon was in bad shape by then and the three ex–mountain men were wondering if their achievement had been worth the effort. But so far as Manifest Destiny and the Westward Course of Empire were concerned, the trio of ex–mountain men had proved that wheels could cross the continent.

During the next twenty-five years, thousands more wagons would follow...

OREGON TRAIL DAYS

Eliza Spalding and Narcissa Whitman shared the honor of being the first white women to cross the continent. When her baby, Alice Clarissa, was born at the Whitman Mission in the spring of 1837, it became the first white child to see the light of day in the area. When as a toddler it wandered away from the house, fell into the nearby Walla Walla River and drowned at the age of two years, three months, and nine days, it became the first white child to die and be buried at the Whitman Mission.

As word reached restless Americans back East that wagons could cross the continent, traffic over the Oregon Trail increased year by year. Since the Whitman Mission was the only American settlement between Fort Laramie and the Willamette Valley at which ill or indigent emigrants could receive medical attention, food, or supplies, Waiilatpu soon became more of an emigrant-aid station than a religious mission to the Cayuse. Understandably, this caused resentment among the Indians.

If given time and left alone, it is possible that the missionaries and the Indians could have learned to understand one another and bridge the ages-long cultural gap separating white and red races. But neither time nor isolation was granted them.

Since theirs was a hunting-gathering culture in which their people killed game, caught fish, and gathered roots and berries that required no cultivation, the Cayuse could not understand why the white missionaries plowed, planted, fenced, and jealously protected the small plots of land on which their crops grew and their livestock grazed. Though the Cayuse soon developed a taste for baked bread made from wheat grown and milled at the Mission and enjoyed such staples as potatoes, corn, fruits, and melons, they could see no point in spending days of hard labor digging irrigation ditches, plowing, planting, and weeding.

Being human, missionaries living at Lapwai, Tshimakain, and Waiilatpu sometimes argued with one another, then, seeking moral backing, wrote complaining letters to the American Board back in Boston. Disappointed because of the apparent lack of success of the Far Western missions and the repeated appeals for more funds and people, the Board decided to make some changes. Putting their decision into a letter delivered to the Whitman Mission in September, 1842, the Board decreed:

The Spaldings were being be recalled...

Waiilatpu was to be closed and sold...

The Whitmans were to move to Tshimakain...

Because at least a year was required for a letter and reply to cross the continent and return, the causes of dissension among the missionaries had long since been acknowledged, forgiven, and corrected by the time the letter from Boston arrived. Dr. Whitman called a meeting of all parties concerned, then made an astounding proposal.

He would leave for the East at once, confront the Board, and persuade its members to change their collective mind.

Impatiently brushing aside objections that the trip would be too dangerous, Whitman, a man named Asa Lovejoy, and the dog Trapper, which had been the pet of the drowned little girl, Alice Clarissa Whitman, left Waiilatpu and headed East October 3.

Ten days later, the trio reached Fort Hall, a distance of five hundred miles. Already the early mountain winter was closing in on the high country; it promised to be a bitter one. Ahead, they were warned by the Hudson's Bay Company factor, Peter Grant, the Sioux and Pawnees were at war, making a crossing of the plains an extremely risky business. Better go back to Waiilatpu and wait for spring.

No, Whitman said, they must go on now. Instead of taking the direct route, they would swing south to Taos and Santa Fe, then back north to Bent's Fort. True, this detour would add a thousand miles to the trip. But he could not wait for spring.

Minus a mule and the family pet, Trapper, both of which had been eaten, Whitman and Lovejoy reached Taos in mid–December. Both men were suffering from exhaustion, frost-bite, and starvation. After resting two weeks, they moved on to Bent's Fort, Whitman impatiently leaving Lovejoy behind there in his haste to join a party heading for St. Louis.

Still wearing the heavy buffalo coat that had kept him from freezing in the snow and cold of the high country, Whitman reached Washington, DC in early March, 1843. Congress had just adjourned. After a brief stay there, he went on to New York, where a cabman, taking him for a hick from the sticks, fleeced him out of two dollars of his almost exhausted funds. He had a session with Horace Greeley, who admired his courage and principles but thought anybody fool enough to go to Oregon was out of his mind.

Broke and shaggy, he reached Boston in early May and pre-sented himself to Secretary David Greene of the American Board. Greene was so shocked by his appearance and smell, he hastily gave him some money and told him to get a bath and some decent clothes.

There is ample evidence that the Board did not approve of Whitman's fantastic journey. But the drama of what he had done overpowered the committee's conservatism. After due considera-tion, it granted him his two most important requests.

Waiilatpu would be continued...

Spalding would be retained "on trial..."

Thus, the legend that "Marcus Whitman Saved Oregon for the United States..." was born. During the few years of life left him, he made no such claim himself. In a memorial to Congress, sent through influential friends, he did stress the importance of the Oregon Country and proposed that the military establish a chain of forts along the Oregon Trail to supply and protect emigrants.

By coincidence, on his return to Waiilatpu he encountered at Westport the first of the Great Emigrations, that of 1843, and rendered it valuable assistance on its way West. But he was not the Saviour of Oregon that a few fanciful writers later painted him to be.

With his twelve-year-old nephew, Perrin, Dr. Marcus Whitman reached Westport May 31, 1843, homeward bound. During previous years, annual migrations to the Far West had been very small, consisting mostly of reinforcements for the missions: fourteen people in 1839; six people in 1840; fifty-four people in 1841; one hundred twelve in 1842—and some of these were bound for California. But this year there was astonishing evidence that a movement unparalleled in the nation's history was under way.

One hundred twenty wagons, over a thousand men, women, and children, and five thousand oxen, horses, and cattle were preparing to move west, the surprised Dr. Whitman found. To the leaders of the migration, his name and feats were well known, and his appearance at this time and place was regarded as the greatest of good fortune. Eager questions peppered him from every quarter.

Was he returning to his mission station? Could wagons get through to the Columbia? Would he travel with them and give them the benefit of his medical services and advice?

To all questions, he answered yes.

As already noted, Whitman neither claimed nor should be given credit for directly inspiring the Great Emigration of 1843, but his services to it were beyond dispute. Jesse Applegate, a member of the party who became a prominent citizen of Oregon, later wrote:

> His constant advice, which we knew was based upon a knowledge of the road before us, was *"travel, Travel, TRAVEL"*—nothing else will take you to the end of your journey; nothing is wise that does not help you along; nothing is good for you that causes a moments' delay.

THE WHITMAN MASSACRE

What had been a trickle of American emigration to Oregon turned into a flood during the next ten years; so it is understandable that the bewildered Indians and the handful of white settlers living in the path of the unprecedented movement of people west were overwhelmed by its volume. While completely accurate figures cannot be obtained, estimates made of a few sample years are of interest:

1844...1,475 people
1845...3,000 people
1846...3,300 people
1847...3,700 people
1849...25,000 people
1852...23,000 people
1853...15,000 people

At Waiilatpu, the nature and purpose of the mission changed drastically, for it lay directly on the route of the Oregon Trail. Since the Whitman Station was the only place emigrants could get supplies and medical services from a fellow American for over a thousand miles, the demands on its resources were becoming increasingly burdensome.

Though Narcissa had no children of her own now, she soon acquired a large adopted family. The ex–mountain man, Jim Bridger, sent his half-blood Ute daughter, Mary Ann, to the Whitman Mission to be schooled and raised like a lady. Joe Meek, on his way to the Willamette Valley, dropped off his half-blood Shoshone daughter, Helen Mar. Part–Indian children from the nearby Hudson's Bay Company post of Fort Walla Walla enrolled in the Mission school, which was being taught by Narcissa and an occasional literate emigrant who could be persuaded to stay and teach for a while.

A bachelor too sick to travel was housed, nursed, and fed until he regained his health. Other indigents were taken in for short or long periods of time. And what, in God's name, could you do with seven young brothers and sisters, ranging from five months to thirteen years of age, whose parents had died along the way? Well, you could say—as Narcissa did—that you would take in only the girls. Then, when you saw the looks in the eyes of the parentless children about to be parted, you could say—as Marcus Whitman did— "In God's name, we'll take them all."

In November, 1847, Narcissa was caring for eleven children, four of whom were part Indian. There now were sixty-nine more or less permanent residents with white blood in their veins living at Waiilatpu. The main concern of the mission now was not saving Indian souls, but feeding the hungry, clothing the naked, and nursing the ill Americans moving west. Understandably, the

Cayuse resented the ever-growing white community occupying their lands.

But resentment changed to horror when one of the ill Americans, sick with black measles, inadvertently passed on the disease to the Cayuses, who had no natural immunity to measles whatsoever.

Like many Indian tribes, the Cayuse had their medicine men—*tewats*—to whom they turned when they became seriously ill. For a fee of a few horses or other articles of value, the *tewat* would provide potions, stage dances, or shake magic charms over his patients in hopes of effecting a cure. As the medicine men well knew, the price of failure could be high, for by the Cayuse code an aggrieved relative was entitled to kill the *tewat* who failed to make his patient well—unless the medicine man could place blame for his failure on some person or evil influence beyond his control.

Dr. Whitman was aware of this custom, yet went on treating sick Indian patients who requested his help regardless of the risk. Among the Cayuse Indians who did believe in Whitman was an influential chief named Stickus. Impressed by the first sermon Whitman preached following his arrival at Waiilatpu, Chief Stickus decided he and all his family members would become Christians. Though not formally taken into the church (for reasons already noted), they would remain converts for as long as they and the Whitmans lived—as later events amply proved.

Normally, the camp in which Stickus lived was located on the Umatilla River in the foothills of the Blue Mountains, some twenty-five miles south of Waiilatpu. Directly adjacent to the Mission was the largest Cayuse village in the area, its headmen answering to the Indian names *Tiloukaikt, Tomahas, Ish-ish-kais-kais, Clokamas,* and *Kia-ma-sump-kin.* Of all the local Indians, these men had opposed the Whitmans most bitterly and had listened most eagerly to the rumors now being spread against them.

The main sources of these negative stories were two recent arrivals from the East: a full-blood Delaware Indian named Tom Hill and a half–French–Canadian, half–Iroquois Indian named Joe Lewis, both of whom had suffered real or imagined abuse at the hands of white men in time past. Siding with them, of course, were the *tewats*, who feared that Dr. Whitman would steal their patients and their fees.

John Mix Stanley Painting, Courtesy Washington State Historical Society
SOURCE OF THE PALOUSE, 1847

Having by now put over three hundred acres into cultivation, the Mission not only was able to feed its growing horde of people, it also had a surplus to sell to the stream of emigrants passing through. The two troublemakers asked the Cayuse several loaded questions: Could the Cayuse not see that the Whitmans were getting rich by using *their* land? Why don't you make them give you a share of the food they raise? Why don't you insist that they pay rent?

Have you not noticed that when Dr. Whitman treats sick white people, they usually get well, while, when he treats Indians, they often die? This is because he has two kinds of medicines in the black bottles on his shelf, with the good medicine going to white people, while Indians are given poison.

Sooner or later, Hill and Lewis warned, the Whitmans will open a black bottle full of deadly disease, kill all the Cayuse Indians, and then take their lands. What can you do about it? The answer is simple.

Kill the whites before they destroy you!

When the epidemic of black measles brought in by an emigrant train began to spread through the Cayuse village, the few natives who still believed in Whitman as a doctor lost what little was left of their trust. Falling back on treatment by the *tewats,* which consisted of raising the temperature of an already-feverish body to an even higher degree by taking a sweat bath then plunging into an icy stream, the Cayuse people suffered appalling casualties. In a band numbering four hundred souls, 198 Indians died before the epidemic ran its course. Of these, most were children.

Unable to treat the sick in the Cayuse village adjacent to Waiilatpu, Dr. Whitman quickly responded to an appeal from Chief Stickus that he visit the Umatilla River area twenty-five miles to the south and minister to ill Cayuse and Umatilla adults and children living there. In contrast to what Tom Hill and Joe Lewis were saying about the doctor, Stickus had good reason to believe in the efficacy of Whitman's treatment. Some years earlier when Stickus became ill, he called in a *tewat,* who failed to cure him. Discharging the native medicine man, Chief Stickus called in Dr. Whitman—who made him well. From that time on, the Cayuse chief would not permit a native healer to practice in his territory.

Stickus had given further evidence of his friendship for Dr. Whitman when in late summer, 1843, he heard that the large wagon train Whitman was guiding west was having trouble in the desert just west of Fort Boise. With several of his young men, Stickus had ridden across the Blue Mountains and down to Snake River near Farewell Bend, then helped guide the emigrants the rest of the way to Waiilatpu.

Concerned about the health of his ten-year-old daughter, Eliza, who was enrolled in the Whitman Mission school, the Reverend Henry Spalding had arrived from Lapwai a few days ago. Though several other children were sick, his own child was in good health, he learned, so he prolonged his visit and accepted Whitman's invitation to ride down to the Stickus village on the Umatilla River.

Though the hour was past midnight when Whitman and Spalding reached his lodge, Chief Stickus lighted a lamp as they approached, came out, and shook their hands. Ordering one of his sons to unsaddle and care for their horses, he brought the two men into his tepee, which was warm and dry, fed them a good meal and provided a comfortable bed. Following prayers and breakfast next morning, Stickus warned Whitman that the Cayuses at Waiilatpu were plotting against him.

Gustaf Sohon Sketch, Courtesy Washington State Historical Society
STICKUS, CAYUSE CHIEF, 1855

"I will give you the names of the men who talk of killing you," he said. "Tiloukaikt, Tamsucky, and Joe Lewis. These are the leaders. And there are half a dozen more."

"I appreciate the warning," Whitman said. "But right now there are sick people to be cared for. I must visit the camps of Five Crows and Young Chief on the south side of the river."

"You will not like what you find in the camp of Young Chief," Stickus said gravely. "He has given his house to the Black Robes to use as a mission. They call it St. Anne."

"So I have heard. Well, it's a free country. While I'm there, I may talk to the priests about the advisability of asking the Cayuses to decide what kind of missionaries they want, Protestant or Catholic."

Ironically, on a personal basis missionaries of rival faiths got along well enough, though on matters of dogma neither sect would give an inch. As an example, two days earlier Whitman and Spalding had visited the Hudson's Bay Company post, Fort Walla Walla, where they had dined with Factor William McBean and two visiting Catholic priests. Having heard that the well-to-do Walla Walla chief, Peo-peo-mox-mox, had given the Catholics permission to establish a mission nearby, Whitman and Spalding agreed to sell them food and supplies both here and at Lapawi, should they build a mission there as they talked of doing.

Spalding then got into a heated argument with one of the priests on the subject of "Transubstantiation" (which the Catholics and several Protestant churches observed during communion, in which bread and wine are supposed to represent the body and blood of Jesus Christ). In his journal, Spalding later detailed the argument and pronounced himself the victor in it by writing, "I convinced him that any person who practiced transubstantiation was either a dissembler or a cannibal."

Returning to Chief Stickus's tepee in late afternoon, Whitman said he had treated the Indian sick, then taken tea with Bishop Blanchet and Fathers Brouillet and LeClaire.

"We had a good conversation. I suggested that it would be helpful if one of them came to Waiilatpu and talked to the Indians with me, showing them that despite our different religions we both have their welfare in mind. Father Brouillet said he would pay us a visit in a couple of days."

When Whitman asked Spalding if he were ready to ride back to Waiilatpu with him, Spalding, who had injured a leg the night before when his horse slipped and fell on a muddy trail, said that if Chief Stickus had no objections he would stay here and rest for a few days. Stickus told him he was welcome to stay as long as he liked.

So Whitman rode home alone.

At noon, next day, the Cayuses took the course of action Tom Hill, Joe Lewis, and grief for their own dead long had urged them to take. By the time their bloody work was done, Marcus Whitman, his wife Narcissa, and twelve more white people were dead, fifty-one whites were being held captive, and terror stalked the land.

Due to a freak of fate Spalding remained alive and free. But the Cayuses knew where he was—and had sworn to kill him.

AFTERMATH—THE CAYUSE WAR

Though eventually the Indian side of the killings would be better understood, white reaction at the time was horror and outrage. Ironically, many American lives were saved by the courage and cool-headedness of two men who were not even citizens of the United States. One of them was the Catholic priest, Father J.B.A. Brouillet; the other a Hudson's Bay Company factor, Peter Skene Ogden.

As he had promised Whitman he would do, Father Brouillet stopped by Waiilatpu early Tuesday evening, the day after the massacre. He was shocked by what he saw. Assisted by two of the survivors, he gave the victims a Christian burial service, reading the Roman Catholic rites in Latin. As a Catholic and a foreigner, he was immune to Cayuse wrath for the time being, but he knew that the moment he appeared to be taking the side of the Americans, the Cayuse would kill him.

He also knew that Henry Spalding planned to ride this way Wednesday morning. If the Cayuse encountered him, he would die. But if Father Brouillet were caught helping Spalding evade the fate the Indians had decreed for him, the priest's own life would be forfeit.

Riding with him as he left Waiilatpu next morning was a friendly Cayuse chief named Camaspelo—"Big Belly"—whom Young Chief had assigned as a guide and interpreter. On the outskirts of the village, they were joined by a tall, arrogant young Indian named Edward Tiloukaikt, son of one of the chiefs who had plotted the massacre. Five or six miles along the trail, they saw a lone rider coming toward them. As he drew nearer, Father Brouillet realized that the man was Henry Spalding. When they met, Spalding shook the priest's hand and asked, "Have you been to the doctor's?"

"Yes."

"What news?"

Giving Edward Tiloukaikt a sidelong glance, Father Brouillet answered tersely, "Sad news, I fear."

"Have more of the children died?"

From the way Edward was glowering at Spalding, Father Brouillet suspected that the young Cayuse was debating whether to kill him now or ride back to the Cayuse village to confer with his elders. Not wanting to upset either Edward or Spalding,

Brouillet spoke to Camaspelo in French, which the friendly Indian understood while Edward and Spalding did not.

"Beg him, in my name, not to kill Mr. Spalding."

Intimidated by the presence of Camaspelo and the priest, the young Cayuse wheeled his horse around and rode back toward Waiilatpu to tell his father he had met Spalding. As soon as he left, Father Brouillet informed Spalding of the massacre, warned him he must leave the area, and gave the white missionary what food he had to sustain him during his flight. Fortunately, the day was cold and a low-hanging fog limited visibility, which would help Spalding evade capture.

When a party of Cayuses rode up a few minutes later, looking for Spalding, they were angry that he had been warned to flee. Camaspelo took the blame for that, saying it had been he and not the priest who had told Spalding what had happened. Unfortunately, in time to come Spalding forgot this personal act of bravery on the part of Father Brouillet, bitterly castigating the Catholics in speeches and in print for having been one of the principal causes of the massacre.

Meanwhile, at Fort Walla Walla, Factor William McBean had received word of the killings and taken measures to rescue the survivors who were being held captive. Since the boundary between the United States and Great Britain had been settled in 1846 at the 49th parallel, with the Hudson's Bay Company agreeing to close its posts and withdraw, Company personnel no longer had the slightest vestige of authority in this part of the country. Nevertheless, McBean wrote a letter to Fort Vancouver, relating what had happened. The messenger who carried the letter was instructed to give it to the man best qualified to deal with such an explosive situation.

That man was Peter Skene Ogden.

Never mind that the "Prince of Good Fellows and Terror of All Indians" was a Britisher living in a country now American; that he was pudgy and old and his muscles and bones were filled with an old man's aches and pains. No person living in the Pacific Northwest was as respected by the Indians of the interior as he. If the situation could be resolved without a massive shedding of white and Indian blood, he would know what to do...

Responding to the appeal, Peter Ogden wrote a note to the Governor of Oregon Territory, George Abernethy, requesting that he do nothing that would disturb the Indians, then he loaded a supply of trade goods into three canoes and headed upriver. His protective force, if such it could be called, consisted of sixteen French–Canadian *voyageurs*—men notorious for their dislike of violence—and a well-earned reputation for never making a promise he did not keep.

His mission was successful. Deeply regretting what a handful of revenge-seeking Cayuses had done, most members of the tribe offered to hand over the forty-seven captives that had survived for a token ransom and the promise that white settlers living in the Willamette Valley would not come upriver and make war on them. Peter Ogden quickly agreed on the quantity of ransom goods to be paid. But he would not promise that no armed volunteers would come upriver seeking revenge, for this was a promise he knew he could not keep.

Soon after the captives were released and out of harm's way, hundreds of Oregon Volunteers marched upriver and began making relentless war on the shattered remnants of the Cayuse tribe. Former mountain man, Joe Meek, whose half-blood daughter Helen Mar had died as a result of the massacre, was appointed a special representative from Oregon to the United States, and made a dramatic journey across the continent to the nation's capital. There, still in his well worn buckskins, he appeared before Congress and visited with expansionist-minded President James Knox Polk, who just happened to be a "shirttail" relative of his.

Securing an appointment as United States Marshal for Oregon, plus an assurance that Congress would quickly approve a bill officially organizing Oregon Territory, Joe Meek returned to the Willamette Valley. One of his first duties was to accept the surrender of the five Cayuse leaders judged by their own people to have been responsible for the killings: Tiloukaikt, Tomahas, Ishish-kais-kais, Clokamas, and Kia-ma-sump-kin.

Tried, found guilty, and sentenced to hang in late May, 1850, the five Indians were taken into the Catholic Church and renamed Andrew, Peter, John, Paul, and James. Because hanging was so abhorrent a way to die in the Indian mind, legend has it that Joe Meek stiffened their spines and helped them stand erect and die like men by whispering just before he cut the rope that sprang the trap that they had murdered his daughter, Helen Mar, and he was taking blood vengeance, as any father had a right to do. Having

Bill Gulick Photo
GREAT GRAVE MEMORIAL, WHITMAN MISSION

lost children of their own, this was the kind of retribution the Indians could understand.

Thus peace came at last to the Walla Walla Valley and the inland country.

Located six miles west of Walla Walla, the Whitman Mission today is a National Historic Site open to visitors the year round. Because most of the original buildings were burned or destroyed by angry Indians following the massacre, Park Service historians decided that none of them should be rebuilt. By following the walks of a self-guided tour, the visitor can see preserved remnants of the Emigrant House, the blacksmith shop, the gristmill, the Great Grave where remains of the fourteen victims are buried, and a white granite marker atop a hill overlooking the mission grounds.

Appropriately, most of the exhibits in the Visitor Center are displays of Cayuse costumes, tools, and items used in everyday Indian life, while Dr. Whitman's medical instruments, Narcissa's kitchen and table ware, and the spinning wheels, churns, looms, and other household furnishings of a bygone time are also on display.

Courtesy Washington State Historical Society
ARRIVAL OF THE NEZ PERCES, WALLA WALLA COUNCIL, 1855

STEVENS TREATIES OF 1855

Following his appointment as Governor of Washington Territory in 1853, one of the first things Isaac Ingalls Stevens attempted to do was to settle the Indian problem by negotiating with native leaders and making treaties under the terms of which the tribes would agree to give up their claims to large areas of land and go on much smaller designated reservations. After spending several months west of the Cascades in 1854 making such treaties, Governor Stevens and General Joel Palmer, Superintendent of Indian Affairs for Oregon Territory, moved east of the Cascades to the Walla Walla Valley in late May, 1855, where they had scheduled talks with five important inland tribes.

Though Stevens was a West Point graduate and had resigned from the Army when appointed Governor, Palmer's honorary military rank derived from service as a commander of Oregon Volunteers during a minor Indian war, following which all enlisted men invariably were called "Colonel" and all officers "General" for the rest of their lives.

Gustaf Sohon Sketch, Courtesy Washington State Historiaal Society
LAWYER, HEAD CHIEF OF THE NEZ PERCES IN 1855

West of the Cascades, Stevens had experienced little difficulty persuading the small though numerous tribes living there to accept reservations near where they had lived for generations. They were already "settled" Indians to a degree. But the tribes east of the Cascades—the horse Indians—were quite another matter. In order to deal with them, Stevens and Palmer would have to convene large numbers of well-armed warriors belonging to the most powerful tribes in the Pacific Northwest, impress them with the strength of the American government, and negotiate treaties that would put them in their place forever and open the rest of their lands to settlement by the whites.

The spot chosen for the meeting was an ancient, traditional Indian council grounds six miles east of the abandoned Whitman Mission. Invited to the treaty talks were members of five tribes: Nez Perce, Cayuse, Umatilla, Walla Walla, and Yakima. Between five and six thousand Indians came to the council, which lasted

Gustaf Sohon Sketch, Courtesy Washington State Historical Society
CHIEFS AT DINNER, WALLA WALLA COUNCIL, 1855

nineteen days. The whites numbered one hundred, only forty of whom were soldiers.

Making a verbatim record of all that was said during the nineteen days was the professional white secretary, James P. Doty. While there is no question that the Indians were put under a great deal of pressure to sign the treaties, the documents did become the best legal claim they had to their land, water, fish, timber, and sovereignty rights, for once approved by the United States Senate and signed by the President, the treaties became the highest law of the land.

In fact, the Indian leaders of the five affected tribes agreed in 1955—the one-hundredth anniversery of the Stevens Treaties—to a renactment of the negotiations in Walla Walla, for which I was asked to write a historical outdoor drama as an observance of the event. At that time, all five tribes were negotiating with the federal government for financial compensation for loss of their "usual and accustomed fishing places" at Celilo Falls, soon to be flooded by the building of The Dalles Dam.

Directing the 1955 event was Charles Luce, who at the time was acting as attorney for the Umatilla Confederation in attempting to reach a settlement of several million dollars for loss of their traditional fishing places. He obtained for me a verbatim transcript of the treaty talks as recorded by the white secretary, James Doty. For those interested, copies of this transcript are available in the National Archives, in Penrose Library at Whitman College, and at a number of the larger regional libraries.

What is not so well known is the fact that for a time at least an Indian record of the talks also existed. It was made by a literate, Christianized Nez Perce Indian named Timothy, who was present during the talks and set them down in the Nez Perce tongue. When I learned that fact, I immediately set about trying to obtain a copy from the superintendent of the Nez Perce National Historic Park, Jack R. Williams. This was his reply to my query:

> According to Mylie Lawyer, a grandaughter of Chief Lawyer, Timothy worked very closely with Chief Lawyer [who in 1855 was head chief of the Nez Perce Tribe]. Both were students of the Rev. H.H. Spalding, and though Timothy could write for some unknown reason he always signed papers with an X—his mark! Chief Lawyer's wife, Mylie's grandmother, told Mylie that Timothy was a crier (which is not well known) and he did record the 1855 proceedings. When Timothy died and was buried in Alpowa in 1890 the family followed the custom of disposing of the deceased's property by giving away and burning. Unfortunately, all his papers were burned and the document you seek was among them.

It was the custom among most Indian tribes to appoint a strong-voiced man as a "crier" who would walk up and down the village streets proclaiming the news of the day and move around in the crowd when a large council was being held repeating what was said by the principals in a loud voice so that the people sitting or standing in the back rows could hear it all. If several different languages or dialects were involved, the process could become, as Captain William Clark described it, "tegious."

In any case, the only record that is left is the one made by Secretary Doty. For the most part, he seems to have recorded what was said by the Indian and white leaders during the official daytime meetings with commendable accuracy and completeness. Whatever threats and pressures were made or brought to bear during unrecorded talks after the official meetings, are a different matter, of course—one of which I have already noted, when Governor Stevens supposedly told Yakima Chief Kamiakin that if

Gustaf Sohon Sketch, Courtesy Washington State Historical Society
TU-EKA-KAS
The father of Chief Joseph, Tu-Eka-Kas was also known as Old Joseph. The drawing dates from the Walla Walla Council, 1855.

he did not sign the treaty his country "would run knee-deep in blood..."

Some of the speeches made by the Indians were poignant and colorful, even in translation. For example, the Walla Walla chief, Peo-peo-mox-mox, whose son had been killed by a white man during a trip to California, with the murderer never brought to trial, said:

> I know the value of your speech from having experienced it in California, having seen treaties made there... From what you have said, I think you intend to win our country, or how is it to be? Suppose you show me goods? Shall I run up and take them...? Goods and the earth are not equal; goods are for using on the Earth. I do not know where they have given lands for goods.

Young Chief said, "I wonder if this ground has anything to say? I wonder if the ground is listening to what is said? I hear what this earth says...

"The earth says, God has placed me here to produce all that grows upon me, the trees, fruit, roots, and grass. It was from her that man was made. God on placing men on earth desired them to take good care of the earth and do each other no harm. God said, `You Indians who take care of a certain portion of the country should not trade it off unless you get a fair price.'"

"My friends, I wish to show you my heart," Stickus said. "How is it that I have been troubled in mind? If your mother were here in this country who gave you birth, and suckled you, and while you were sucking some person came and took away your mother, how would you feel then? This is our mother, this country, as if we drew our living from her."

In the end, of course, the only thing the objections raised by the Indians accomplished was getting the white commissioners to agree to set up three rather than the two reservations they first had planned to establish. Because both were large tribes, the Nez Perces and the Yakimas agreed to go onto relatively large reservations, while the reserve of what became the Umatilla Confederation—Cayuse, Walla Walla, and Umatilla—was considerably smaller.

As noted earlier, the boundaries of the Yakima Reservation today remain substantially the same as set in the 1855 treaty, though pieces of land sold to non–Indians within the borders of the reserve have become an ongoing problem.

To a lesser degree, individual members of the Umatilla Confederation, whose reservation lies in the foothills of the Blue Mountains east of Pendleton, Oregon, caused similar problems when they sold or leased lands held in severalty to white farmers or ranchers.

First given title to a ten-thousand-square mile reservation covering parts of southeast Washington, northeast Oregon, and north–central Idaho, the Nez Perces appeared to have fared better than any other tribe, for they had retained almost all of their traditional tribal lands. But the discovery of gold in 1860 in the heart of their country soon changed that, with the white intruders insisting that the reservation be reduced to twenty-five hundred square miles, all of it in Idaho.

In a classic piece of political skullduggery in 1863, one-third of the members of the Nez Perce Tribe signed away seven-eighths of the traditional tribal lands in what became known among the dissenting bands as the "Steal Treaty." Because a gentle, peace-loving Wallowa chief named Old Joseph refused to give up his homeland and instilled the same love of the "Land of the Winding Waters" in his son, Young Joseph, a bitter war would be fought in 1877 whose details are outside the scope of this book but whose origin was in the Treaty of 1855 made in the Walla Walla Valley.

THE STEPTOE DISASTER

With white trespassers violating stipulations in the Stevens Treaties that they would not cross Indian lands without permission, brutal incidents of whites abusing Indians and Indians killing whites in retaliation occurred. Two years after the military post of Fort Walla Walla was established in 1856, its commandant, Lieutenant Colonel Edward J. Steptoe, decided that the time had come "to show the flag," demonstrating to whites and Indians alike that the army was here to keep the peace.

Heading toward Spokane and the Colville area in May, 1858, the colonel led a column of 159 men and a large pack train. Legend has it that so much food, forage, and useless equipment was taken along that when all the pack animals were loaded the ammunition had to be left behind. This is a slight exaggeration. In actuality the three companies of dragoons and the partial company of infantry carried forty rounds per man, along with two mountain howitzers. But as events soon proved, the arms, training, and leadership of the expedition were very poor.

When swarms of belligerent Indians, led by Chief Kamiakin, challenged the passage of the troops in the Palouse Hills area near what later would be called Steptoe Butte, the colonel agreed to halt the forward march, turned his column around, and started to leave what the Indians regarded as their country. Taking the army's retreat as a sign of weakness, the Indians first harassed, then attacked, and finally slaughtered one isolated detachment down to the last man.

With seventeen officers and men killed, fifty more wounded, and the two howitzers and a large amount of supplies and arms lost, what became known as the "Steptoe Disaster" made the fighting ability of the US Army look very bad indeed. This was a

Courtesy Penrose Library, Whitman College

SKETCH OF WAIILATPU, WHITMAN MISSION, PRIOR TO 1847

state of affairs not to be tolerated by the War Department. To correct it, the next commander of an expedition against the Indians would be a martinet without mercy, Colonel George Wright.

At the head of a company of dragoons and six companies of artillery—over seven hundred men in all—Colonel Wright marched northeast from Fort Walla Walla across the sun-scorched hills of the Snake River country on August 7, 1858. Armed with brand-new "rifle muskets" firing a minie ball that could kill at six hundred yards, these soldiers represented the kind of well-led, well-trained, well-equipped force the Indians had never faced before. Made overconfident by the ease with which they had turned back the Steptoe expedition, a thousand hostiles led by Chief Kamiakin eagerly awaited the first engagement in the pine and lake-dotted country just south of present–day Spokane.

This time it was their turn to suffer a disaster—which will be covered in more detail a little later in this book.

GOLD, RAWHIDE, AND IRON

It is matter of record that the discoverer of the rich gold mines of northern Idaho, Elias Davison Pierce, first predicted the bonanza-to-be while drinking with three prospector friends in a Walla Walla saloon. If a historian were so inclined, it could also be proved that, while no gold ever was dug within the city limits of Walla Walla, a larger share of north Idaho gold ended up in the safes, tills, and cash boxes of Walla Walla bankers, merchants, saloon keepers, and proprietors of places of entertainment than of any other inland city in the Pacific Northwest.

A veteran prospector from California, E.D. Pierce had told the three friends drinking with him in the Walla Walla saloon about meeting a Nez Perce Indian who described a brilliant, fist-sized rock he had seen glittering in a cliff wall in the wilds of the Nez Perce country. Suspecting that the rock was a diamond beyond price, Pierce told his friends that there also ought to be gold in that part of the country; so, even though the North Fork of the Clearwater was within the boundaries of the Nez Perce Reservation, he and his friends made up an expedition to go prospecting there.

Caught and ejected by Agent Andrew J. Cain and the Indian Police, Pierce and his friends bribed Timothy's daughter, Jane, to act as their guide and take them into the forbidden country by a

Courtesy Washington State Library
ANNIE FAXON AT A SNAKE RIVER LANDING, 1880s

back route. Once there, they began digging, struck good color, forgot all about the diamond, sent two members of the party back to Walla Walla for supplies, and settled in for the winter. With the coming of spring, they paid their debts to the Walla Walla merchants with $1,200 in gold dust which, when sent downriver to Portland, "...set off a blaze of excitement..."

The gold rush was on.

Like all gold finds in the West, the permanent benefactors were the merchants, farmers, and suppliers rather than the miners themselves. Let the mere word "gold" be whispered, and settlements down in the lowlands where supplies could be purchased and miners could winter boomed and prospered. Walla Walla was such a place. Blessed with the mildest climate in the inland country, its farmers, merchants, saloonkeepers, and professional people could supply just about everything the prospectors needed—for a price.

Drawn to the town from the Willamette Valley by the gold boom, Dorsey Syng Baker was a doctor, while his business associate, John F. Boyer, was a merchant. Opening a general merchandise store in Walla Walla, the two men soon found themselves giv-

Courtesy Penrise Library, Whitman College
DORSEY S. BAKER

ing credit to prospectors heading for the north Idaho mines and stashing pouches of gold for men who had struck it rich in their big iron safe when the the miners returned to town for winter. While the partners never revealed how many prospectors failed to pay their grubstake bills, it was common knowledge around town that no person who had left a poke in their care ever lost a dime.

Still in existence, the Baker–Boyer Bank makes that same boast today, for the independently-owned bank did not close it doors for a single hour during the depths of the 1930 Depression when banks all over the country were failing, nor has it done so since.

Doc Baker also was renowned for building and operating what legend later called "The Rawhide Railroad." Like many isolated frontier towns back in the 1860s and 70s, Walla Walla dreamed of the day when a transcontinental railroad would pass through the community and open the world's markets to its farmers. Blessed with rich soil and a long growing season, the Walla

Courtesy Penrose Library, Whitman College
FIRST LOCOMOTIVE ON THE BAKER RAILROAD

Walla Valley soon had enough surplus wheat to feed all the population living west of the Cascade Mountains, with some left over for export to China. But getting the grain to market without rail transportation was a problem.

In 1868, Doc Baker and a few of his independent–minded friends raised $2,000 which they used to persuade Northern Pacific engineers to estimate how much it would cost to lay 32 miles of track from the city of Walla Walla to Wallula Landing, where river steamers owned by the Oregon Steam and Rail Navigation Company loaded grain. The estimate the engineers came up with exceeded $600,000, which was far more than the Northern Pacific felt freight traffic would be worth.

Sharpening his own pencil, Doc Baker figured *he* could build a line for a total cost of only $356,134.85. Persuading a few local businessmen and farmers to back the project, he organized the Walla Walla & Columbia River Railroad Company, scrambled and scrounged for funds, began building, and finally completed the

Courtesy Penrose Library, Whitman College
LOCOMOTIVE HAULING LOGS ON THE BAKER RAILROAD, 1800s

railroad. In his intriguing book: *Walla Walla, Portrait of a Western Town, 1804–1899,* local historian Robert A. Bennett, writes:

> To save money Baker used narrow gauge locomotives rather than the more expensive standard gauge. Baker also had most of his rolling stock manufactured locally and purchased his engines from the East and shipped around Cape Horn. The only passenger car on the small railroad was a homemade box car with small windows, and it became affectionately known to townspeople as the "hearse."
>
> The first rails used were made of wood and then topped with strap iron. Iron rails were used on turns, trestles, and other stress points. The strap iron had a nasty habit of breaking loose from the rail, rolling up and crashing through the floor of the car. They were called snakeheads and made riding the train a real adventure. The economic necessities of completing the railroad led to many humorous stories about the railroad, and it became known as Dr. Baker's "Rawhide Railroad."

Requiring two-and-a-half hours to travel from Walla Walla to Wallula, the first train made its run October 23, 1875. Bennett writes, "The town was now connected by a silver thread to the river, where its products could be exported to the world."

Courtesy Penrose Library, Whitman College
DORSEY S. BAKER NEAR WALLULA GAP ON THE COLUMBIA, 1880s

With a monopoly on freight traffic from one of the most productive grain-growing regions in the West, the railroad was a
moneymaker from the start. Being a man who did not believe in
borrowing funds unless it was absolutely necessary, Dr. Baker, as
president of the company, made sure that construction costs and
rolling stock were paid for within three years, for his shrewd
banker's judgment told him that such transportation giants as the
O.R.S.N. and the Northern Pacific Railroad Company would
move in and try to take over once they realized that his little railroad was a success. In a day when big corporations were unregu-
lated, they would push him to the edge of bankruptcy, then buy
him out for ten cents on the dollar.

Owning every boat, landing, and portage on the Snake and
Columbia Rivers between Lewiston, Idaho and the sea, the
O.R.S.N. Company directors were fond of saying, "He who owns
the shipping facilities, owns the river."

Doc Baker quietly disagreed. His view was that shipping
facilities were worthless without freight revenue—which could
only come from shippers of products such as wheat.

"He who owns the approaches to the river controls it," he said.

Time proved him right. When he offered to sell his railroad to the O.R.S.N. for $1 million, the directors laughed at him. Very well, he said, he would build his own river boats and shipping facilities. Knowing he had the resources to do it, the O.R.S.N. quit laughing, accepted his offer, and paid him a million dollars for his railroad. This was in 1878, only three years after its completion. On behalf of his stockholders, of which he was the major one, he had made a 400 percent profit on the investment. As a tribute to what they called, "The stubbornest man in Washington Territory," the O.R.S.N. Company named its newest addition to the Columbia River grain fleet the *D.S. Baker*.

Eventually, both the railroad and the steamship line were taken over by the Northern Pacific Railroad, which substituted standard-gauge iron rails for the wood stringers topped with strap iron. By then stories being told about Doc Baker's Rawhide Railroad had been repeated, magnified, and elaborated upon so many times by so many people that the railroad and its builder had passed into the realm of legend.

Many years later in a biography of her grandfather, *Gold, Rawhide and Iron*, Helen Baker Reynolds retold a number of those tall tales, which she said her father, Frank Baker, who had worked on the railroad as a young man, had enjoyed hearing.

According to the legend, Doc Baker had never even seen a raiload or a locomotive when he decided that was what the Walla Walla Valley needed. Hiring an Irish surveyor who liked his toddy but was short of surveying instruments, Doc Baker, who was a teetotaller, let him use a half-full bottle of whiskey as a level in selecting the thirty-two mile route. Better equipped surveyors declared later that the grade was perfect.

Not knowing how far apart the rails should be, Doc Baker had one rail laid first, then sent an Indian runner to wherever a narrow-gauge line was operating in the Northwest, with instructions to measure the distance between the tracks, cut a notch in a stick, then come home and show the construction superintendent what the width should be. Ordering a locomotive shipped around the Horn and up the Columbia River, Doc Baker realized that carrying it past the fourteen-mile portage around Celilo Falls would be a problem. But the Indians living in the area could be hired to pack things, if the wage was right. In his store, Doc Baker just happened to have a thousand black silk plug hats that had not sold.

Bill Gulick Photo
CHINESE GRAVEYARD IN WALLA WALLA
Here the Chinese burned tokens to the spirits of their ancestors.

Knowing that Indians loved fancy headwear, he gave a thousand of them a hat apiece to rig carrying poles with which they packed the locomotive around the Falls.

Not able to afford strap iron with which to top the rails, Doc Baker killed and skinned a few hundred cattle, then used the rawhide—which as every pioneer knows wears like iron—to top the wooden stringers. This worked fine until an unusually cold winter came along, with the snow so deep that it drove the coyotes down out of the hills. The animals were so hungry that they ate all the rawhide off the rails, forcing Doc Baker, who had accumulated a little capital by then, to reluctantly spend some of it for less tasty strap iron.

As an economy, Doc Baker had not equipped his locomotive with a cow-catcher. Instead, he trained a collie dog to precede each train, barking a warning to stray cows, horses, and pigs that a locomotive was bearing down on them and they had better get out of the way. When the problem of the strap iron "snake heads" working loose and curling up through the floors of the cars arose, the collie was trained to spot them and warn the engineer by raising his tail, to which a red flag was attached.

Though derailments were frequent, they seldom were serious because of the slow pace at which the train moved. When they did happen, the train crew and whatever passengers happened to be aboard got out and helped lift the derailed car back onto the track.

On one such occasion, so legend had it, a derailment occurred on a westbound train ten miles short of Wallula Landing. When a strong-backed pedestrian who happened to be passing by proved helpful in getting the train back on the track, the conductor offered him a free ride the rest of the way as a reward.

"No thanks, I'll walk," the pedestrian said. "I'm in a hurry."

THE WALLA WALLA JESUS

From my study window as I write this, I can look out and see the foothills of the Blue Mountains, just six miles away. A long, sloping ridge where wheat fields merge with the fir and pine of the mountains higher up is called "Mormon Grade." This is something of a misnomer, for the colony of forty or so families that settled there back in 1867 definitely was not Mormon but a group of people that had left Utah because they differed strongly with the Mormon faith and came further west to set up a communal society that would be distinctly their own. Regarding the settlement established there by William Davies, Russell Blankenship wrote in his colorful book *And There Were Men,* which was published by Alfred A. Knopf in 1941: "It is probable that his colony was one of the last if not the last religious communes founded in the United States, though this statement should not be accepted as authoritative."

It is a good thing that he did qualify the statement, for as later "hippie" colonies during the 1960s and 70s and the well-publicized Rajneesh venture in central Oregon between 1981–85 amply proved a hundred years later, efforts at communal living still did

Courtesy Penrose Library, Whitman College
WILLIAM W. DAVIES
The founder of the Davisite Colony is pictured with sons David and Arthur.

and do go on. But there is a poignant, haunting quality to the Walla Walla interlude that deserves special mention here.

Searching for a spot on which to locate his forty families, Davies was shown eighty acres on a ridge overlooking the Walla Walla Valley; like Brigham Young earlier, he said, "This is the place."

Bothering no one, the families built simple shelters for themselves and the livestock they had brought with them, began to farm, plant vegetable gardens and fruit orchards. A simple, thrifty people who turned all their money, worldly goods, and title to the land over to their leader, they sought no converts locally, though from time to time people with like beliefs did arrive from places such as California.

Courtesy Penrose Library, Whitman College
BIRTH AND BURIAL PLACE OF "THE MESSIAH" IN THE LATE 1800S

On February 11, 1868, Mrs. Davies became the mother of a son, who was given the name Arthur. Shortly thereafter, the father announced to the community that the child was the reincarnation of Jesus. On September 28, 1869, another son was born, this one pronounced to be the spirit of God the Father. Blankenship writes:

> Davies then proclaimed himself as the Holy Ghost. All three of these assertions were accepted without question by the members of the colony. No attempt whatever was made at concealment of their beliefs from the outside world, and the faithful showed neither a sense of shame at believing their strange doctrines nor a feeling of arrogance and superiority toward the unbelievers who lived outside the colony.

For thirteen years, the Davisites (as members of the colony were called) lived in harmony with one another, though all were poor in material things. Then came evil days. Mrs. Davies took sick and died. Following that tragedy, the great killer of children in the 1880s, diptheria, swept through the region in an epidemic that took a ghastly toll.

On February 15, 1880, the stricken father announced that his youngest son—the child named God—had died. A week later, he had to tell his followers that the Walla Walla Messiah named Jesus had just passed away.

So in brief week's time, William Davies had to announce to the colony that both God and Jesus were dead.

That was the beginning of the end. Their faith shaken, individual members of the colony brought lawsuits against Davies and one another, seeking to salvage what they could. By the time the courts finally sorted out who was entitled to what, the $3,200 judgments in favor of three plaintiffs barely were satisfied by a sheriff's sale in which the livestock brought $1,757.25 and the land $1,975.

During the ensuing years, some members of the colony moved away while others stayed, finding anonymity by marrying into local families of non–members and bearing children and grandchildren who either felt uncomfortable with their history or simply forgot it.

As county records have a way of doing in small communities, the Superior Court records of the 1881 litigation and trial are missing a number of documents and pages—a fact noted by Russell Blankenship back in the 1930s and confirmed by my own research five or six years ago. All that is left of the colony today is a wheat field on Mormon Grade in which there are a few rotting stumps of what may have been fruit trees a hundred and twenty-five years ago.

Standing on the ridge overlooking the wide, fertile valley, a person can imagine how William Davies must have felt after an absense of many years when he returned to Walla Walla for a brief stay. When asked by one of his former neighbors if anything looked familiar, he replied with a touch of regret, "Only the sky and the hills. All else has changed."

LOWER SNAKE RIVER

Between Burbank near its mouth and Clarkston at the head of navigation, the elevation of Snake River increases from 340 to 740 feet—approximately one hundred feet every thirty-five miles. Because this stretch of the Snake now is tamed by four dams—Ice Harbor, Lower Monumental, Little Goose, and Lower Granite— the river is a drab series of tranquil pools, with locks at each dam lifting tug and barge traffic, as well as pleasure boats, in stairstep stages of one hundred feet, requiring little effort on the part of the engines propelling the boats.

But the four dams built between 1955 and 1975 are relatively recent changes in a stretch of river that ran downhill in a hurry between the time the Lewis and Clark party first floated it in 1805 and the end of steamboat days in the 1940s. Stimulated by the discovery of gold in north Idaho in 1860, a colorful breed of men called river pilots fought the rapids, snags, rocks, shoals, ice jams, and floods of the wild Snake River in an era as romantic as the one recorded by Mark Twain on the Mississippi half a continent away at about the same time.

Downriver on the Columbia, steamboat traffic began in 1836, when the Hudson's Bay Company side-wheeler *Beaver* began plying the lower river, much to the disgust of Factor John McLoughlin, who hated the stinking thing. Year by year through the 1840s and 50s, boat traffic increased on the lower, middle, and upper river, until by 1860 regularly scheduled runs were being made to Wallula Landing, eleven miles downstream from the mouth of the Snake. But no boat-builder or pilot was foolhardy enough to risk navigating the Snake—until William H. Gray came along.

To say that Gray had a contentious nature, only begins describing him. A carpenter by trade but ambitious to be a doctor, a missionary, a politician, a businessman, an empire-builder or whatever else might occur to him in this land of limitless opportunity, he had come west with the Whitmans and the Spaldings in 1836 supposedly as a helper at the missions. Certainly he was skillful with his hands when it came to building a house, a gristmill, a blacksmith shop, or a boat. Trouble was, he could not get along with anybody—for the simple reason that he never tried.

A man of positive opinions, he had this to say of his first son, William Polk Gray, who was born in 1845:

> I named him after President Polk. When I named him, the President had taken a strong stand on 54–40 or fight. Polk reversed his attitude on that question and I have been sorry I called my boy after him ever since. Sometimes I have a notion to wring the youngster's neck, I am so disgusted with President Polk...

Fortunately for Snake River navigation history, young William Polk Gray did not get his neck wrung by his irate father; instead, he began learning the ways of rivers at the tender age of thirteen. During the ensuing fifty years, he became the most colorful and experienced riverman in the Pacific Northwest. His education began in the rapids of the lower Snake River.

With the merchants of Lewiston clamoring for goods and no steam-powered boats willing to risk the hazards of the river, William H. Gray built a modest-sized sailboat, mortgaged everything he owned in order to buy a stock of merchandise to be transported to the Idaho mines, hired a crew at Umatilla Landing, and headed upriver. Hearing that he intended to go up the Snake, the entire crew quit, judging the project to be too dangerous. From that point, William Gray, Jr., who was then fifteen years old and a veteran of two years experience on big rivers, tells the story:

> Father secured a new crew of seven men and on September 20, 1861, we left Wallula. It took us three days to reach the mouth of the Snake, a distance of only 11 miles. The prevailing winds were directly across the current, so that it was necessary for us to cordel the boat almost the entire way.
>
> Another boy and myself took ropes in a skiff up the stream and found a place where the rope could be made fast. We would then come downstream bringing the rope to our boat where the rope was made fast to the capstan and the rope would be slowly wound up. We had a difficult trip to Lewiston and before we got there my comrade and myself in the skiff had demonstrated that there was not a single rapid in the Snake River that could not be swum...

Below Five Mile Rapids, young Gray told his father that the current was too dangerous to be swum and that it would be impossible to find any place to secure a rope by which the unwieldy boat could be pulled upriver.

> "My son," his father replied, "'can't' isn't in my dictionary. Anything can be done if you want to do it badly enough. If you are overturned, you and the skiff will both come downstream. You may not come down together, but you will both come down. You will then go back and make another attempt and continue to do so until you have succeeded..."

How many unsuccessful attempts were made to secure the rope around the rapids-surrounded rock and how many times the two boys and the skiff came bouncing downstream separately or together are details young Gray did not record. But he wrote, "After that experience there has never been any combination of wood, iron, or water that has ever scared me."

Forty days of wet, gruelling, dangerous work brought the boat to Lewiston, where the goods it carried were sold at a substantial profit. Inspired by the example, shallow-draft sternwheelers that could run on "a light dew" began to navigate the lower Snake, though in times of high or low water or during the ice breakup of early spring the boats had to wait for days in such sheltered coves as Ice Harbor, ten miles above the mouth of the Snake, for the hazards to clear out.

By the summer of 1864, steam had replaced sail on the upper Columbia and the Snake; so young Gray went to work as a cub pilot on the sternwheeler *Yakima*. While in port in Lewiston one day, he was approached by a mill-owner from Asotin, a few miles up the Snake on the Washington side. Lumber here was worth only $15 per thousand, the mill-owner said, while at the booming port of Umatilla Landing on the Columbia, it could be sold for $55. Did young Gray think it possible to take a raft of lumber down the Snake without its being broken up and lost as all previous rafts floated into the rapids had been?

Gray thought it possible "...if you will get the right man..." and told the sawmill owner who the right man was—himself. Given a leave of absence from his job as a cub pilot, Gray picked up a raft containing fifty thousand board feet of lumber at the Asotin mill, floated it down to Lewiston, added another ten thousand board feet there, then embarked on the 180–mile journey down the Snake and Columbia. Atwood, the mill-owner, was aboard, as apprehensive as Gray was confident.

During previous unsuccessful attempts to float lumber rafts down the river, crews had tried to manage them with side sweeps; all Gray used was a steering oar at the rear. When approaching a rapid, his predecessors had made desperate efforts to keep to the edge and avoid the faster water; in the same situation, Gray steered the raft directly into the center of the rapid, where the current's force gave the clumsy raft such impetus that it quickly shot through into slack water. If worst came to worst, Gray knew that for him all the rapids were swimmable—a piece of information likely of small comfort to Mr. Atwood.

As they barreled down the Snake at a brisk nine miles an hour, Gray cheerfully told his employer that they would get along all right until they came to the Palouse Rapid. There they were going to have a serious time of it, he warned, for the water poured through a narrow chute and emptied into an eddy, which boiled back toward the current from the south shore. Gray wrote:

When we got to the Palouse Rapid I sent the raft into the center. The current was so swift it shot us into the eddy. The forward part of the raft went under water. We stayed on the raft until the water was up to our knees. The skiff which we had on the raft started to float off, but I caught the painter and we got aboard. We brought the skiff over where the raft had been and felt down with the oars but we could not touch the raft.

We floated down with the current. All I attempted to do was keep the skiff on its course. Atwood said, `I knew you couldn't do it. With such rapids as the Palouse, it was foolish to think you could.'

I felt pretty serious, for I was afraid the eddy had broken the fastenings on the raft and we soon would run into the wreckage of floating boards. About a half mile below the rapids our skiff was suddenly lifted out of the water by the reappearance of the raft. Both had gone with the current, and, oddly enough, the raft had appeared directly under us.

You never saw a man more surprised or delighted than Mr. Atwood...

Small wonder that Mr. Atwood was pleased. Young William Polk Gray had brought a raft of lumber worth $900 at Lewiston to Umatilla Landing in two days' time, where it sold for $3,300. Since Gray's wages were ten dollars a day, Mr. Atwood had made a net profit of $2,400 on his $20 investment in the cub pilot's service.

THE WHEAT SLIDES

For most of its length between Burbank and Clarkston, the Snake flows between immense lava bluffs which rise two thousand feet above the surface of the river. Much of the country in the area raises fabulous yields of wheat year after year, but because of the topography of the land getting the grain downriver to Portland and overseas markets always has been a problem.

Between the 1870s and '90s, the grain was placed in burlap sacks, which, when sewn shut, weighed one hundred pounds. Hauling a wagon load of sacked grain down the narrow, rutted switchbacks of the ungraded roads behind several teams of draft horses was an extremely risky business that only the most skillful professional teamsters would undertake—at great expense to the farmers. So a few inventive geniuses came up with schemes devised to use the law of gravity to transport the grain from the plateau on which it grew down to the landings where the river boats could load it.

Courtesy Idaho Historical Society
CAPTAIN WILLIAM POLK GRAY

One of these men was a Walla Walla civil engineer named Major Sewell Truax. Building a 3,200 foot long wooden tube four inches in diameter from the heights down to river level, he poured the wheat into a hopper, slid it down to the waiting cargo boat, and emptied it into sacks on the landing. As he anticipated, gravity did the work, all right. But the wheat slid downward so fast and created so much friction that by the time it reached the waiting boat it was toasted crispy black.

So he went back to the drawing board.

This time he installed baffle plates in the tube at one-hundred foot intervals, open at the top so that the air being carried downward with the wheat could be vented, thus eliminating problems created by a vacuum, with an additional bonus that dust, smut, and all foreign matter embedded with the wheat also went out the vents, with the result that the wheat pouring into sacks at river level was clean and pure.

BPA Photo, Courtesy Corps of Engineers
ICE HARBOR DAM, SNAKE RIVER

Patenting the invention, he and the Paine brothers—who came up with a similiar device—had five such grain chutes operating along the river from 1879 till 1900.

Shortly after 1900, another inventor tried a different scheme that put the law of gravity to work. This was a tramway on which a car on a track, with a passing siding halfway down, would carry a load of sacked wheat from the heights down to the landing two thousand feet below, with the weight of the descending car pulling the empty back up to the top of the bluff. Most of the time, the system worked pretty well, though on an occasion or two a reckless man hitching a ride up in an empty car while a loaded car was coming down got injured or killed when the rather primitive braking system failed to work as it should.

As one old timer later observed wryly, "In them days, the only safety system they had was a man with a loud voice who when something went wrong yelled, 'Look out!'"

Though almost all physical evidence of these grain-carrying systems is gone now, a faint scar rising from river level to the bluff above still may be seen in the Mayview area a few miles upstream from Lower Granite Dam.

The most comprehensive book on steamboating in the Pacific Northwest is *Blow For the Landing* by Fritz Timmen, published by Caxton in 1972. He writes:

> By 1878 seven more big steamers had been added to the O.S.N. fleet: the *Harvest Queen, John Gates, Spokane, Annie Faxon, Mountain Queen, R.R. Thompson,* and the *Wide West.*
>
> The *Harvest Queen* was a veritable floating palace, the finest and fastest steamboat on the upper river. She was two hundred feet long with a thirty-seven foot beam and seven and one half foot depth of hold. She could carry five hundred tons of cargo. Command of the *Queen* was given to twenty-three year old Captain James W. Troup. Some years later, when she left the upper river run, Captain Troup took her full steam ahead over the falls at Celilo in one of the river's more memorable passages.

Now and then, one of the river boats ended its career suddenly and dramatically, as did the big sternwheeler *Annie Faxon* on April 14, 1893. Historian Timmen writes:

> At Wade's Bar Captain Harry Baughman pulled the whistle cord and headed in to pick up a bit of freight and a lone passenger. Purser Tappan left his cabin, where his new bride sat, to collect the dollar fare and check the manifest. As the *Annie Faxon* neared the bank, Captain Baughman rang down the engines. Almost immediately there was a low, ominous rumble from below decks and the cabin of the steamboat collapsed upon itself.
>
> Purser Tappan turned to speak to a deckhand standing by the gangway and saw him dead on the deck. Captain Baughman's pilot was beheaded by a sliver of flying wreckage, and the Captain a moment later found himself dazed and injured on the bank, blown there by the explosion.
>
> Purser Tappan survived, but not his bride, who was thrown into the river and drowned.

As a result of the boiler explosion, eight people were killed and the *Annie Faxon* was a total loss.

WAYS TO SEE THE LOWER SNAKE RIVER

The best way to see the river between Burbank and Clarkston is by boat, either private, charter, or working tug. Only in that way will you get an idea of how big the locks are and how effortlessly water can lift any size craft from a twenty-foot-long pleasure boat to a six-hundred-foot-long combination of a tug pushing three massive barges, each one of which can carry enough cargo to fill a hundred-car freight train.

When the dams were first built, the Corps of Engineers, which operates them, was required to lock a craft upstream or downstream with no more than a fifteen-minute wait, no matter what its size. If the hundred-foot tall steel gates were closed and the red traffic light was against you when traveling upstream, all you had to do was maneuver your little power boat to the traffic light rope-pull and give it a jerk. Within minutes, the massive gates would unfold, the light would turn from red to green, and you would putt-putt majestically into the 650–foot long, 84–foot wide, 100–foot high lock. There, you secured your boat to a side-anchor that rose with you and the water flooding in so that you did not toss about unduly in the minor turbulence as the lock filled.

Whether alone or sharing the lock with a monstrous tug-and-barge tow, the amount of water needed to fill the lock, the time required, and the toll charge (none) were the same. Within twenty minutes, your boat and whatever other craft shared the lock would be lifted a hundred feet, the upstream gates would swing open, and you would be free to cruise another thirty-five miles or so before you reached the next dam, where the process would be repeated. Coming downriver, the procedure was reversed.

Because a large amount of water is used for each lockage, the process has been modifed during recent years so that the wait may extend to an hour or so and the water may be saved for power generation or fish passage. But the toll charge for all boats is still the same—zero.

During the summer season, weekly charter boats run out of Portland to Lewiston, while briefer trips can be booked out of marinas in the Tri–Cities area. If you are able to hitch a ride on a tug and barge tow, it will be slow, not as exciting as in stern-wheeler days when the river ran free, but the food will be great, for tugboat crews forced to spend long periods of time on the river will not tolerate a poor cook.

Many of the sights along the lower Snake are not visible from water level; but they can be seen with a little time, patience, and back-country driving on roads that are good though not well marked. Measuring from Sacajawea State Park at the mouth of the Snake, Ice Harbor Dam is located at Mile 10; Lower Monumental

BPA Photo, Courtesy Corps of Engineers
LOWER MONUMENTAL DAM, SNAKE RIVER

at Mile 40; Little Goose at Mile 80; and Lower Granite at Mile 105.
Paved roads lead to all four dams from both sides. If you wish,
you may cross on the tops of the dams themselves during daylight hours, but you must limit your speed to ten miles an hour.

At each dam, tours of the power plants and fish-ladder facilities are self-guided, and Corps of Engineers brochures explaining
some of the benefits and problems created by the dams are available.

BENEFITS AND PROBLEMS

On the plus side, the rapids and hazards of the once-wild river
have been smoothed out so that slack-water navigation with a
fourteen-foot deep channel is available year-round as far upriver
as Lewiston, Idaho, 470 miles from the mouth of the Columbia.
This gives bulk shippers of grain, oil, and other cargo the cheapest possible freight rates.

Storage dams in eastern Idaho, the 150–mile-long Grand
Coulee Reservoir, and dam pools in British Columbia and western Montana have such a large holding capacity that floods such
as the one that devastated Portland in 1948 with a great loss of
property and life can never happen again. As an additional bene-

fit, spring and early summer runoff from snowmelt that once ran wasted to the sea can be stored and used for irrigation.

Installed in most of the 161 dams on the Columbia and Snake River watersheds, power-generating facilities give the Pacific Northwest the lowest electrical rates in the nation, attracting industry and people to a region with lots of room and an equable climate.

On the minus side, the swift-water rapids and the white sand beaches that once were such an attraction to nature lovers on the lower Snake are gone. Runs of anadromous fish such as salmon, steelhead, and sturgeon have dwindled alarmingly during the past forty years, reaching the point where one species, the sockeye salmon, has been placed on the endangered list, to which another, the chinook salmon, may soon be added. This unhappy event has come as a surprise to some of the experts, though others are saying grimly, "We warned you this would happen but you would not listen."

In justice to both sides, it should be said that the changes made by man in the Columbia and Snake River systems have been so extensive over the past fifty years that none of the experts could have forseen their results. For example:

In order to permit salmon and steelhead to migrate upstream to their remote mountain spawning beds, fish-ladders were built below all the dams downstream from Grand Coulee. These are stairstep pools rising a foot at a time, up which the fish can easily jump as they formerly did in the natural rapids of swift-flowing rivers. Experiments showed that ladders work well when the dams are no more than one hundred feet high, with the fish loss at each dam in the neighborhood of fifteen percent. By building hatcheries at several upriver sites, it was anticipated that the number of fish lost at the dams could easily be replaced by hatchery-raised smolt (young salmon and steelhead) which are released when eight inches long.

For several years, the plan seemed to be working well. But as the number of dams on the Columbia and Snake between the Pacific Ocean and the central Idaho spawning grounds increased from one to eight, the runs began to dwindle. Not only that, but fish taken out of pools below the dams began to sicken and die from a disease that finally was diagnosed as "nitrogen poisoning."

Forming nearly four-fifths of the atmosphere, nitrogen in normal amounts is harmless. In excessive amounts, it is lethal, causing an ailment in human divers called the "bends." It affects fish the same way.

Whether natural or manmade, all waterfalls pick up nitrogen from the air and carry it into the pools below. This causes the water in these pools to become "supersaturated" with up to half again the normal nitrogen level. Below a natural waterfall, river water gives up its nitrogen when it strikes shallows and rapids, acquires oxygen, and resumes a normal balance of the elements. But below each manmade dam on the Snake and Columbia there is typically only a quarter-mile or so of free-flowing river before another still, deep pool up to fifty miles long is encountered. In these pools, the nitrogen content reaches a level far above the 110 percent that anadromous fish can tolerate for a brief period of time.

To assure propagation of the species, at least 22,500 adult steelhead must pass through the counting station at Lower Granite Dam on the Snake River. It is the eighth dam pool (following Bonneville, The Dalles, John Day, and McNary on the Columbia, Ice Harbor, Lower Monumental, and Little Goose on the Snake) that the fish must swim through before they reach their spawning beds. So the nitrogen supersaturation problem—added to the stress of negotiating eight sets of fish ladders— proved deadly to the fish runs.

In the autumn of 1974, only 10,000 steelhead made their way through the counting station at Lower Granite Dam. Faced with the stark prospect that this seagoing trout most prized by fishermen would vanish forever from the upriver streams, the Fish and Game Departments of Idaho, Oregon, and Washington closed the season to all sports fishermen in early October that year. For three years, the season remained closed, while fish experts and the Corps of Engineers took desperate measures to restore the runs.

Since the major cause of nitrogen supersaturation is water pouring over dam spillways, where it falls a hundred or so feet, the Corps experimented with several devices intended to reduce the amount of nitrogen absorbed by the falling water—perforated gates, fliplips, and others—but none worked very well. Because the loss of a few adult fish could be tolerated, while the preservation of the young smolt was vital, the fish experts concentrated on saving the young fish, which would be the breeding stock of the future.

Several unique methods of transporting the steelhead smolt around the downstream hazards were tried. A few made the trip down the Snake and Columbia in deluxe style—by air, in a specially equipped tanker plane. Others were transported around the dam pools by tanker trucks whose refrigerated, oxygen-enriched water kept the fish in the best possible environment during the long ride from eastern Washington to western Oregon. Each of the four tanker trucks in the Corps of Engineers' *Save the Steelhead* fleet could carry 30,000 smolts; during the crises of the first few seasons, the trucks were constantly on the move.

Soon after the completion of Lower Granite Dam in 1975, another method of transporting smolt downstream was tried— hauling them by tug and barge. Since two million smolt can fit into a barge filled with specially conditioned water, this has proved to be the most efficient and successful of all the methods yet tried.

By September, 1977, the steelhead count; at the Lower Granite counting station had increased to 45,000; so, after three closed seasons, sports fishing in the three states was reopened. The problem seemed to be solved. But during the late 1980s, Mother Nature taught us another lesson regarding what happens when we make drastic alterations in the natural environment.

Hatchery-raised fish, the biologists learned, did not possess the natural immunity to disease that wild fish whose ancestors had lived in Pacific Northwest waters for millenia did. Consequently, when a virus or germ that would not affect a wild fish got into a batch of hatchery-bred fish, they all sickened and died.

The solution to that problem, biologists realized, was to increase the number of wild fish spawning and going to sea in Pacific Northwest rivers. But this was not happening. Instead, one species—the sockeye salmon—which for eons had migrated from the mouth of the Columbia River almost a thousand miles to the white-graveled beds of Redfish Lake at the foot of the Sawtooth Mountains in Idaho—had dwindled almost to the vanishing point.

The shocking discovery that in the fall of 1991 only *five* sockeye salmon—that's right, five—remained alive caused the species immediately to be put on the endangered list.

BPA Photo, Courtesy Corps of Engineers
LITTLE GOOSE DAM, SNAKE RIVER

Since that time, state and federal fish and game officials have become aware of the fact that the most valuable anadroumous fish of all, the chinook salmon, is also in trouble. Whether blame for the diminishing runs should be placed on the increased number of dams, industrial pollution, the siltation of spawning beds by poor logging practices, or a combination of all these factors, remains to be seen.

But the situation is so serious that at this writing (early October, 1994), all commercial and most sports fishing off the coasts of Oregon and Washington has been closed down completely. What is involved here is the shutdown of a food and sports industry that generates a billion dollars annually.

Though none of the experts have come up with a solution for this massive problem, one school of biologists has suggested that if a way could be found to move downriver-migrating smolt to the sea more quickly, a larger number of them might survive the hazards of the dam pools. At present, it takes fifty-three days for the smolt to travel from the Lower Granite pool to saltwater, biologists estimate. By releasing more water from each dam pool, the Corps of Engineers suggested, they could imitate the seasonal spring flooding of the rivers that existed before the dams were built, reducing the fifty-three–day period by half.

After a great deal of discussion and controversy, a month-long experiment called a "drawdown" was tried during March, 1992, and will be repeated in the years to come. What its overall results will be cannot be known until all the facts and figures are put together by the experts. But the screams of the people affected by the   March,   1992,   drawdown—which   in   the Lewiston–Clarkston sector of the Snake was twenty-eight feet— were immediate and loud.

Port districts and tug-and-barge companies whose shipping was suspended for thirty days felt they were being badly abused. Private marina operators whose docks were damaged and whose users now found several hundred feet of mudflats where deep water used to be were outraged. Because the large releases of water could not be used to generate electricity, the Bonneville Power Administration said it might have to raise electrical rates, which displeased all their customers. Even though the the irrigation season had not yet come, farmers pumping out of the dam pools feared they might have to add to the length of their intake pipes, install new pumps, or pay higher pumping costs.

For a time, threats were made by a number of interests to sue somebody for damages—though exactly who should be sued for what was not clear. Now that the first experiment has ended and the Snake and Columbia Rivers have been raised to their normal level, the complaints have subsided. But they illustrate how complicated the regulation of a great river system has become.

HISTORY AND CHANGE

Though the names Central Ferry on State Highway 127 from Dodge Junction to Dusty and Lyons Ferry on State Highway 261 from Starbuck to Washtuckna remain on the map, both ferries across the Snake were replaced by bridges some years ago. As a person who often has gone miles and hours out of my way to take a ferry of any kind, I am sorry this is so, but at least I can remember riding some of the old ferries before the advent of bridges and dams.

One of these was Lyons Ferry. Built in 1860 and operating until 1955, this was one of the last of the cable ferries, whose motive power was the current of the river itself. Before a dam pool downstream created slack water at this point on the Snake, which here was a quarter-mile wide, thick ropes ran from a huge wooden wheel on the scow-like boat to a wire cable strung from bank to bank on twin towers far overhead.

By turning the wheel, the pilot of the ferry tightened one rope while loosening the other, which altered the angle of the ferry to the current, thus thrusting the vessel across the river without requiring any propulsion power. Established when the Mullan Military Road connecting Fort Walla Walla with Fort Benton on the Missouri River was built, the Lyons Ferry was operated by the same family for three generations.

Being located in remote country, it did little more business when I first rode it in 1950 than it had done when first licensed by the Territorial Legislature ninety years earlier. From its appearance, the narrow, twisting, rutted road leading down from the bluff top to the ferry approach had not been graded since stagecoach days, it looked to me.

After driving aboard and watching the lean, weathererd, middle-aged ferryman manuever the scow into the current at the proper angle, I saw him resume his seat in a canvas chair, put his feet up, and again contemplate the thumb-thick fishing rod set in a bracket near the rail.

"What are you fishing for?" I asked.

"Sturgeon," he said laconically.

"How big a sturgeon can you handle with that kind of gear?"

"Oh, I've pulled 'em in up to eleven foot long."

"What does it feel like hooking onto an eleven-foot sturgeon?"

He thought about that for a while, then said, "Kind of like hooking onto a horse."

Though at the time I thought he might be pulling my leg, I learned in years to come that he was not, for the white sturgeon to be found in the lower Snake River used to grow to a monstrous size. Of course there are some sturgeon stories in regional folklore that may be slight exaggerations. For instance, the one about the farmer who baited an immense hook on a thick line, then tied the end of the line around the trunk of a sturdy tree and left it overnight.

Checking the line, next morning, he found it quivering like a taut violin string. Pulling on the rope with all his strength, he was unable to budge the monstrous fish on the other end even a lttle bit, so, leaving the rope still tied to the tree, he went to his barn, hitched up a strong draft horse, brought it down to the river bank,

Courtesy Yakima Nation Collection

CELILO FALLS

untied the rope from the tree trunk, and attached it to the big draft horse.

Though it pulled its best, the horse also failed to budge the fish. So, leaving the horse tied to the fish, the farmer went back to the barn and got another horse. When he returned to the river bank, the first horse was gone—never to be seen again.

In a more modern version of the story, the fisherman is driving a pickup truck, which he hitches to the unseen fish. Unable to budge the monster with the truck, he goes to the nearest farm and persuades a friend to drive a caterpillar tractor down to the river bank. When the two men get there, the pickup is gone...

Just off State Highway 261 on the north side of the the Snake are Lyons Ferry State Park and Palouse Falls State Park. Because of its mild climate and plentiful food supply, this area was the prehistoric home of indigenous people living in what was called the "Marmes Rock Shelter" 10,000 to 12,000 years ago, making theirs

Courtesy Corps of Engineers
JUVENILE FISH TRANSPORTATION BARGE
It is at the starting point, the Lower Granite Collection Station, near Lewiston, Idaho.

one of the oldest cultures ever found in the Pacific Northwest. Before the artifacts buried in the floor of their cave could be completly excavated and classified by experts, rising waters of the Lower Monumental Dam pool threatened to flood the site.

In a belated effort to keep it dry so that research could continue, the federal governent appropriated $1,000,000, which the Corps of Engineers used to throw up an earthen dike around the site. Unfortunately, the dike leaked and the site flooded anyway. But at least the archaeologists know that the artifacts are still there and safe from vandals unless they are skilled scuba divers.

A few miles to the north, the Palouse River, which has cut a deep, narrow gorge through the lava overlay covering this part of the country, plunges over a spectacular waterfall. Considerably higher than Niagara at 198 feet, Palouse Falls is a small-sized replica of what the world's greatest waterfall in the Grand Coulee area must have been during the glacial-age meltdown, but it is so far off the tourist track that relatively few people have seen it.

The same thing may be said for another interesting area, the Juniper Dunes Wilderness, lying just to the north of Ice Harbor Dam. With an annual rainfall of seven inches, this is desert country where a low-sprawling, scraggy juniper tree only a few feet tall must save up every drop of moisture it can acquire even to exist, let alone grow. Yet there is a beauty and tenacity of life in this desert area that many nature lovers feel must be preserved.

In contrast to this parched, arid desert, scientifically cultivated fields lying on either side of the lower Snake River make better, more productive use of the vast amount of irrigation water available in the river than any other region in the inland Pacific Northwest. Instead of depending on gravity-fed reservoirs such as those in the Columbia Basin and Yakima River projects, water is drawn directly out of the pools behind Ice Harbor and Lower Monumental Dams by large-capacity pumps which lift the water a thousand or more feet then put it on the land with fully automated circle irrigation sprinklers that can cover a quarter-section of land.

From the air, these circles look like huge lily pads, with marked contrast between the tawny acres of desert outside and the fertile fields of potatoes, corn, wheat, and other crops growing inside the circles. Of recent years, still another kind of irrigation has encouraged the planting of another kind of crop—grapes. Though it long has been known that this area of abundant sunshine, excellent soil, and a long growing season could produce good juice grapes such as the Concord variety, it was not until twenty years ago that wine grapes were tried. Once far down on the list of wine-producing states, Washington now ranks just behind California and New York as the third-largest wine-producing state in the Union. Ninety-eight percent of those wines are made from grapes raised in the Columbia and Snake River watersheds, with a number of them winning international awards for their excellence.

The lower Snake River area also is becoming renowned for new innovations its grape growers are using—drip irrigation—to put water directly to the roots of the vines, which absorb the exact quantity needed by capillary action and no loss of moisture by evaporation. Despite having more than enough water available in

Courtesy Corps of Engineers
LOWER GRANITE DAM, SNAKE RIVER

the Snake and Columbia Rivers, the irrigators are demonstrating
the fact that they can raise excellent wine grapes with only twenty-five percent of the water now used in California vineyards,
many of whose managers of recent years have been making pil-
grimages to eastern Washington to see how it is done.

Instead of letting Pacific Northwest water be exported to
thirsty southern California—as some Los Angeles politicians have
urged be done—eastern Washington farmers may teach the "foreigners" how to make better use of what water they already have.

THE PALOUSE HILLS

Because the origin of the name Palouse and that of the horse
called the Appaloosa are controversial, I might as well attempt to
settle both matters here—though I seriously doubt that advocates
on either side of the question will agree with me.

Covered with nutritious bunchgrass for as far as the eye could
see, the gently rolling hills of this part of the country were marvelous wild-horse graze, so the first explorers—who were
French—called the region *le pelouse*, which is French for lawn,

grass-plot, or greensward. On this rich and nutritious grass, the Nez Perce Indians—one of the few tribes that practiced selective breeding—raised such excellent horses that British and American fur trappers gladly paid twice the price that they would pay for any other breed. Some of these horses bore distinctive markings such as spots and patches and were prized for their toughness and endurance on mountain trails. Usually the trappers called them "Nez Perce" horses.

When westering Americans began to settle the country and a newcomer asked an old settler, "What kind of horse is that?" the answer likely would be, "Oh, that's a Pelouser." Many years later when the breed was officially recognized, it became the Appaloosa. For persons interested in a more detailed explanation, headquarters and the national museum of the Appaloosa Horse Club of America is located in the heart of the Palouse Hills at Moscow, Idaho, just a few miles east of Pullman, Washington.

Geologically, the brown, fertile soil—which is called *loess* (Greek for windblown)—has been eroded over eons of time off the Cascade Mountains two hundred miles to the west and deposited in the area. Containing all the minerals and trace elements needed to grow wheat, lentils, and peas, the Palouse Hills boast some of the richest soil on earth; in places, a well-driller's bit will not encounter a single rock to a depth of fifty feet. Flatland farmers from Plains states such as Kansas marvel when they see fields with a grade as steep as twenty percent being farmed with Caterpillar tractors and self-leveling combines.

"Doesn't the soil wash in heavy rains?" they ask. "Don't the combines ever fall over on those steep hillsides?"

The answer to both questions is the same: "Sometimes—but not often."

The reason the soil does not often wash in heavy rains is that in this part of eastern Washington rain usually falls in fine droplets, taking all day or night to deposit less than an inch, with most of the moisture soaking in. As to combines falling over, they have a self-leveling feature so that the wheel support on the downhill side is much longer than the one the uphill side. Furthermore, long years of experience have taught their operators how steep a slope can be safely farmed.

Before the advent of tractors, the plows, drills, and combines were pulled by triple spans of horses or mules—that is, three abreast and eleven spans to a hitch. Managing the thirty-three animals as a unit required a skill that became a lost art in the 1920s. To some degree, that art may be seen and appreciated today in the Fort Walla Walla Park Frontier Farm Museum, where the late Carl Penner, who for many years drove such a hitch, left a permanent memorial of his times by commissioning the Walt Disney Studio to manufacture thirty-three lifelike wax mules, which he then harnessed to a combine and placed in a specially constructed building on the Farm Museum grounds.

STEPTOE BUTTE

As already noted, the settlement adjacent to the new military post of Fort Walla Walla first was called Steptoeville in honor of its commander, but was hastily changed when an army force under his command suffered a stinging defeat at the hands of the Indians. But a cone-like butte rising stark and lonely 1,600 feet above the surrounding plains, as well as a small town nine miles north of Colfax, now share the dubious honor of perpetuating the unfortunate colonel's name.

Planning merely to impress the Indians with a military presence in May, 1858, Colonel Steptoe picked up Chief Timothy and three Nez Perce braves as guides at the Alpowa Creek crossing of the Snake. Ninety miles north of the river and surrounded by large numbers of increasingly hostile Indians, Colonel Steptoe began leading his command in what he thought would be a peaceful, strategic withdrawal. But near present–day Rosalia, the Indians attacked.

At first, the retreat was orderly. Then, according to historian George W. Fuller:

> Indians fired upon them from the timber on the south side and from various elevated points along the line. Lieutenant Gaston, without waiting for orders, charged with his men and cleared an opening in front to the high lands on the south, and was followed by the entire force...Colonel Steptoe was in advance with "H" troop and the pack animals.

As the morning passed and Indians continued to attack the column from all directions, the pace of the retreat quickened. Captain Taylor and Lieutenant Gaston with their troops fought a desperate rearguard action. Fuller writes:

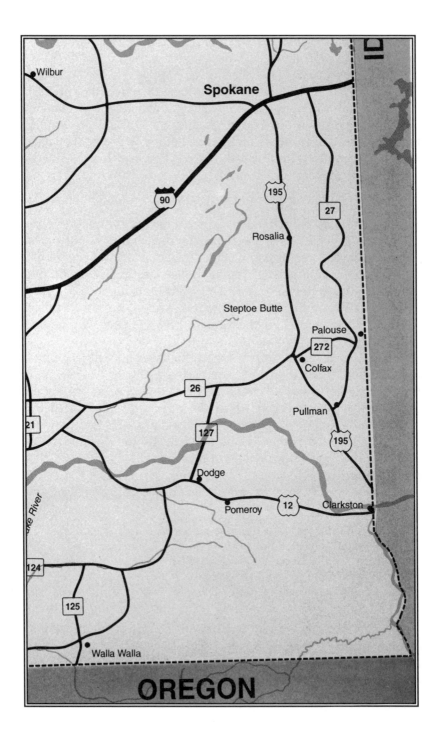

Wilbur

Spokane

ID

90

195

27

Rosalia

Steptoe Butte

Palouse

272

Colfax

26

Pullman

21

127

195

Dodge

ake River

124

12

Pomeroy

Clarkston

125

Walla Walla

OREGON

Wearied, exhausted, and with their ammunition all gone, they still maintained their moving position. At last Lieutenant Gaston sent a courier named Tickey Highland, asking Colonel Steptoe to halt the command and give his men an opportunity to reload their guns. His request was not granted.

Out of ammunition, badly outnumbered, and deserted by the rest of the command, Captain Taylor, Lieutenant Gaston, and members of the rearguard were reduced to fighting the Indians hand to hand, using clubbed pistols and empty muskets against the knives, lances, bows and arrows, and guns of the Indians. It was in this battle that Crimean and Algerian wars, began a legend when he cried as he swung his clubbed musket at the Indians, "My God, my God, for a saber!"

Wounded so badly that he could not ride or bear to be carried by a comrade on a horse, DeMoy asked that he be placed in a sitting position on the ground, with a loaded revolver in his hand. After killing or wounding several Indians, he used the last bullet on himself.

Sure that they had the troops surrounded, the Indians broke off the siege as darkness fell, went into camp and spent the night dancing, chanting, and celebrating. Checking on the supply of ammunition, Colonel Steptoe learned that the soldiers averaged only four rounds to the man. There was nothing to do but run for it.

State 127, 26—Dodge to Colfax
  44 miles
US 195—Colfax to Rosalia
  26 miles
State 271, 27—Rosalia to Pullman
  46 miles
US 195—Pullman to Clarkston
  30 miles
US 12—Clarkston to Pomeroy
  35 miles
State 129—Clarkston to Oregon Line
  36 miles

According to some accounts, it was at this point that Timothy led the command by a narrow, difficult trail known to few Indians and no whites, through the lines of the hostiles, with such stealth that the escape was not discovered until daylight. Other accounts, including official army reports, do not even mention Timothy's presence.

Whatever act of heroism, carelessness, or chicanery was involved, the escape attempt was successful. Leaving behind the dead and badly wounded, muffling spurs, bridle chains, and any metal that would clink, covering light-colored horses with dark blankets, and moving through the darkness with the silence of ghosts, the soldiers filtered one by one through the loosely manned lines of the hostiles until they were out of earshot, then mounted and rode for safety as fast as their horses would run.

Following this defeat, Colonel George Wright replaced Steptoe. Later that summer Wright mounted a successful campaign that settled the Indian problem in the region once and for all.

As the country settled up, the winding road to the top of Steptoe Butte—from which a spectacular view could be seen—became so popular that a local capitalist named "Cashup" Davis because of his insistence on always settling bills owed or owing with "cash up" on the line, built a large, rambling resort hotel on top of the butte, which for years was quite a regional attraction despite its problems with a water supply. Eventually, it burned to the ground, though by then it had fallen into disuse.

Now a State Park reached by way of a narrow, paved road that circles up to the crest of the 3,613 foot high butte, the view from the top on a clear day is still spectacular.

WASHINGTON STATE UNIVERSITY

Like most Western states, institutions of higher learning in Washington originally were set up under the plan that there should be one big university that would educate doctors, lawyers, and scientists, a slightly smaller "cow college" that would train farmers and rural people in the few skills they might need, and a scattering of small "normal" schools that would give potential teachers the two years of education required to qualify them to teach students in high school and grade school.

With the University of Washington established in the metropolis of Seattle, the cow college obviously should be located in the wide-open spaces of eastern Washington, reasoned the legislature, as should the state prison. At that time, Walla Walla was the most populous and important city east of the Cascades, so it was offered its choice between the cow college and the prison. Legend has it that the Walla Walla city fathers judged crime to be a more dependable industry than education, so they chose the prison. This left the college for Pullman—with the jury still out as to which city made the wiser decision.

Today, of course, all colleges have become universities, as have all normal schools, which have been replaced by community colleges now well along the road to becoming branch universities themselves. But the location of Washington State University, like that of its nearby neighbor the University of Idaho at Moscow, Idaho, just ten miles to the east, is ideal in that it is situated in the heart of the richest, most productive agricultural district in the world. Just as its big-city counterpart in Seattle has pioneered in remarkable achievements in engineering and medicine, so has the Pullman institution of higher learning made outstanding contributions to the science of feeding a hungry world.

How these contributions in the field of education should be measured against the quality of the two football teams of the cross-state rivals in the field of sports is a matter best left to more scientific minds than mine.

THE BLUE MOUNTAINS

On their westbound trip in October, 1805, Lewis and Clark left their horses with the Nez Perces on Weippe Prairie, made dugout canoes at the forks of the Clearwater, then floated down that river and the Snake to the Columbia and the sea. When they reached the mouth of the Walla Walla River on their eastbound trip in May, 1806, the Snake was running in full spring flood, so they took the advice of their Nez Perce guides, abandoned the canoes, and proceeded by land up the Walla Walla Valley and across a spur of the Blue Mountains along the route now followed by US 12 to the present–day town of Clarkston, Washington.

For most of their length, the Blue Mountains are an Oregon range, gaining their name from the blue haze hanging over them in late summer and early fall. During Oregon Trail days, crossing the rugged Blues was a challenge to worn-out people, oxen, and wagons. Today, Interstate 84 between Ontario and Pendleton makes crossing the Blue Mountains much easier for truckers and motorists. But the relatively small segment of this formidable mountain range that extends northward into Washington as the Wenaha–Tucannon Wilderness still is so rugged that it demands respect from hunters, hikers, and fishermen who venture into it.

Crests such as Oregon Butte and Diamond Peak, which loom 6,300 feet, cool and condense air rising off the low-lying Columbia Basin plain to the west, dramatically altering the rainfall pattern. Along the Columbia River at the western edge of Walla Walla County the annual average rainfall of seven inches makes this desert country. Fifty miles to the east in the foothills of the Blues, this portion of the county receives an average of thirty inches, turning it verdant and green.

South of Clarkston on the Snake River, the backwaters of the Lower Granite Dam pool extend six miles up the Snake to Asotin. Moving up and away from the river, State 129 climbs over open prairie land to Field Springs State Park, then drops in winding loops down into the canyon of the lower Grande Ronde River, a stream beloved by steelhead and salmon fishermen back in the days when those fish were still abundant.

Climbing again up to the high tableland near the Oregon border, the highway goes on south to Enterprise, Joseph, and Wallowa Lake.

An alternate blue-line road at river level leads south from Anatone to the mouth of the Grande Ronde River 35 miles away. Here, the Snake River still runs free for ninety miles through the spectacular gorge called Hells Canyon. From the marina at Hellers Bar, a few brave souls launch private prop or jet boats and risk the hazards of the rapids-filled river; but unless the boater is experienced in white water, the safer way to see Hells Canyon is to take a four-hour to three-day charter and let a pro do the driving.

Traditionally, the low-lying sandbars on either side of the Snake in the Grande Ronde area were the winter homes of the Nez Perce Indians, who in summer and fall moved their villages and livestock into the beautiful grass-covered high Wallowa country, then came down to the sheltered canyons of the Snake to spend winter and spring in comfortable longhouses built in sunken pits on the sandbars. This habit of moving their dwelling places and livestock with the seasons seemed far more sensible to them than did the white man's way of building houses and barns, cutting firewood and hay, and combating the ice, snow, and cold of high-country winters or enduring the drought, dust, and heat of low-country summers.

Basically, this was the philosophy that caused white politicians to accuse the Indians of having a roving nature and no desire to live in fixed abodes. In 1877, the federal government's attempt to change the Nez Perce way of life by forcing the Chief Joseph band to leave their beloved Wallowa Valley, move to an Idaho reservation, and become "settled" Indians, led to a bitter, tragic war.

Perhaps it is fitting that the Hells Canyon sector of the Snake River should have become the scene of the final great battle to preserve a piece of wilderness in the Pacific Northwest. Having been personally involved in that battle for a number of years, I am pleased that the river itself and some of the country through which it flows has been preserved as the Hells Canyon National Recreation Area so that future generations can see what a river looks like in its natural state.

From its far northwest corner on Cape Flattery at the entrance to the Strait of Juan de Fuca to the depths of Hells Canyon in the southeast corner, Washington is a big, beautiful, rugged state, which must be seen to be believed.

My hope is that the reader will get as much pleasure traveling across it as I have enjoyed living in it and writing about it.

THE END

Acknowledgements

For a book of this nature, a writer requires access to a good library. I have used one of the best—Penrose Library at Whitman College—for many years, first as an outside researcher, then, after my wife Jeanne went to work there, as a "Friend of the Library" in more ways than one.

During that time, Larry Dodd, Archivist, Marilyn Sparks, Reference Librarian, Gerde Tugman, Circulation Librarian, and Henry Yapel, Head Librarian, not only have given me invaluable assistance but have become personal friends. Locally and regionally, Professor Thomas Edwards, who recently completed a term as a member of the Board of Directors of the Washington State Historical Society, has done me a number of favors.

In Tacoma, where the State Historical Society is located, Librarian Elaine Miller provided me quick access to the Ashael Curtis photographs, a number of which are used in the book, while Director David Nicandri also was most helpful. During one of my visits to Tacoma, I was pleased to hear that a new building has been approved and is in the planning stage; it will be erected in the vicinity of the Union Station on Pacific Avenue, which has been preserved as a historical landmark.

At the Washington State Library in Olympia, Gayle Palmer and Ellen Levesque were most accommodating in giving me access to the historic photographs in the Washington State Room, which was supposed to be closed the morning of my final visit but whose door somehow opened just long enough to let me in for a couple of hours. Why our political leaders tax and spend so generously in all other areas, then try to save a few dollars by cutting the staff budgets of the State Library and Historical Society is a mystery to me.

During the celebration of the one hundredth birthday of Washington State in 1989, State Librarian Jeanne Engerman and Project Coordinator Karen Goettling persuaded me to take part in a program in which regional authors toured the state and talked to audiences about their experiences as writers. Until then, it did not occur to me that thirty-five years of writing about the Pacific Northwest had made me something of a historical landmark myself. During those years, for example, I had seen a million acres of desert land in the Columbia Basin turned green and productive by the magic of irrigation. I had observed a generation of young Indians neglecting their traditions and language—which the older generation respected— then a still younger generation taking a renewed interest and starting again to study their people's language and ways.

In my talks to various groups, by far the liveliest audience was one made up of 240 fourth-and-fifth-graders at Edison School in Walla Walla who showed by their attention and questions that they can and do read and are very much interested in history.

At the Burbank Community Library, Anitra Breit was a most kind hostess, as were Regan Robinson at the Spokane County Library, and Cynthia A. Garrick at the Yakima Valley Regional Library. Later, I visited Yakima again searching for historical photographs and was directed to a real treasure, the Click Relander Collection, by Carolyn Norton, who had Diana Tufts lead me downstairs and open up the collection for me, from which I chose a number of excellent historic photographs.

Here, I must acknowledge my great debt to writers and local historians who have gone before me—first, for the accuracy and excellence of their writings; second, for their generosity in turning over to libraries and regional historical societies the photographs, scrapbooks, letters, and newspaper clippings they have gathered over the years. The late Click Relander was one of the best of these. For many years a reporter in the Yakima area, he wrote articles and books about Indians at a time when nobody else cared about preserving the traditions and history of the native Americans. His *Drummers and Dreamers* (about the little-known Wanapum tribe), for example, has become a classic in its field.

Whether my longtime friend Robert Pace, who lives in Yakima, should be called a writer, a photographer, or both, I cannot say. Certainly he is well qualified in both fields and has helped me tremendously whenever called upon to do so.

In the Puget Sound area, writer friends Archie Satterfield and Lucile McDonald have done me much-appreciated favors, as have Vance Orchard and Robert Bennett in Walla Walla. The late Nard Jones and Don Pugnetti, who lived and wrote both east and west of the mountains and were good friends, unfortunately are gone now but I have showed my appreciation for their writings by quoting them at length with due credit.

At the Ilwaco Heritage Museum, Director Noreen Robinson kindly opened the photographic files during a hectic period of remodeling, then supplied me with a number of excellent photos. Across the river at the Columbia River Maritime Museum in Astoria, Oregon, Curator Anne Witty helped me obtain some fine historic photos. During one of our visits there, I took part in an anniversary celebration attended by a number of regional writers during which Patricia Longnecker, who managed the book store, told me the pleasing news that my books on the Pacific Northwest continue to sell well. People taking the week-long cruise from Portland downriver to Astoria, then up the Columbia and Snake through eight sets of locks and dams 470 miles to Lewiston, Idaho, are particularly interested in the region's history. Having covered most of the area by boat myself, this is a trip I highly recommend.

Since many federal agencies are involved with the resources and regulation of the Columbia and Snake Rivers, I have requested information and photographs from several of them and have been given their full cooperation. At the Bonneville Power Administration office in Walla Walla, local manager Steve Lee and engineer Robert Gorenson were most helpful. In the Portland office, Nick Christmas III, Photo Lab foreman, and Ron Holeman, Project Engineer in charge of the Wind Energy experiment near Goldendale between 1981 and 1987 supplied me with photographs of all the major dams in the State of Washington and a detailed report on the Wind Energy effort.

In Goldendale, Mary Jean Lord, Energy Research Specialist for the Klickitat County Public Utility District, gave me excellent photos of the wind generators while they were still in operation, as well as information regarding some of the problems and future prospects for this kind of power.

Because of the impact of the 1980 Mount Saint Helens explosion and its aftermath on the state of Washington, we visited the area from all possible approaches eight times during the researching and writing of this book. As noted in the text, on our first visit to the newly opened Visitor Center on the brink of the volcano at Coldwater Ridge our guides were Duane Chatham, Director of the Center, and Mike Nitsch, Chief of Security for the Mount Saint Helens National Monument District of the Forest Service, who answered all our questions in a most satisfactory fashion—except why the sun did not shine the day of our first visit.

During the spring of 1994, Jeanne and I spent five weeks in the Washington, DC area researching several subjects for information not available in the Pacific Northwest. Back in 1980 while writing my nonfiction book *Chief Joseph Country: Land of the Nez Perce,* I had received a great deal of help locating historical photographs from Paula Fleming at the Smithsonian's Museum of Natural History. Visiting the Smithsonian fourteen years later, we were pleased to find that she not only was still there, but that she remembered me, knew exactly what we were looking for (an unpublished dictionary of the Nez Perce language), located it, and arranged to have it microfilmed at a reasonable cost and mailed to us before we got home.

Since the other subject I was interested in was sailing ships of the Pacific Northwest between 1790 and 1850, all of which were built on the East Coast, I sought help at the Library of Congress. Fortunately, I found it in Virginia Steele Wood, who long has been an archivist, reference librarian and the Recommending Officer for Naval and Maritime History. She kindly made me a printout of several dozen titles of books written on the subject, including her own, *Live Oaking: Southern Timber For Tall Ships.* The fact that the Jefferson Building of the Library of Congress complex was closed to the public because of remodeling during my several visits to it, I was given a pass to find my own way through its baffling tunnels and halls, which only added to the pleasure of my explorations of its vast store of treasures.

In Walla Walla at the Corps of Engineers Public Information office, James Hackett and Nola Conway were most helpful. At Grand Coulee Dam, Bureau of Reclamation officer Craig

Sprankle, Public Affairs, not only furnished me prints of the building of the dam but suggested I get in touch with L. Vaughn Downs, a B. of R. engineer who worked on the Grand Coulee project from its first authorization in 1934 until his retirement in 1975. Now living in Ephrata near the lower end of the irrigation project that has turned a million desert acres green, he has written a book about his experiences, which, though out of print, I found at Penrose Library after having the pleasure of meeting and talking with him in his Ephrata home.

In Ellensburg, the Director of the Public Library, Carolyn Willberg, supplied me with several interesting photos of haying, harvesting, and irrigation flumes. Having an interest in Western Art, we were pleased to see that the John Clymer Museum (he was a native of Ellensburg) is being developed on schedule. Darwin Goodey, President of the Western Art Association which sponsors the annual Western Art Show in Ellensburg, Jo Leal Clark, Executive Director, and Marilyn Krueger, Board Member—all of whom are old friends—did me several favors, not the least of which was putting me in touch with Sculptor David Govadere, whose cliff-top depiction of the Indian legend "Grandfather Cuts Loose the Ponies" has been erected just off I–90 east of Vantage.

Another artist, Dave Manuel, and his wife Lee—who are also good friends—take almost as much pleasure in selling my books as they do his paintings and sculptures. Their gallery/museum in Joseph, Oregon is filled with their artistic treasures—as well as my books.

Finally, to my wife, Jeanne, who has borne with me during all my travels and travails for lo, these many years, a mere "thank you" is not enough. But I believe she knows how much her help and support have meant to me.

Bill Gulick

Bibliography

Alt, David D. and Hyndman, Donald W., *Roadside Geology of Washington*. Missoula: Mountain Press,1984.

Andrew, Chas. E., *Tacoma Narrows Bridge*. Olympia: 1962.

Bancroft, Hubert Howe, *History of Washington*. San Francisco: 1890.

Bauer, E.E., *Boeing in Peace and War*, Enumclaw: TABA Publishing Company, 1990.

Bennett, Robert A., *Walla Walla, Portrait of a Western Town, 1804–1899*. Walla Walla: Pioneer Press Books, 1980.

Boyne, Walter, *Boeing B–52, a Documentary History*. Seattle: Janes Publishing Company, 1981.

Bowers, Dawn, *Expo '74 World's Fair in Spokane*. Spokane: Expo Corporation Publ., 1974.

Canady, Lewis, and Doward, Jan S., *Cloud Country*. Mountain View, California and Portland: Pacific Press, 1953.

Carson, Rob, *Mount Saint Helens: the Eruption and Recovery of a Volcano*. Seattle: Sasquatch Books, 1990.

Clark, Norman H., *Mill Town, a Social History of Everett*. Seattle: University of Washington Press, 1970.

Doig, Ivan, *Winter Brothers: a Season at the Edge of America*. New York: Harcourt, Brace, Johanovich, 1980.

Douglas, William O., *My Wilderness: the Pacific West*. New York: Doubleday, 1960.

Downs, L. Vaughn, *The Mightiest of Them All: Memories of Grand Coulee Dam*. Fairfield: Ye Galleon Press, 1986.

Drury, Clifford. M., *A Tepee in His Front Yard*. Portland: Binford & Mort, 1949.

Eells, Myron, Edited by George Pierre Castile, *Indians of Puget Sound: The Notebooks of Myron Eells.* Originals at Penrose Library, Whitman College, Walla Walla. Seattle: University of Washington Press, 1985.

Espy, Willard R., *Oysterville.* New York: Clarkston Potter Co., 1977.

Ewe, W. Storrs, *Washington State, a Literary Chronicle.* New York: Funk and Wagnalls, 1969.

Fahey, John, *The Inland Empire.* Seattle: University of Washington Press, 1986.

Fargo, Lucile F., *Spokane Story.* New York: Columbia University Press, 1950.

Fuller, George W., *A History of the Pacific Northwest*, Second edition, revised. New York: Alfred A. Knopf, 1938.

Gibbs, James A., *Shipwrecks off the Pacific Coast.* Portland: Binford and Mort, 1957.

Gulick, Bill, *Snake River Country.* Caldwell: The Caxton Printers, Ltd., 1971.

——— *Chief Joseph Country: Land of the Nez Perce.* Caldwell: The Caxton Printers, Ltd., 1981.

Harris, Stephen L., *Fire Mountains of the West.* Missoula: Mountain Press, 1988.

Hildebrand, Lorraine Barker, *Straw Hats, Sandals, and Steel.* Tacoma: Washington State Bicentennial Commission, 1977.

Hult, Ruby E., *Untamed Olympics.* Portland: Binford and Mort, 1954.

Jeffrey, Julie Roy, *Converting the West.* Norman: University of Oklahoma Press, 1991.

Johansen, Dorothy O. & Gates, Charles M., *Empire of the Columbia.* New York: Harpers, 1957.

Jones, Nard, *Seattle.* New York: Doubleday, 1972.

———*Evergreen Land.* New York:Dodd Mead and Company, 1947.

Kirk, Ruth, and Namkung, Hohsel, *The Olympic Rain Forest.* Seattle: University of Washington Press, 1966.

Meany, Edmund S., *Mount Rainier: a Record of Exploration.* New York: MacMillan, 1916.

Meeker, Ezra, Pioneer Reminiscences of Puget Sound. Seattle: Logman & Hanford Printing Company, 1905.

Morgan, Murray, *Puget's Sound*. Seattle: University of
Washington Press, 1979.
————*South on the Sound: an Illustrated History of Tacoma*. Tacoma:
Windsor Publ., 1984.
————*The Dam*. New York: Viking, 1954.
————*Skid Road, an Informal Portrait of Seattle*, New York: Viking,
1951.
Moser, Don, *The Peninsula*. San Francisco: Sierra Club, 1962.
Murray, Keith A., *The Pig War*. Tacoma: Washington State
Historical Society, 1968.
McDonald, Lucile, *Coast Country: a History of Southwest
Washington*. Seattle: Superior, 1966. Reprint by
Ilwaco: Ilwaco Heritage Foundation, 1989.
Prosser, William Farrand, *A History of the Puget Sound Country*,
Vol. 1. New York: The Lewis Publishing Company,
1903.
Pugnetti, Frances Taylor, *Tiger by the Tail*. Tacoma: Mercury Press,
1975.
Reynolds, Helen Baker, *Gold, Rawhide, and Iron, the ....Biography of
Dorsey Syng Baker*. Palo Alto: Pacific Books, 1955.
Richardson, David, *Pig War Islands*. Orcas: Orcas Publishing
Company, 1970.
Ripley, Thomas Emerson, *Green Timber*. Tacoma: American
West/Washington State Historical Society, 1968.
Rosen, Shirley, *Truman of Saint Helens: The Man and His Mountain*.
Bothell: Rosebud Publishing Company, 1981.
Ruby, Robert H., & Brown, John A., *Half-Sun on the Columbia, a
Biography of Chief Moses*. Norman: University of
Oklahoma Press, 1965.
Satterfield, Archie, *Backroads of Washington*. Rand McNally and
Company, 1980.
Solberg, Carl, *Conquest of the Skies*. New York: Little Brown, 1979.
Splawn, A.J., *Kamiakin, Last Hero of the Yakimas*. Yakima: 1917.
Strahorn, Carrie Adell, *Fifteen Thousand Miles by Stagecoach*. New
York: Knickerbocker Press, 1911; Reprint by Lincoln:
University of Nebraska Press, 1988, 2 vols.
Strickland, Rob, *Whistlepunks and Geoducks, Oral Histories from the
Pacific Northwest*. New York: Paragon House, 1990.
Swan, James G., *The Northwest Coast*. Fairfield: Ye Galleon Press, .
1966.

Sundbertg, George, *Hail Columbia*. New York: MacMillan, 1954.
Syckle, Edwin Van, *They Tried to Cut It All*. Seattle: Pacific Search Press, 1980.
———*The River Pioneers: Early Days on Gray's Harbor*. Seattle: Pacific Search Press, 1982.
Thomas, Edward Harper, *Chinook, a History and Dictionary of the Northwest Coast Jargon*. Portland: Binford and Mort, 1935.
Timmen, Fritz, *Blow For the Landing*. Caldwell: The Caxton Printers, Ltd., 1973.
Tosaw, Richard T., *D.B. Cooper; Dead or Alive?* Ceres: Tosaw Publishing Company, 1984.
Tuhy, John E., *Sam Hill, the Prince of Castle Nowhere*. Portland: Timber Press, 1983.
Van Syckle, Edwin, *The River Pioneers: Early Days on Grays Harbor*. Seattle: Pacific Search Press, 1982.
Weinstein, Robert A., *Grays Harbor: 1885–1913*. New York: Viking Press, 1988.
Williams, John H., *The Mountain That Was God*. New York: G.P. Putnam's Sons, 1911.
Wood, Robert L., editor, *Exploring Expedition Into Olympics by Christie, 1889–90*. Seattle: University of Washington Press, 1967.
Wood, Virginia Steele, *Live Oaking: Southern Timber for Tall Ships*. Boston: Northeastern University Press, 1981.

Index